An Artist
a Day

An Artist a Day

A Daily Diary of Artists' Birthdays

With texts by Michael Semff

PRESTEL
Munich · London · New York

Cover: Henri Matisse, *Spray of Leaves, 1953*

© Prestel Verlag, Munich · London · New York 2025
A member of Penguin Random House Verlagsgruppe GmbH
Neumarkter Strasse 28 · 81673 Munich

1st edition 2025

produktsicherheit@penguinrandomhouse.de
(The above information is mandatory information according to GPSR and
should be used for all queries relating to the safety of our books)

A CIP catalogue record for this book is available from the British Library.

Copy-editing German: Dr. Petra Kunzelmann
Translation: Alexandra Cox and Lance Anderson
Copy-editing English: Dr. Tas Skorupa
Picture editing: Sieveking Agentur, Munich

Editorial direction Prestel: Katharina Haderer
Production management: Martina Effaga
Production, Typesetting and Project management: Sieveking Agentur, Munich

Printing and binding: Livonia Print, Latvia

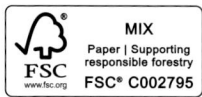

Penguin Random House Verlagsgruppe FSC® N001967

Printed in Latvia

ISBN 978-3-7913-9169-4 (English edition)
ISBN 978-3-7913-9168-7 (German edition)

www.prestel.com

Foreword

This book would like to introduce you, dear readers, to artists both famous and less known, from all continents of the world. It does not aim for academic perfection but is intended to serve as a small, handy reference book. May it awaken your interest in the endless diversity and various media of artistic creativity. The timeline extends from the Old Masters to the young, vibrant artists of today. Each entry introduces an artist who was born on that day with a short introductory text and an illustration of one characteristic work. The result is an easily accessible collection of texts that contain information on the activity of the artists presented – and sometimes even personal details.

Alfred Stieglitz

1864–1946 | Photographer, gallerist and patron | United States

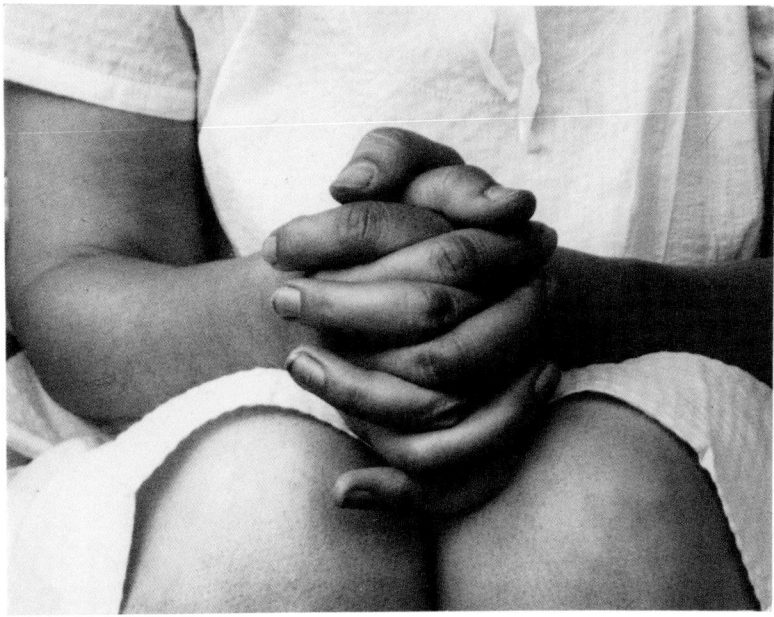

Margaret Prosser's Clasped Hands in Lap, 1933

As a publicist and author, successful gallerist and the organizer of major exhibitions of both photography and modern art, Alfred Stieglitz was one of photography's most influential pioneers and an inspired advocate of the avant-garde. His close ties to Europe – through extended stays as a youth and numerous study trips to countries including Germany – and his mature years in New York were formative. At the age of sixty, he married the painter Georgia O'Keeffe, who achieved fame largely through exhibitions organized by Stieglitz.

1 JANUARY

Robert Smithson

1938–1973 | Painter and land artist | United States

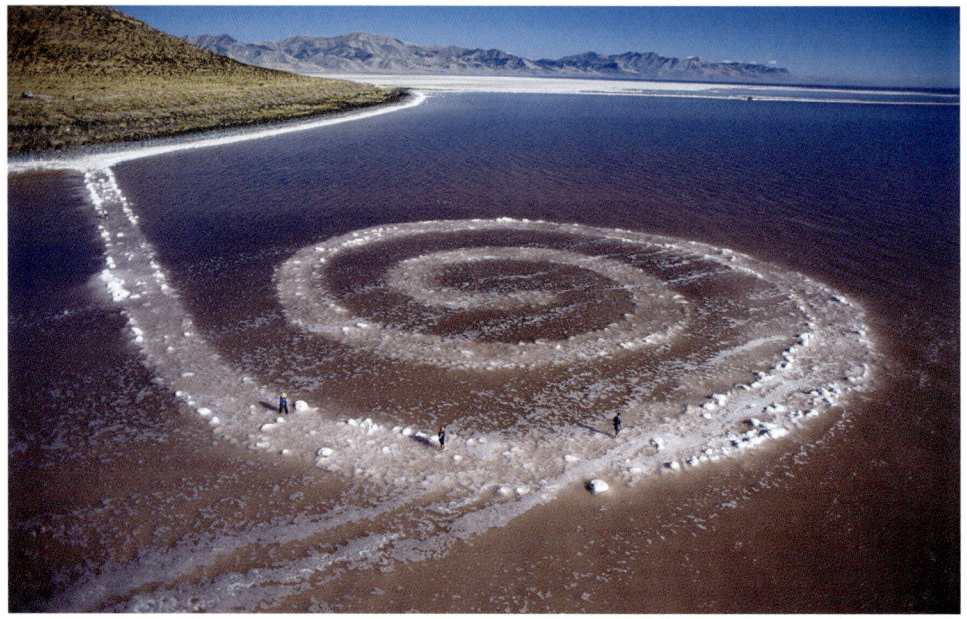

Spiral Jetty, 1970

Robert Smithson's early work consists of paintings in the style of Abstract Expressionism. After 1964, he considered himself solely a sculptor. His encounters with authoritative Minimalist artists such as Carl Andre, Donald Judd and Richard Long, and later with Bernd Becher in Germany, had a major influence on his work. As his international renown grew, in 1970 he began his probably most famous piece, *Spiral Jetty*, an approximately five-hundred-metre-long spiral made of natural materials, which he created on the shore of Great Salt Lake in Utah.

2 JANUARY

August Macke

1887–1914 | Expressionist painter | Germany

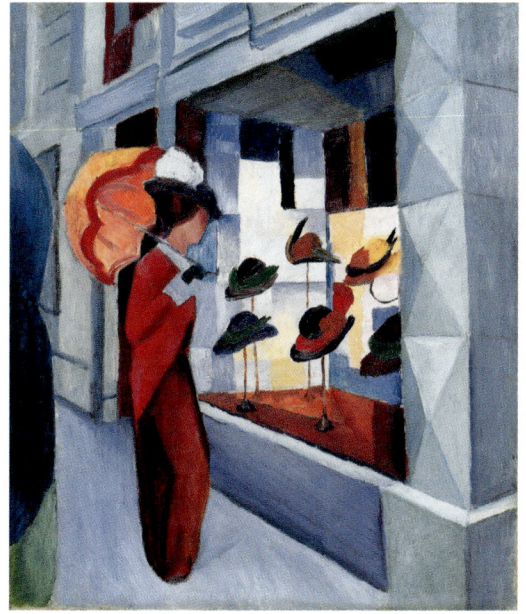

Woman with Umbrella in Front of a Hat Shop, 1914

Amid the widely diverging art movements of the early twentieth century, August Macke had little more than a decade to create his own distinctive oeuvre. He was a close friend of Franz Marc from 1910. His journey to Tunisia with Paul Klee and Louis Moilliet in 1914 became famous. It was during that trip that he matured into one of the great colourists in German painting. His early death as a soldier on the Western front in 1914 abruptly ended his burgeoning career.

3 JANUARY

Wilhelm Lehmbruck

1881–1919 | Sculptor and graphic artist | Germany

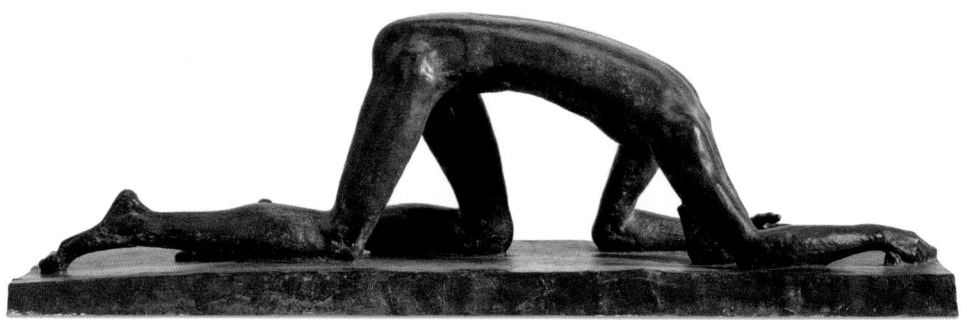

Fallen Man, 1915/1916

Wilhelm Lehmbruck is one of the most significant German sculptors of the twentieth century. He lived and worked mostly in Paris, Berlin and Zurich. His best-known pieces include *Pensive Woman* (1913), *Rising Youth* (1913) and *Fallen Man* (1915/1916). His unmistakable style, with its often expressively extended proportions is characterized by a unique etherealness combined with a high degree of formal abstraction.

_____

_____

_____

_____

4 JANUARY

Yves Tanguy

1900–1955 | Surrealist painter | France, United States

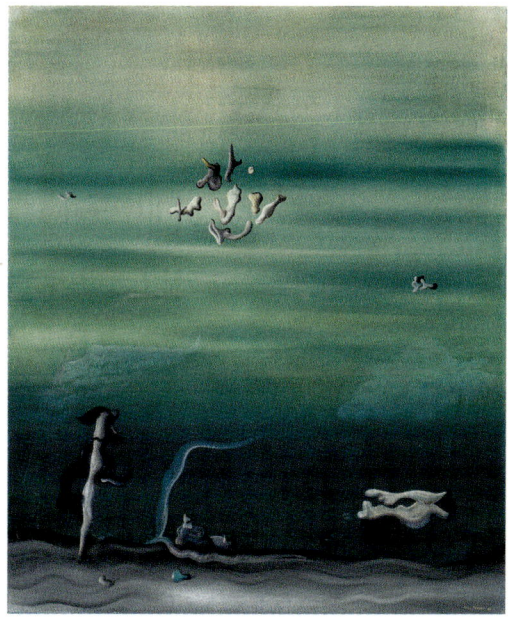

The Lovers, 1929

A self-taught artist, Yves Tanguy first started drawing and painting in watercolours in around 1923/1924. After Expressionist and Cubist beginnings, he devoted himself to Surrealism in 1925, keeping up lively contact with its protagonists in Paris. In late 1939, following the outbreak of the Second World War, Tanguy emigrated to the United States, where he died in 1955. His surreally coded, often ghostly lit visual worlds burgeon like mysterious plants in endless spaces and spellbinding, hyperreal dream landscapes.

5 JANUARY

Gustave Doré

1832–1883 | Painter, graphic artist and illustrator | France

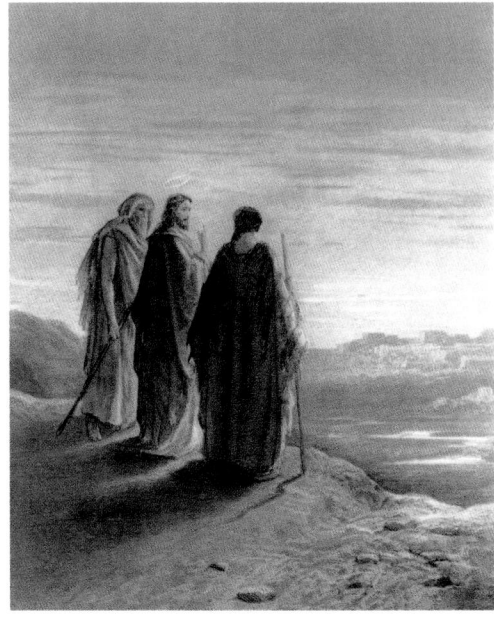

Christ with the Two Disciples Going to Emmaus, 1866

A precocious Gustave Doré tried his hand at illustrating Dante's *Divine Comedy* at the age of nine. Over the course of his career, he produced illustrations of some ninety works of world literature. His best-known creations include his Bible illustrations from 1866. Doré was one of the nineteenth century's great masters of illustration, and he had a considerable influence on quite a few artists, including Salvador Dalí.

6 JANUARY

Fahrelnissa Zeid

1901–1991 | Painter | Turkey

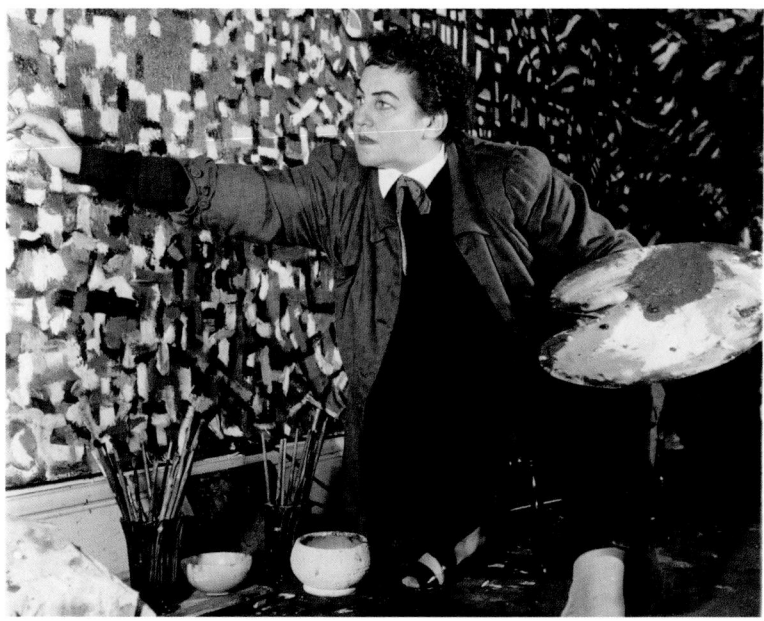

Fahrelnissa Zeid working on one of her large-format paintings, 1962

Zeid was one of the most significant Turkish painters of the twentieth century. Her life was defined by frequent relocations and global travels. Alongside traditional subjects, her abstract pictures with their kaleidoscopic synthesis of elements of Islamic, Byzantine and Western art were the foundations of her personal style that earned her global recognition.

7 JANUARY

Elisabetta Sirani

1638–1665 | Painter and engraver | Italy

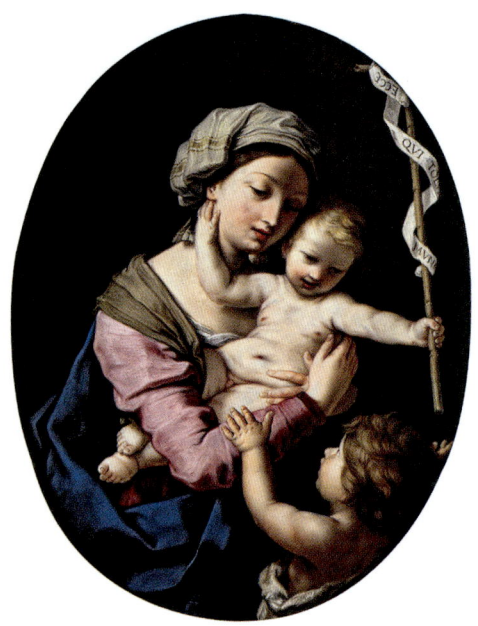

Madonna and Child with the Infant St John, undated

Sirani began working professionally as an artist at the age of seventeen. She set up an academy exclusively for female pupils in Bologna, her home city. The fruits of her brief but productive years of activity were some two hundred paintings, chiefly religious works, portraits and history paintings, as well as numerous drawings and some etchings. Most of her clientele came from Bologna's prosperous bourgeoisie and Italian and European aristocracy.

8 JANUARY

Gottfried Seelos

1829–1900 | Painter | Austria

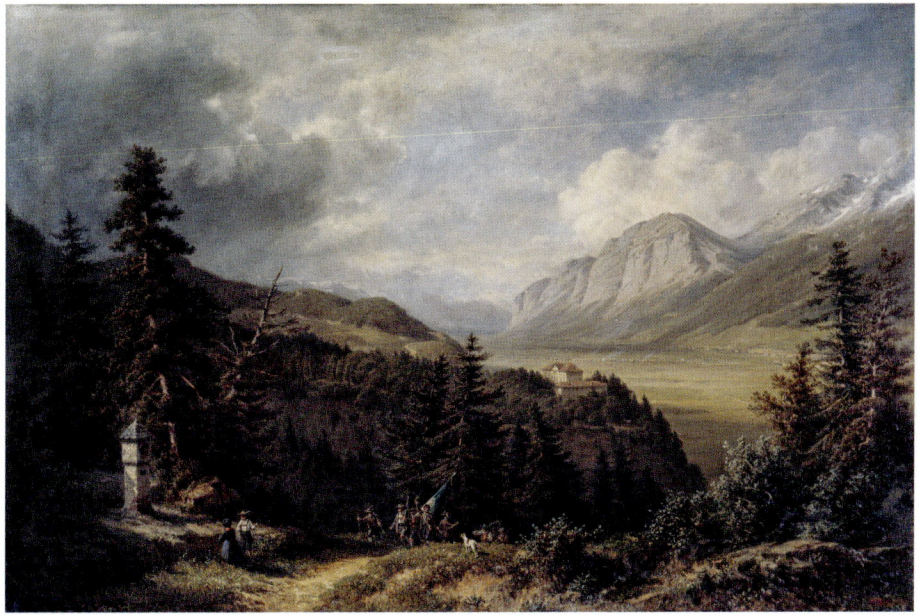

Bergisel, 1880

Following his studies at the Vienna Academy with a focus on landscape painting, Seelos embarked on the first of several study trips to Italy. His preferred themes were landscape depictions comprising northern Italian and Austrian motifs. He also made monumental murals such as the ones for Vienna's imperial palace, the Hofburg. Many of his landscapes were published as lithographs in large albums.

9 JANUARY

Barbara Hepworth

1903–1975 | Sculptor | Great Britain

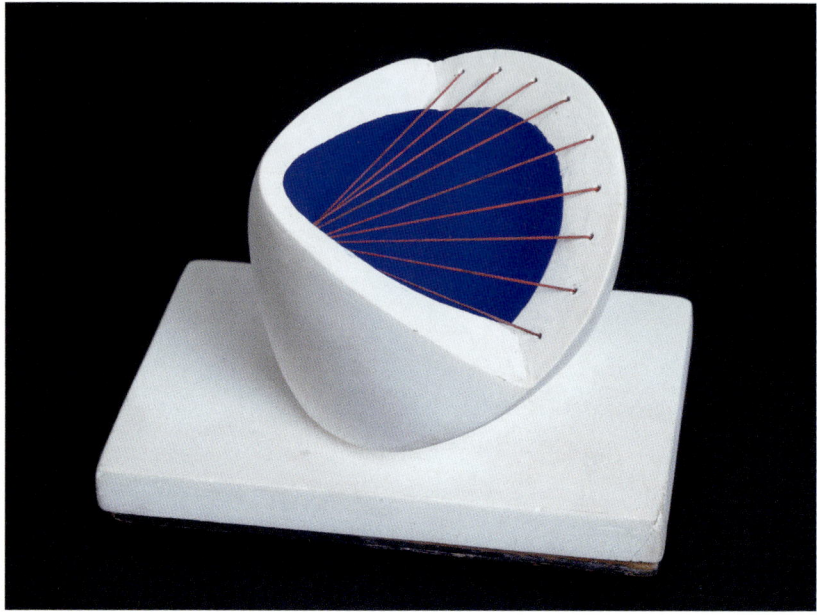

Sculpture with Colour (Deep Blue and Red), 1940

Hepworth, an English sculptor, earned international fame with her abstract sculptures. During her second marriage – to the painter Ben Nicholson, the father of her triplets – she created an independent oeuvre that is deeply indebted to influences by artists such as Constantin Brâncuşi and Jean Arp. Hepworth was one of the few female artists of her day to create her own distinctive style in the early avant-garde. Two museums dedicated to her oeuvre exhibit the artist's work on a permanent basis.

10 JANUARY

Parmigianino

1503–1540 | Painter and etcher | Italy

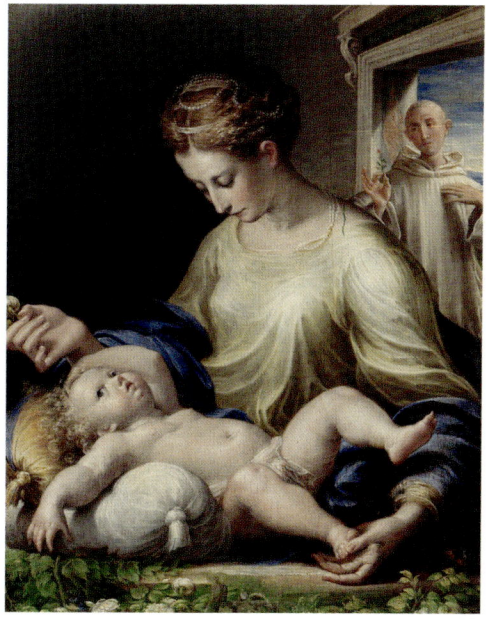

Madonna and Child with a Monk, c. 1530

Known as "The Little One from Parma", Parmigianino was one of the most important Mannerist artists in Europe. Despite his short life he was remarkably prolific. He is best known for his *Self-Portrait in a Convex Mirror*, which drew comparisons to Raphael when he arrived in Rome around 1524. He later worked in Bologna and Parma, producing frescoes and panel paintings that reveal his distinctive ideal of the human figure – elegantly elongated and exaggerated in proportion. His religious, mythological and portrait works are held in museum collections around the world. Parmigianino died in 1540, likely of malaria, at the age of thirty-seven.

11 JANUARY

John Singer Sargent

1856–1925 | Portrait painter | United States

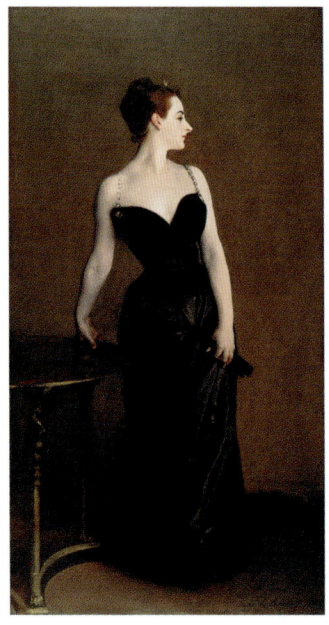

Madame X (Virginie Amélie Avegno Gautreau), 1883/1884

Sargent, an American, was regarded as the greatest portraitist of his time. His life was in constant flux, due to his parents' many relocations and his own numerous journeys across Europe to the Middle East and Morocco. Following an apprenticeship in Paris, he lived primarily in London from 1886. Working in the style of American Impressionism – and considerably influenced by the great Spanish painter Diego Velázquez – he made hundreds of technically dazzling oil paintings, watercolours and drawings, and was the international aristocracy's most coveted portrait painter.

_____

_____

_____

_____

12 JANUARY

Lilla Cabot Perry

1848–1933 | Impressionist painter | United States

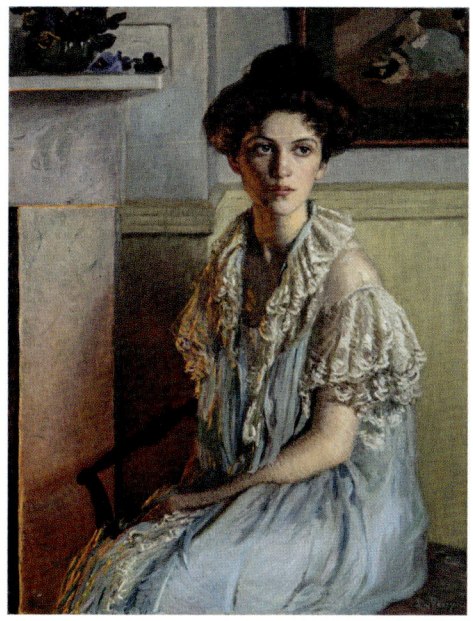

Lady with a Bowl of Violets, c. 1910

A friend of Claude Monet and Camille Pissarro, this American painter was a highly esteemed advocate and promoter of Impressionism in her home country. She spent an extensive period living in Europe from 1887, chiefly in Paris, before returning to Boston and then living in Japan for three years. Her painting style ingeniously combines Western aesthetics and Far Eastern traditions.

13 JANUARY

Berthe Morisot

1841–1895 | Impressionist painter | France

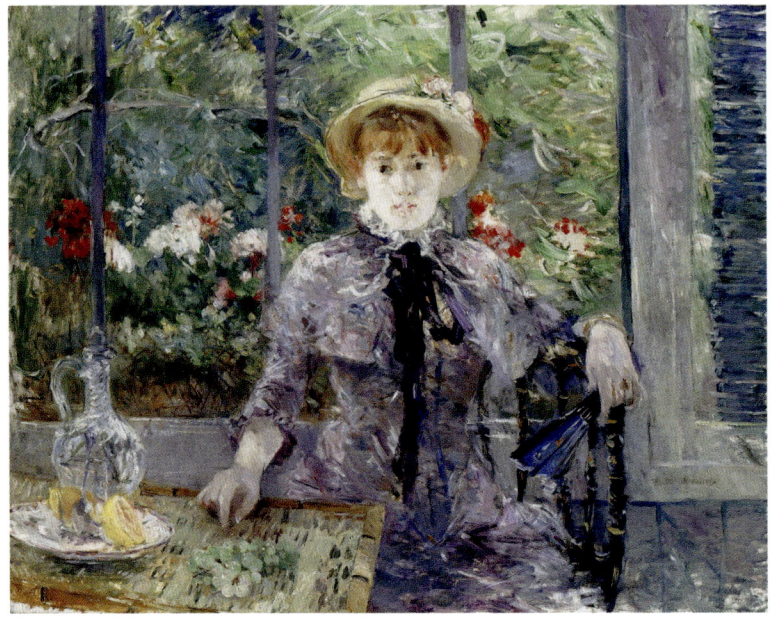

After Lunch, 1881

Family scenes and portraits in colours suffused with light were among the preferred subjects of this French painter, who is among the handful of professional female Impressionists. Born into a prosperous family, she cultivated contacts to the French art scene at an early age and exhibited in the Paris Salon from 1864. Among her many acquaintances were Edgar Degas and Édouard Manet – the latter painted her portrait many times and she married his brother in 1874. She was a founding member of the Impressionist group and took part in seven of the eight Impressionist exhibitions, through which she achieved great recognition at an early stage.

14 JANUARY

Andreas Gursky

Born 1955 | Photographer | Germany

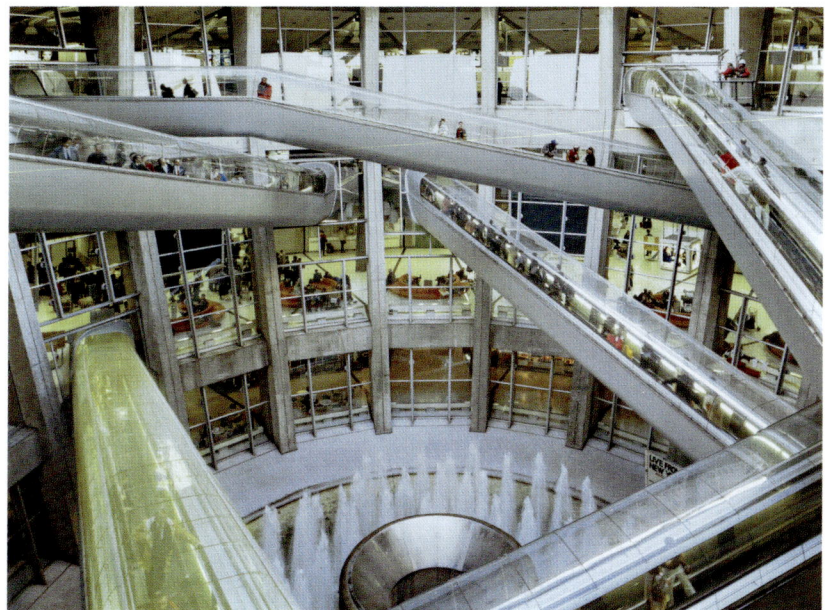

Charles de Gaulle, 1992

Andreas Gursky, the son and grandson of commercial photographers, was born in East Germany the year that his family fled to the West. They settled in Düsseldorf, a pivotal location for West German photography due to the local art academy and not least the activity of Bernd and Hilla Becher. Gursky became one of the world's most successful photo artists whose work has sold for record prices at auction. He is famous for his large formats that use subtle montage to confuse the optics in a practically imperceptible way. In a world of media and consumerism, Gursky incessantly explores the relationship between illusion and reality in the image.

15 JANUARY

Gerta Overbeck

1898–1977 | Painter of New Objectivity | Germany

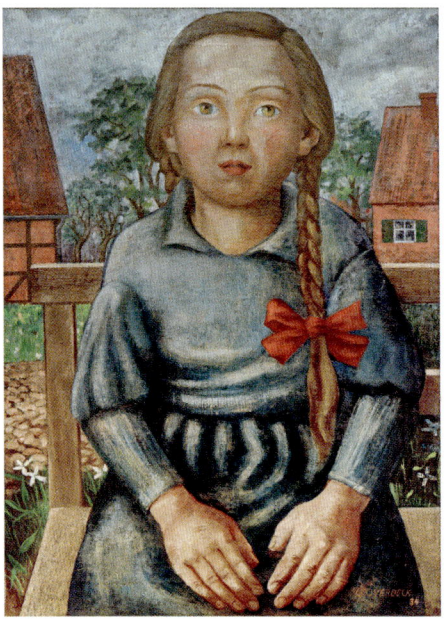

Young Girl, 1934

Overbeck is among the most renowned protagonists of Neue Sachlichkeit (New Objectivity) in Germany. Initially employed as a drawing teacher, she later worked as an independent painter. In 1932, twenty-three of her paintings were shown in the exhibition *New Objectivity in Hanover*. A close associate of the Communist Party, she was a member of the Reich Chamber of Fine Arts during the Nazi period. She spent her later years isolated and almost penniless in Cappenberg near Lünen in northern Germany. Her first solo exhibition took place in Hamburg one year before her death.

16 JANUARY

Giustiniano degli Avancini

1807–1843 | Painter | Italy

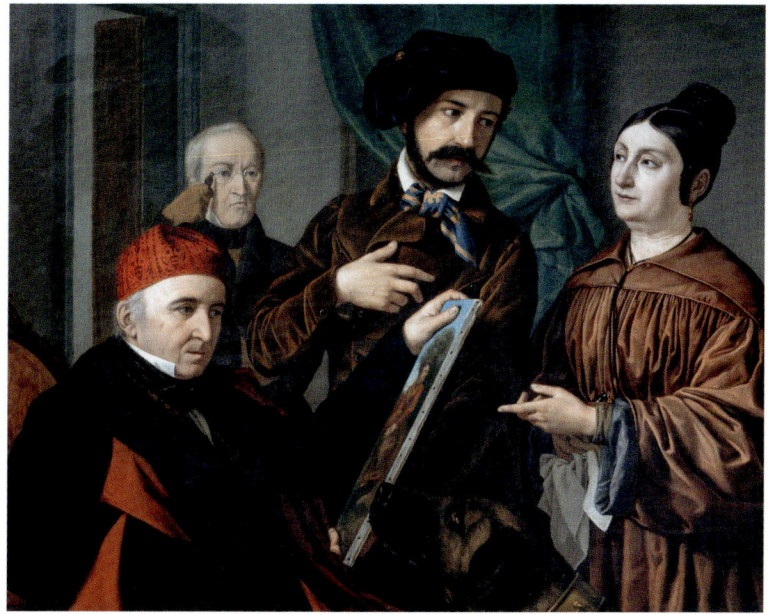

In the Artist's Studio, undated

The scion of an aristocratic family from Trento, Degli Avancini was born in Levico in northern Italy. He studied painting in the 1820s, first in Padua and then in Milan, and later spent time in Rome, where he rubbed elbows with major artists such as Jean-Auguste-Dominique Ingres and Eugène Delacroix. He became prominent mainly as a history painter, but also as a man of letters. Before settling in Venice, where he died prematurely, he travelled all over Europe.

17 JANUARY

Kiki Smith

Born 1954 | Sculptor and printmaker | Germany, United States

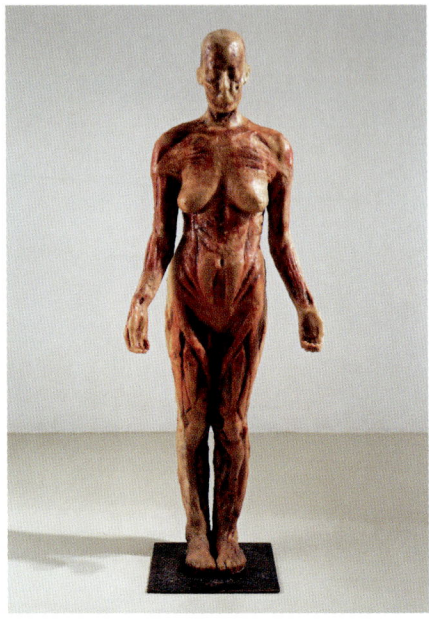

Virgin Mary, 1992

Born in Nuremberg and raised in the United States, Smith is recognized globally for her multidisciplinary practice through which she explores embodiment and the natural world. Smith's influential oeuvre examines the body, mortality, regeneration and gender politics, as well as the interconnection of spirituality and the natural world. Her expansive practice resonates personally and universally, manifesting in sculpture, glassmaking, printmaking, watercolour, photography and textile, among other art-making forms.

18 JANUARY

Paul Cézanne

1839–1906 | Painter | France

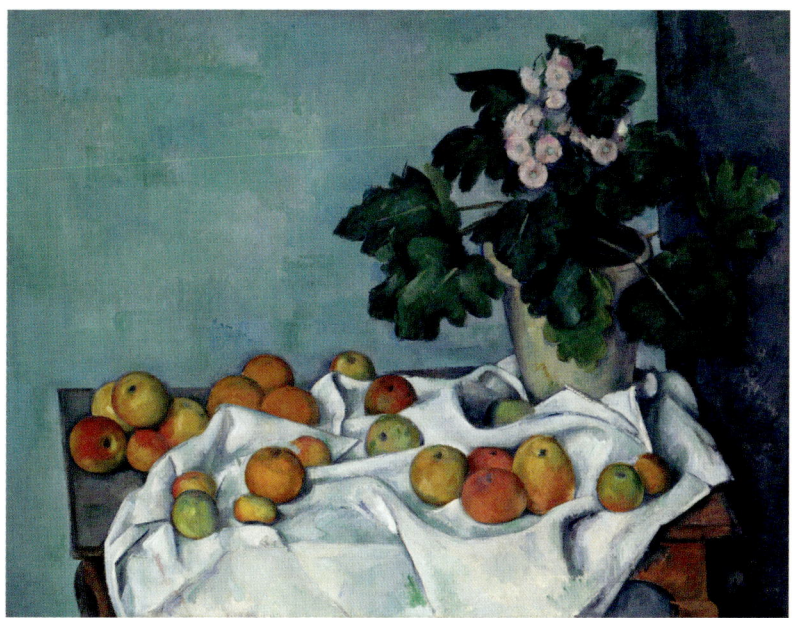

Still Life with Apples and a Pot of Primroses, c. 1890

Cézanne's modest and reclusive life produced a unique body of work that was long misunderstood and judged largely on formal and pictorial criteria. For him, "nature" was an essential starting point, and painting was a means of visually constructing the world. Turning away from Impressionism's interest in optics, Cézanne pursued – with radical intent and a "constructivist" spirit – a flattened pictorial space that challenged traditional perspective, in which nature and form were inextricably intertwined. In doing so, he became the father of modern art, to whom many later artists felt deeply indebted.

19 JANUARY

Antônio Parreiras

1860–1937 | Painter, draughtsman and illustrator | Brazil

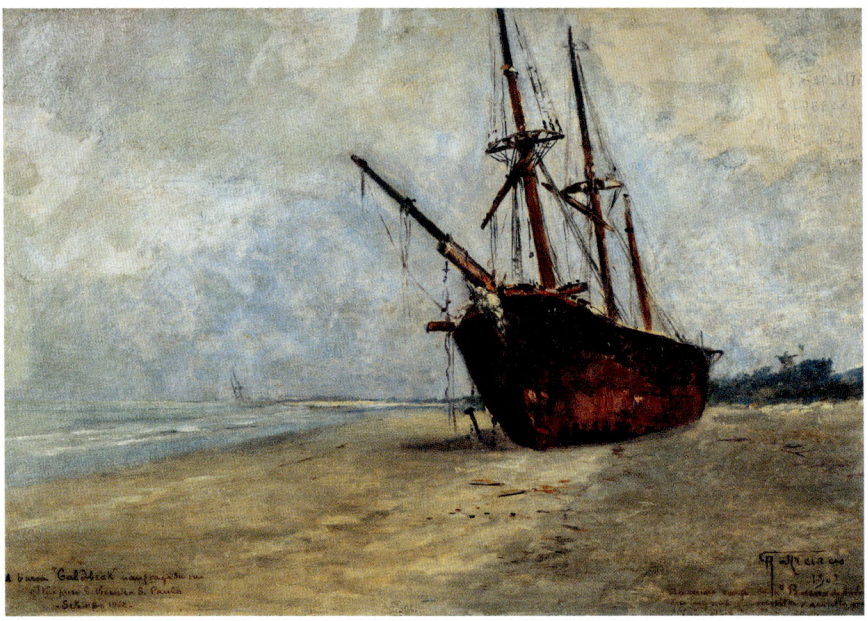

Seascape, 1902

After studying painting in Rio de Janeiro, this Brazilian artist travelled to Europe in 1888 to hone his skills at the Academy in Venice. Upon his return to Brazil, he was appointed professor of landscape painting in Rio. He subsequently received commissions for prestigious history paintings in public buildings. He also painted nudes of delicate sensuality. In the mid-1920s, he was one of his country's best-known painters, and he published his autobiography in 1926. A museum dedicated to his work was established after his death.

_____

_____

_____

_____

20 JANUARY

Jeff Koons

Born 1955 | Artist | United States

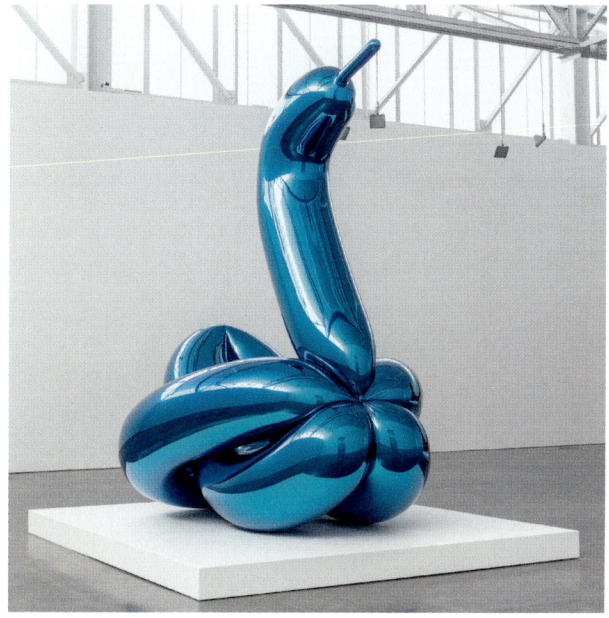

Balloon Swan (Blue), 2004–2011

Around the globe, this American is one of the most popular artists, a darling of the press and an often controversial crowd-pleaser. Situated between art and kitsch, his works ironically reference objects of consumer culture, which by means of defamiliarization and imitation take on a new, unprecedented presence. One of his best-known pieces is *Rabbit*, an inflatable bunny cast as a sculpture in stainless steel. At an auction price of more than ninety million dollars, this became the most expensive piece by a living artist in 2019.

---

21 JANUARY

Francis Picabia

1879–1953 | Painter and graphic artist | France

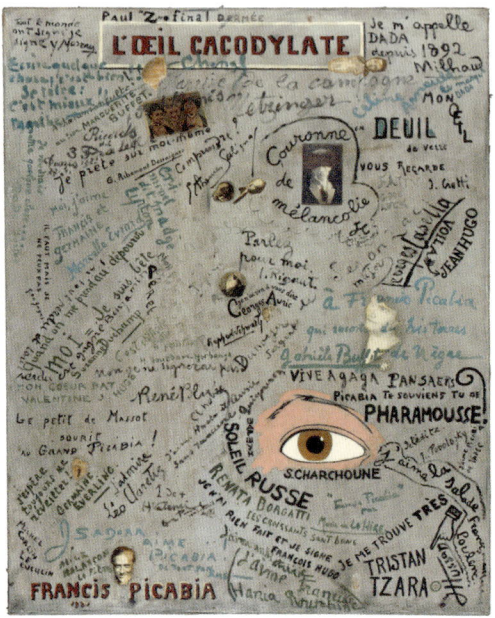

The Cacodylic Eye, 1921

On his father's side, Picabia was of Cuban descent; his French mother died prematurely. Financially independent, this eccentric artist refused to be defined by any particular political movement or to be categorized under the doctrine of any particular style. He frequently changed his style of painting between Impressionism, Cubism, abstraction, Dada, Surrealism and figuration. He lived in New York, subsequently in Barcelona, in Southern France and, after the war, in Paris again. His chameleon-like, protean character remained an enigma to many people, but it had a highly seminal impact on modern art.

22 JANUARY

Georg Baselitz

Born 1938 | Painter, sculptor and graphic artist | Germany, Austria

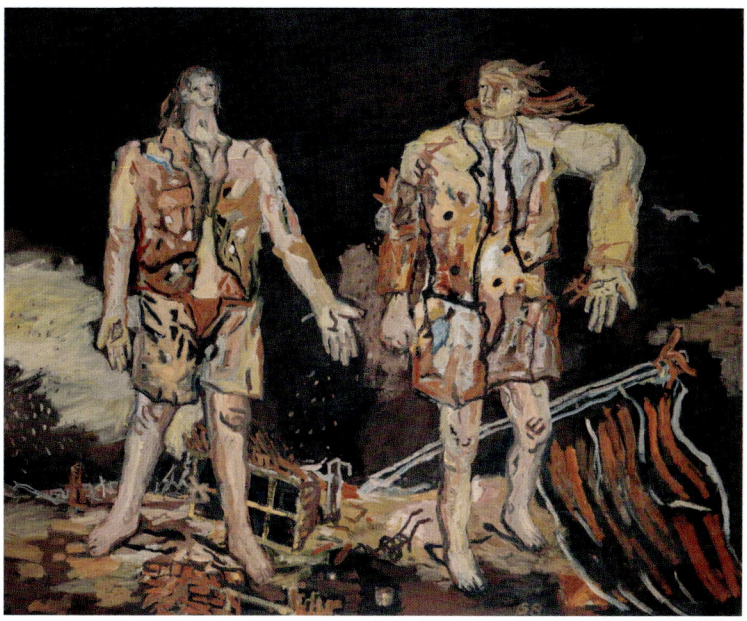

The Great Friends, 1965

This artist from Saxony has enjoyed international renown since the 1970s. He created his first upside-down picture in 1969, and these inverted images have since become the painter's trademark. Baselitz's concern was to devalorize the traditional reading of painting in favour of the independence of the genre. In 1965, twenty years after the end of the Second World War, Baselitz developed his series of *Heldenbilder*, or "hero paintings", in which he processed the experience of the Third Reich and his own biography in the communist German Democratic Republic. The artist has radically broken taboos, provoked and disrupted conventions in his oeuvre throughout his career.

23 JANUARY

Ruth Asawa

1926–2013 | Artist | United States

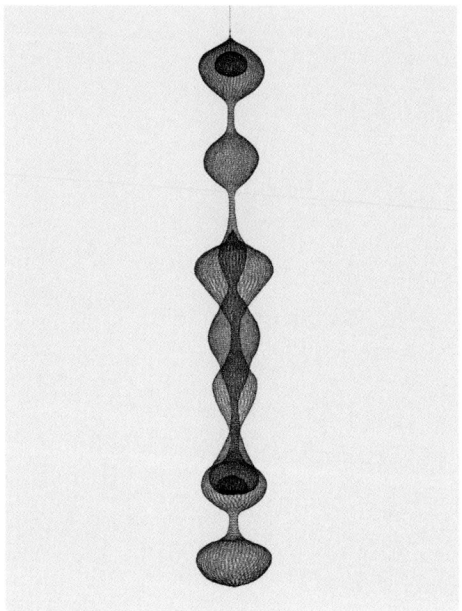

Untitled (S. 272, Hanging Seven-Lobed Continuous Interlocking Form with Spheres in the First and Sixth Lobes), *c.* 1954

Asawa, the daughter of Japanese immigrants in the United States, studied under the German émigré Josef Albers at the famous Black Mountain College between 1946 and 1949. Among other skills, she learned to work with everyday materials such as wire. In the 1950s and 1960s, she became famous for her spatially transparent wire sculptures. In 1968, she created her first fountain in bronze; it was followed by more, earning her the nickname "Fountain Lady" in San Francisco.

---

24 JANUARY

Tomioka Tessai

1837–1924 | Painter and calligrapher | Japan

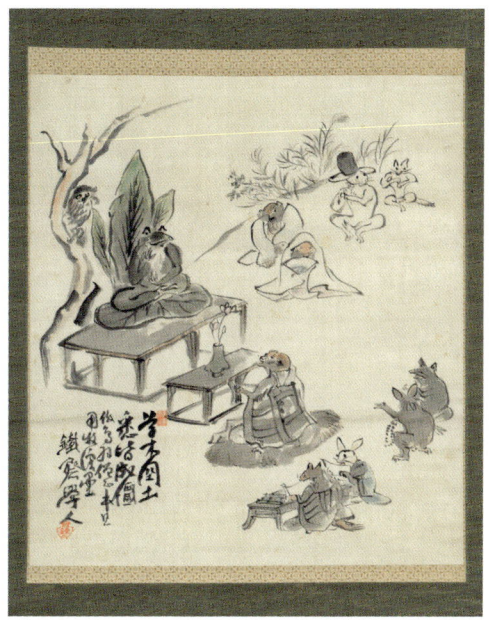

Scene Inspired by the Scrolls of Frolicking Animals and Humans, 1890s

This Japanese painter and calligrapher studied classical Japanese literature and sinology from an early age. He lived in a monastery as a Shinto monk for a while. Back in his home city, he obtained a teaching position; in 1917, he earned the distinction of court painter and, shortly after that, he became a member of the Imperial Academy of the Arts. He was self-taught, influenced by the style of Chinese and Japanese old masters. As a calligrapher he developed a highly individual brushstroke.

25 JANUARY

Paula Rego

1935–2022 | Painter and graphic artist | Portugal, Great Britain

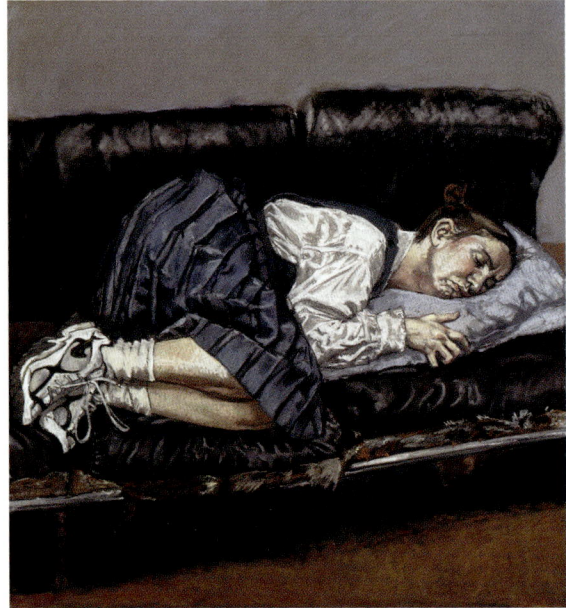

Untitled No. 4, 1998

Paula Rego, born in Lisbon into an Anglophile family and trained in London, was one of the most important painters of her day, initially creating pictures of controversial political content in the form of collage. Her magical realist painting style is unmistakeable: her predominant theme in often dramatic images is the role of women, as well as (her own) grief and suffering. In later works, mostly executed in pastel, she devoted herself with harrowing bluntness to the topic of abortion. A museum dedicated to Paula Rego was opened in Cascais near Lisbon in 2009.

26 JANUARY

Jozef Israëls

1824–1911 | Painter and graphic artist | The Netherlands

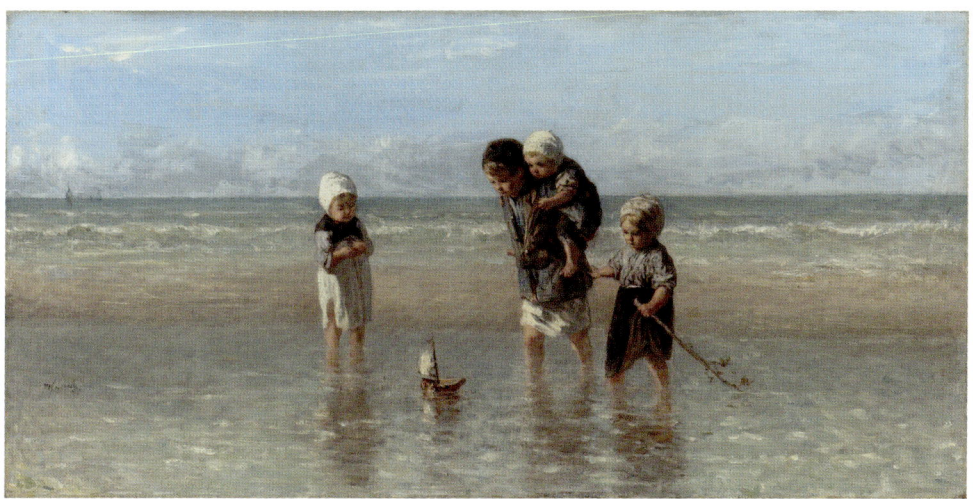

Children of the Sea, 1872

This Netherlandish painter and graphic artist lived initially in Amsterdam and later worked chiefly in The Hague. In the mid-1940s, he spent two years in Paris, where he learned to make history paintings in the Romantic style. Back in The Hague, pictures of simple fishermen from Zandvoort made him famous. He became one of the most important protagonists of what was known as the Hague School, was a member of various academies and wrote a book about Rembrandt, published in 1905.

27 JANUARY

Jackson Pollock

1912–1956 | Painter, performance artist, etc. | United States

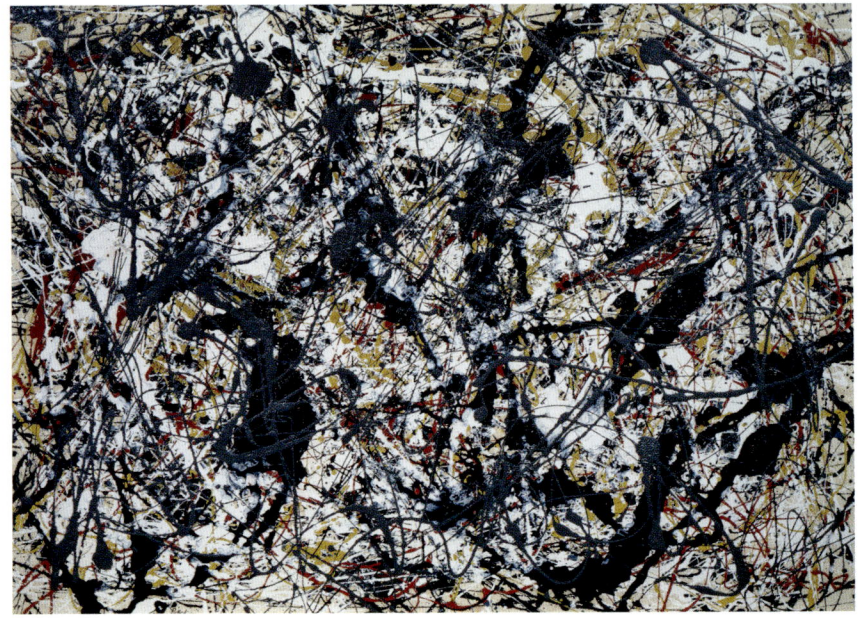

Painting (Silver over Black, White, Yellow and Red), 1948

Due to the uncompromising nature of his work, which was rooted in a life lived with intense urgency, Pollock was regarded as a legend. After 1946, the Surrealist-inspired figurative elements of his earlier paintings gave way to a radically new mode of psychological improvisation. Using "drip painting" – a technique in which he poured or flung paint from a can or stick rather than using a brush – Pollock worked with the canvas laid flat on the floor, applying paint in a process involving the entire body. As he remarked, "It doesn't make much difference how the paint is put on as long as something has been said. Technique is just a means of arriving at a statement."

28 JANUARY

Barnett Newman

1905–1970 | Painter and sculptor | United States

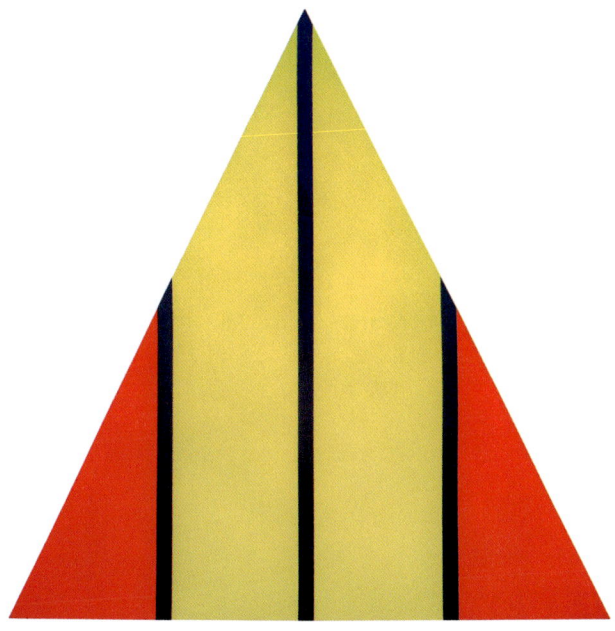

Chartres, 1969

The son of Jewish immigrants from Poland, Newman made chiefly Abstract Expressionist paintings in the 1940s. Later – together with painters such as Mark Rothko and Robert Motherwell – he developed Colour Field Painting as well as Hard Edge Painting, in which shape and colour appear starkly reduced. His first New York solo exhibition in 1951 received scathing reviews, causing the artist to withdraw for several years. Newman became famous all over the world for his large monochrome paintings that reflect his aesthetic search for the absolute and the sublime. They are scored by sharp lines, which he called "zips".

_____

_____

_____

_____

29 JANUARY

Amrita Sher-Gil

1913–1941 | Painter | Hungary, India

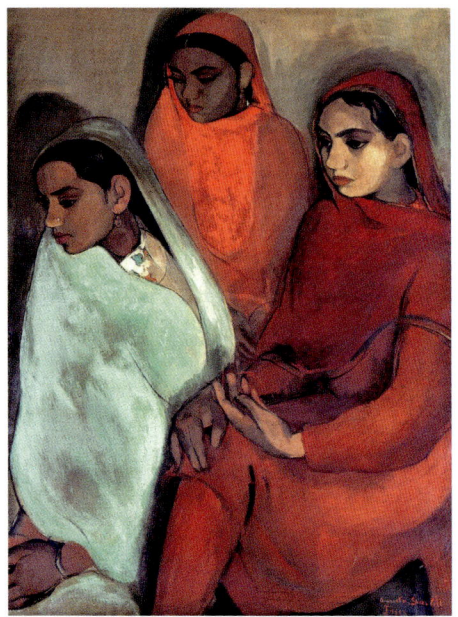

Group of Three Girls, 1935

Amrita Sher-Gil was born into an artistic, intellectual, bourgeois family in Budapest, and she grew up in India. In 1929, her family moved to Paris, where their art-loving daughter could study. Some sixty of her approximately two hundred paintings in total were made by 1932. One of her sources of inspiration was Paul Gauguin. Her self-portraits revolved thematically around her own – sexual – identity. In 1934, she returned to India, where she found her personal style and became one of the pioneers of Indian modern art. She died in Lahore at the age of only twenty-eight.

30 JANUARY

Betty Parsons

1900–1982 | Painter and gallerist | United States

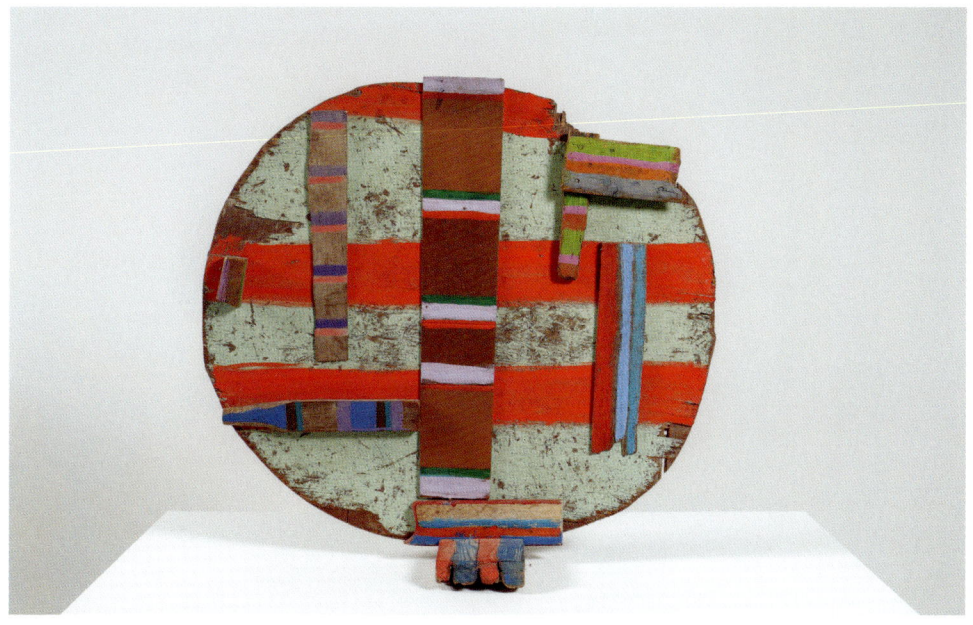

Il Oglala, 1979

Betty Parsons initially studied art against her parents' wishes. She married young and embarked on a month-long honeymoon through Europe; the couple divorced a short time later. She then studied in Paris and cultivated friendships with celebrities. After losing her money on Black Friday in 1929, she returned to the United States in 1933, working in various galleries but still pursuing her artistic work. In 1949, she opened her own gallery in Manhattan, where she represented Abstract Expressionist painters in particular.

31 JANUARY

Takashi Murakami

Born 1962 | Artist | Japan

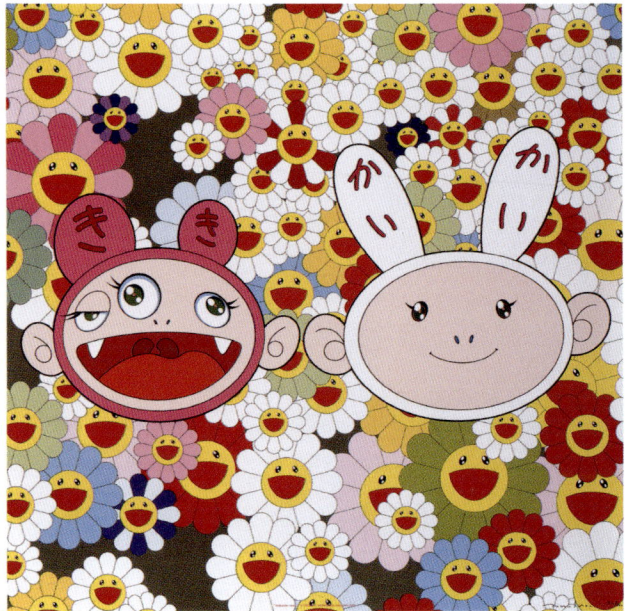

Kaikai Kiki News, 2002

Murakami was born in Tokyo. In addition to being a painter, he is active as a film director, animation producer, gallerist and hip-hop artist. He operates a gallery, a merchandise shop, a café and a confectionery studio, and serves as the president of his own company, Kaikai Kiki Co., Ltd. He has attracted international attention through a wide range of collaborations with luxury fashion brands such as Louis Vuitton, as well as musicians including Kanye West and Billie Eilish. Murakami is also known as the founder of the "Superflat" theory, which connects the aesthetics of traditional Japanese art with the flatness found in post-war Japanese anime and manga.

1 FEBRUARY

Oswald Achenbach

1827–1905 | Painter | Germany

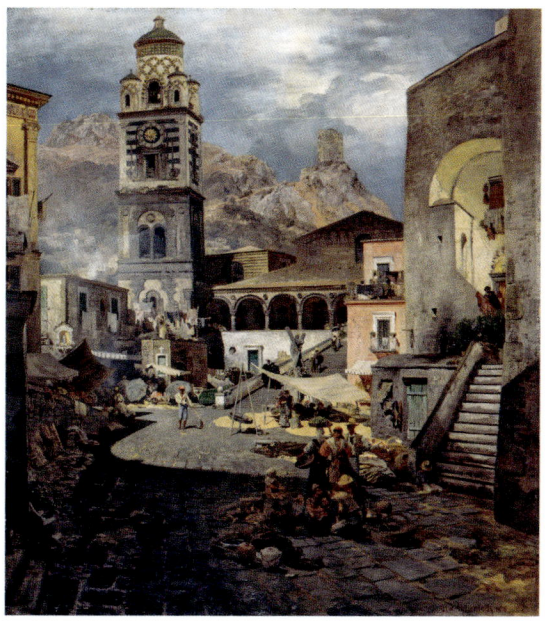

Marketplace in Amalfi, 1876

Achenbach, who was born and died in Düsseldorf, was one of the best-known land-scape painters in Europe during his lifetime. He was also an influential personality as professor of the art academy in his home city, which awarded him honorary citizen-ship in 1897. From the 1840s onward, he travelled extensively, especially to Italy. His painting style was rather conservative and, with an oeuvre comprising around two thousand paintings, tended to repeat motifs, which led to varying critiques of his art almost immediately after his death.

2 FEBRUARY

Daisy Campi

1893–1979 | Painter | Germany

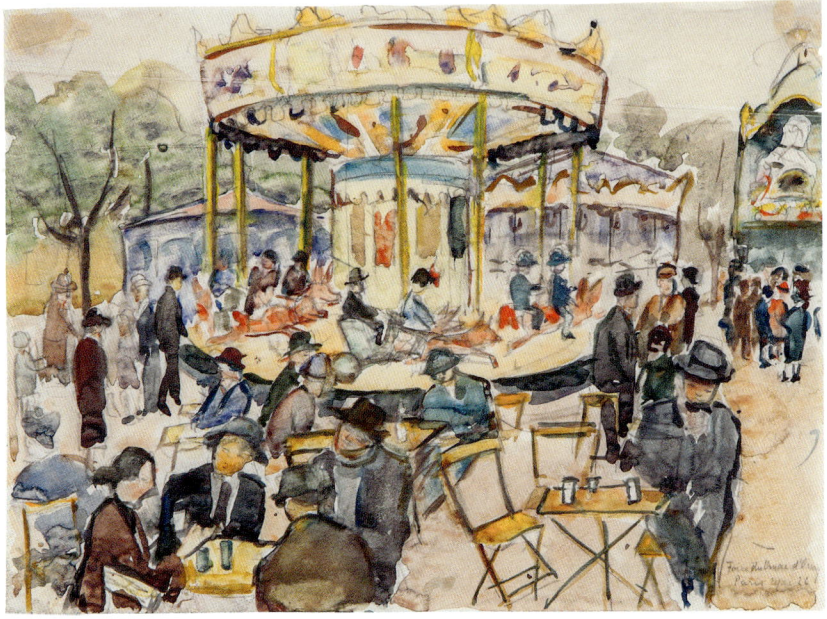

Fair in Paris, 1926

The daughter of a French diplomat, Campi was born in Port Said, Egypt, and spent her childhood in London, Shanghai and Paris. She began her training as an artist in 1914 in Lausanne, and later in Geneva and at the Art Academy in Munich. That was where she met the painter Hermann Euler, whom she married in 1928 and with whom she lived for the rest of her life in a farmhouse near Rosenheim in Upper Bavaria. Her oeuvre comprised still lifes and travel paintings, predominantly of southern landscapes, which were distinctly individual in terms of composition and colouring.

3 FEBRUARY

Georgina de Albuquerque

1885–1962 | Painter, graphic artist and academy professor | Brazil

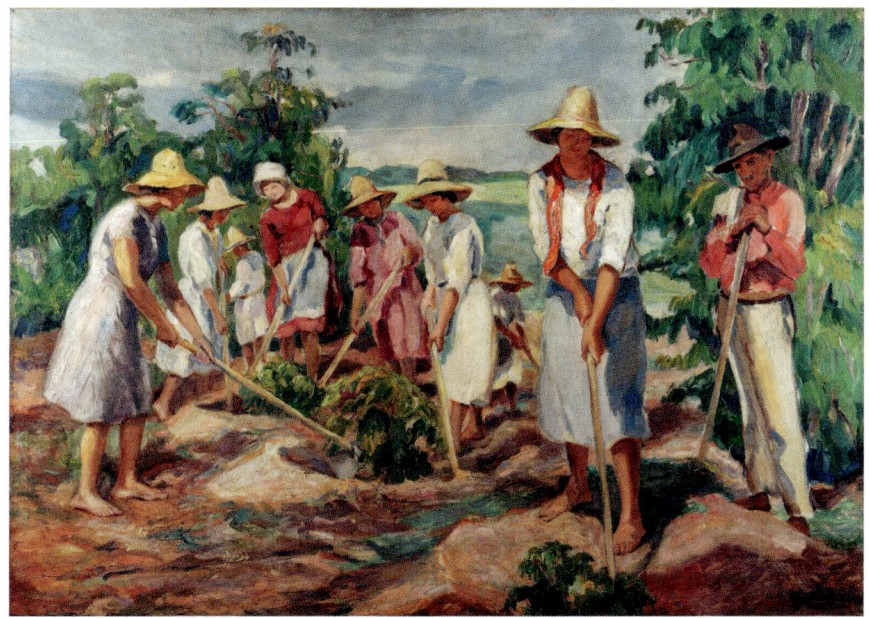

On the Coffee Plantation, c. 1930

Following initial teaching assignments and studies in São Paulo and Rio de Janeiro, where she met Lucílio de Albuquerque, whom she married, de Albuquerque travelled with her husband to Paris, where they both enrolled in the academy. Back in Brazil, she held various exhibitions of her Impressionistic landscape and genre paintings. Between 1927 and 1948, she taught artistic drawing at the Escola de Belas Artes, where she was later principal. After her husband's death, she established a museum dedicated to his work.

4 FEBRUARY

Olafur Eliasson

Born 1967 | Artist | Denmark, Iceland

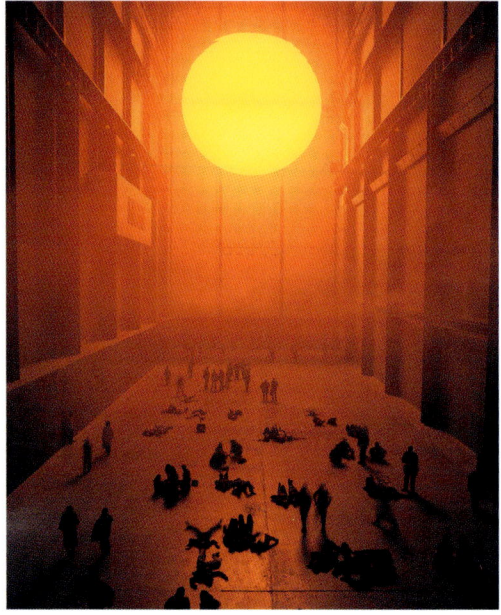

The weather project, 2003, installation view: Tate Modern, London, 2003

The Icelandic-Danish artist Eliasson spent his childhood in Iceland and now lives in Copenhagen and Berlin, where he runs a studio in which he elaborates his projects with a large team of co-workers from a wide variety of disciplines. His inventive mind endeavours to make physical natural phenomena come alive in large public spaces. The works, situated somewhere between art and nature and exhibited in prominent places across the world, are always widely covered in the media.

5 FEBRUARY

Achille Devéria

1800–1857 | Painter and lithographer | France

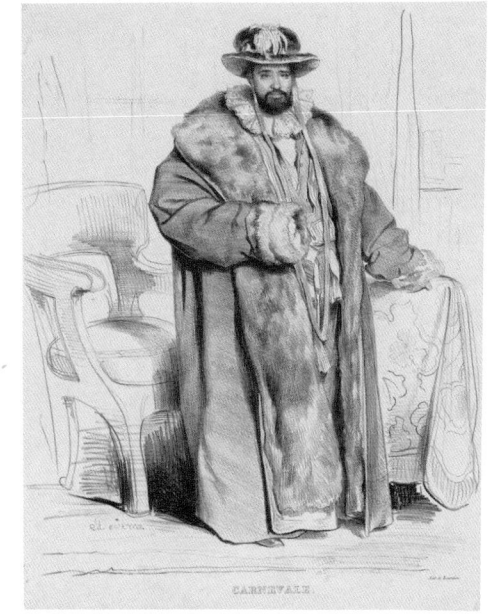

Carnival, 1830

The French painter and lithographer was invited to take part in the Paris Salon at the young age of twenty-two. He founded a successful private music school with his brother in 1830. After giving up painting, he devoted himself to lithography and worked as an illustrator of works that included *Don Quixote* and Goethe's *Faust*. The most coveted portrait-painter of his time, he had numerous celebrity sitters. In 1849, he was appointed director of the collection of drawings and prints at the Bibliothèque Nationale and curator of the Egyptian collection at the Louvre.

6 FEBRUARY

Henry Fuseli

1741–1825 | Painter and publicist | Switzerland, Great Britain

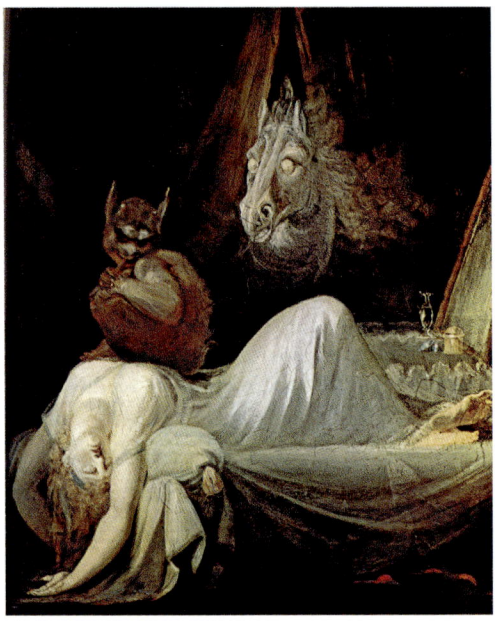

The Nightmare, 1790/1791

Born in Switzerland, Fuseli initially studied theology in Zurich and became a priest at the age of twenty. He went on to translate some of Shakespeare's dramas and, in 1765, decided to move to London, backed by an all-round education and speaking several languages. Joshua Reynolds ultimately encouraged him to pursue painting. Following a sojourn in Rome between 1770 and 1779, he returned to London as a celebrated artist. He was a painter and draughtsman, illustrator, poet and publicist. His painterly oeuvre ranges from surreal dreams to bizarre fantasy. An eccentric visionary, he was far ahead of his time.

———

———

———

———

7 FEBRUARY

Paula Modersohn-Becker

1876–1907 | Painter | Germany

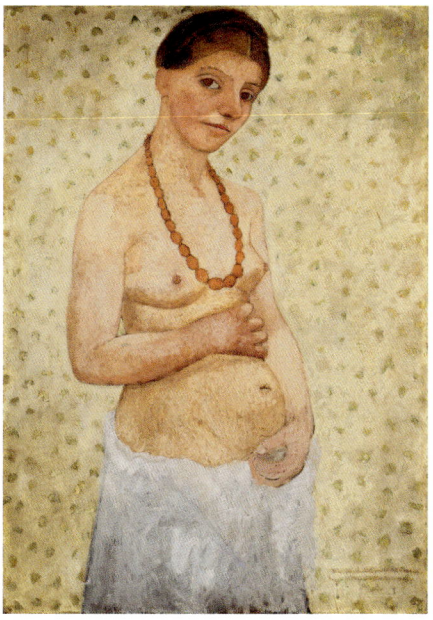

Self-Portrait on Our Sixth Wedding Anniversary, 1906

Following her early years in Dresden, Paula Becker moved with her family to Bremen. In the mid-1890s, she attended painting and drawing classes in Berlin. The artist colony in Worpswede, where she met her husband, Otto Modersohn, became a place of inspiration for her. She stayed there on multiple occasions from 1897 until her death. Paris, where she lived for four extended periods between 1900 and 1906, became her second home, where she cultivated many contacts, including to Rainer Maria Rilke and Auguste Rodin. One of the most significant painters of the early modern period, Modersohn-Becker died in childbirth at the age of only thirty-one.

8 FEBRUARY

Gerhard Richter

Born 1932 | Painter and photographer | Germany

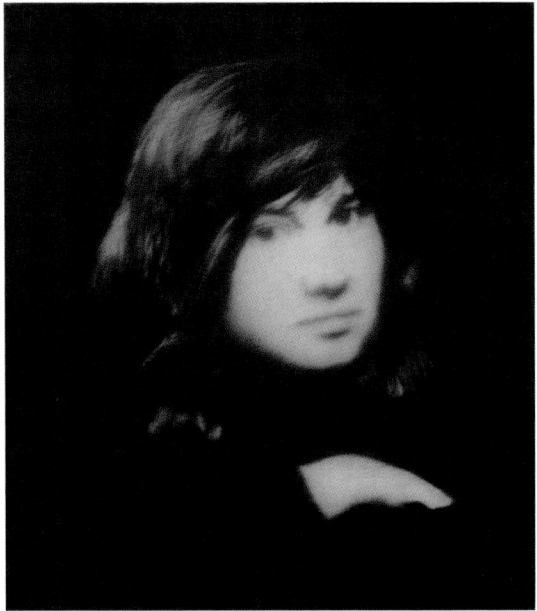

Portrait of a Young Woman, from the cycle "18 October 1977", 1988

Born in Dresden, Richter fled to West Germany in 1961. Between 1971 and 1993, he was professor at the Düsseldorf Art Academy. Early highlights of his oeuvre are his pictures from the 1960s, based on photographs that are defamiliarized by means of blurring. This phase came to an end with *18 October 1977*, a politically controversial cycle of paintings dedicated to the members of the Red Army Faction. Abrupt changes in style dominate as an enduring principle in the work of this internationally acclaimed artist, whose paintings have set price records at auction. Richter's oeuvre is contingent on his experimental dealings with objectivity between abstraction and realism.

9 FEBRUARY

Wilhelm Thöny

1888–1949 | Painter, graphic artist, etcher and illustrator | Austria

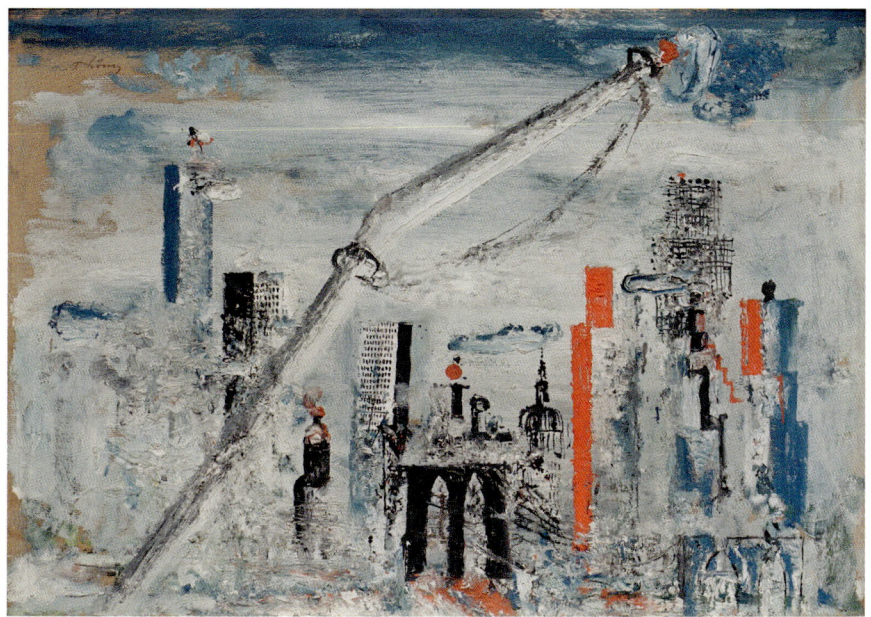

New York, Manhattan with Crane, 1935–1938

Between 1908 and 1912, Thöny, who was also a talented musician, studied in Munich, where he met the draughtsman Alfred Kubin, among others. Starting in 1915, he served in the war, working as a frontline draughtsman. When he returned to his birthplace, Thöny became president of the Graz Secession in 1923. The period between 1931 and 1938 he spent in Paris and the South of France before moving to New York with his Jewish wife. He lost a major part of his life's work to a fire in 1948. Graphic elements and a light colour scheme between white, blue and grey shades dominate in many of his works, forming an exquisite lyrical harmony.

10 FEBRUARY

Mona Hatoum

Born 1952 | Artist | Lebanon, Great Britain

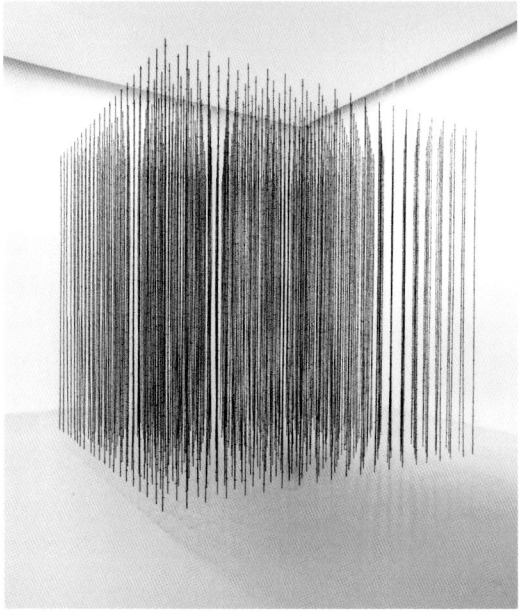

Impenetrable, 2009

In the 1980s, the Palestinian-British artist Hatoum became famous for her performances, videos, sculptures and installations. Many of her works focus on the body,
which she uses – often in a dramatic way – to express aspects of violence, power-
lessness, injustice and strategies of resistance. Much of her oeuvre relates to political
events as well as her own biography. She is interested in visualizing universally
valid experience through the involvement of the body, senses, mind and emotions.
Numerous prizes, including the Praemium Imperiale in 2019, attest to her global fame.

---

11 FEBRUARY

Max Beckmann

1884–1950 | Painter, graphic artist, sculptor and author | Germany

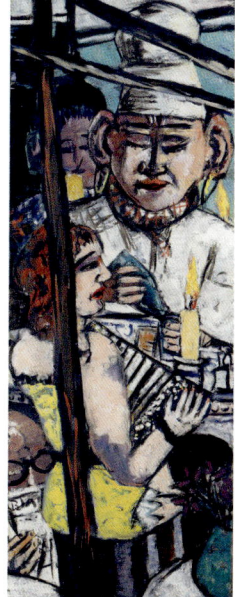 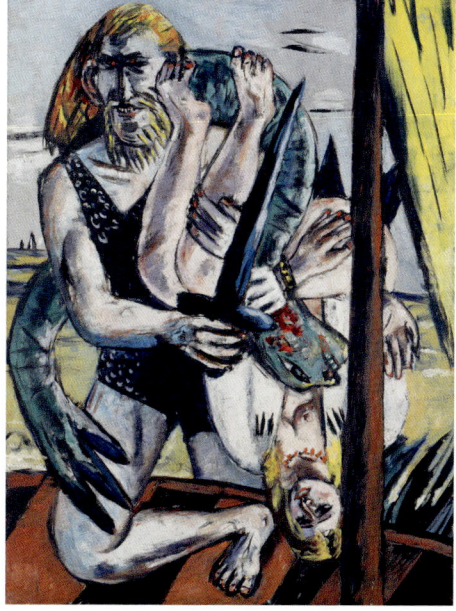 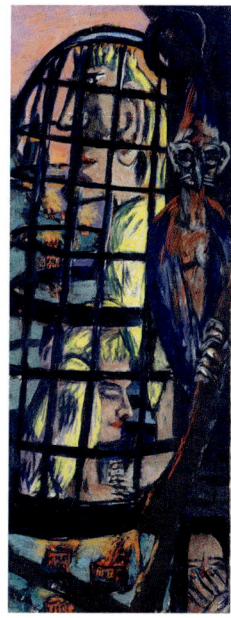

Perseus, 1941

Beckmann is one of the great painters, draughtsmen and graphic artists of Classical Modernism. As he rejected Expressionism, it was Beckman's aim to oppose the emerging abstraction with a modern form of figurative painting. The First World War signified a momentous experience for him. After years in Frankfurt am Main and Berlin, he emigrated to Amsterdam in 1937 and, from 1947, lived in the United States, where he died in New York in 1950. By his own statement he wanted to capture the "magic of reality" and translate it into painting. His narrative, myth-creating painting culminated in nine triptychs.

12 FEBRUARY

Grant Wood

1891–1942 | Painter | United States

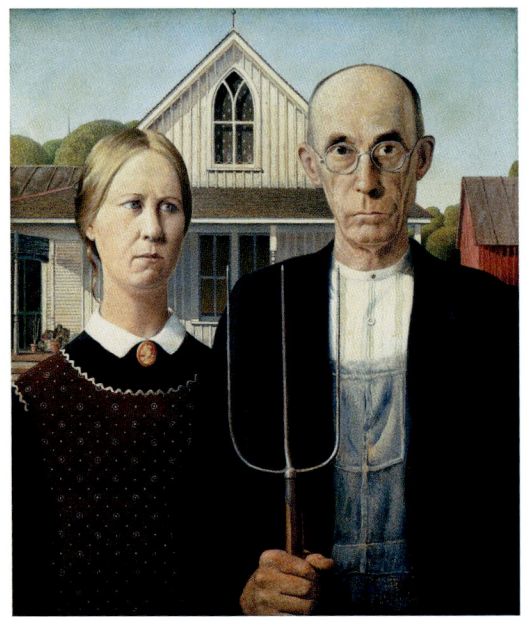

American Gothic, c. 1930

This American painter was a well-known protagonist of 1930s Realism. A stay in Munich during a commission for a stained glass window in 1928 was decisive for his evolving painting style. In Munich's Alte Pinakothek, the early German and Flemish masters impressed him so deeply that he copied them in part. He may also have been influenced by works of Neue Sachlichkeit (New Objectivity). His best-known work, *American Gothic*, which he painted in 1930, brought him overnight fame. Wood was appointed a professor at the University of Iowa in 1934. He died of cancer on the day before his fifty-first birthday.

13 FEBRUARY

Leon Battista Alberti

1404–1472 | Art theorist, architect, etc. | Italy

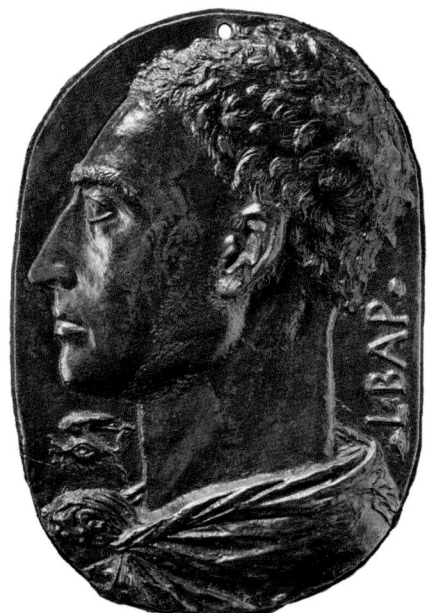

Self-Portrait, c. 1435

One of the fifteenth century's great polymaths in Italy, Alberti was highly regarded as an architect, writer, mathematician and art theorist of the Early Renaissance among rulers and princes as well as in humanist circles in northern Italy. In around 1435, he penned the pioneering texts *On the Art of Painting* and *On the Statue*, as well as, a few years later, *On Construction*. As an architect, engaging freely and creatively with precepts from antiquity, he designed major churches and palaces in Rimini, Florence and Mantua.

14 FEBRUARY

Charles-François Daubigny

1817–1878 | Painter and graphic artist | France

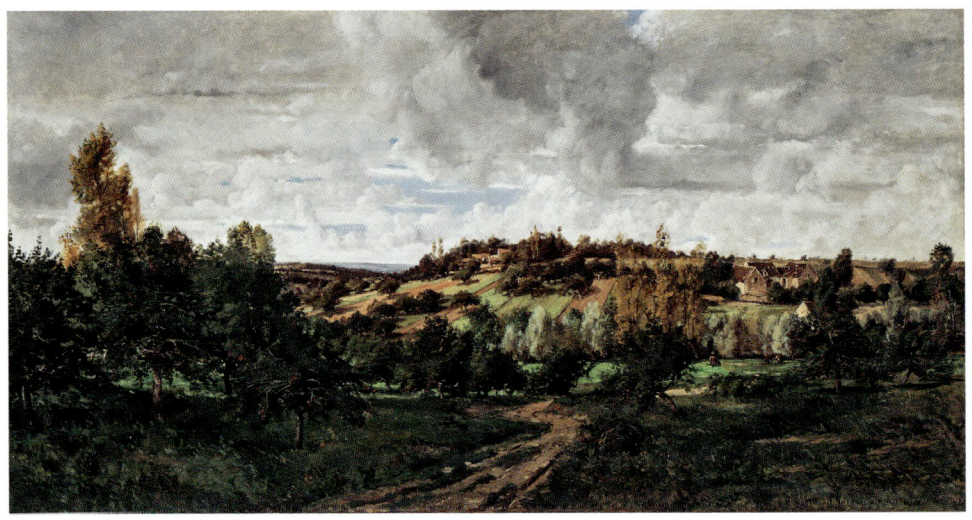

Landscape near Auvers, c. 1860–1870 (?)

As his father's pupil, Daubigny exhibited classical landscapes starting in 1838 but only began to achieve general recognition in the 1850s. Along with a number of other painters, he was part of the Barbizon School. His open-air painting had a considerable influence on Impressionism. In 1860, he settled in Auvers-sur-Oise, his departure point for trips in his studio-boat on the Seine and the Oise in search of suitable natural motifs, something which Claude Monet later did too.

15 FEBRUARY

Kanō Eitoku

1543–1590 | Painter | Japan

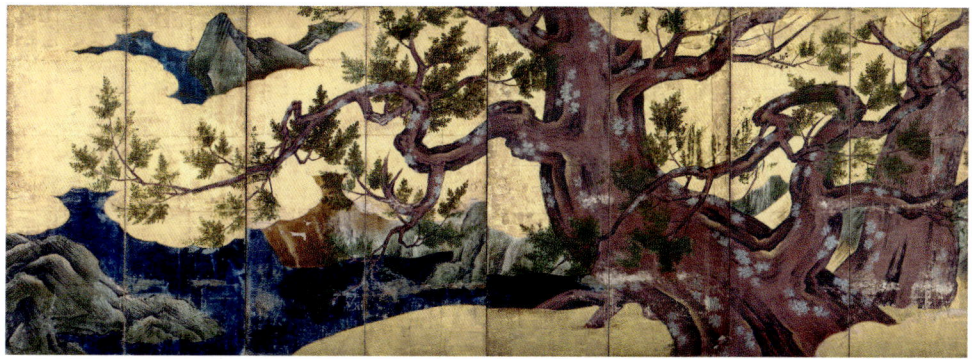

Cypress Trees, c. 1590

Eitoku is regarded as a major Japanese painter of the sixteenth century: some of his works were elevated to the rank of Japanese national treasure. He demonstrated his artistic prowess at a young age with paintings on wooden sliding doors and wall screens. His *Views In and Around Kyoto* are understated masterpieces painted on gold ground. Sadly, many of his creations were lost when the palaces were destroyed. In Eitoku's art, the paint ingeniously mingled with the lines of black ink against grounds of rich gold.

16 FEBRUARY

Raphaelle Peale

1774–1825 | Painter | United States

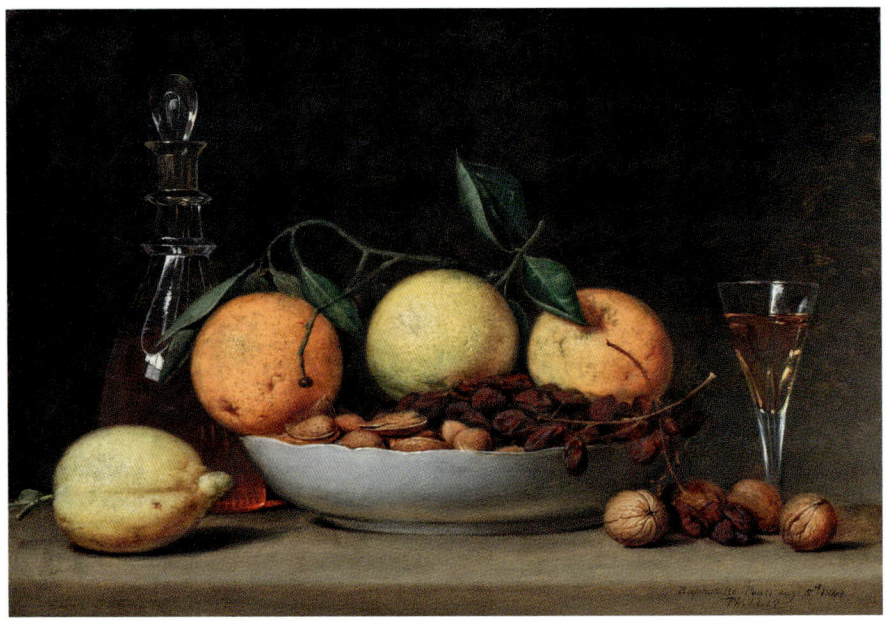

A Dessert, 1814

Named, like many of his siblings, after a famous painter, Raphaelle was taught painting by his father. Even as a young man he suffered from poor health and was plagued by gout. He was reliant on crutches from 1813 onward. From that time, Peale devoted himself mainly to still lifes and *trompe l'œil* painting, which his father disapproved of, wanting to see him focus on portrait painting. Peale died after a night of binge drinking at the age of just fifty-one. He is regarded as the father of still-life painting in America.

17 FEBRUARY

Max Klinger

1857–1920 | Sculptor, painter and graphic artist | Germany

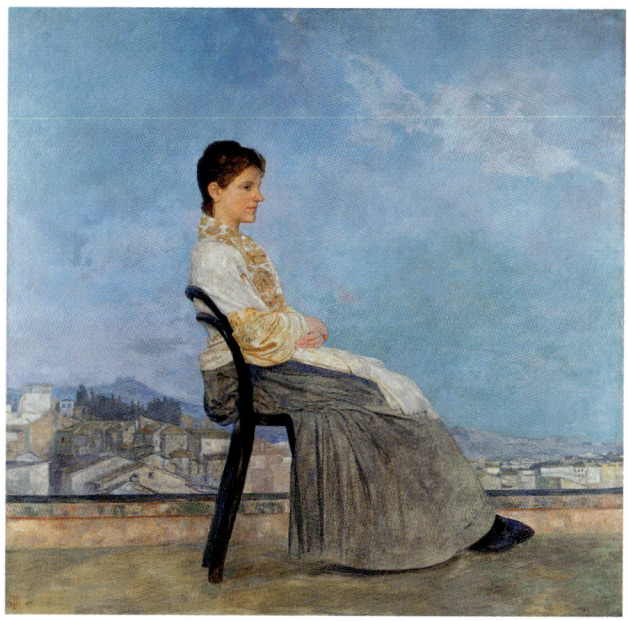

Portrait of a Roman Woman on a Flat Roof in Rome, 1891

A man of letters and a scholar, Klinger studied in Karlsruhe and Berlin, lived in Paris from 1883 to 1886 and then in Rome from 1888 to 1893. In his polemic *Painting and Drawing*, published in 1891, he explored the idea of the *Gesamtkunstwerk* or "total work of art" within the intellectual framework of Nietzsche and Wagner. Although he worked as a sculptor and painter, his true calling was printmaking. Numerous graphic cycles exploring Symbolist themes such as longing, solitude, love, eroticism and death had a marked influence, decades later, on modern artists including Giorgio de Chirico, Max Ernst and Max Beckmann.

18 FEBRUARY

Constantin Brâncuși

1876–1957 | Sculptor and photographer | Romania, France

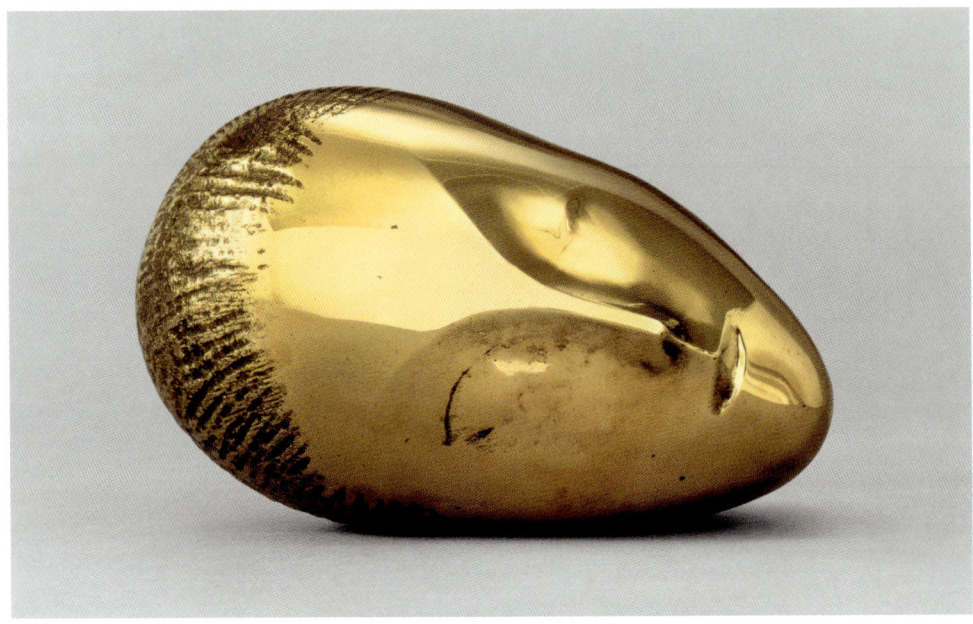

Sleeping Muse, 1910

One of the twentieth century's most influential sculptors, Brâncuși lived in Paris from 1904. He spent his whole life searching for the perfect shape. He created his archetypical basic shapes, inspired by popular art in Africa and Romania, in various materials such as marble, wood and bronze. The gleaming surface achieved by means of polishing meant, for him, transparency and opening to the space. Light, to him, was a design element. One highlight of his oeuvre is the soldiers' memorial built in 1938 in Târgu Jiu, Romania, with the *Endless Column* as its centrepiece.

19 FEBRUARY

Josefa de Óbidos

1630–1684 | Painter | Portugal

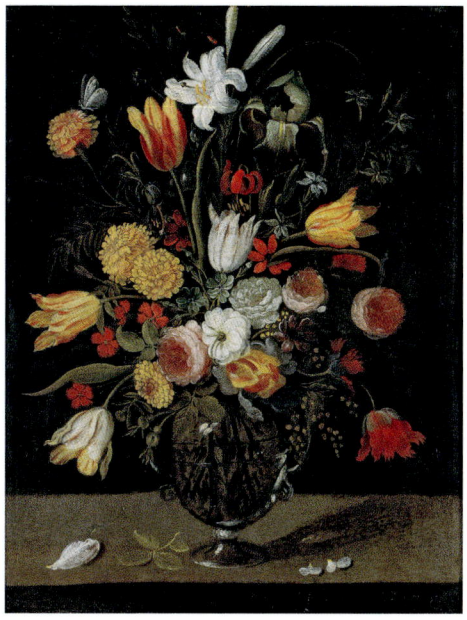

Still Life with Flowers in a Vase, second half of seventeenth century

Born in Seville, where her father – a Portuguese painter – was working, Josefa de Óbidos arrived in Portugal at the age of five. After spending her childhood in Coimbra, she later lived and worked in Óbidos. In addition to portraits and miniatures, she painted still lifes. She is considered the most significant woman artist in Portuguese painting of the seventeenth century. Her work was rediscovered in a 2015 solo exhibition at the Museu de Arte Antiga in Lisbon.

20 FEBRUARY

Félix Resurrección Hidalgo

1855–1913 | Painter | Philippines

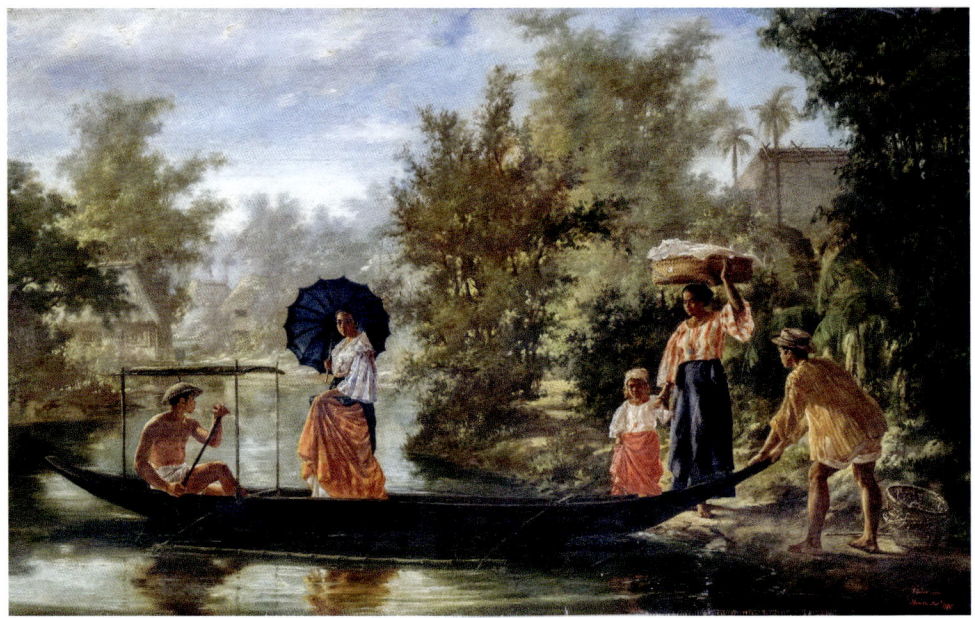

The Indigenous Boat, 1876

The recipient of a grant from the Spanish government, Hidalgo studied at the Real Academia de Bellas Artes de San Fernando in Madrid between 1879 and 1881. Some of his paintings, executed in a style that fuses Impressionism and Neoclassicism, were later distinguished with medals in Madrid, Paris and Barcelona. He participated in exhibitions in Chicago, Bilbao, Manila and, in 1904, in St Louis, Missouri. He died in Barcelona in 1913.

21 FEBRUARY

JR

Born 1983 | Photographer and street artist | France

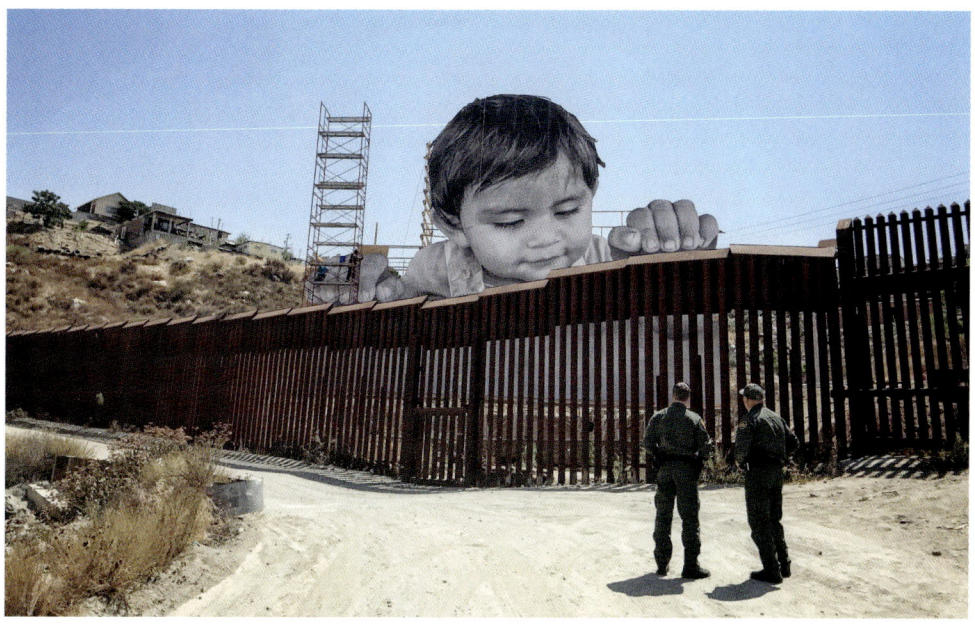

Giants, Kikito, US-Mexico Border, 2017

JR began doing graffiti in public space at a young age. In 2004/2005, he photographed other street artists at work in various cities and published the photos, complete with journal entries, in his first book, *Carnet de Rue*. Several of his documentary films have won prizes at major festivals. Pasted on building façades around the world, his photographs attract public attention to the faces of people whose lives were shaped by the likes of suffering, oppression, war, displacement and loss.

22 FEBRUARY

Franz von Stuck

1863–1928 | Draughtsman, painter and sculptor | Germany

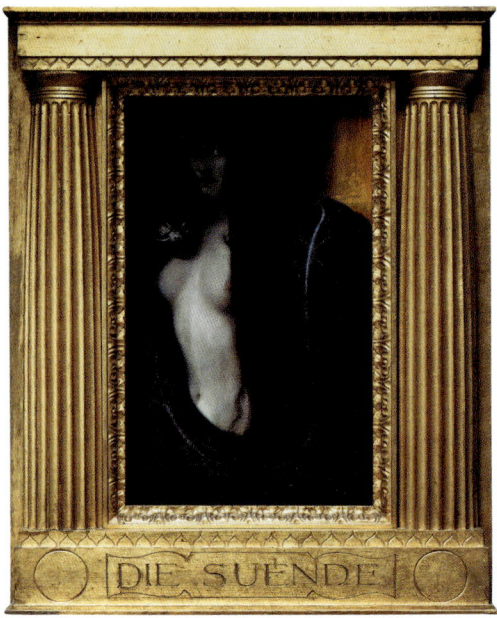

Sin, 1893

A series of caricatures for the magazine *Fliegende Blätter* catapulted Stuck to fame. He began his first experiments in oil painting in around 1887. From 1895, Stuck was a professor and teacher at the Art Academy in Munich; his students included Josef Albers, Giorgio de Chirico, Wassily Kandinsky and Paul Klee. His pictorial world was characterized by allegorical, symbolic content with erotic shades. In addition to being a protagonist of Munich Jugendstil, he was a major proponent of German Symbolism who was able to implement his visions of a *Gesamtkunstwerk*, or total work of art, in his villa in Munich, which is now a museum.

23 FEBRUARY

Etel Adnan

1925–2021 | Writer and painter | Lebanon, United States

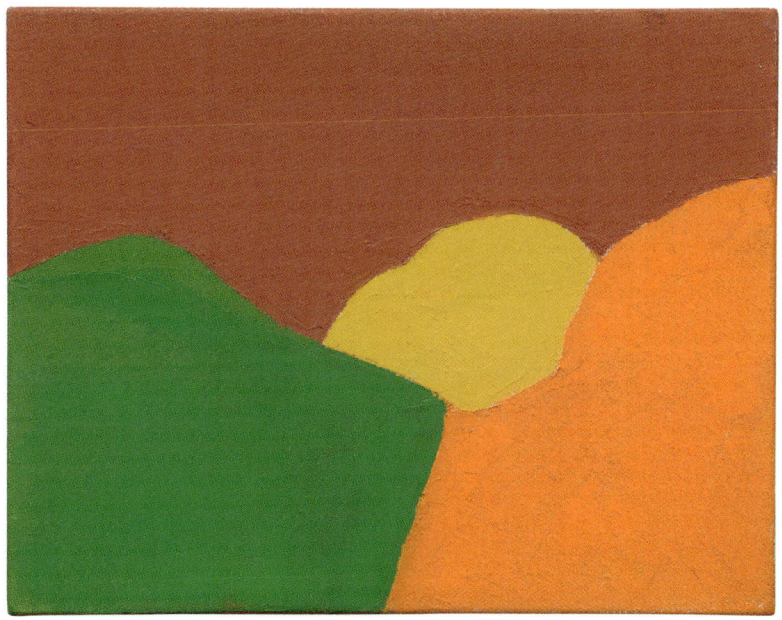

Untitled, 2010

Born in what was then French-controlled Lebanon, Adnan relocated many times. In 1949, she went to Paris, where she studied philosophy; she was later a student at the University of California, Berkeley, and Harvard. She met her life partner following her return to Lebanon in 1972. In 1976, she moved back to Paris; from there she moved to California and to Paris again. She applied her multicultural talents to books, radio dramas, plays and abstract paintings; her creative output fluctuates between Arabic and Western influences.

24 FEBRUARY

Pierre-Auguste Renoir

1841–1919 | Painter | France

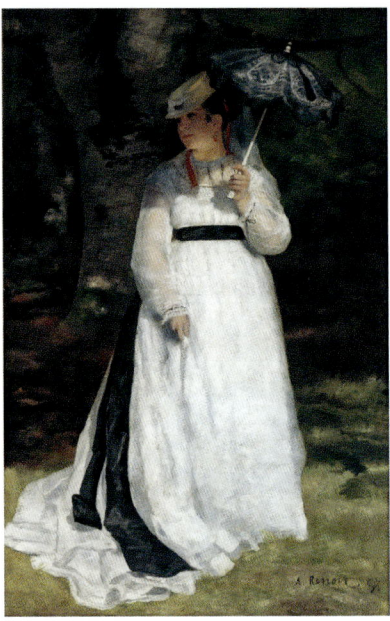

Lise with a Parasol, 1867

One of the most significant French painters of Impressionism, Renoir began studying painting in 1861 and befriended other artists, including Monet, with whom he worked outdoors. His vibrant and light-suffused paintings – including landscapes, portraits, still lifes, nudes, family portraits and pictures of social leisure pursuits – are one big celebration of life and the outdoors. In 1917, owing to his arthritis, the father of three sons moved near to Nice, where he painted into his final years in a wheelchair.

25 FEBRUARY

Mihri Müşfik Hanım

1886–1954 | Painter | Turkey

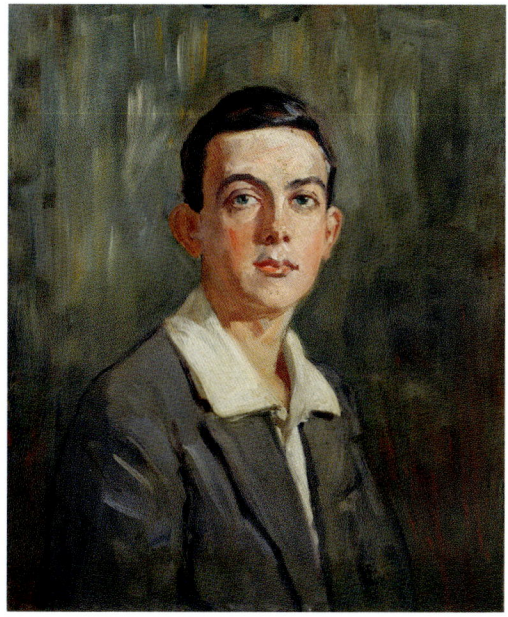

Portrait of a Young Man, undated

This Turkish painter is regarded as one of the leading artists of the Late Ottoman period. Her life was spent discontinuously in Istanbul, Rome, Paris and later the United States. At her initiative, an art academy for women was founded in Istanbul in 1914; she later became its principal. Hanım's painting was considerably inspired by French art. She became famous for her likenesses of women and for portraits of celebrities such as Atatürk and Pope Benedict XV. There are no records of her in the US after the war ended. She was buried in a pauper's grave in 1954.

26 FEBRUARY

Joaquín Sorolla

1863–1923 | Painter | Spain

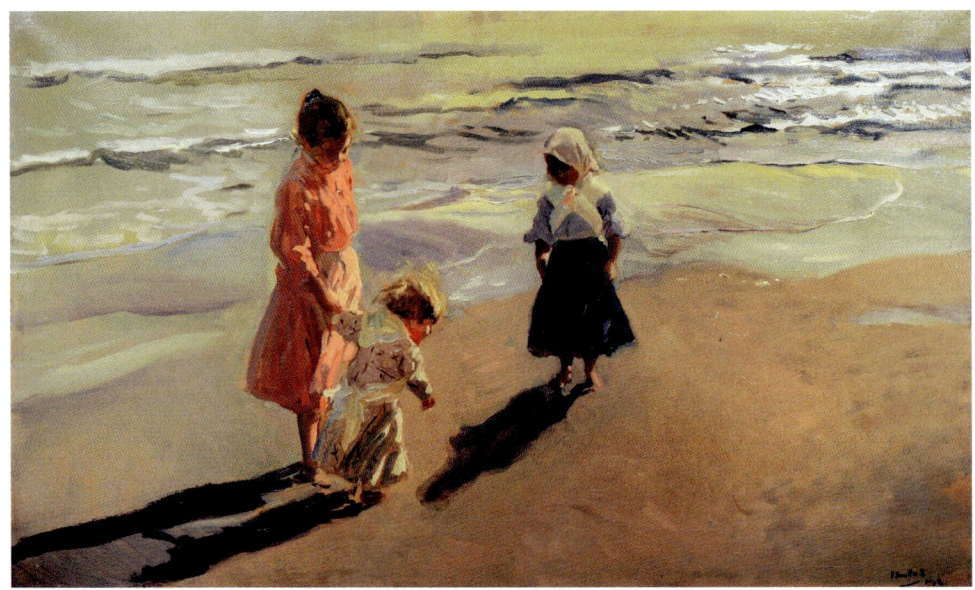

Girls on the Beach, 1908

Sorolla grew up an orphan with his aunt. In 1885, the recipient of a grant, he went to Rome and travelled to Paris, where he saw works by the Impressionists. International awards and exhibition successes mounted up, for example, between 1909 and 1911 in the United States. By 1919, he created fourteen large paintings for the library of the Hispanic Society of America. Inspired by the French Impressionists, he painted sun-drenched beach pictures, genre scenes, portraits and landscapes. He left his legacy to the Spanish state. The Museo Sorolla was established in his house in Madrid.

27 FEBRUARY

Guillaume Delisle

1675–1726 | Cartographer | France

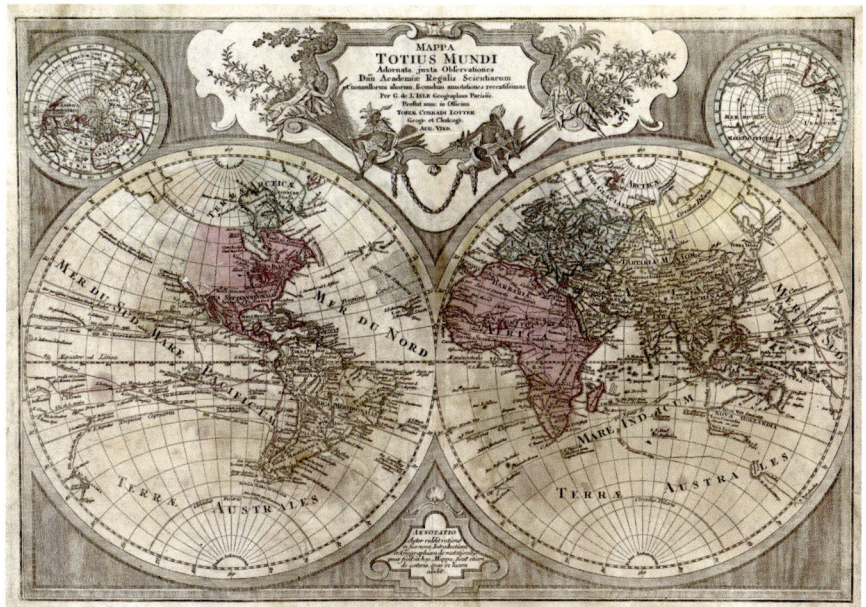

Map of the World, 1775

Delisle, who came from a scientifically inclined family, is credited with having been the first to initiate scientific comparative geography, which also included travel reports and findings by naturalists. Due to their vivid sharpness and aesthetics, the globes and maps that he published differed greatly from earlier maps. As a member of the academies in Paris and Berlin, he created a comprehensive map of the Caspian Sea for Peter the Great.

28 FEBRUARY

Augusta Savage

1892–1962 | Sculptor | United States

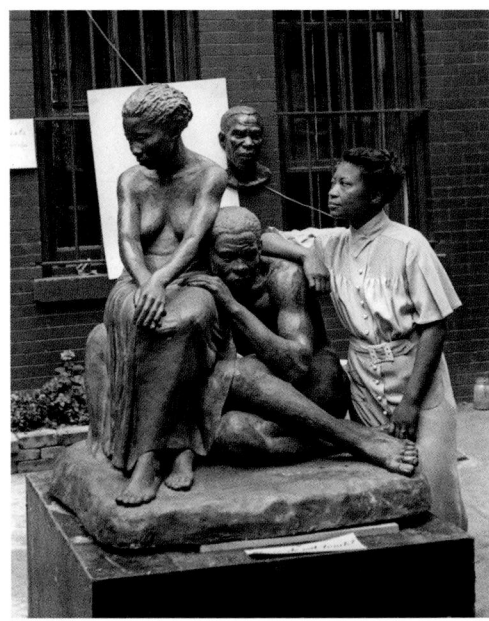

Augusta Savage with her sculpture "Realization", c. 1938

Modelling in clay was one of Savage's early passions. Later, she moved to New York and, after protracted first attempts, she succeeded in working in Paris, where she met, among others, the sculptor Charles Despiau. Exhibitions and travels ensued. When she returned to New York, she taught lessons in her own studio. In 1937, her school was opened at a new location as the Harlem Community Art Center, of which she was principal. She made a monumental sculpture for the World's Fair in 1939. Savage fought heroically for Black rights throughout her life.

29 FEBRUARY

Oskar Kokoschka

1886–1980 | Painter and graphic artist | Austria i.a.

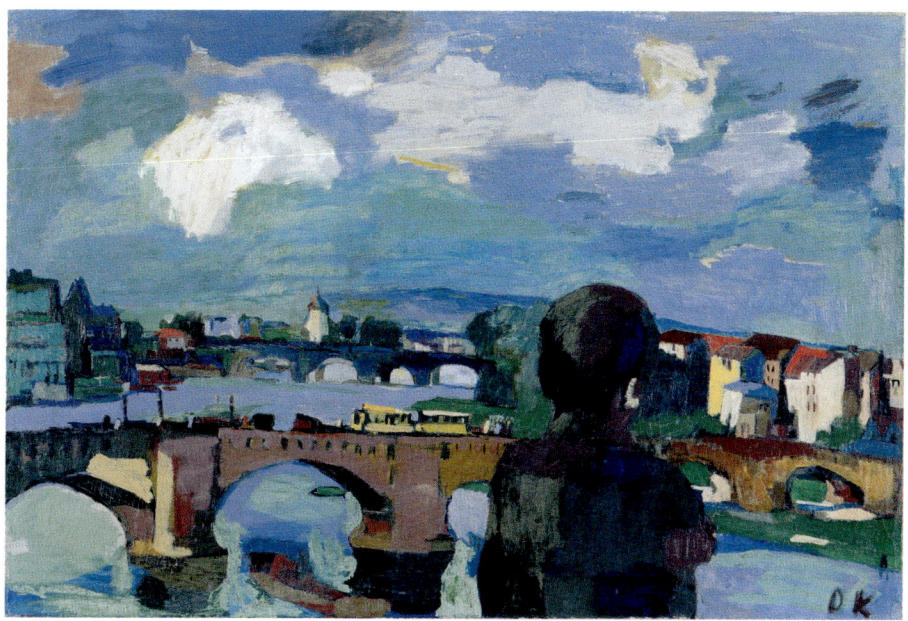

Dresden, Augustus Bridge with Figure from Behind, 1923

Kokoschka, an Austrian, was among the foremost painters, graphic artists and writers of the twentieth century. He lived first in Vienna and in Berlin from 1910. In 1919, he began a passionate relationship with Alma Mahler. Wounded in the First World War, he went to Dresden in 1917 and became an academy professor. He took part in international exhibitions and travelled through Europe, North Africa and the regions surrounding the eastern Mediterranean. Following exile in Prague and England, he relocated to Switzerland in 1953. Major exhibitions and awards ensued. His portraits, still lifes and urban paintings are found in museums around the world.

1 MARCH

Al Taylor

1948–1999 | Painter, sculptor and graphic artist | United States

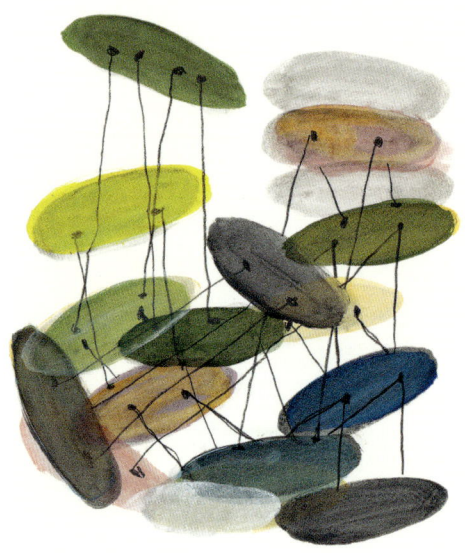

Untitled (Without Riggers), c. 1998/1999

From 1966, Taylor studied at the Kansas City Art Institute and often visited New York, where he lived from 1970. Between 1975 and 1982, he was Robert Rauschenberg's assistant and became acquainted with many prominent artists through this role. A journey through Africa radically altered his artistic thinking. Taylor cultivated important contacts in Europe from 1987 and was given his first museum exhibition in Bern in 1992. Alongside his paintings and sculptures, Taylor's drawings occupy a special rank in his oeuvre.

2 MARCH

Anne Ratkowsky

1903–1996 | Painter | Germany, United States

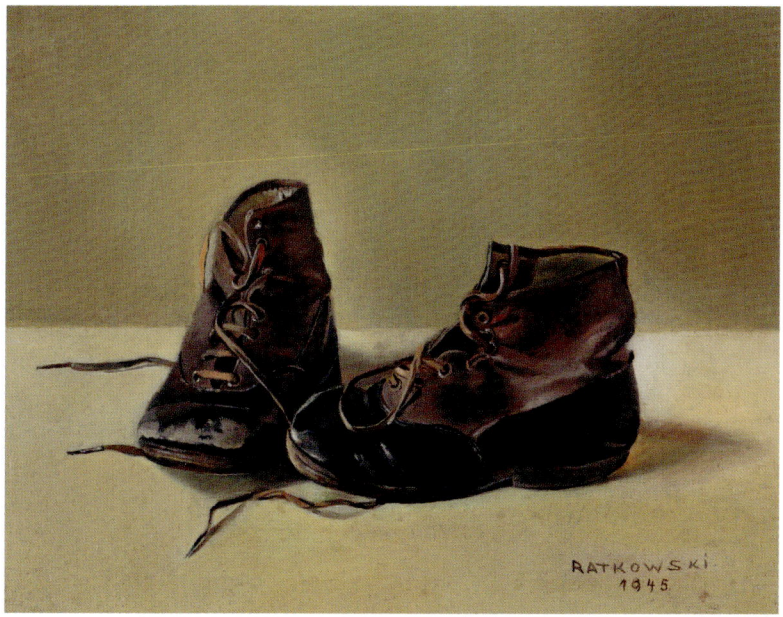

Still Life with Children's Shoes, 1945

In the 1920s, Anne Ratkowsky took private lessons from Arthur Segal in Berlin. During that period, she presented her works at the *Great Berlin Art Exhibition* and enjoyed initial successes with her paintings in the style of New Objectivity. As a Jew, she was obliged to emigrate. She was able to have her son from her first marriage brought safely to England. She herself went to Belgium, where she remarried. The couple moved to New York in 1948. Ratkowsky's work was only recently rediscovered in Germany.

3 MARCH

Mies Elout-Drabbe

1875–1956 | Painter and draughtswoman | The Netherlands

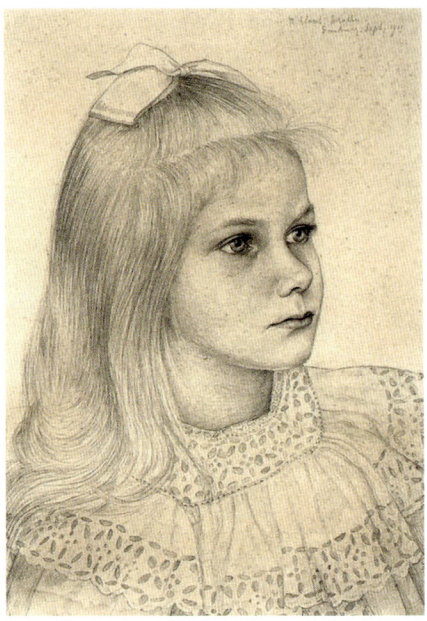

Portrait of a Girl, undated

From 1895 until shortly before her death, Elout-Drabbe lived in Domburg, a Dutch coastal resort. In 1898, she met the painter Jan Toorop, with whom she remained friends until his death in 1928. His influence over her unfolding career was considerable. In Domburg, she took part in exhibitions and kept up a lively dialogue with other artists, including Piet Mondrian. Her light-filled oeuvre, which is tempered by Neo-Impressionism and Pointillism, consists of portraits, landscapes, still lifes and figure paintings.

_____

_____

_____

_____

4 MARCH

Giovanni Battista Tiepolo

1696–1770 | Painter and graphic artist | Italy

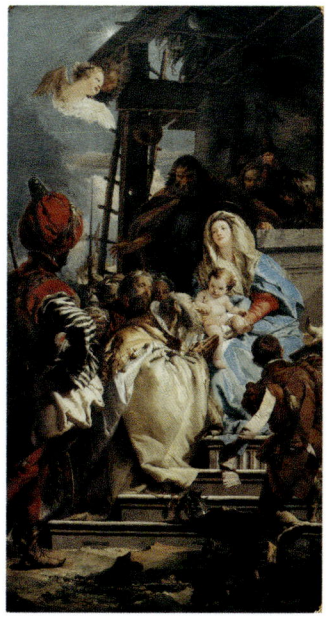

Adoration of the Magi, 1753

As one of the leading masters of eighteenth-century Venetian painting, Tiepolo was an artist of European standing. Having become famous at a young age, he received numerous public commissions, including projects outside of Venice in Udine, and later in Milan and Würzburg. His frescoes in the Residenz in the latter city are considered his masterpiece. He spent the period between 1762 and his death in Madrid, where among other works he executed the ceiling fresco in the Palacio Real. He had nine children, of whom Domenico was a well-known painter. His pictures and works on paper can be found in many museums around the world.

5 MARCH

Michelangelo Buonarroti

1475–1564 | Sculptor, painter and architect | Italy

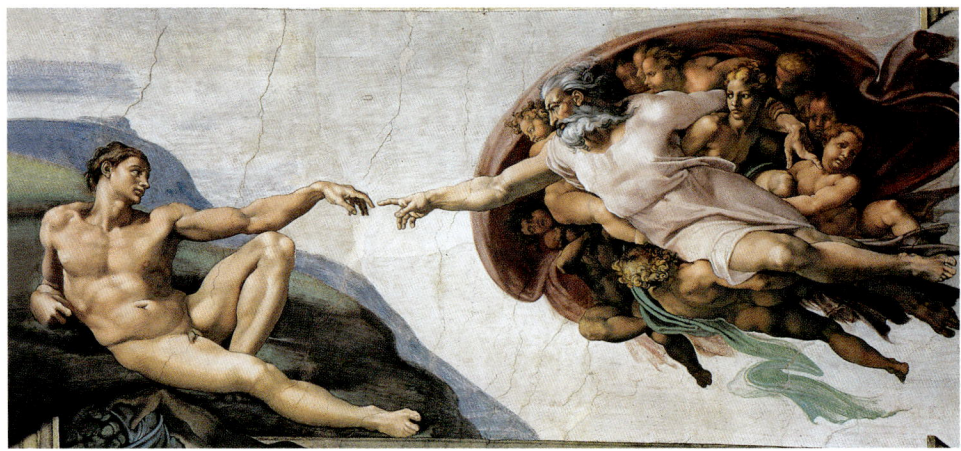

The Creation of Adam, 1510

Michelangelo was one of the greatest polymaths in all of art history. He was a sculptor, architect, builder, painter, draughtsman and man of letters. Everything he accomplished in these disciplines was exemplary. Throughout his life he alternated his place of work between Florence and Rome, depending on the projects he was commissioned for. Famous individual pieces include the *Pietà* in St Peter's in Rome or *David* in Florence. His frescoes in the Sistine Chapel in the Vatican are admired to this day. Michelangelo never married and died aged eighty-eight in Rome.

_____

_____

_____

_____

6 MARCH

Piet Mondrian

1872–1944 | Painter | The Netherlands

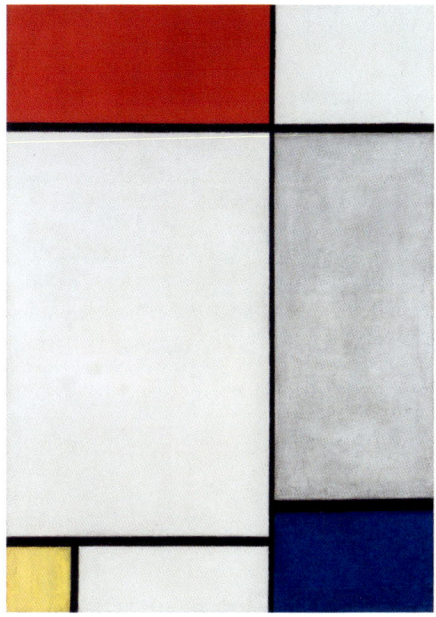

Composition with Red, Yellow and Blue, 1927

Mondrian, one of the most influential abstract painters of Classical Modernism, lived in Paris between 1911 and 1938, then from 1938 until 1944 in London and New York. He explored the mystical, religious movement of theosophy for his whole life. As a painter he sought reduction and a balance between the individual and the universal. His paintings' grid structure with their characteristic fields in the primary colours red, yellow and blue became well-known across the world and has been reproduced countless times to this day.

_____

_____

_____

_____

7 MARCH

Rosso Fiorentino

1495–1540 | Painter | Italy

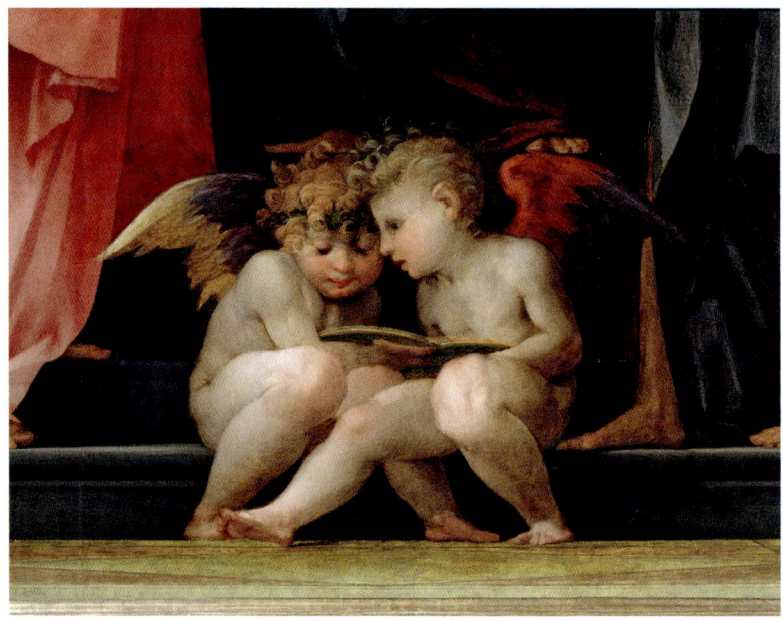

Madonna and Child with Saints (detail), 1518

A member of the Florentine painters' guild from 1516, Rosso stayed in Volterra in 1521, where he created his famous *Deposition* for the city's cathedral, a painting characterized by impassioned theatricalism and gleaming colours. After a number of years in Rome, which he left after the city was sacked in 1527, François I, the king of France, summoned him to Fontainebleau, where he was responsible for the château's interior until his death. His decoration of the gallery there became famous. Rosso is regarded as one of the founders of the Fontainebleau School as a centre of Mannerism.

8 MARCH

Constance Mayer

1775–1821 | Painter | France

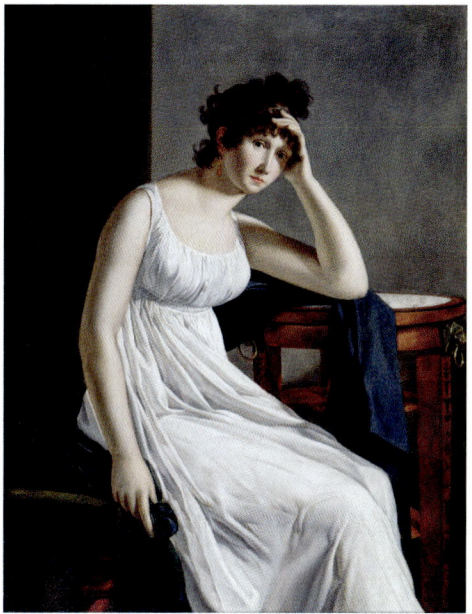

Self-Portrait, c. 1800

As a pupil of Jean-Baptiste Greuze, Mayer exhibited in the Paris Salon at a young age. Her entire life was influenced by her meeting the painter Pierre-Paul Prud'hon, with whom she fell in love. Many of her paintings – especially classical portraits – were sold as works by Prud'hon to achieve higher prices. Constance Mayer later lived and worked in close proximity to Prud'hon's studio. One year after her death, the latter dedicated a comprehensive retrospective to her creative oeuvre.

9 MARCH

William Etty

1787–1849 | Painter | Great Britain

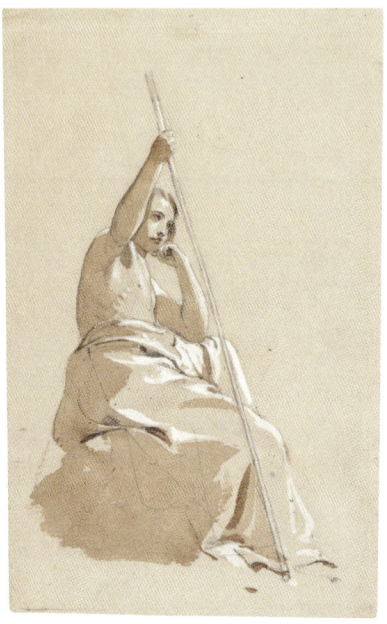

Seated Youth with a Staff, c. 1815

Etty commenced his painting studies at London's Royal Academy of Arts in around 1807 and was a pupil of, among others, John Flaxman and Thomas Lawrence. Having attracted public notice, he travelled to Paris, Florence, Rome and Venice in the early 1820s. On the way, Etty copied the Old Masters and studied female nudes in particular, which were to become the main feature of his subsequent paintings. His successes mounted up from the 1820s. In 1848, he returned to York, where he died one year later.

10 MARCH

Henri Rivière

1864–1951 | Graphic artist, painter and set designer | France

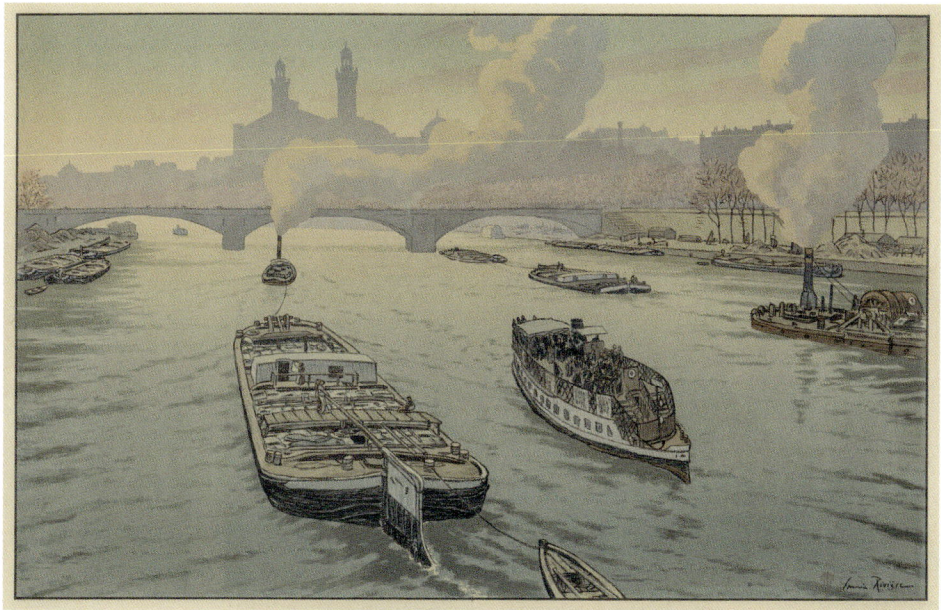

The Trocadéro, 1900

Initially influenced by Gustave Doré, Rivière tried his hand at etching and woodcarving.
From 1886, he was director of the Parisian artists' establishment Le Chat Noir, for
which he produced colourful shadow theatre until the establishment's closure.
He began taking an interest in Japanese woodcarving from 1897. In 1921, he had an
exhibition in the Musée des Arts Décoratifs in Paris. He spent his later years with his
wife in Provence. By then completely blind, he died at eighty-seven and left behind a
large number of watercolours and prints.

11 MARCH

Anton Raphael Mengs

1728–1779 | Painter | Bohemia, Germany

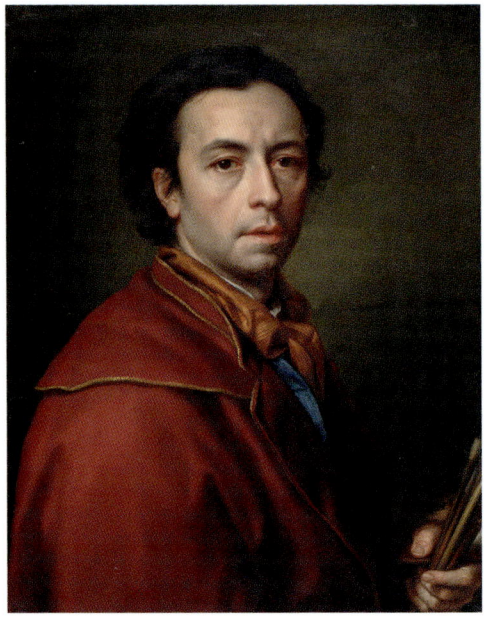

Self-Portrait, 1773

From 1741, Mengs stayed on multiple occasions in Rome, initially to study the Old Masters and antiquity. There, in 1755, he met the archaeologist Johann Joachim Winckelmann, who as a close friend had a major influence on his painting. Mengs became famous across Europe as a leading painter of German Neoclassicism and a coveted portraitist of influential figures. In 1761, he was summoned to decorate the royal palace in Madrid. Many regarded him as the greatest painter of his day.

12 MARCH

Alexej von Jawlensky

1864/65–1941 | Painter | Russia, Germany

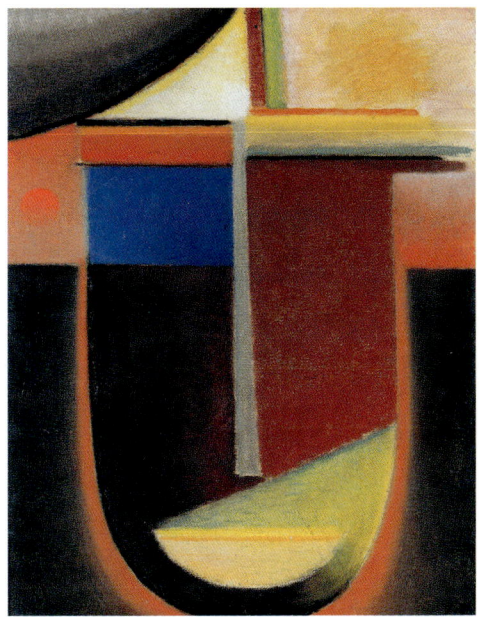

Abstract Head: Last Light, 1925

During his studies under Ilya Repin in St Petersburg, Jawlensky, a Russian, met the painter Marianne von Werefkin, who moved with him to Munich in 1896. Jawlensky belonged to the community of the artists' collective Der Blaue Reiter; his oeuvre shows influences mainly by Wassily Kandinsky and Henri Matisse. In 1914, he emigrated to Switzerland, and in 1917, he began painting faces and heads, which developed into the modern icons of his *Meditations* from 1934. In 1941, he died – entirely paralysed – in Wiesbaden, where he had been living since 1921.

_____

_____

_____

_____

13 MARCH

Ferdinand Hodler

1853–1918 | Painter | Switzerland

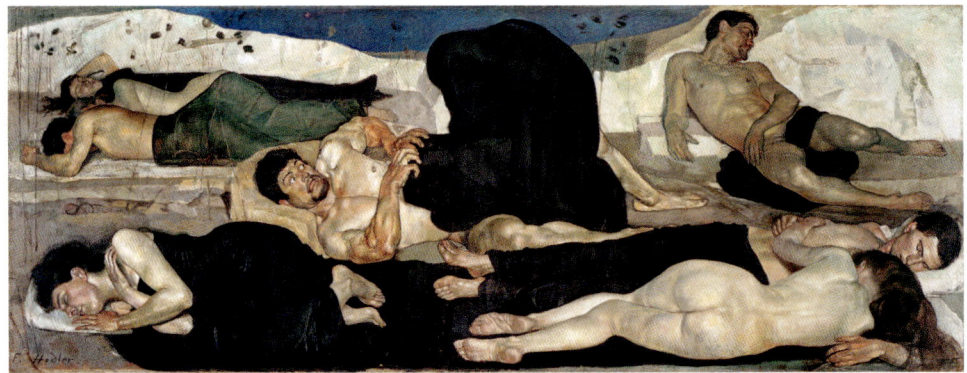

Night, 1889/1890

Having grown up in poverty, Swiss-born Hodler attended the art academy in Geneva in 1871. A journey to Spain ensued in 1878. Two-dimensional figure painting is the expansive format for his pathos that leans towards the mystical. 1889 saw the creation of *The Night*, which marked his breakthrough in its combination of sleep, death and sexuality. Hodler's best-known expressive and pathos-laden pictures were made in the 1890s. His numerous self-portraits and later landscapes of Lake Geneva also became famous.

14 MARCH

Shibata Zeshin

1807–1891 | Painter | Japan

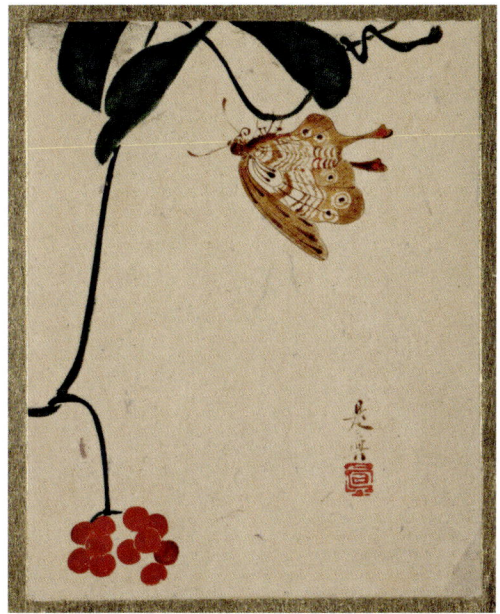

Red Berry Plant and Butterfly, undated

Zeshin, a Japanese artist, learned the art of lacquerware under the master of the Koma School. In 1830, he went to Kyoto to continue his training and visited mainly temples and shrines to study antique lacquerware. Following the Meiji Restoration in the 1870s, Zeshin exhibited at the world's fairs in Vienna, Philadelphia and Paris and earned distinctions in Japan. As one of the great masters of the art of lacquerware in the nineteenth century, his concern was to preserve traditional Japanese values.

15 MARCH

Silvia Bächli

Born 1956 | Draughtswoman | Switzerland

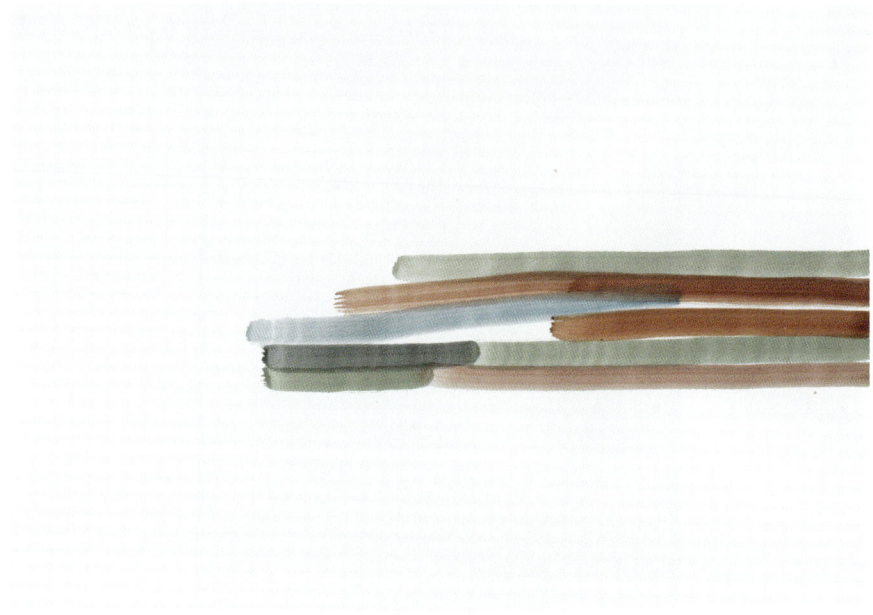

Untitled, 2019

Bächli, from Switzerland, ranks among the internationally most significant draughts-people of the present day. Following studies in Basel and Geneva, she began to explore drawing as a medium, an endeavour that has continued for nearly five decades. The sparingness of her means effected an increasingly radical reduction in terms of form. Using lines, strokes and, occasionally, planar agglomerations, she consolidates what she has seen, causing physical, scenic and musical structures to resonate. Bächli's work displays a mutability that has not waned to this day.

_____

_____

_____

_____

16 MARCH

Mikhail Vrubel

1856–1910 | Painter, sculptor and ceramicist | Russia

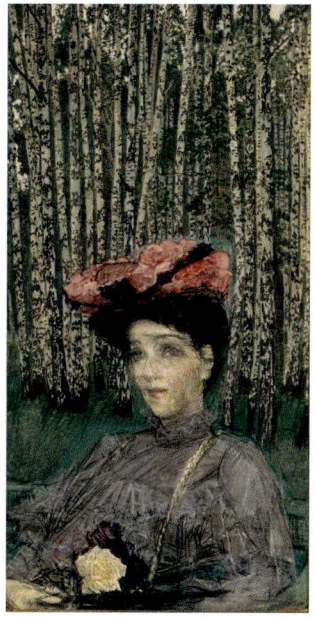

Nadezhda Zabela-Vrubel with Birches in the Background, 1904

Following studies in St Petersburg, Vrubel lived in Kyiv and Moscow. His works, a blend of subjectively mystical and allegorical elements, with motifs from traditional Russian fairy tales and heroic epics as well as classic Western literature, established his fame as one of the leading representatives of Russian Symbolism. He also worked as a ceramicist, set designer and illustrator of poems by Lermontov and Tolstoy's novel *Anna Karenina*.

---

17 MARCH

Hugo Charlemont

1850–1939 | Painter | Austria

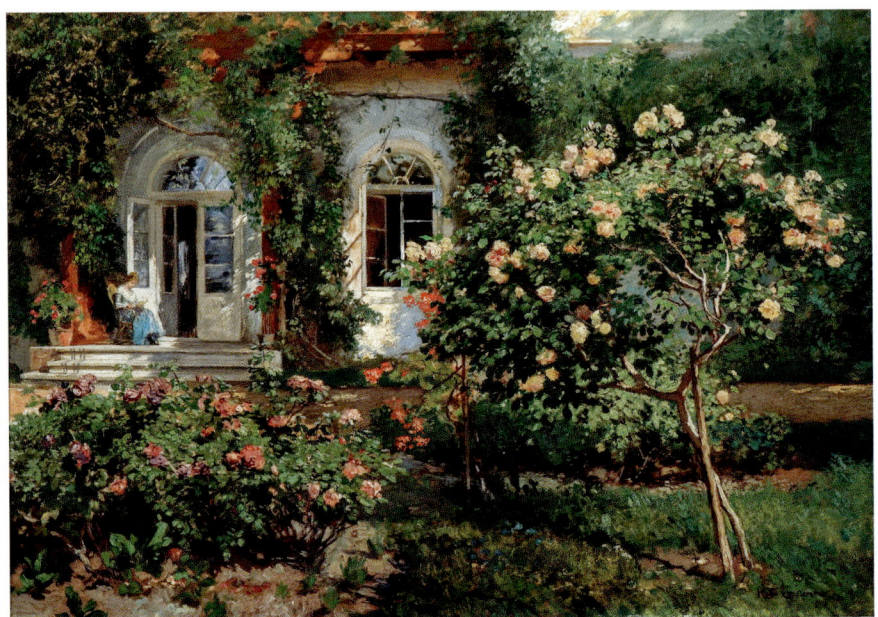

In the Rose Garden, 1906

Born into an Austrian family of artists, Charlemont began his studies at the Vienna Academy in 1873. He later continued his training under Hans Makart and spent several years in Venice. Charlemont's subjects were diverse, including still lifes, portraits, genre and animal paintings. His Impressionism-tinged landscapes with frequently occurring motifs from the Brijuni Islands are of particular note. Charlemont remained true to his traditional painting style into his later years.

18 MARCH

Josef Albers

1888–1976 | Painter | Germany, United States

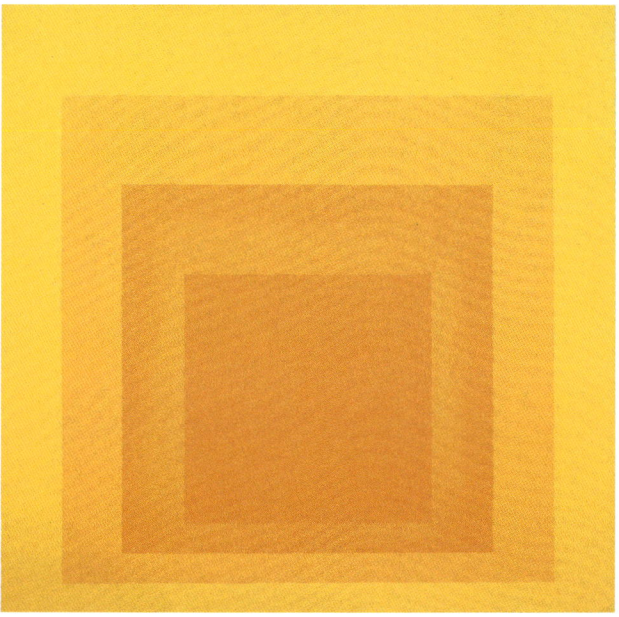

Homage to the Square, 1967

Albers taught at the Bauhaus between 1920 and 1933, first in Weimar and, from 1925, in Dessau. Together with his wife, Anni, a textile and graphic artist, Albers fled to the United States in 1933, where he taught at Black Mountain College until 1949 and then at Yale University. Numerous study trips ensued starting in 1935, to places including Mexico, which had a crucial influence on both artists. In the series *Homage to the Square*, which he began in 1950, Albers explored perception and the synergy of colour planes. He was one of the most influential theorists and educators of the twentieth century.

19 MARCH

Edward Poynter

1836–1919 | Painter, designer and draughtsman | Great Britain

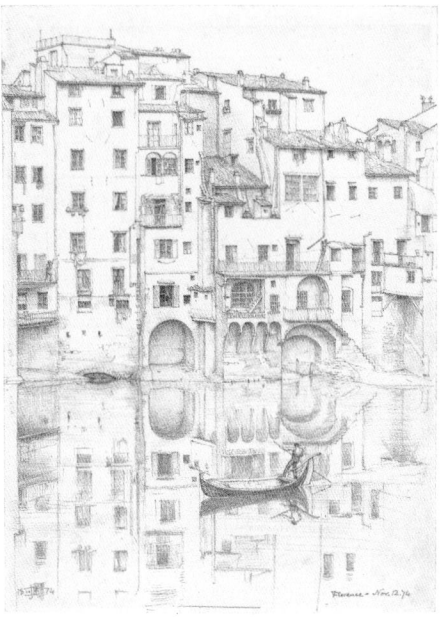

A View of the Arno, Florence, 1874

Poynter, an English painter and draughtsman, became known for his large paintings featuring historical themes. He also held important offices such as the directorship of the National Gallery and the presidency of the Royal Academy of Arts in London. For the National Gallery, Poynter compiled its first comprehensive catalogue and acquired major paintings, including works by Titian and Rembrandt. He was interred in St Paul's Cathedral in London in 1919.

20 MARCH

Bartholomeus Spranger

1546–1611 | Painter | Flanders

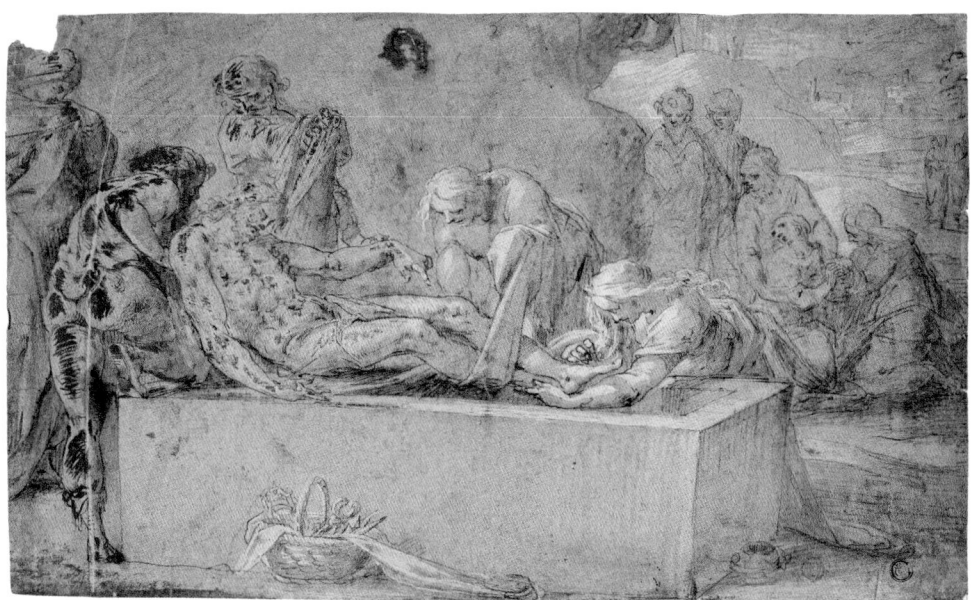

Entombment, undated

Spranger, a Fleming famed as a painter and draughtsman, was an important propagator of Italian Mannerism beyond the Alps and a precursor of Baroque painters, including his countryman Peter Paul Rubens. Working between 1565 and 1575 in Italy and particularly in Rome for the Pope, he later went to the Viennese court and, in 1580, moved to Prague, where he encountered many prominent artists. His contribution played a fundamental role in the flourishing of art and culture at the court of Rudolph II.

21 MARCH

Yayoi Kusama

Born 1929 | Artist | Japan

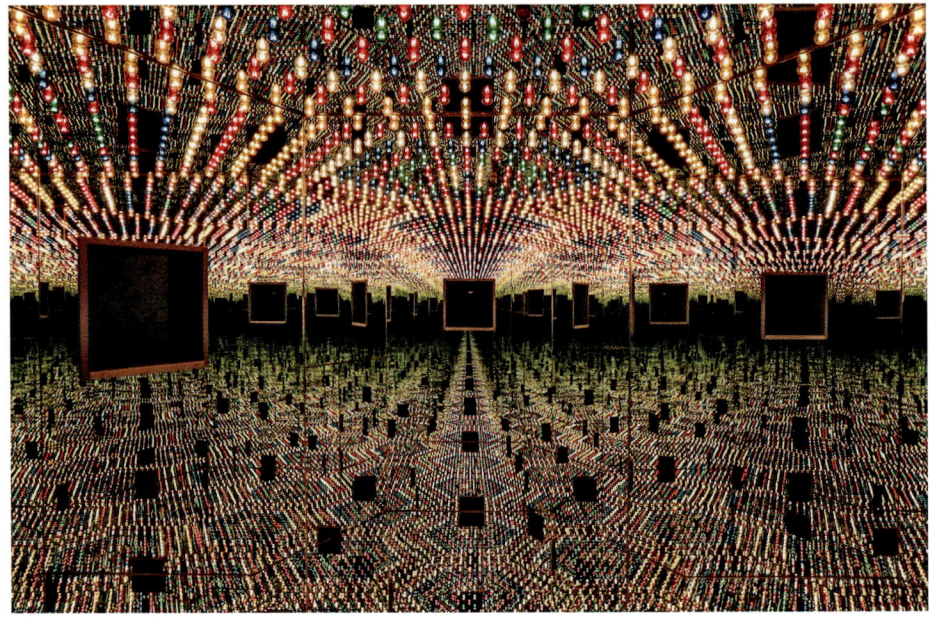

Infinity Mirrored Room – Love Forever, 1966/1994

Kusama suffered pathological hallucinations of dot and net patterns from an early age. In addition to sexual anxieties, these left a lasting impression on her art. Kusama was very active in the Japanese art scene, and then moved to New York in 1957. She has created textile soft sculptures with stuffed phallic shapes and collages, accumulations of stickers, toy bills and pieces of her work photographs since the early 1960s. Kusama has lived and worked in a psychiatric clinic in Japan since 1977. She was awarded the Praemium Imperiale in 2006 and received Japan's Order of Culture in 2016.

22 MARCH

Juan Gris

1887–1927 | Painter | Spain

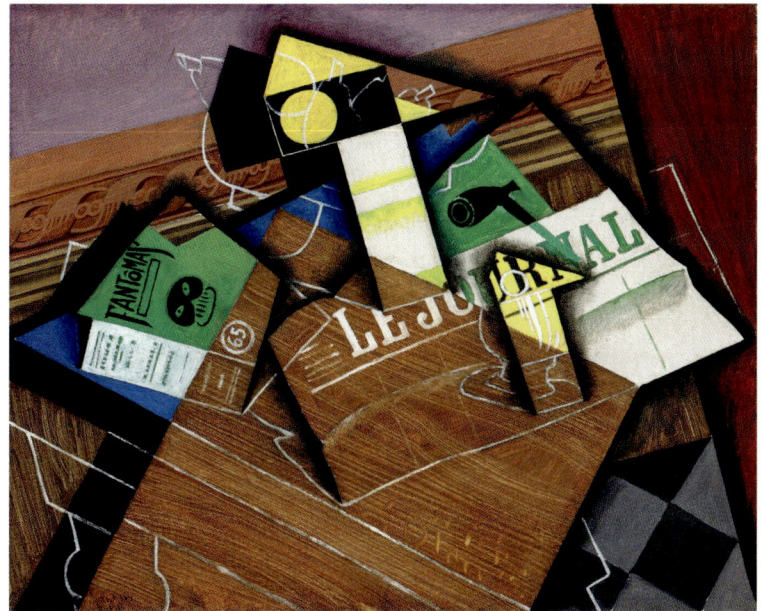

Fantômas, 1915

After studying in Madrid, Gris, a Spaniard, moved to Paris in 1906. Inspired by Pablo Picasso, he painted his first works in the style of analytical Cubism in 1911. The influential art dealer Daniel-Henry Kahnweiler signed him up. In 1913, he made his first synthetic works using collage techniques with newspaper, wallpaper and glass shards. He was later influenced by Henri Matisse. His vibrantly coloured pictures are found in museums around the world.

23 MARCH

Rebecca Horn

1944–2024 | Sculptor, action artist, etc. | Germany

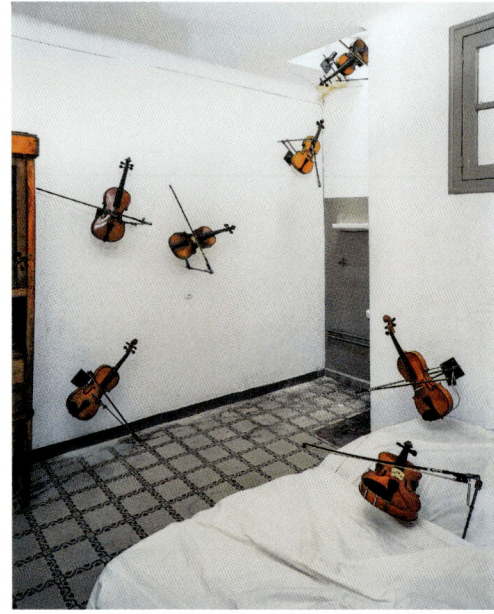

The River of the Moon, 1992

Horn was one of the most internationally influential contemporary artists from Germany and was honoured around the world. In 1993, she became the first woman to have a solo exhibition at the Guggenheim Museum in New York, and in 2010, she was awarded the Praemium Imperiale in Tokyo. As a student in Hamburg in 1967, she suffered severe lung poisoning while experimenting with polyester resin, which is why she used lighter and predominantly organic materials from that point on. Based in New York and Berlin, Horn later created poetic, sometimes ambiguous installations, performances, kinetic objects and films.

24 MARCH

Juan Carreño de Miranda

1614–1685 | Painter | Spain

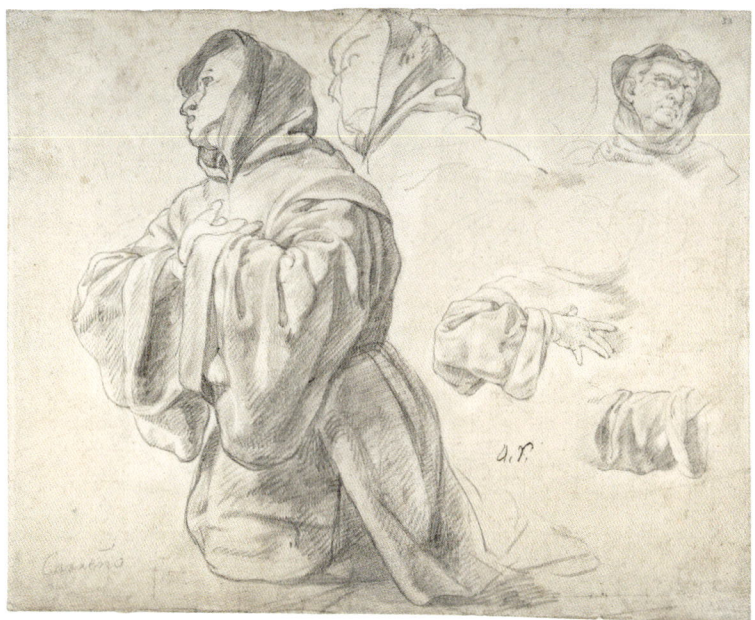

Figures of Monks, undated

This Spanish artist was a prominent seventeenth-century painter, one of the protagonists of what is known as the Golden Age in Madrid. Under Carlos II he created large
altar paintings and frescoes. *The Assumption of the Virgin*, which he painted in about
1657, is a free interpretation of Peter Paul Rubens's picture of the same subject in
Antwerp. In 1671, Carreño succeeded Diego Velázquez as court painter and portraitist.
He was commissioned to paint numerous works all over Spain. Late portraits of
Carlos II and his mother brought him particular fame.

25 MARCH

Shirin Neshat

Born 1957 | Artist, filmmaker and photographer | Iran, United States

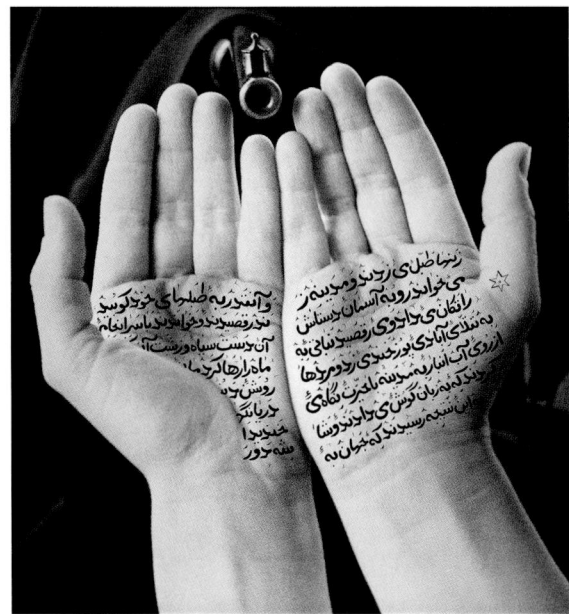

Guardians of Revolution, from the series "Women of Allah", 1994

Born into a Western-oriented family in Iran, Neshat left her country before the Islamic Revolution began in 1979 and went to the United States. She began her politically motivated work with the photo series *Woman of Allah*, which she created between 1993 and 1997. In these black-and-white photographs, she shows women wearing chadors that only reveal the face or parts of it. As an advocate of women in the Muslim world and an intermediary between the cultures of East and West, she won international fame and accolades with her films. Today she is based in New York.

26 MARCH

Kathleen Scott

1878–1947 | Sculptor | Great Britain

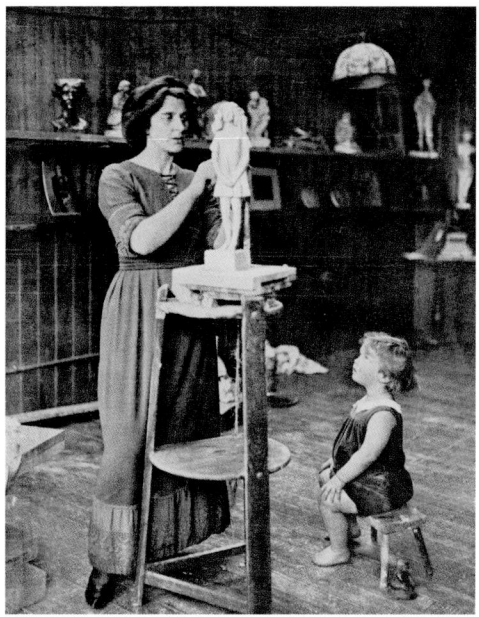

Kathleen Scott working on a statue, 1912

Following training in London and Paris, Scott made numerous portraits and busts as well as a number of larger public monuments. She counted several prominent artists, including Rodin, among her friends. In 1925, Scott participated in the Salon de Paris and was awarded a medal. Despite poor health she travelled all over the world in later life. Her sculpting remained consistently traditional.

27 MARCH

Fra Bartolommeo

1472–1517 | Painter | Italy

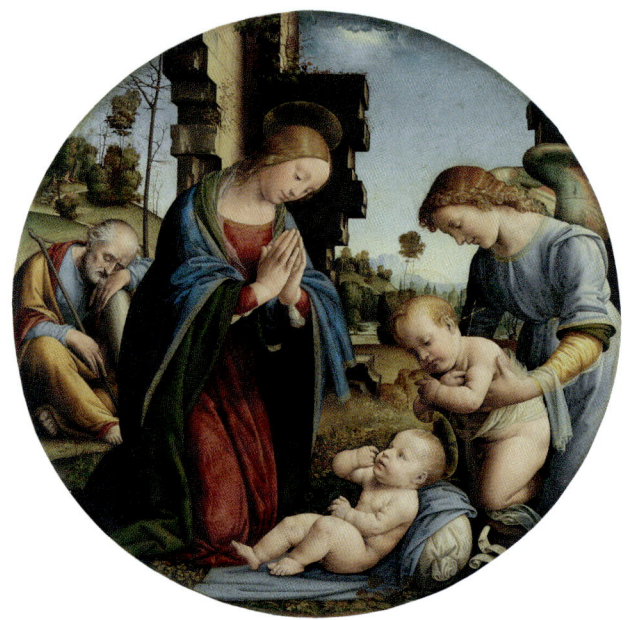

Adoration of the Child, c. 1495

This Tuscan painter was among the most loyal devotees of Girolamo Savonarola, burning during the latter's campaign in 1497 all of his own works that did not conform to the values of Savonarola's strict religious teachings. Savonarola himself was burnt on the bonfire soon afterwards, which devastated Fra Bartolommeo. He became a monk and from 1501 lived in the San Marco monastery in Florence, where he accepted a series of commissions. On visits to Venice and Rome, he took inspiration from painters such as Michelangelo and Raphael. He was celebrated as both a painter and draughtsman.

28 MARCH

Edward Burra

1905–1976 | Painter | Great Britain

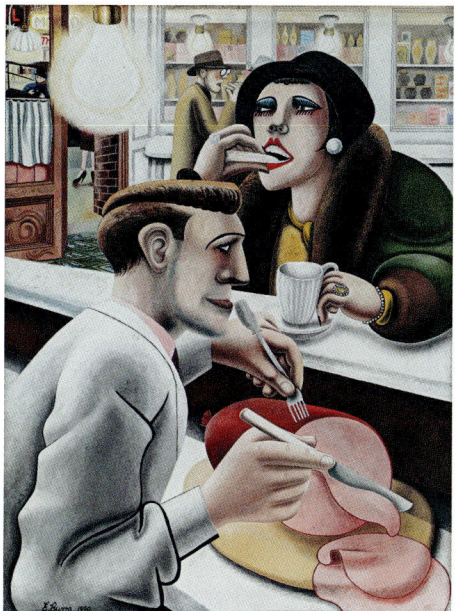

The Snack Bar, 1930

After training in London, Burra travelled to France in 1927. He loved the harbour environment of Marseilles and painted everyday motifs, often with a socially critical, disreputable background. More travels to New York and Spain followed. His innate tendency towards the bleak and depressing grew stronger during the Second World War. Burra made large-scale watercolours in particular but also experimented with collages and later devoted himself to landscape painting. In some ways his early socially critical works are reminiscent of the oeuvre of George Grosz.

29 MARCH

Francisco de Goya

1746–1828 | Painter and graphic artist | Spain

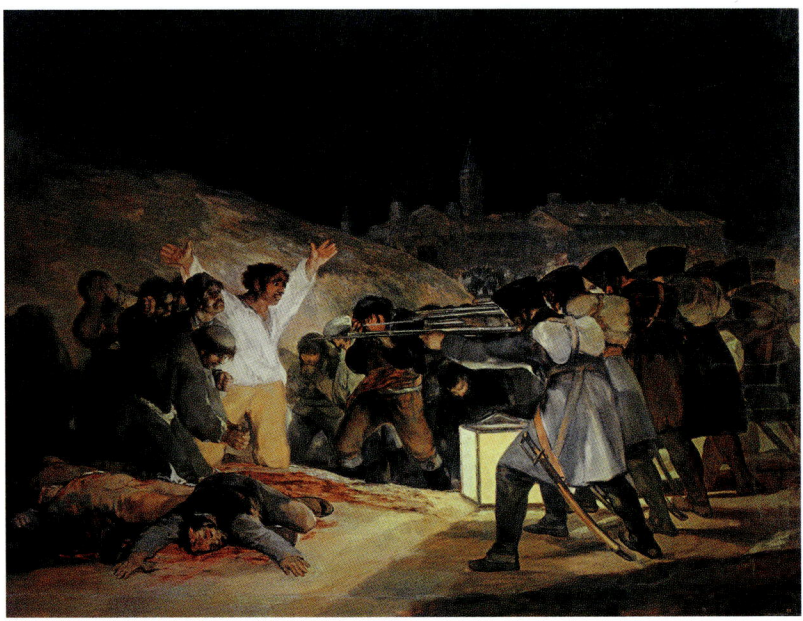

The Third of May 1808, 1814

As a painter, draughtsman and graphic artist, Goya was one of the greats in art history, enduring beyond his lifetime. He worked chiefly in Madrid, became a court painter and, among other subjects, painted numerous portraits for the nobility and the royal family. In the 1790s, his work changed: he renounced representational court depictions and devoted himself to political themes. His famous series of etchings ensued, featuring stark portrayals of atrocities, misery and war. In 1824, having come under political pressure, he moved to Bordeaux, where he died in 1828.

30 MARCH

John La Farge

1835–1910 | Painter and glass artist | United States

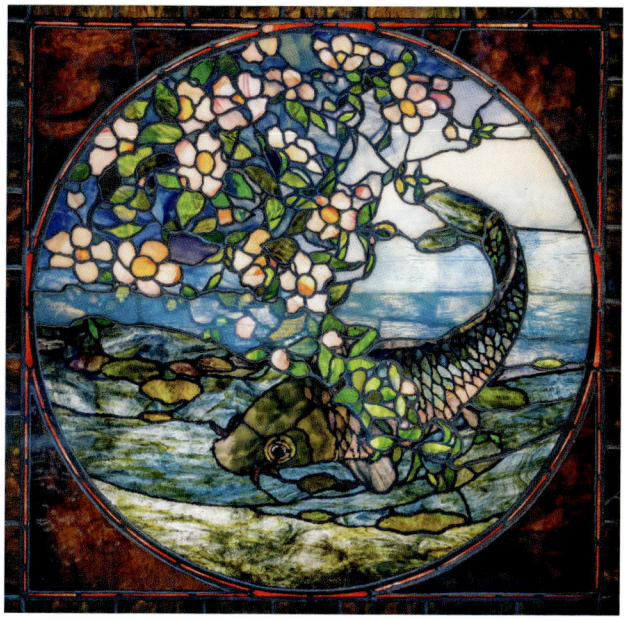

The Fish or The Fish and Flowering Branch, c. 1890

La Farge painted portraits, mythological and religious subjects; starting in 1873, he painted murals for churches and explored Japanese art. Extended travels took him to Asia and the South Pacific. From the late 1870s, he specialized in the production of opalized glass. This material was the object of patent disputes between La Farge and his competitor Tiffany. A great number of stained glass windows can be found in American churches.

31 MARCH

Dan Flavin

1933–1996 | Minimalist artist | United States

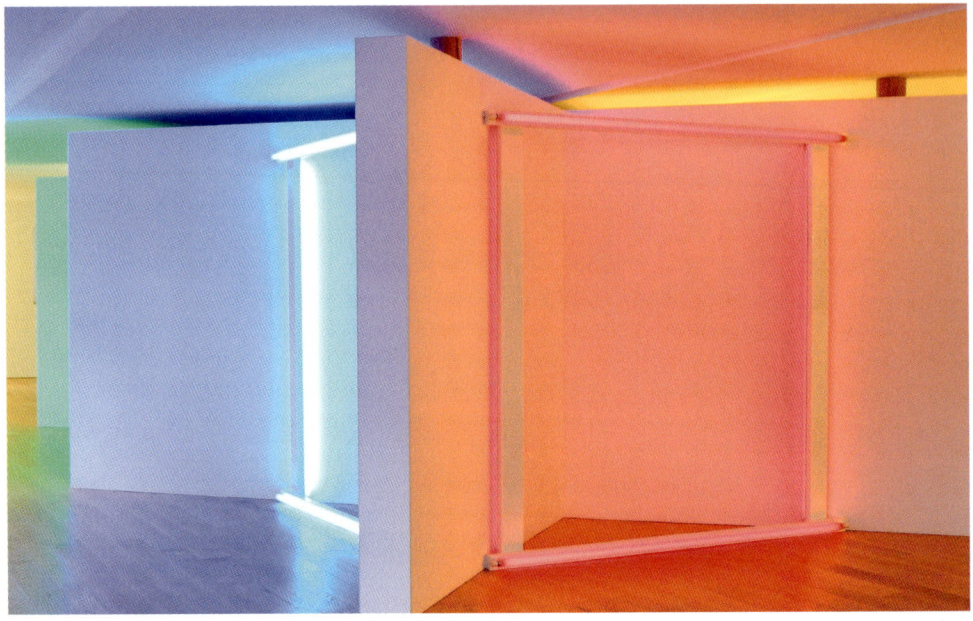

Untitled, from the series "To European Couples", 1966–1971

Flavin studied at Columbia University in New York between 1957 and 1959. He made his first installations using fluorescent tubes in 1961 and began working in themed series in 1963. Flavin's focus in his immersive light sculptures was the perception of space and the effect of light on the observer. He garnered international fame with his Minimalist light installations; his works were shown in many exhibitions, including twice at documenta in Kassel.

1 APRIL

Maria Sibylla Merian

1647–1717 | Naturalist and artist | Germany

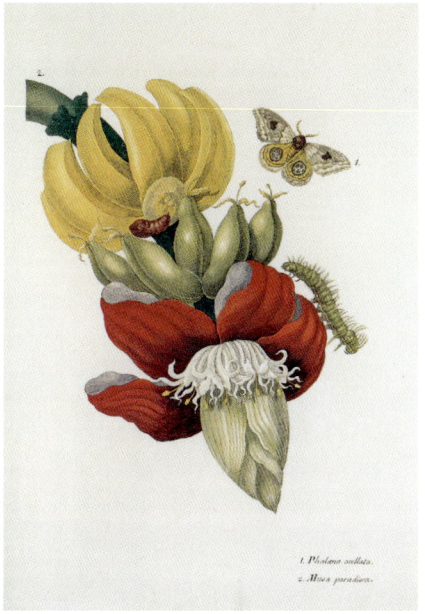

Banana Tree Flower with Io Moth, sheet XII from the "Insect Book", 1705

Highly regarded during her lifetime and well into the eighteenth century after her death, Merian was one of the first to systematically research insects and their metamorphosis. Her two main works – the *Caterpillar Book* and the *Insect Book* – had multiple print runs. Her two-year research trip to South America's rainforest as a woman alone, accompanied only by her daughter, was utterly unusual at the time. Merian was also famous for her Dutch-style flower paintings. Merian died in 1717 in Amsterdam, where she had lived since 1701.

2 APRIL

Henry van de Velde

1863–1957 | Painter, designer and architect | Belgium

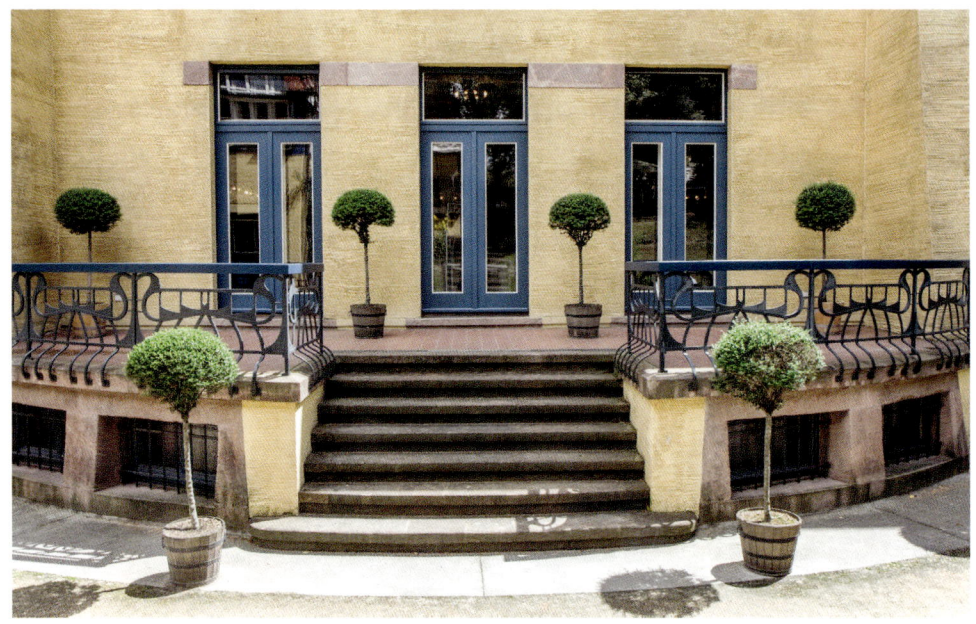

Villa Esche, Chemnitz, 1902/1903

Van de Velde was one of the most significant Art Nouveau artists. Unhappy with his painting, he turned to architecture and applied art in 1894. Early private commissions for interior decoration and furnishings came from Paris. These were exhibited in 1897 at the *International Art Exhibition* in Dresden. His own workshops in Brussels were funded by patrons. In 1901, Van de Velde moved to Berlin and later to Weimar, where he was director of the arts and crafts school until 1915. In 1918, he moved to Switzerland, before returning to Belgium; in 1947, his path led back to Switzerland, where he died in 1957 at a grand old age.

Constance Marie Charpentier

1767–1849 | Painter | France

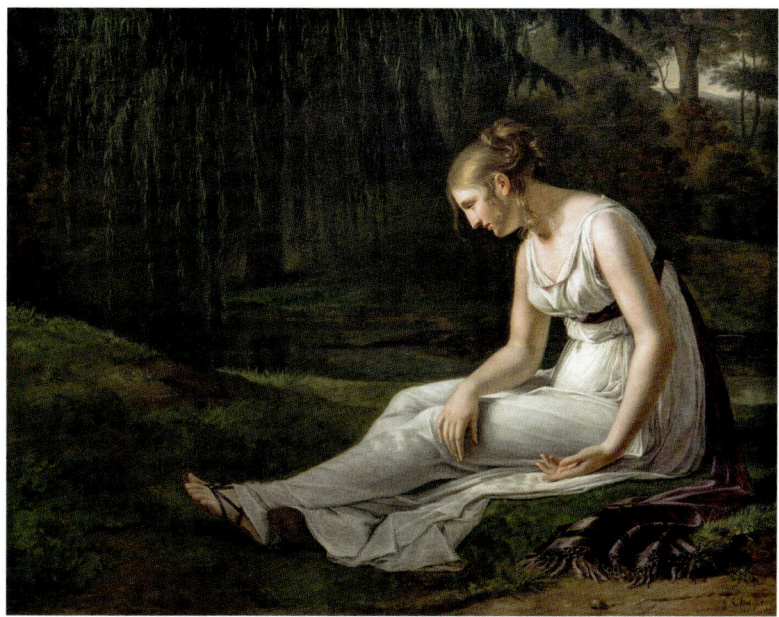

Melancholy, 1801

Charpentier, from France, studied painting with artists including Jacques-Louis David. Between 1795 and 1819, she took part in the Paris Salon, where she won a gold medal in 1814. Her painting focused on genre scenes and, above all, portraits of women in the style of Neoclassicism. She later gave up participating in exhibitions and taught painting and drawing to young women in her Paris home. One of her best-known paintings is *Melancholy* from 1801, which depicts a woman mourning at her father's grave.

Jean-Honoré Fragonard

1732–1806 | Painter, draughtsman and etcher | France

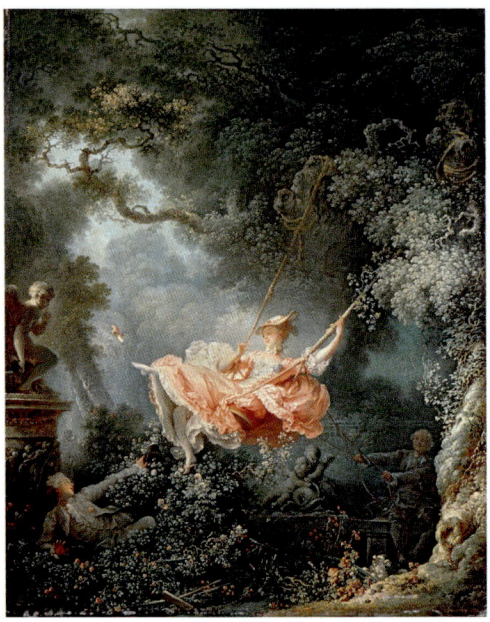

The Swing, 1767

In 1756, after studying with Jean Siméon Chardin and François Boucher, Fragonard went to Rome, where he copied the works of seventeenth-century Italian masters of Neoclassicism. Beginning in 1761, in Paris, he turned from religious and historical subject to depictions of domestic and family scenes as well as playful and suggestively erotic works. His loose, light brushwork and virtuoso drawing style made him, alongside Antoine Watteau and Boucher, one of the great masters of the French Rococo, and was often reproduced in engravings. He lost his fortune during the Revolution and died in poverty in 1806.

_____

_____

_____

_____

5 APRIL

Leonora Carrington

1917–2011 | Painter and sculptor | Great Britain, Mexico

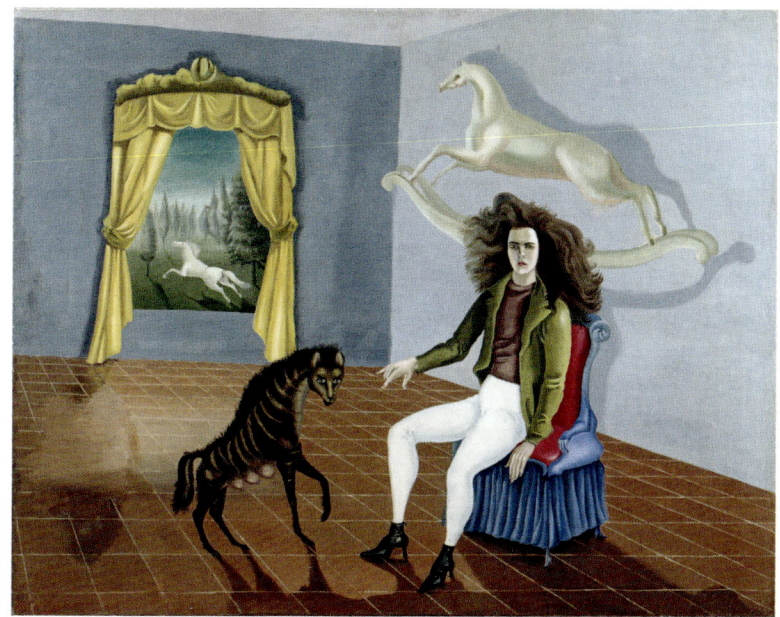

Self-Portrait, 1937/1938

As a student, Carrington met the painter Max Ernst, who influenced her. She exhibited her Surrealist pictures in Paris with other prominent painters. In 1941, Carrington emigrated to New York and, shortly after that, to Mexico, where she met her second husband, the Hungarian photographer Emérico Weisz. Carrington's Surrealist style both as a painter and sculptor is highly individual. An auction in 2024 made her one of the five most expensive artists worldwide.

Gerrit Dou

1613–1675 | Painter | The Netherlands

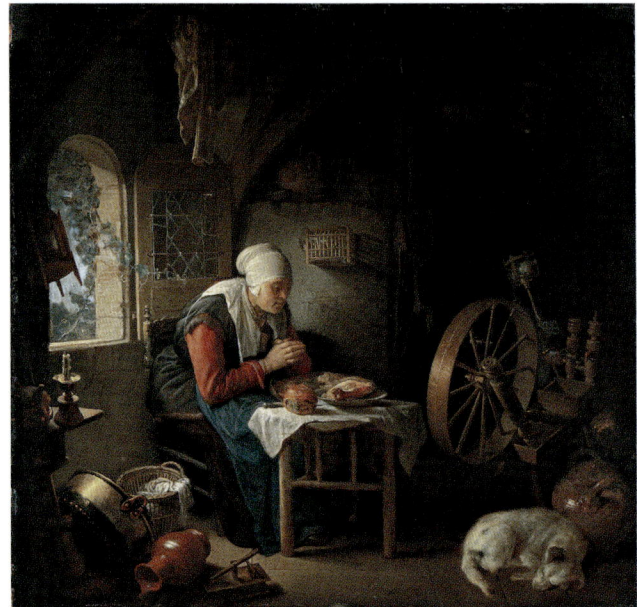

The Prayer of the Spinner, c. 1645–1650

From 1628 until 1631, Dou was apprenticed to Rembrandt, who greatly influenced him. After that, he worked independently in Leiden, where he became a member of the Guild of St Luke. Famous even in his lifetime, he created around two hundred works, including outstanding portraits and small genre paintings, most of which are found in the top museums in Amsterdam, Paris, London and Dresden. Due to his meticulous painting technique, he is considered the founder of the Leiden school of *fijnschilderij*, or fine painting.

7 APRIL

Mahmoud Saïd

1897–1964 | Painter | Egypt

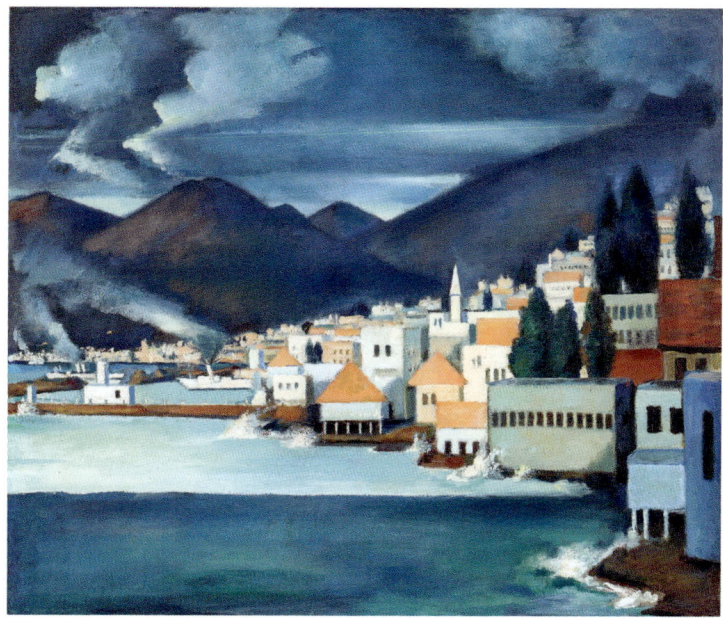

The Port of Beirut, 1954

The son of the former Egyptian prime minister, Saïd was born in Alexandria and graduated from university with a law degree in 1919. At that time he began painting and travelled throughout Europe, attending the Académie Julian in Paris. When he returned to Egypt, he continued to work as a magistrate into the 1950s. He participated in many exhibitions, with shows in places such as New York and the Venice Biennale, with his figurative and expressive works that include portraits and landscapes. Saïd is considered one of the founders of modern Egyptian painting. A Saïd Museum was opened in Alexandria in 1973.

8 APRIL

Eadweard Muybridge

1830–1904 | Photographer | Great Britain

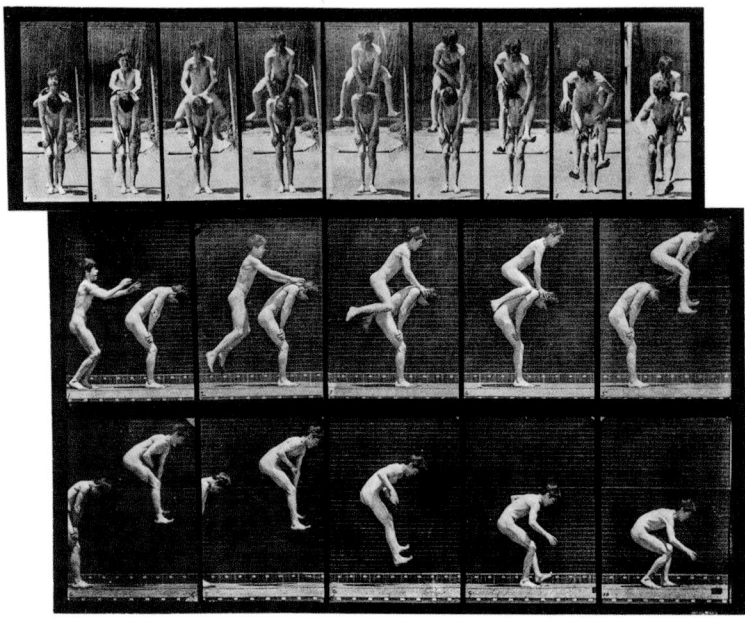

The Human Figure in Motion: Boys Playing Leapfrog, undated

Muybridge was a pioneer in nineteenth-century photography. His influential studies in motion inspired artists such as Edgar Degas, Marcel Duchamp and Francis Bacon. He emigrated to the United States as a young man and became famous for his panoramas of San Francisco. In 1878, he devised a technique for visually recording the individual stages of motion of a galloping horse, which he later used to photograph naked and lightly clad people.

Alfred Kubin

1877–1959 | Graphic artist, writer and book illustrator | Austria

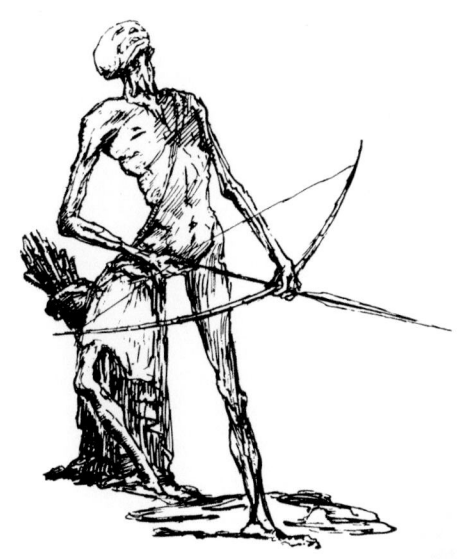

Death, 1926

In 1906, after his marriage, Kubin moved to Zwickledt Castle, where he lived until his death. This was also where he wrote his famous novel *The Other Side*, in which the author conjures up dreams, fantasy and hallucinations. Kubin illustrated many books, including editions of Fyodor Dostoevsky, Edgar Allan Poe and Elias Canetti, and left behind numerous portfolios comprising graphic works as well as thousands of drawings. He participated in exhibitions during the Nazi period, although many of his works were confiscated as "degenerate". Kubin's oeuvre had a major influence on modernism in the early twentieth century.

10 APRIL

Adélaïde Labille-Guiard

1749–1803 | Painter | France

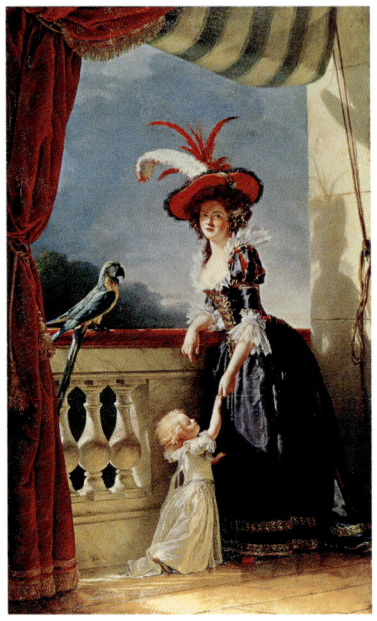

Portrait of Louise-Elisabeth ot France and Her Son Ferdinand, 1788

Labille-Guiard wanted to become a painter from the age of fourteen and learnt minia-ture painting and the fashionable pastel technique. She was not admitted to the Royal Academy until 1783, when she was accepted, along with her rival Elisabeth Vigée-Lebrun, who is better-known today. Labille-Guiard was particularly successful with her portraits of artists and aristocracy, and she founded Paris's first school for women painters. Her quality as an artist has recently been rediscovered.

11 APRIL

Robert Delaunay

1885–1941 | Painter | France

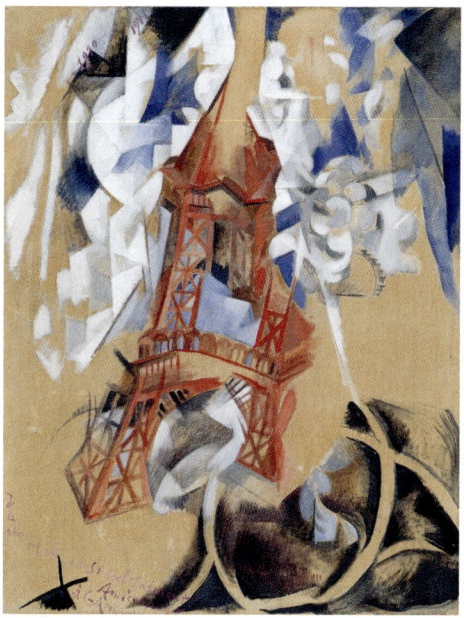

The Eiffel Tower, 1910/1911

Delaunay taught himself to paint in the style of Neo-Impressionism. In 1909, after seeing works by Pablo Picasso and Georges Braque in Paris, he devoted himself to Cubism. His series of *Eiffel Towers* became famous, with their colours characterized by an almost Futuristic dynamism. He often collaborated with his wife, the painter Sonia Delaunay, and held joint exhibitions with her. Delaunay began to make series of abstract pictures in 1912. The couple spent the First World War in Spain and Portugal, and in 1940 they moved to the South of France, where Delaunay soon died of cancer.

12 APRIL

James Ensor

1860–1949 | Painter, graphic artist and draughtsman | Belgium

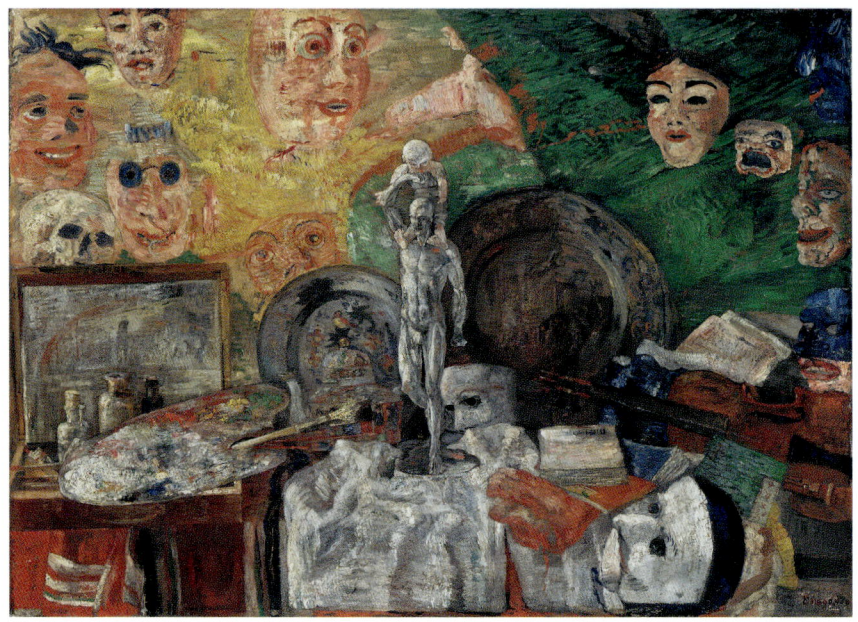

Still Life in the Studio, 1889

One of the modern era's great outsiders, Ensor studied briefly at the Brussels Academy and then returned to Ostend, where he remained for the rest of his life. His first works were portraits, still lifes and interiors painted with loose brushstrokes. In 1883, he painted his first picture of people transformed into masks. His subjects became increasingly grotesque and fantastical, with the planes of dream and reality becoming ever more interchangeable. The graphic arts were an integral part of his oeuvre. His fame came late in life, and he was honoured with a state burial.

13 APRIL

Wilhelm Busch

1832–1908 | Draughtsman and painter | Germany

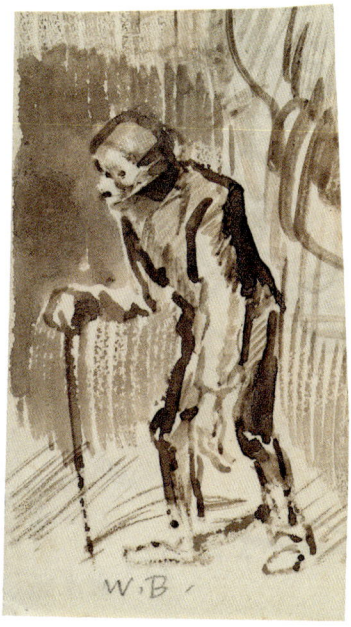

Old Man with a Cane, undated

Busch was a humorous poet and draughtsman who remains beloved in Germany to this day. He became known as early as the 1870s for his drawings and verses with popular appeal: his story *Max and Moritz*, for example, was later described as a forerunner of modern-day comics. His often grotesque and macabre humour also contained subtle cruelties. Busch was introverted and led a quiet life; his financial situation improved only gradually. Besides poems and prose, he also made hundreds of small-format paintings.

14 APRIL

Leonardo da Vinci

1452–1519 | Painter, sculptor, architect i. a. | Italy

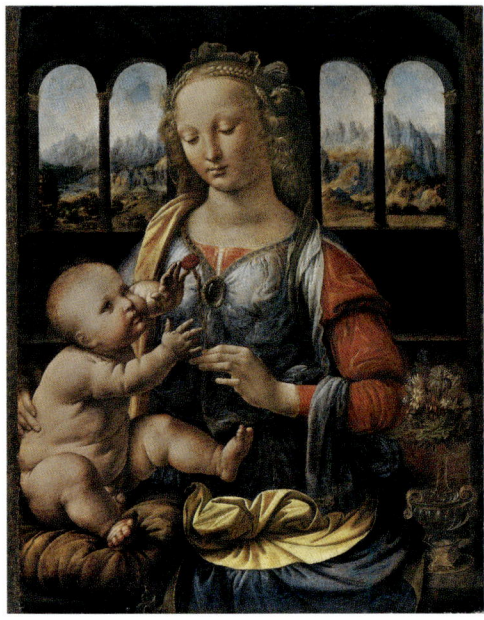

Madonna with Carnation, c. 1475

With his manifold skills, Leonardo was one of the greatest polymaths of all time. His fame has endured for centuries to the present day, through such works as his *Last Supper* in Milan or the *Mona Lisa*, which has hung in the Louvre in Paris since 1804. He is equally known for his unique drawings and studies, both scientific and anatomical. Leonardo considered himself a moral and natural philosopher, which is reflected in his pictures as well as his literary and poetic work. He spent his final years at the invitation of the king of France at his palace in Amboise.

15 APRIL

Élisabeth Vigée-Lebrun

1755–1842 | Painter | France

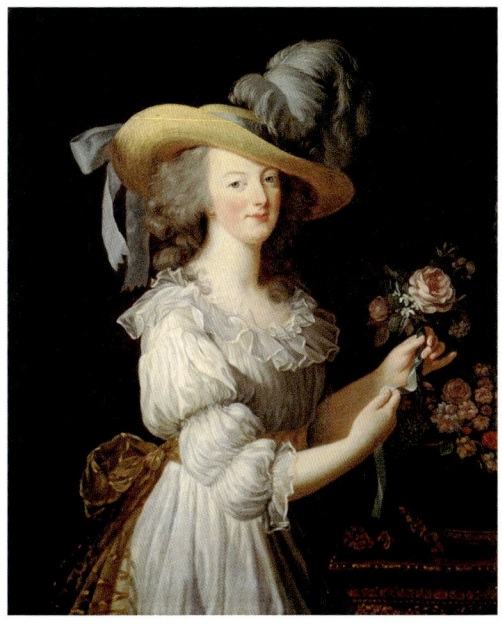

Portrait of Marie-Antoinette in Muslin Dress, 1783

In 1776, the painter married a descendant of Charles Le Brun, court artist under Louis XIV. She found prosperity through numerous commissions for portraits of the aristocracy, not least of Marie-Antoinette. In the course of the French Revolution, she fled with her daughter to Rome, where she later moved in aristocratic circles. She had lost all civic rights in France, and her property was in jeopardy. Following her divorce, she travelled to St Petersburg, where she was supported by the tsar's family. In 1802, she returned to Paris, where she lived until her death. Her legacy consists of hundreds of paintings in Neoclassical style.

16 APRIL

Alf Lechner

1925–2017 | Sculptor and draughtsman | Germany

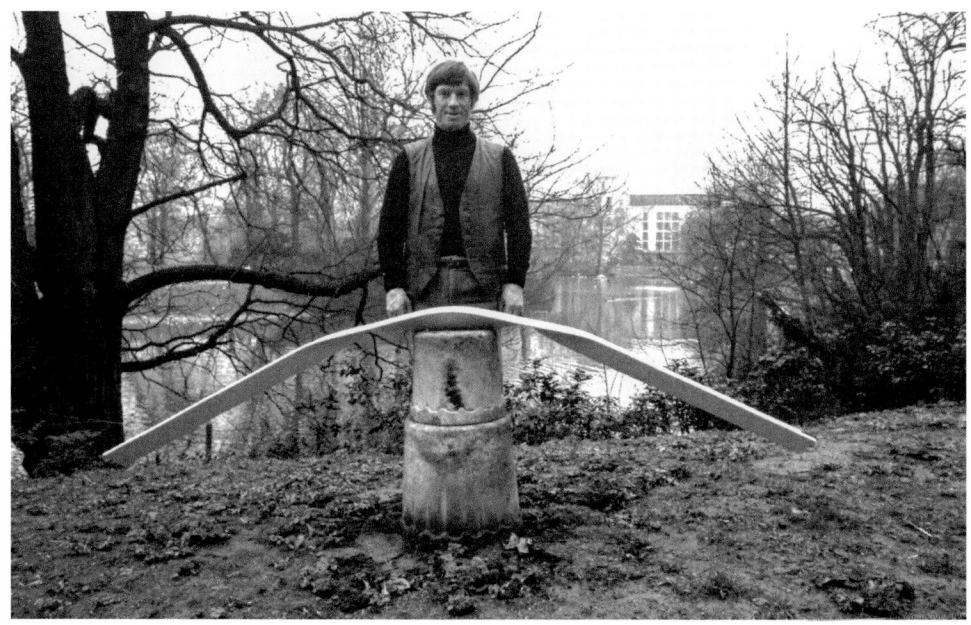

Alf Lechner with one of his sculptures, 1969

This Munich native was one of the great German steel sculptors of his time. After studying conventional painting techniques, he apprenticed as a locksmith, founded a company and had his inventions patented. Starting in the 1960s, he created an extensive oeuvre that aspired to the greatest simplicity in his analysis of basic geometric shapes. Lechner united rational and sensuous forms in sculptures that weighed tons to create aesthetic structures of playful lightness and succinct power. The Lechner Museum opened in Ingolstadt in 2000.

_____

_____

_____

_____

17 APRIL

Neo Rauch

Born 1960 | Painter | Germany

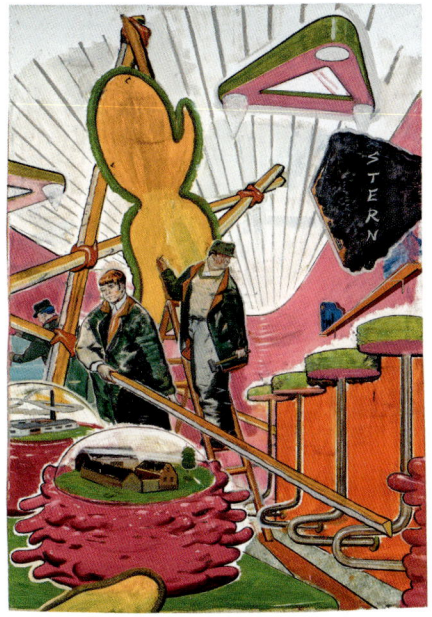

Star, 2001

Rauch is one of the most successful German painters in the world today. In the 1990s, he became known for his unique expression in pictures and prints whose realistic content – including motifs from the everyday and working world – employ idiosyncratic shifts in size as well as surreal and magical elements. Between 2013 and 2016, he made *Neo Rauch – Gefährten und Begleiter*, an artist's portrait and film documentary about his work. In 2018, partnering with his wife, the painter Rosa Loy, he designed the set of *Lohengrin* for the Bayreuth Festival.

18 APRIL

Fernando Botero

1932–2023 | Painter and sculptor | Columbia

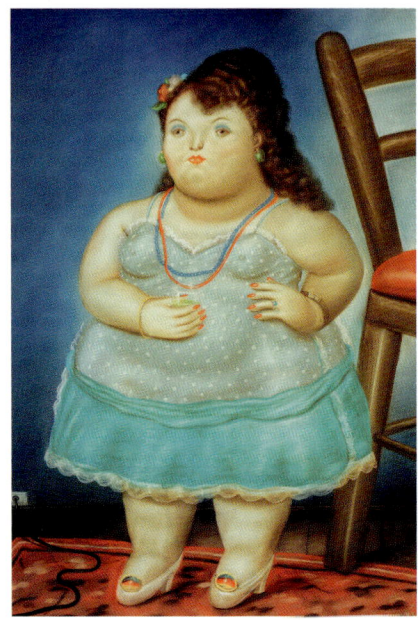

Prostitute, 1975

One of Latin America's best-known artists, Botero found his unmistakeable personal style using voluminous, sensuous shapes at an early stage. All his depictions of both people and animals derive their presence from this exaggeration of form. Something grotesquely "naive" and not rarely a subtle humour often resonates in his protagonists' overblown corporeality. Botero lived for a long time in Pietrasanta, Italy, and died at an extreme old age. His fame is assured through numerous exhibitions and sculptures on squares worldwide.

19 APRIL

Joan Miró

1893–1983 | Painter, graphic artist, sculptor and ceramicist | Spain

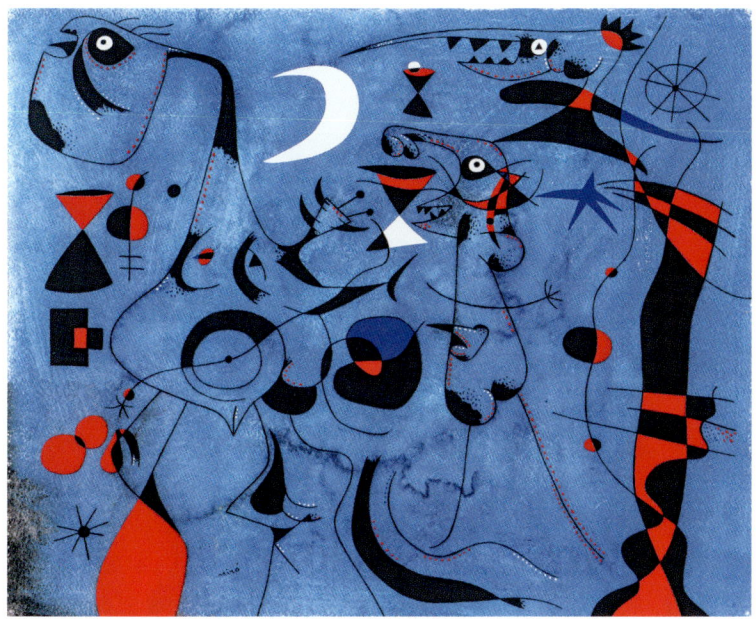

People at Night Guided by the Phosphorescent Trails of Snails, 1940

The Catalan Miró was one of the most popular artists of the twentieth century. Miró's early landscapes were highly poetic pictures of nature. Once he had become friends with Pablo Picasso, among others, in Paris in 1919, he sought to transform the figurative into a more abstract visual language. He was inspired by Surrealism as well as by Paul Klee. In the 1930s, Miró created large paintings featuring fantastical beings thrusting towards metamorphosis. During the Spanish Civil War Miró lived in Paris until 1940; he later returned to Spain, settling in 1956 in Majorca, where he died aged ninety.

20 APRIL

Dod Procter

1890–1972 | Painter | Great Britain

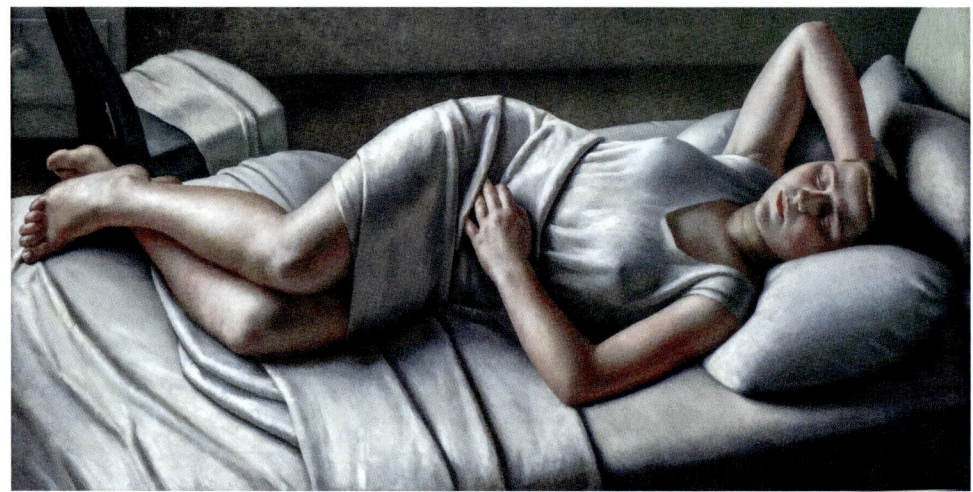

Morning, 1926

Dod Procter was a fellow student of Ernest Procter, whom she married in 1912, in Paris, where Impressionism influenced them both. She first exhibited at the Royal Academy in 1913. During the 1920s, she painted portraits and sensual female figures. *Morning*, her most famous painting, was acquired in 1927 by the Tate Gallery in London. Following her husband's death in 1935, she travelled extensively to places including Africa. In her later years, she produced mainly portraits and floral pieces. Her public recognition dwindled during her lifetime but particularly after her death in 1972.

21 APRIL

Odilon Redon

1840–1916 | Graphic artist and painter | France

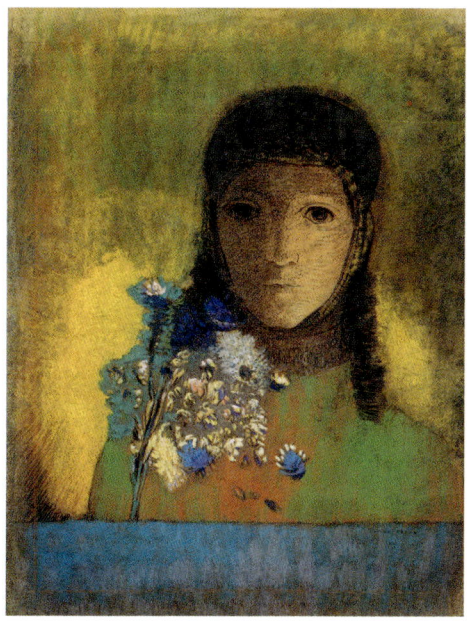

Woman with Wild Flowers, c. 1900

Redon devoted himself to drawing at an early age. In 1870/1871, he fought in the infantry in the Franco-Prussian War. After that, he lived in Paris, made financially secure by money from his parents' vineyard. In 1870s and 1880s, he made his famous black charcoal drawings and series of lithographs, some of which he dedicated to the novelist Gustave Flaubert. Unconscious fears, nightmares and hallucinations fill these works, while later pieces plunge his conceptual world into a surreally iridescent realm of colour. As a Symbolist, Redon inspired many later artists.

22 APRIL

Fritz Wotruba

1907–1975 | Sculptor | Austria

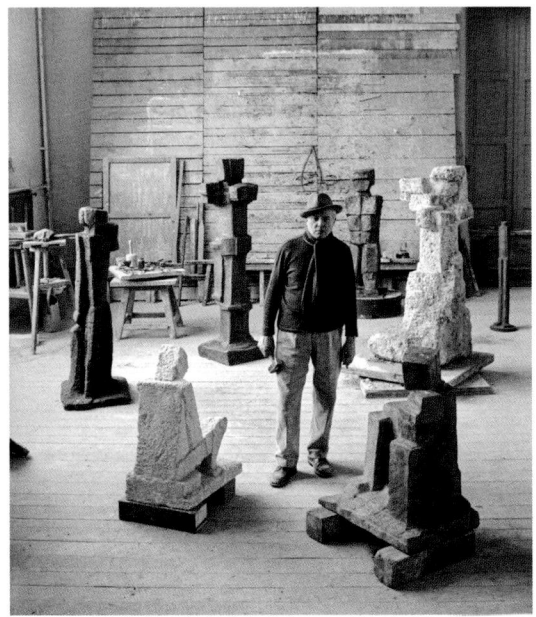

Fritz Wotruba in his studio in Vienna, 1959

Wotruba was one of the leading European sculptors of the post-war period. His life's theme was the human figure; his preferred material, stone. Through a consistent reduction of forms, he achieved his vision of the human figure as architecture. In the 1930s and 1940s, his meeting with Aristide Maillol was formative. Wotruba spent the war living in Switzerland on account of his Jewish wife. His influence as an artist and academy professor grew steadily after 1945. A church that he designed near Vienna was consecrated as his artistic legacy in 1976.

23 APRIL

Bridget Riley

Born 1931 | Op Art painter | Great Britain

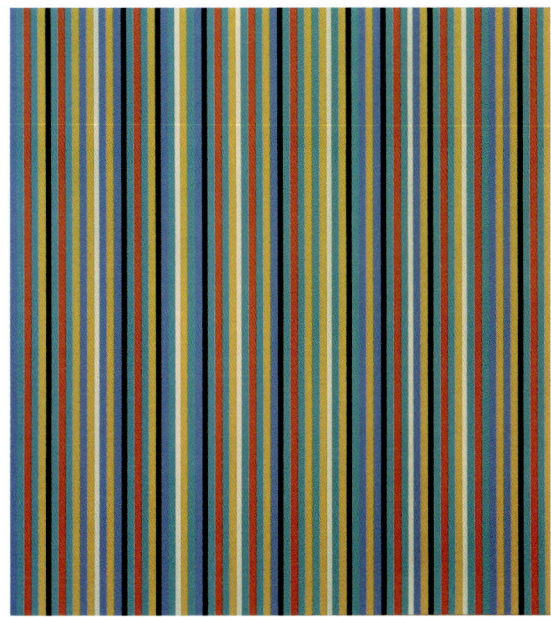

Gentle Measure, 1982

This world-famous British artist is one of the leading protagonists of Op Art. Her exploration of Georges Seurat's Pointillism and Italian Futurism during her studies in London was formative. In 1960, Riley made her first Op Art pictures, consisting of abstract shape patterns and geometric coloured figures, which evoke the impression of shimmering movement and optical illusions in viewers. The artist has been honoured with numerous international exhibitions and awards.

24 APRIL

Cy Twombly

1928–2011 | Painter, photographer and object artist | United States

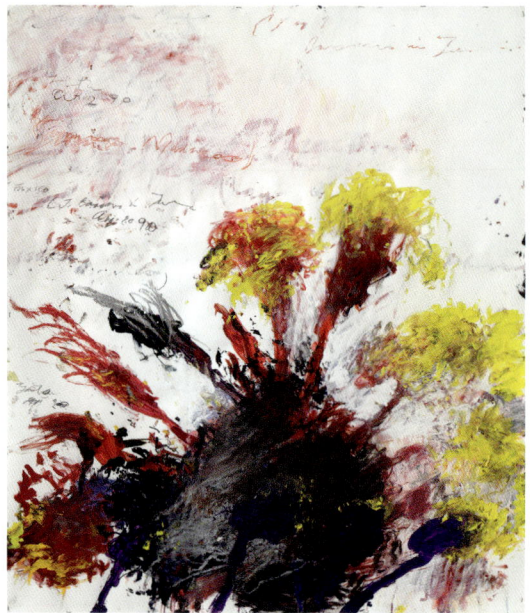

Summer Madness, 1990

Twombly is one of the most famous and expensive artists of the second half of the twentieth century in the world. Early on, he became friends with Robert Rauschenberg, with whom he travelled extensively to places such as Europe, Cuba and Morocco. He lived in Rome starting in 1957. Further travels to Greece and Egypt, among other places, influenced his paintings and drawings, in which often overpainted word fragments and ciphers, pencil traces and elements of collage suggest enigmatic ambiguity. He had a mysterious knack of making subjects from mythology and history "resonate".

25 APRIL

Akseli Gallen-Kallela

1865–1931 | Painter, architect and designer | Finland

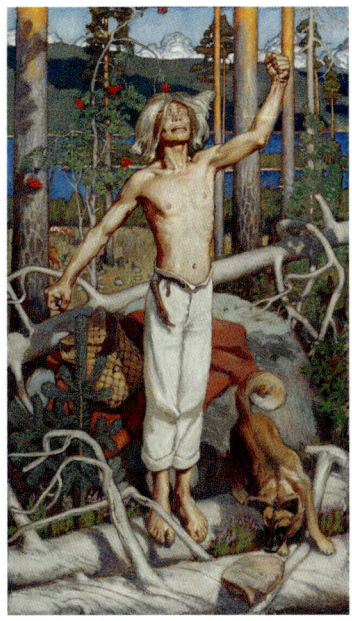

Kullervo's Curse, 1899

After studying in Helsinki and Paris, Gallen-Kallela spent his life exploring subjects from Finnish mythology. Initially working in a Realist style, he later found influences in Symbolism and Art Nouveau. He illustrated works of Finnish literature, in particular the *Kalevala*, the central work of Finnish national Romanticism. Gallen-Kallela was in contact with many influential figures, and international exhibitions made him famous. In the 1920s, he lived in the United States, returning intermittently to Finland, and he died in Stockholm in 1931.

26 APRIL

Emil Jakob Schindler

1842–1892 | Landscape painter | Austria

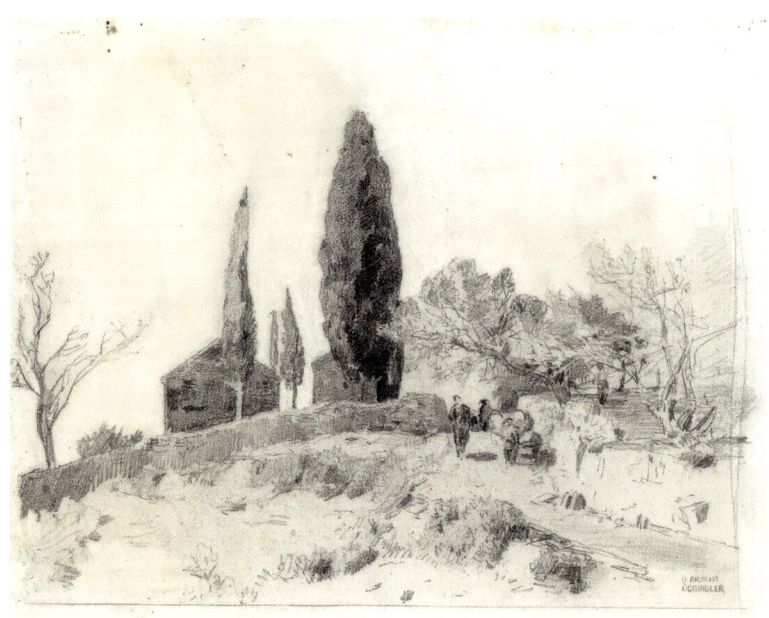

Cypresses near Zara, c. 1887/1888

Following his studies in Vienna, where he was close friends with Hans Makart, Schindler travelled to Venice and Holland. His daughter, born of his marriage with a singer, later became famous as Alma Mahler-Werfel. Starting in the 1880s, he was busy with commissions and received many awards. Among these commissions, he was hired by the crown prince of Austria to travel to Mediterranean resorts and capture them in ink drawings or watercolours. His Impressionistic landscape paintings were particularly popular.

27 APRIL

Yves Klein

1928–1962 | Painter, sculptor and performance artist | France

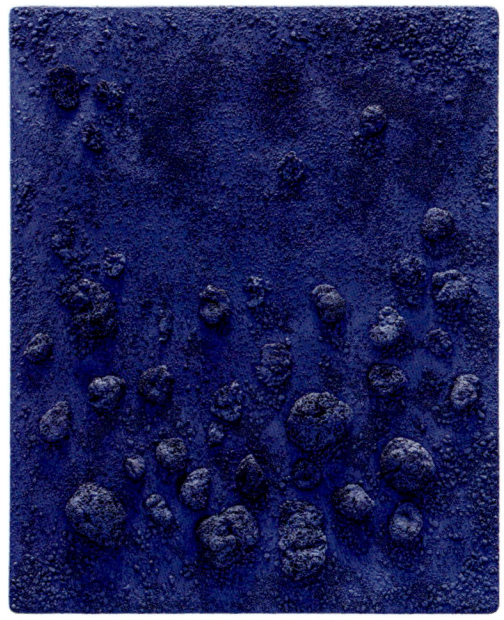

Blue Sponge Relief (Little Night Music), 1960

Klein was obsessed with his radical artistic concepts. At eighteen, lying on the beach in Nice, he created his first immaterial picture, which he declared his first "monochrome". By putting his signature to the blue Mediterranean sky, he anticipated approaches of later Conceptual Art. Klein began making his monochrome paintings after experiencing the blue backgrounds in Giotto's frescoes in Assisi. He was granted a patent for the ultramarine he used in 1960. International exhibitions and performances ensued.

28 APRIL

Frank Auerbach

1931–2024 | Painter | Great Britain

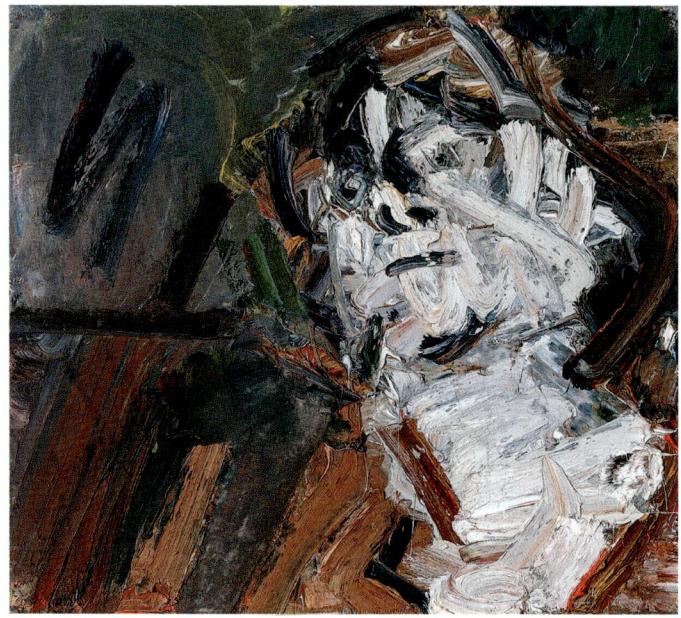

Head of J. Y. M., 1978

Born into a Jewish family in Berlin, Auerbach was sent to England in the *Kindertransport* rescue effort at the age of eight. He never saw his parents again; they were murdered in the Holocaust. Success took a long time coming. It was not until the 1986 Venice Biennale, where he won the Golden Lion, that he made his breakthrough. Despite his fame, he remained one of the most enigmatic artists, shunning any form of publicity. His figurative style was expressive. Sometimes he worked for years on his "heads" and urban landscapes, which often resembled sculptured reliefs due to their thickly applied paint.

29 APRIL

Francesco Primaticcio

1504–1570 | Painter, sculptor and architect | Italy

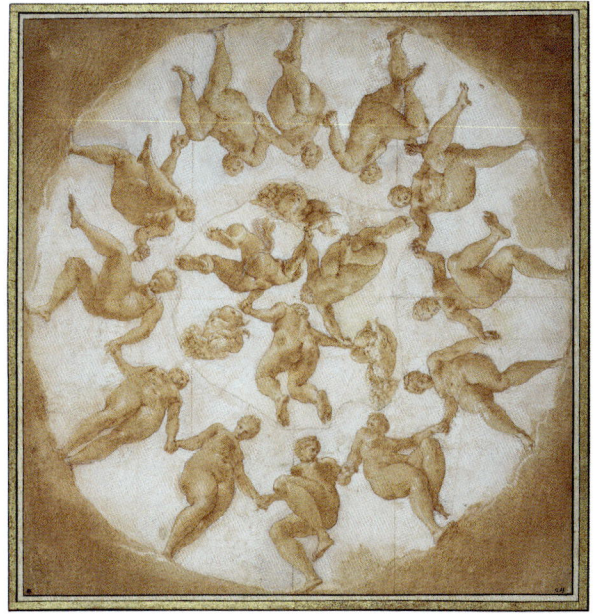

Dance of the Hours, c. 1547/1548

In 1532, François I, the king of France, invited the young Primaticcio to Fontainebleau to work on the castle's decoration with Rosso Fiorentino. After the latter's death, Primaticcio's activity flourished: he became director of the construction and decoration works, of the sculpture collection and of the department of drawings. Later, he was received prestigious commissions from patrons including Catherine de' Médicis. Primaticcio was a prominent protagonist of Mannerism and one of the co-founders of the famous Fontainebleau School.

30 APRIL

Cecilia Beaux

1855–1942 | Painter | United States

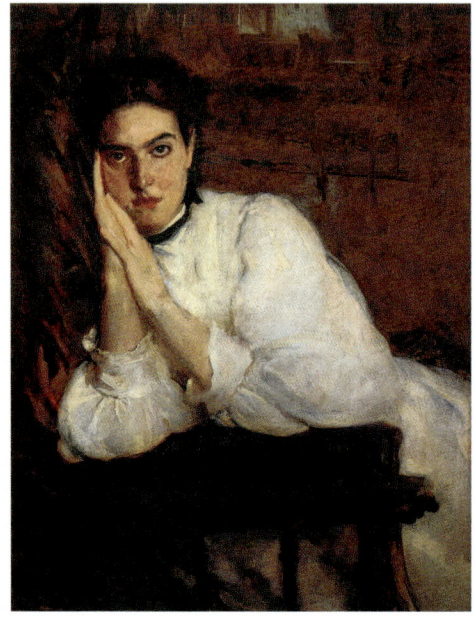

The Dreamer, 1894

Cecilia Beaux, whose father was French, embarked on a journey through Europe after finishing her studies. She attended the relevant academies in Paris, where she studied the great masters in the museums, as she had done in England and Italy. From 1900, she lived in New York, where she exhibited and became known as a portrait painter to the wealthy upper class. Her home was a meeting place of New York's high society. Beaux's sitters included Georges Clemenceau and Edith Roosevelt.

1 MAY

Peggy Bacon

1895–1987 | Painter, graphic artist and author | United States

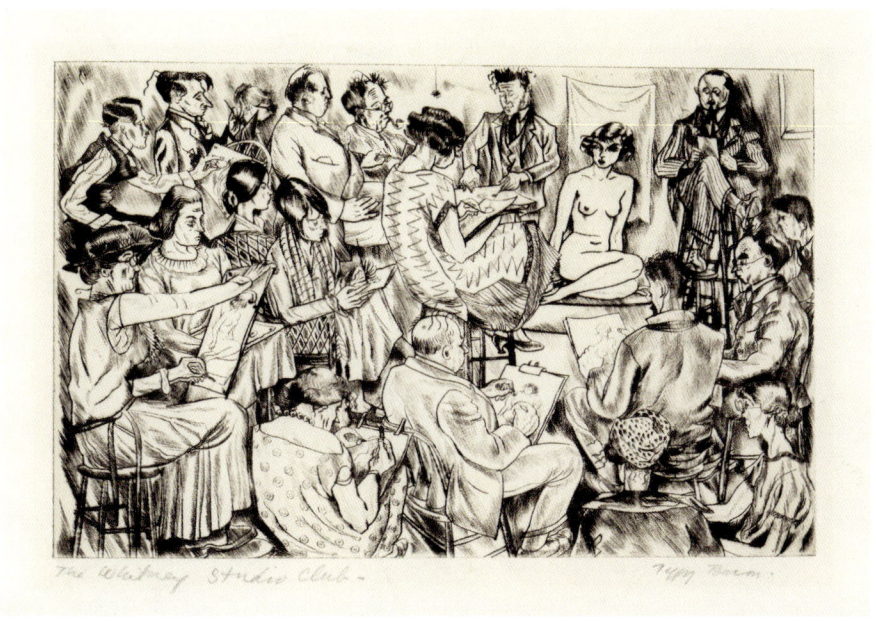

The Whitney Studio Club, 1925

Bacon grew up in a sheltered, artistic parental home with private tutors; her father's suicide in 1913 was a decisive event. Right after that she moved with her mother to New York City and studied painting. She taught herself the technique of drypoint etching. She was prolific as an artist, wrote and illustrated numerous books, and became famous with her satirical prints, which appeared in magazines such as *The New Yorker*. Many exhibitions and accolades ensued, until she died aged ninety-one.

2 MAY

Robert De Niro Sr.

1922–1993 | Painter | United States

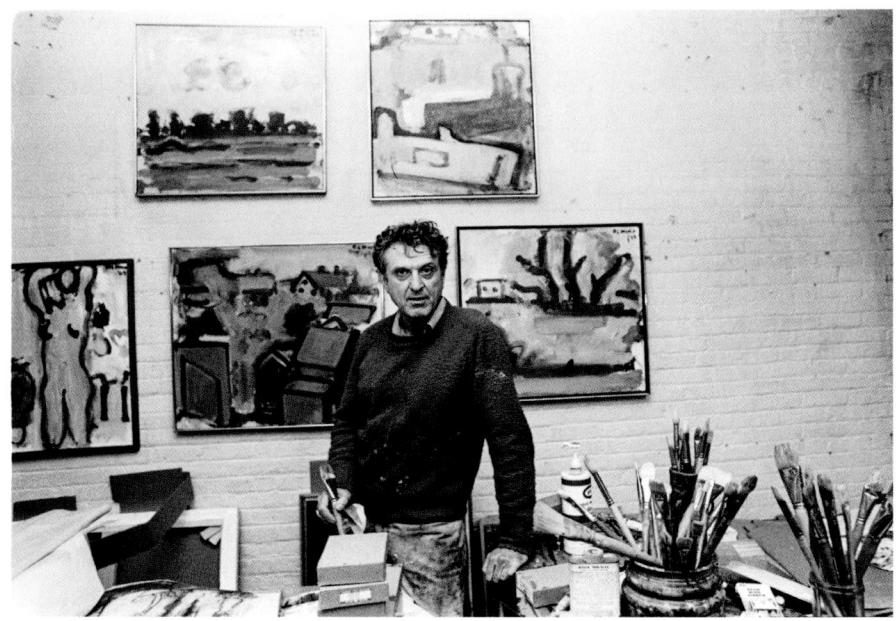

Robert De Niro in his studio in New York, 1982

De Niro studied under Hans Hofmann in New York as well as under Josef Albers at Black Mountain College. Many of his early works were lost in a studio fire in 1949. In 1968, De Niro was awarded a Guggenheim Fellowship. Exhibitions throughout America followed on from that. Shortly after his marriage and the birth of his son he divorced, presumably because he became aware of his homosexuality. His world-famous son of the same name made this public in a film in 2014. A celebrated member of the New York school of painters alongside Mark Rothko, Willem de Kooning and Jackson Pollock, De Niro was known for his unique, bold, gestural style of painting.

3 MAY

Keith Haring

1958–1990 | Artist | United States

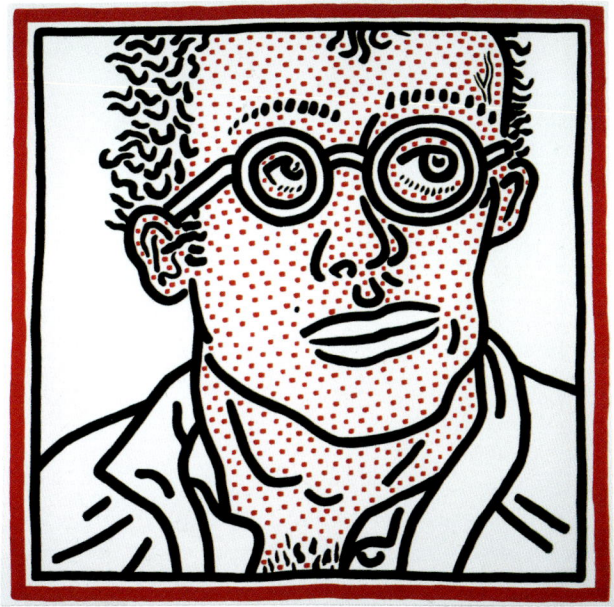

Untitled (Self-Portrait for Tony), 1985

Haring, an internationally famous street artist, was strongly influenced by the graffiti scene. Using simple lines and symbols, he developed a visual language of his very own, often with biting political content. Several thousand works appeared in the corridors of the New York subway between 1980 and 1985, easily and instantly recognizable by passers-by. In 1983, he became friends with Andy Warhol, painted walls worldwide and exhibited internationally. Even before he was diagnosed with AIDS, he was committed to AIDS awareness until his death – a subject that was reflected in his oeuvre before that.

4 MAY

Niko Pirosmani

1862–1918 | Painter | Georgia

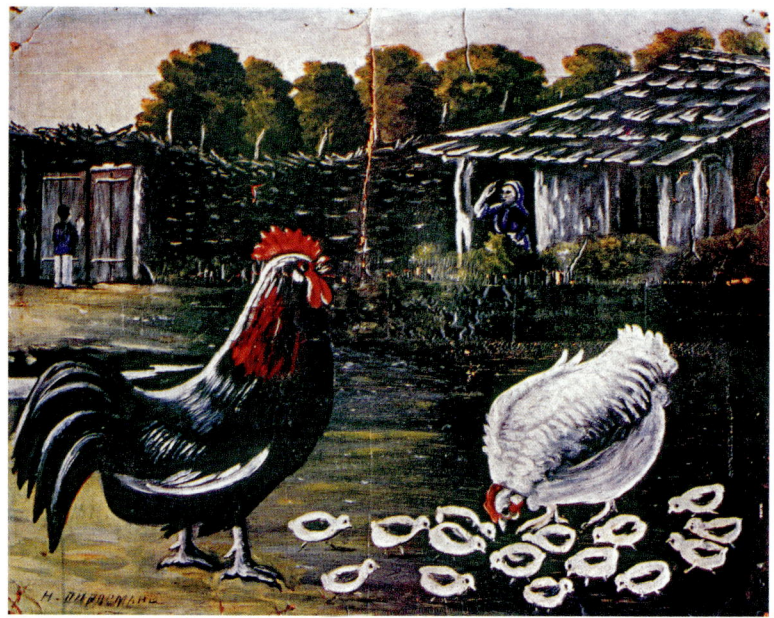

Chicken and Cockerel, 1904

Born to a farming family, Pirosmani taught himself painting. Starting in 1901, he was homeless, living in the train station quarter of Tbilisi and earning his living with occasional jobs, such as painting pub signs. The subjects of his "naive" pictures are countryside scenes, portraits, still lifes and landscapes. His animal depictions are particularly intense. He was internationally acclaimed as one of the great "naive" painters alongside Henri Rousseau, long after his death due to malnourishment and liver failure in 1918.

5 MAY

Lyubov Popova

1889–1924 | Painter | Russia

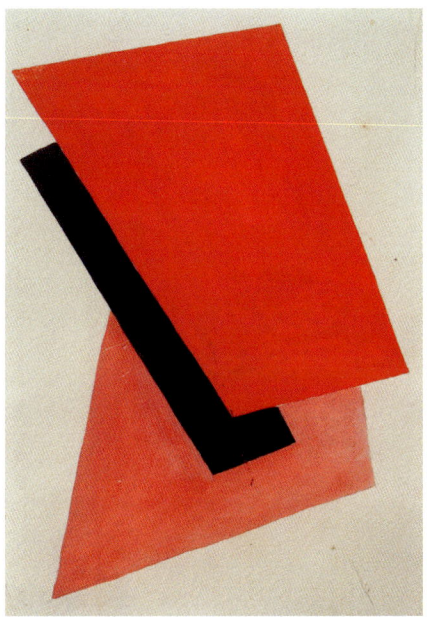

Painterly Architectonics, 1917

Following private studies in Moscow between 1910 and 1914, the Russian painter Popova travelled to Italy and Paris. While she focused on the Futurism of Umberto Boccioni in Italy, in the French capital she partnered with a series of well-known painters. She was sharing a studio with Vladimir Tatlin by 1916. In her exploration of both Cubism and Futurism, Popova was an influential figure in the Russian avant-garde. Starting in 1921, she was active in the field of industrial design and created, among other things, innovative textile designs.

6 MAY

Rabindranath Tagore

1861–1941 | Philosopher, poet, painter, composer and musician | India

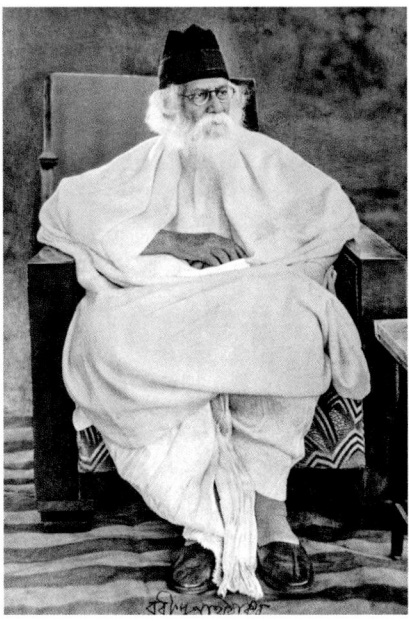

Rabindranath Tagore, c. 1935

Tagore, a Bengali, was partly pioneering in many areas. Alongside his cultural and social reforms, he enriched his home country's literature and art. For example, he modernized Bengali art by breaking down its strict structure and classical formal vocabulary and linking the resultant Indian modernism with European Expressionism. He encountered Western culture during a stay in England and the United States. He received the Nobel Prize for Literature in 1913.

7 MAY

Georg Muche

1895–1987 | Painter and graphic artist | Germany

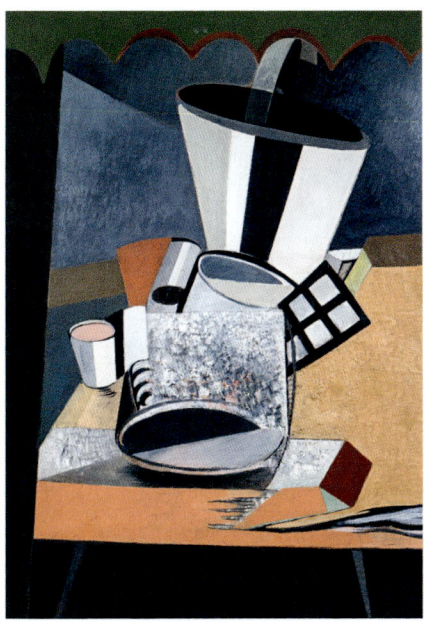

Two Pails, 1923

Following a rejection from the Art Academy in Munich, Muche went to Berlin in 1914. There, Herwarth Walden organized a joint exhibition for Muche with Max Ernst and recruited him as a teacher at Der Sturm's art school. Appointed to the Bauhaus in 1920, he was director of the weaving workshop until 1927. Teaching activities ensued in Berlin and Wrocław. He taught at the textile engineering school in Krefeld between 1939 and 1958. He proved protean in his artist style: following abstract and Surrealist pictures, he devoted himself to poetic depictions of people and plants, and also took up critical subjects in his late oeuvre.

8 MAY

Gustav Blaeser

1813–1874 | Sculptor | Germany

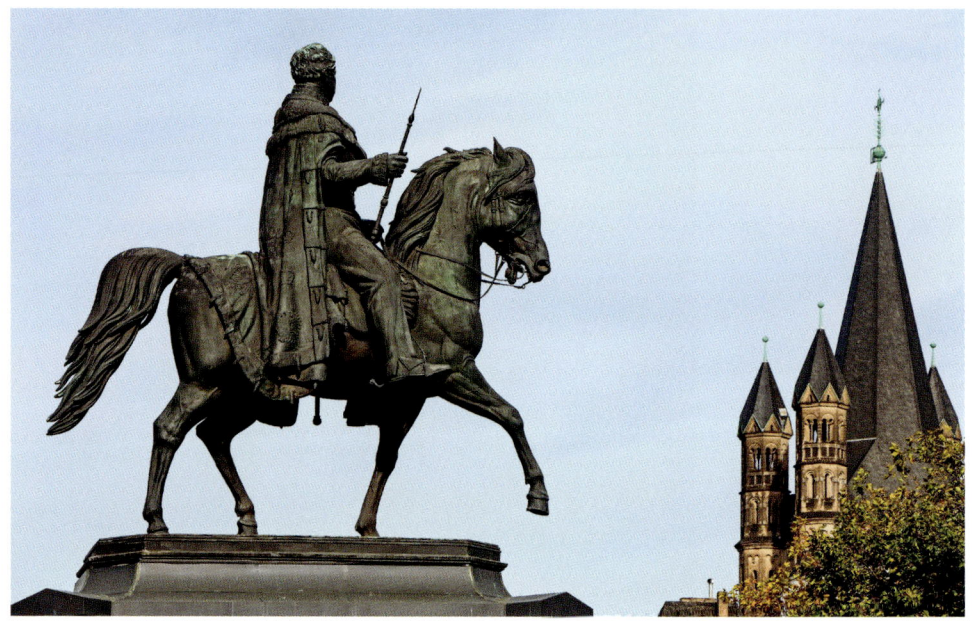

Equestrian Statue of King Friedrich Wilhelm III of Prussia, Cologne, 1864–1878

Between 1834 and 1843, Blaeser was active as a student at the Art Academy in Berlin and employed in the studio of sculptor Christian Daniel Rauch. After a sojourn in Rome, he returned to Berlin, where he was commissioned to create a group of sculptures for the bridge leading to Berlin Palace. This made him very well known as a sculptor. Blaeser sculpted numerous monuments, memorials, statues and busts in public space.

9 MAY

Chang Dai-chien

1899–1983 | Painter | China

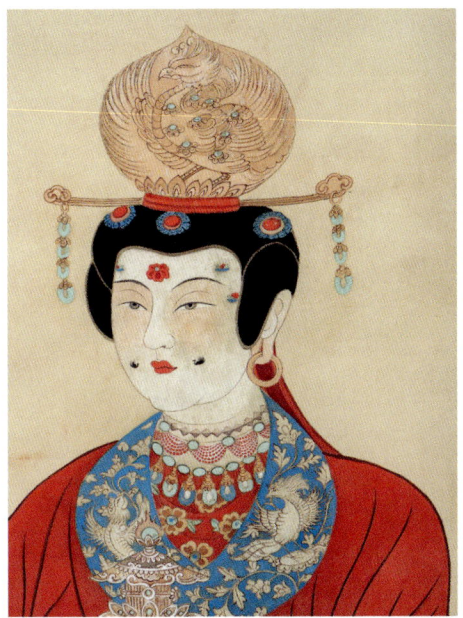

Lady Li, 1943

Dai-chien achieved worldwide fame as one of the best-known Chinese painters of the twentieth century. He began his career learning drawing and textile dyeing in Japan. On his return to China, he devoted himself to literature, calligraphy and painting, was a Buddhist monk for a while and, in 1936, obtained a professorship at the art department of the university in Nanjing. In his painting he was a master of landscapes, figures, flowers and birds. He later lived in Hong Kong, India, South America, the United States and finally in Taipei.

Salvador Dalí

1904–1989 | Painter | Spain

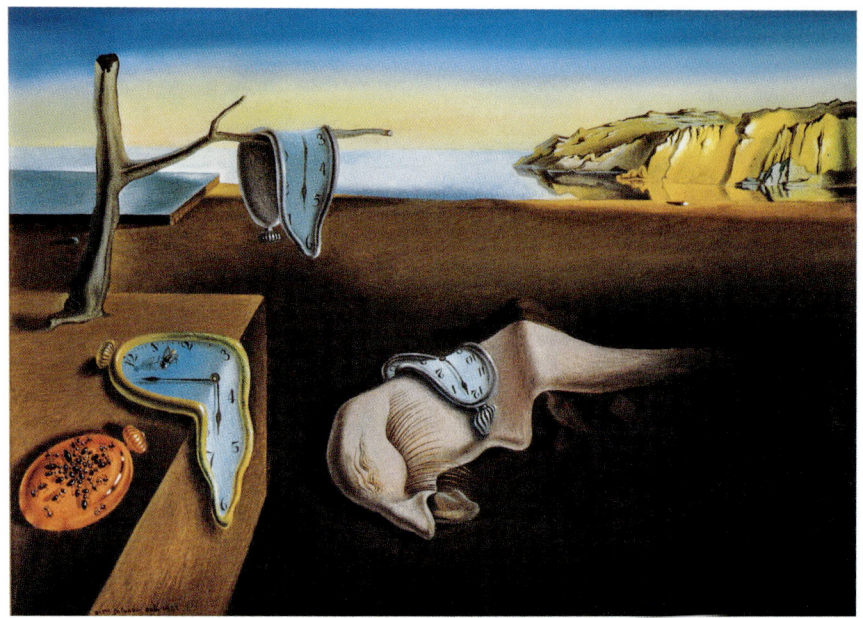

The Persistence of Memory, 1931

Dalí was one of the twentieth century's most famous artists and one of the most prolific, ingenious and simultaneously eccentric figures on the international art scene. In 1929, he joined the Surrealists and fell in love with Gala, who later became his wife and muse. Dalí's pictures revolve around the world of the subconscious; he takes up phenomena such as paranoia, dream and intoxication with clearly sexual undertones. In 1938, Dalí met Sigmund Freud, whose writings he was studying. After a flamboyant life – also in terms of his politics – spent between Europe and the United States, he died at an advanced age in 1989.

11 MAY

Frank Stella

1936–2024 | Painter, sculptor and object artist | United States

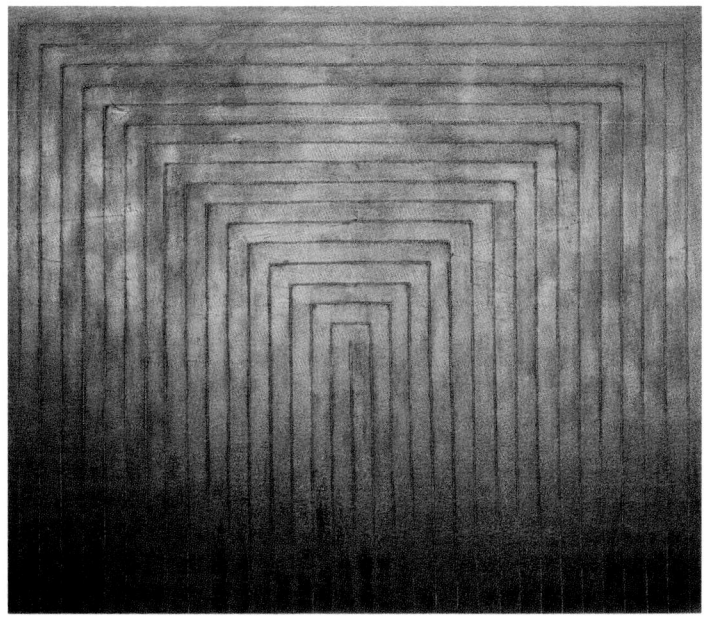

Getty Tomb (First Version), 1959

When Frank Stella died in 2024, he was one of the last great American post-war painters. In 1958, he created the first of his large, Minimalist "Black Paintings", which made him famous in the New York art scene and cleared the way for the three-dimensional expansion of visual space. The change from Minimalism to Maximalism that came about in his almost baroque expanses of his colourful wall reliefs and sculptures starting in the 1980s made Stella one of the most influential American artists of his day. From 1990 onwards, Stella was primarily occupied with architectonic works.

12 MAY

Zofia Stryjeńska

1891–1976 | Painter, illustrator and set designer | Poland

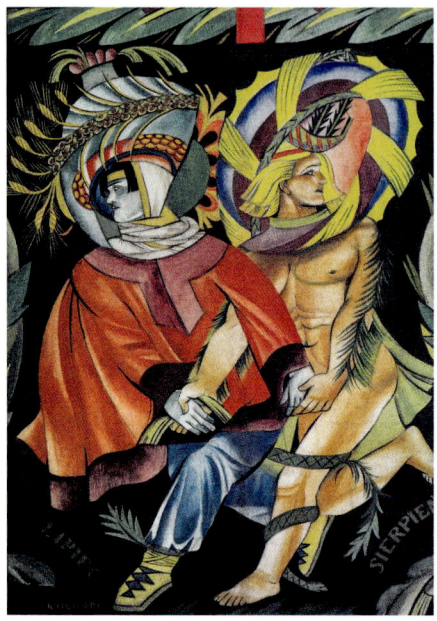

Seasons: July–August, 1925

Disguised as a boy, Stryjeńska began studying at the Art Academy in Munich at the age of twenty. When she returned to Kraków, painting and literature were her main interests. She spent the Second World War living in Kraków and later moved to Switzerland with her children. In addition to her illustrations and tapestries, she became famous across Europe with her paintings for the Polish pavilion at the Paris World's Fair in 1925. Due to her numerous works featuring Slavic gods, she is regarded as the forerunner of Slavic neopaganism.

_____

_____

_____

_____

13 MAY

Thomas Gainsborough

1727–1788 | Painter | Great Britain

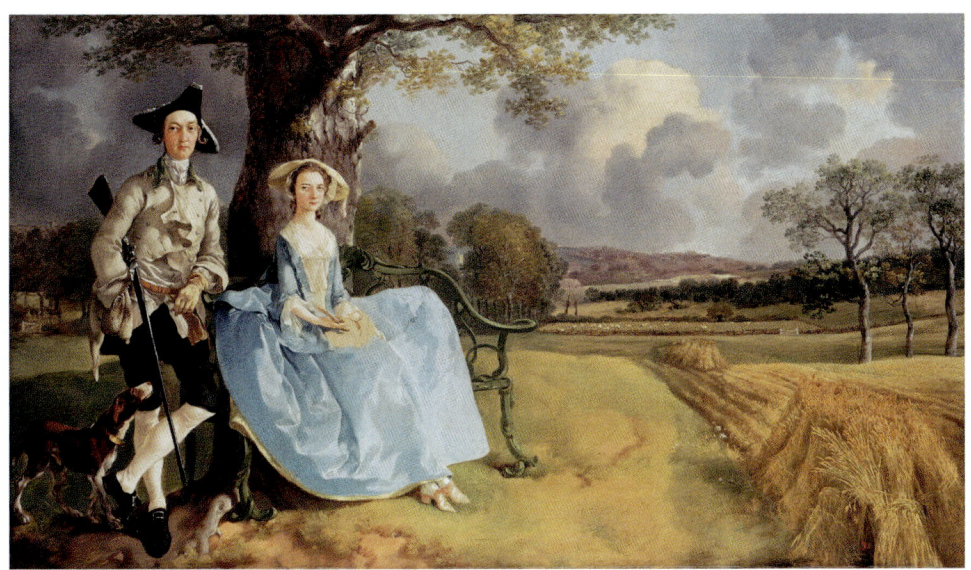

Mr and Mrs Robert Andrews, c. 1750

Gainsborough was already managing his own studio in London at the age of sixteen. Initially unsuccessful, he returned to the country and painted portraits and landscapes. In 1759, he moved to Bath, becoming better-known for his portraits and exhibiting at the Royal Academy of Arts in London. In constant rivalry with Joshua Reynolds, who favoured academic history painting, Gainsborough was able to establish himself as an empathic portraitist in London from 1774. His subtle capturing of character made him one of the foremost English painters of the eighteenth century.

14 MAY

Jasper Johns

Born 1933 | Painter, sculptor, set and costume designer | United States

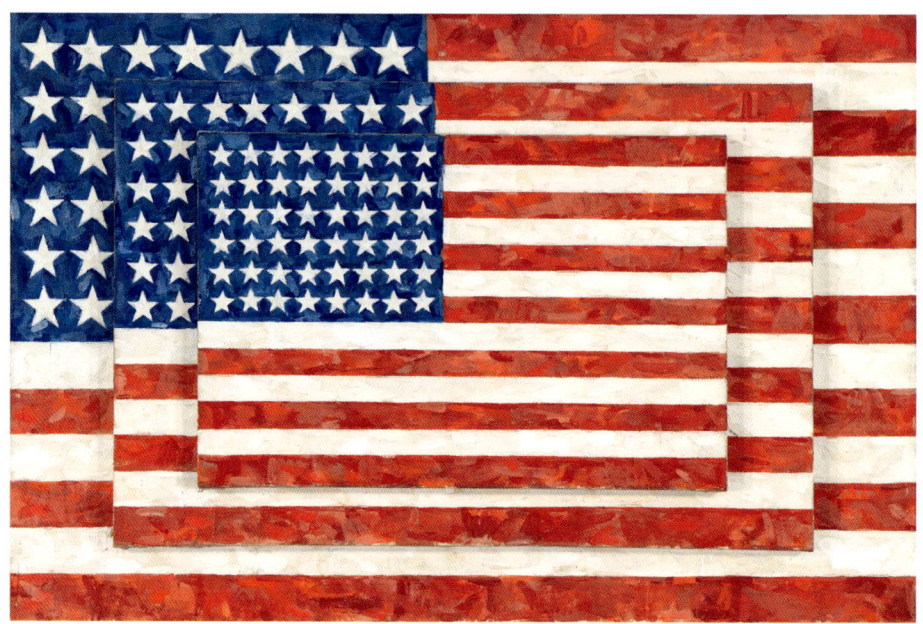

Three Flags, 1958

Johns is one of the most influential post-war American artists. He collaborated with Robert Rauschenberg, who was his life partner for several years. In 1954, he destroyed his early work and began painting flags, maps, shooting targets, letters and numbers. One of his most famous subjects, the American flag, fluctuates between recognizable symbol and painterly medium. In addition to sculpture, Johns was a master of prints. Uncounted exhibitions and global honours testify his fame.

15 MAY

Tamara de Lempicka

1898–1980 | Painter | Poland

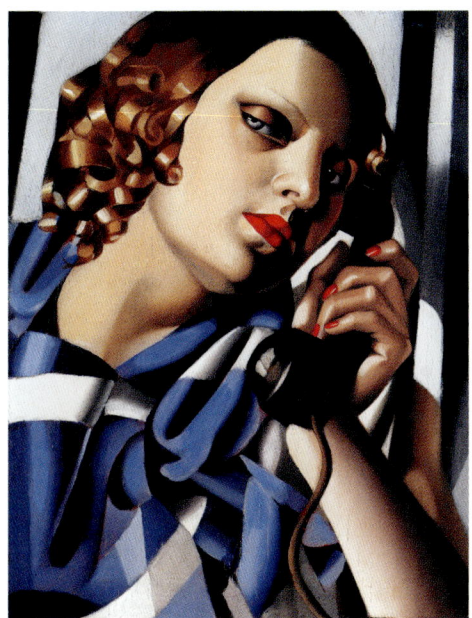

The Telephone II, 1930

Tamara de Lempicka discovered Renaissance painting on a trip to Italy in 1911, and this encounter set the tone for her own art. After studying art in St Petersburg, in 1918 she continued her studies in Paris, where she found success year later at the first Art Deco fair. Her pictures were coveted for their blend of coldness and sensuality; Lempicka circulated in Parisian society as a diva. After 1939, she lived with her second husband in various cities of the United States and Mexico, where she died.

16 MAY

VALIE EXPORT

Born 1940 | Media and performance artist, etc. | Austria

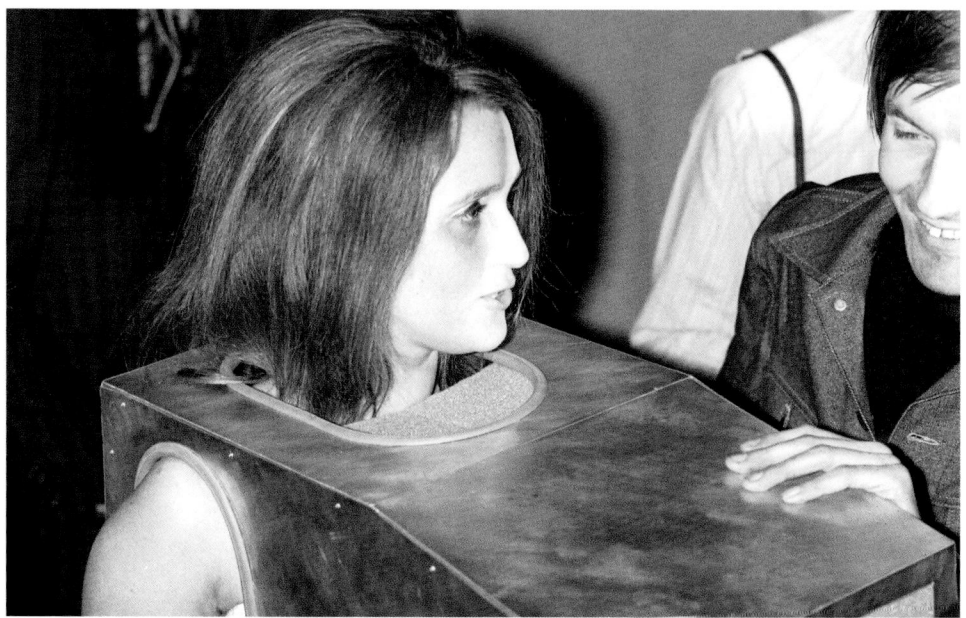

Tap and Touch Cinema, 1968

In 1967, the artist changed her name, not least in order to appear on the art scene with a new identity. She combined her nickname Valie with the logo "EXPORT", the label of a popular cigarette brand at the time. She explored feminism, performance art and the medium of film at an early stage. She presented bold body performances, closely related to Viennese Actionism, jointly with her then husband Peter Weibel as a kind of enfant terrible of the art world. Numerous exhibitions and awards earned her international renown.

17 MAY

Gertrude Käsebier

1852–1934 | Photographer | United States

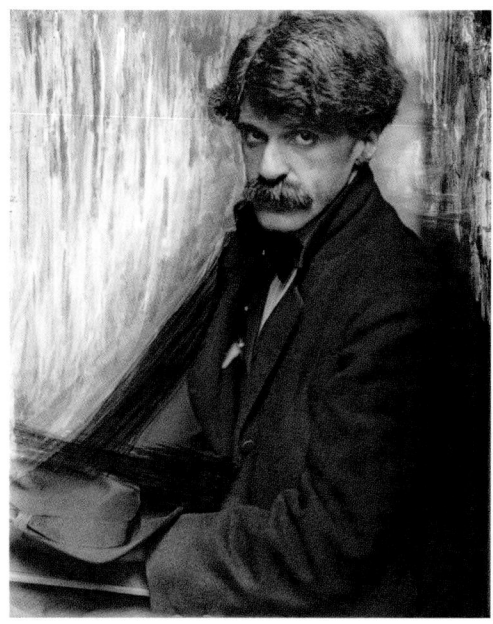

Alfred Stieglitz, 1902

Käsebier received artistic training at Pratt Institute in New York and began taking occasional photographs of her family as a mother of three children in the 1890s. After further studies and opening her own studio in 1897, she had her first success as a portraitist. Alfred Stieglitz published six of her photographs in 1903. However, she later distanced herself thematically from Stieglitz. Alongside portraits and depictions of mothers and their children, she also produced landscapes. Käsebier is regarded as a pioneer of Pictorialism, a painterly, aesthetic movement in photography.

Jacob Jordaens

1593–1678 | Painter | Flanders

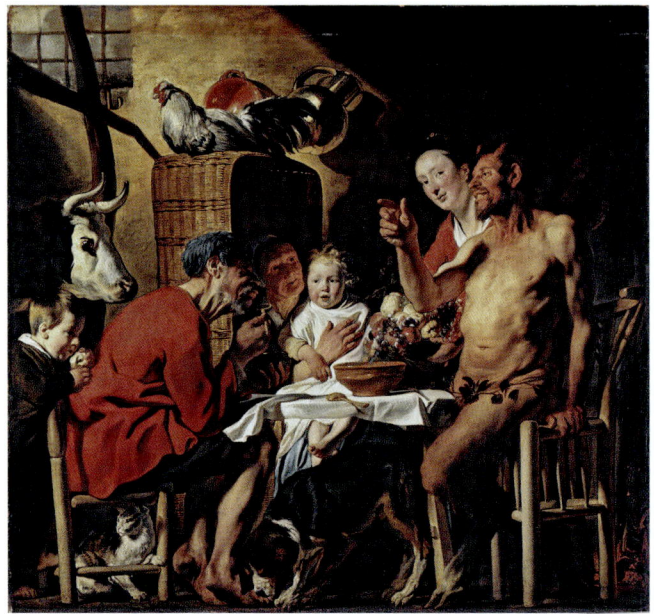

The Satyr and the Peasant, c. 1620/1621

Next to Peter Paul Rubens and Anthony van Dyck, Jordaens is among the influential painters of Antwerp Baroque. He made many genre paintings featuring scenes from bourgeois life, but also altarpieces and both mythological and allegorical subjects. After Rubens's death in 1640, Jordaens became Antwerp's foremost painter, receiving an abundance of court commissions. His income was considerable, enabling him to acquire several houses and enjoy an excellent position in society until his death. He was exceedingly busy; it is sometimes difficult to distinguish works by his own hand from workshop commissions.

19 MAY

Johann Gottfried Schadow

1764–1850 | Draughtsman and sculptor | Germany

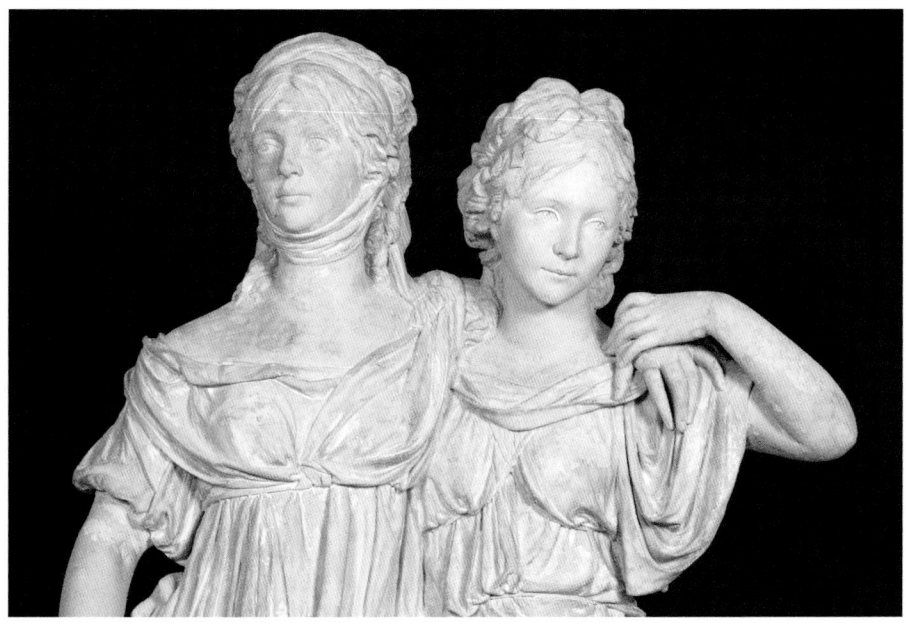

The Princess Group (Princesses Luise and Friederike of Prussia), 1795

One of the main protagonists of Neoclassicism in Germany, Schadow founded the
Berlin school of sculptors. He began his training in 1778 at the Academy of the Arts
in Berlin. He travelled to Italy and married his first wife in 1785. In the subsequent
period, he took on various offices in Berlin and was commissioned to create works
such as the Quadriga on the Brandenburg Gate. He was the director of the academy
from 1816. An eye condition restricted his later sculptural activities. His large oeuvre
includes memorials, busts, monuments and works on paper.

20 MAY

Henri Rousseau

1844–1910 | Painter | France

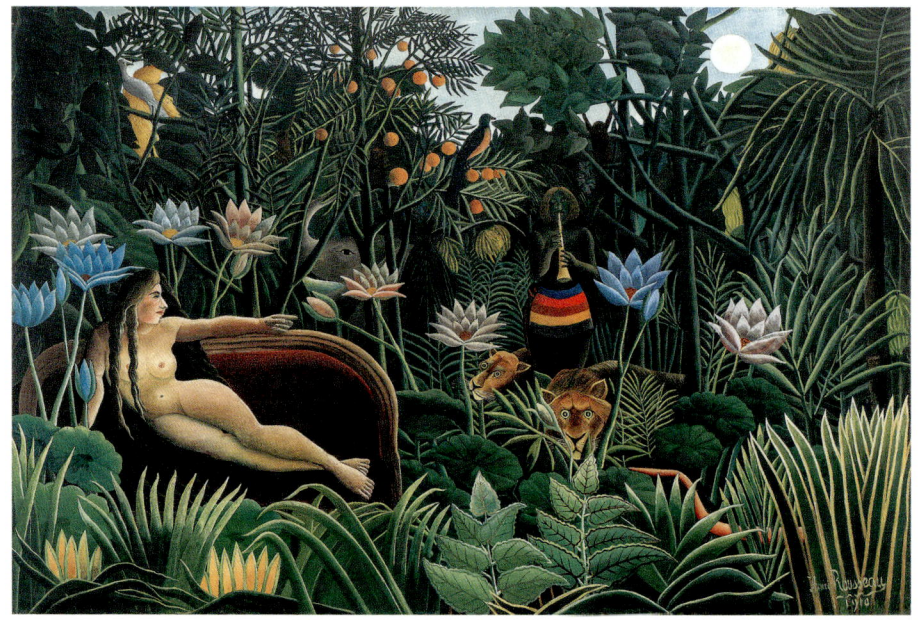

The Dream, 1910

Honoured worldwide as one of the great "naive" artists, Rousseau left a deep impression on the artists of his day. He was interested in poetry and music from an early age. Following military service, he worked in customs, which earned him the nickname "Le Douanier". His jungle pictures, with their magical realism, became famous: paradisaical dreamworlds filled with poetic symbols, both "naive" and of captivating clarity. Rousseau's influence on later generations of artists, including those of Neue Sachlichkeit (New Objectivity) and Surrealism, was huge.

21 MAY

Mary Cassatt

1844–1926 | Graphic artist and painter | United States

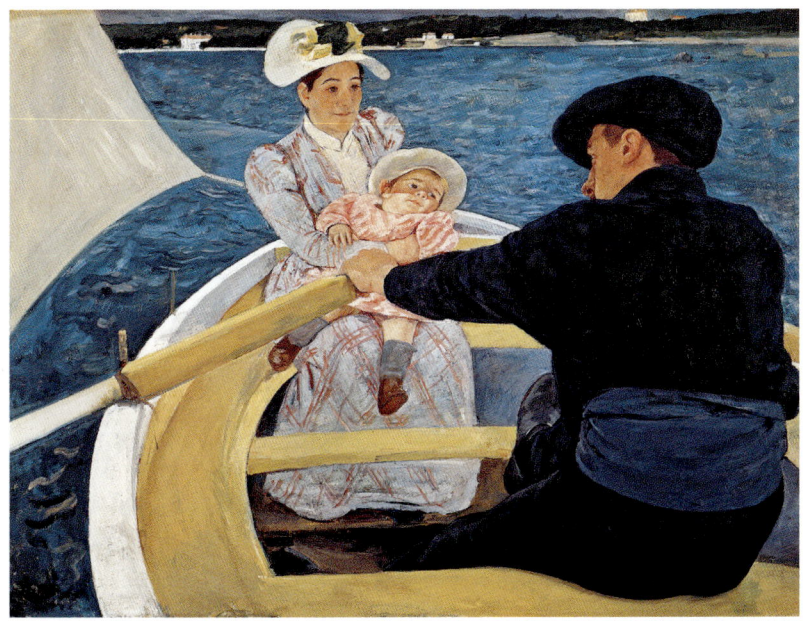

The Boating Party, c. 1893/1894

The daughter of well-off parents, Cassatt came to Europe at any early age, living in Paris starting in 1874 and travelling to Italy and Spain to study the great masters in the museums. A close friend of Degas, she often modelled for him and joined the Impressionists. In addition to her success, she had a major influence on the growing reputation of the Impressionists in the United States. Cassatt became famous with her paintings of women, the theme of mother and child, and with her graphic works. She gave up her painting in 1914, when she became nearly blind.

22 MAY

Franz Kline

1910–1962 | Painter | United States

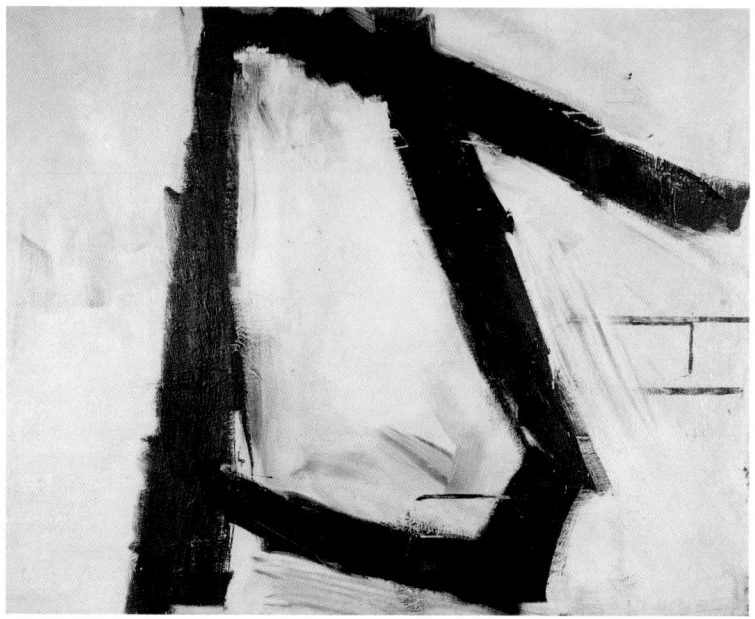

Untitled, 1953/1954

Kline was one of the leading painters of Abstract Expressionism in the United States. After studying in Boston and London, he moved into a studio in New York in 1938 and taught at various institutions. Following early works in a naturalistic, Cubist style, he began to make small ink drawings, which became increasingly abstract. Their dynamism demanded larger canvases in which the powerful structures of heavy, black markings and fragmented, bar-like forms could unfold. Alongside Jackson Pollock and Willem de Kooning, Kline is one of the pioneers of Action Painting.

23 MAY

Jacopo da Pontormo

1494–1557 | Painter | Italy

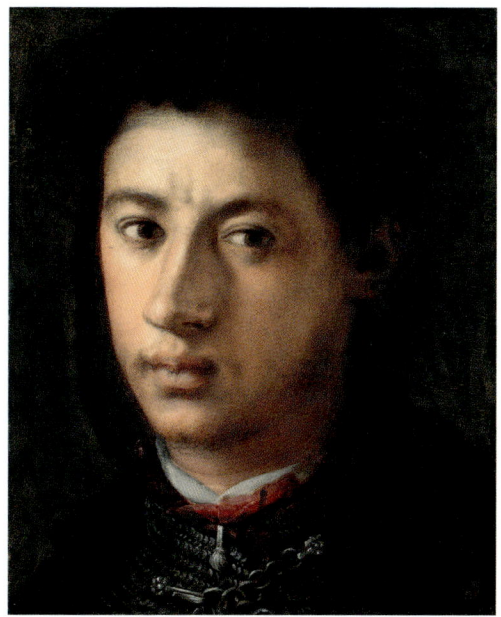

Alessandro de' Medici, 1534/1535

After his parents' early deaths, the young Jacopo went to Florence, where his teachers included Leonardo da Vinci. Praised by Michelangelo, Pontormo later received many commissions from the Medici. One of his best-known works is the portrait of Cosimo de' Medici. He also created frescoes for the Medici summer villa and the *Deposition* in Santa Felicita in Florence. Pontormo was buried in Florence in 1557. He was one of the main protagonists of Florentine Mannerism, a movement that was soon forgotten after his death but became highly esteemed again in the early twentieth century.

24 MAY

Nobuyoshi Araki

Born 1940 | Photographer | Japan

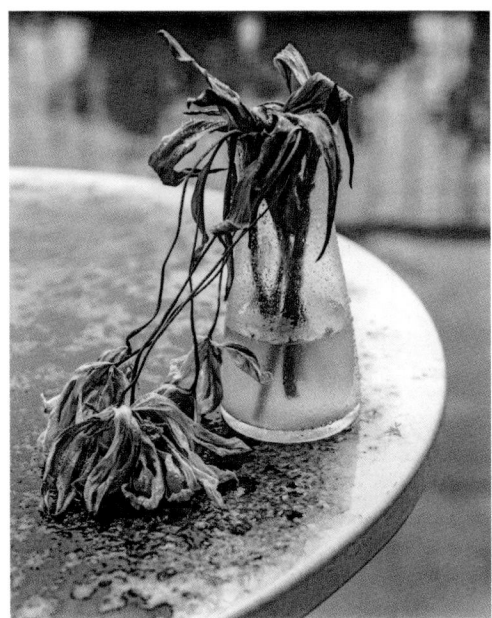

Laments: From Close-range, 1991

Based in Tokyo, Araki is one of Japan's foremost living photographers. He became widely known for his personal photography that documents the honeymoon trip with his wife. After working as a commercial photographer, he devoted himself to various subjects with eclectic style, depicting interpersonal themes and capturing the abysses of the human soul. One of his best-known models is the Icelandic singer Björk. Araki has published numerous photobooks, many of which are diaries that show his everyday life.

25 MAY

Dorothea Lange

1895–1965 | Photographer | United States

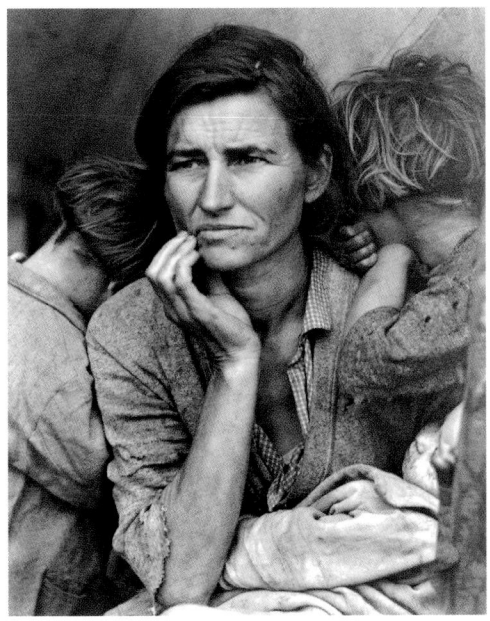

Migrant Mother, 1936

After studying photography in New York, Lange moved to San Francisco, where she opened her own, successful portrait studio in 1919. In 1929, during the Depression, she began photographing people that were unemployed, starving and striking on the streets. This documentation helped her initiate measures for humanitarian assistance. Her photographs of rural living conditions, such as *Migrant Mother*, taken in 1936, made her famous. A few weeks before her retrospective at the Museum of Modern Art in New York, she died of cancer. Lange was one of the foremost figures in documentary photography in the twentieth century.

26 MAY

Wols

1913–1951 | Photographer, painter and graphic artist | Germany, France

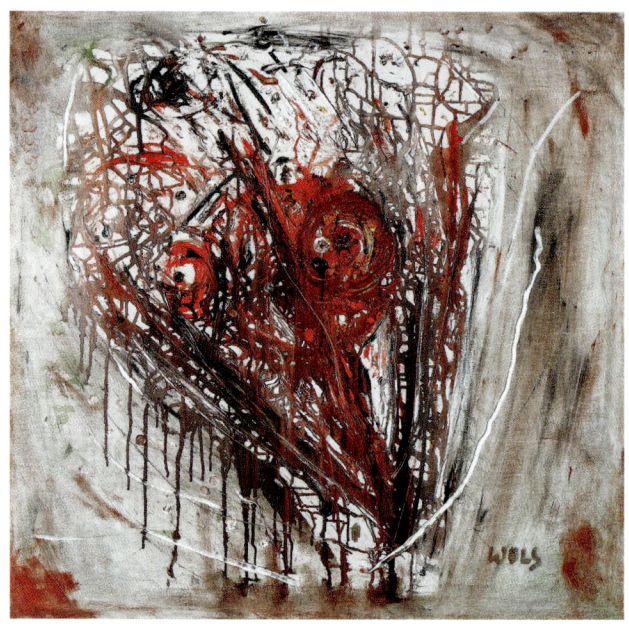

Hallucinogenic Gaze, 1946/1947

Coming from a family of art enthusiasts, Wols proved to be a good student pupil and excellent violinist. His father's early death was a cutting blow. In Paris in 1932, Wols met Grety, who later became his wife, a member of the Surrealist circle. After years in Spain, he worked until 1939 as a portrait photographer in Paris, where had to move frequently and eventually died. Living under permanent existential threat between internment camps, alcoholism and poverty, he created a significant oeuvre of photographs, paintings and works on paper, which later influenced many artists.

27 MAY

Hans Makart

1840–1884 | Painter and decorative artist | Austria

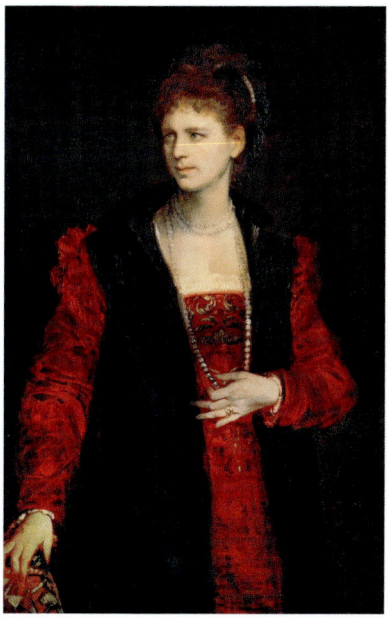

Portrait of the Actress Zerline Gabillon (1835–1892), 1873

After studying the Art Academy in Munich, Makart travelled to places including Rome. In 1869, Emperor Franz Joseph summoned him to Vienna, where he took his own studio and was celebrated as a princely painter. An in-demand society favourite of his day, his self-presentation made him legendary, for example, at roaring artist parties in his studio. He coined what is known as the Makart style, which with its pomp was particularly fashionable among Vienna's upper middle classes of the late nineteenth century.

28 MAY

Behjat Sadr

1924–2009 | Painter | Iran

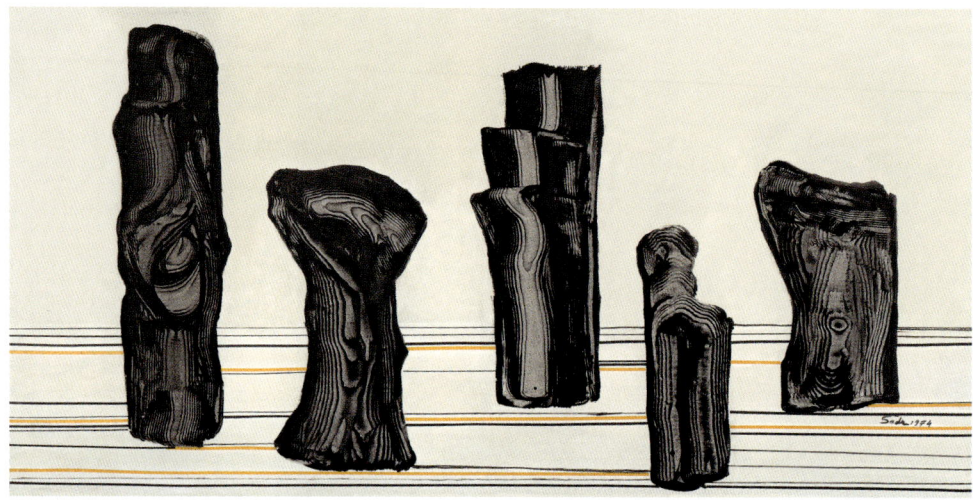

Untitled, 1974

After taking her first artistic steps in Teheran, Sadr studied at the academies in Rome and Naples with the aid of a fellowship. She began painting in an abstract style in Rome, where she had her first major exhibition in 1958; she also participated in the Venice Biennale several times. In 1957, she began teaching at Tehran University, where she remained for nearly twenty years. One year after the Islamic Revolution, she moved to Paris and subsequently had a series of exhibitions in France and Iran. In addition to collages and photographs, she made pictures using a technique in which she directly applied the paint and scraped it off many times, creating idiosyncratic structures.

29 MAY

Robert Ryman

1930–2019 | Painter | United States

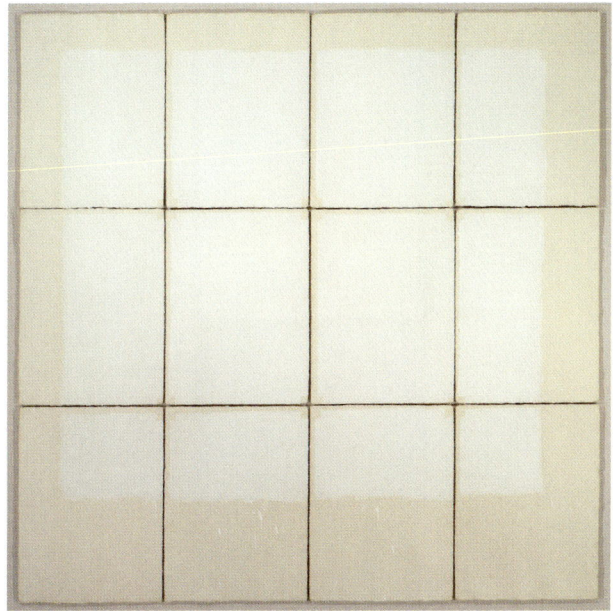

Classico IV, 1968

Initially trained as a jazz musician in New York, Ryman spent the 1950s working as a security guard at the Museum of Modern Art. The works of Paul Cézanne, Pablo Picasso and Henri Matisse impressed him to such a great extent that he began painting in 1954. From the 1960s on, he created an oeuvre in which he engaged in a unique exploration of the colour white and its subtle nuances on the picture surface. Ryman exhibited around the globe and received many awards.

30 MAY

Ellsworth Kelly

1923–2015 | Painter, sculptor and graphic artist | United States

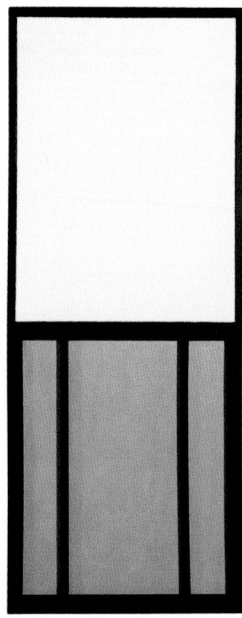

Window, Museum of Modern Art, Paris, 1949

Kelly was a pivotal figure in the development of post-war American abstraction. Following his service in Brittany during the Second World War, he lived in Paris until 1954, where he engaged deeply with his environment. During this period, Kelly produced paintings and sketches inspired by visual phenomena observed in his surroundings – such as architecture, shadows and natural patterns – which he abstracted into simplified forms. Upon his return to the United States, Kelly expanded his practice to include sculpture and printmaking. He developed a distinctive approach characterized by the use of bold, monochromatic colour fields and sharply defined forms.

31 MAY

Terry Winters

Born 1949 | Painter, draughtsman and graphic artist | United States

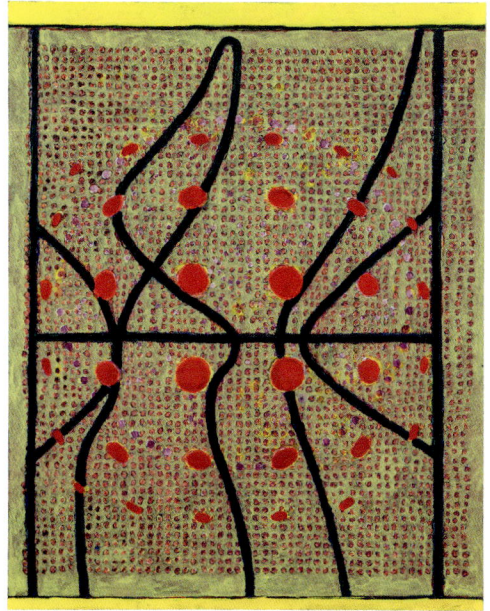

Index 5, 2021

Organic elements and biomorphic interdependence were formative in the work of Terry Winters, the major American painter, draughtsman and graphic artist; after all, nature's vital growth processes are reflected in the creative. Winters translates his speculative imagination into rigorously interconnected pictorial organisms with a specific sense of structure, pattern and system. He considers spatial imagination to be a primary source of energy. Winters's international standing is founded on numerous global exhibitions, projects and publications.

1 JUNE

Richard Long

Born 1945 | Land artist | Great Britain

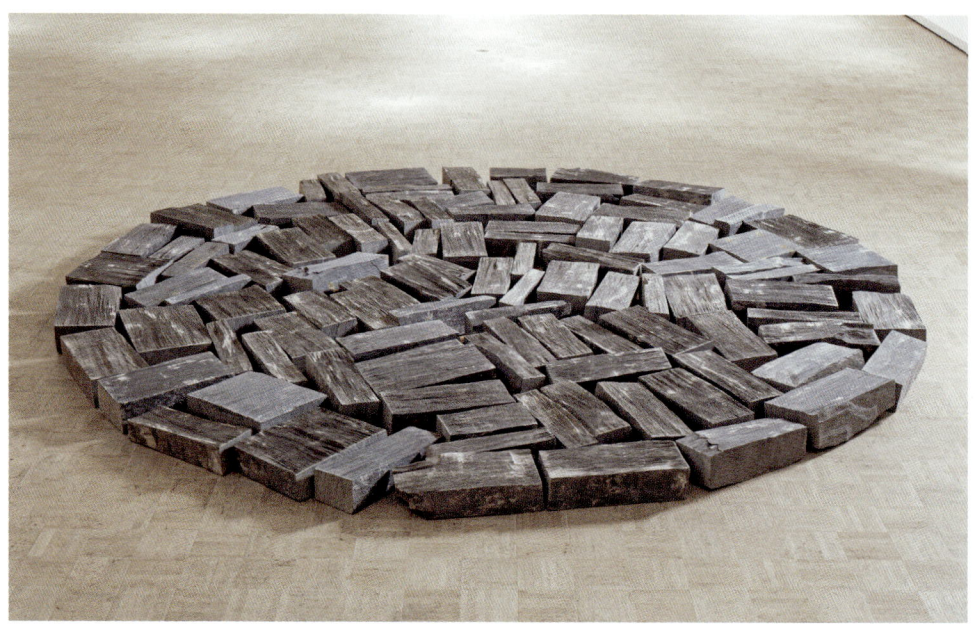

Santa Cruz Circle, 1997

After completing his studies in Bristol and London, Long was the recipient – at a relatively young age – of awards such as the Turner Prize, and in 1972, he participated in documenta in Kassel. His Conceptual oeuvre makes him an important representative of Land Art. He has documented his trips to many parts of the world with photographs and texts. He also makes floor sculptures using wood or stone for museum and outdoor spaces, some of which are only temporary. His documentation of his walks, including maps in which he has indicated his hiking routes, is often part of his exhibition presentation.

2 JUNE

Raoul Dufy

1877–1953 | Painter | France

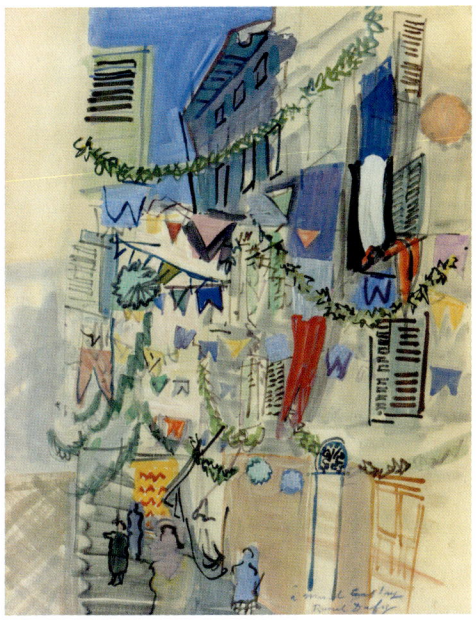

Nice, Festival of Lou Mai, 1947

Inspired by Henri Matisse, Dufy painted in a Fauvist manner but was also influenced by Paul Cézanne, with the result that he did not arrive at his exquisite, bright style of almost refined innocence until around 1918. His work in the field of fashion and interest in fabric painting certainly influenced his arabesque, mannered painting. He collaborated with the fashion designer Paul Poiret and also worked with his brother, Jean, at the Atelier Bianchini, on world-famous fabric designs for the silk mill Bianchini-Férier. In 1937, Dufy painted what was then the world's biggest picture for the Paris World's Fair.

3 JUNE

Robert Jacobsen

1912–1993 | Sculptor | Denmark

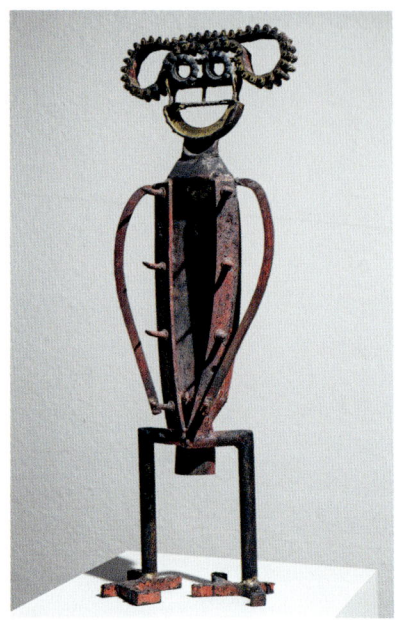

Earthly Nourishment, 1954

A self-taught artist, Jacobsen went to Paris in 1947 and lived there until 1969. In Paris he began making ice sculptures, which brought him international fame as one of the great ice sculptors of his time. His sculptures are structures in a changing dialectic between closeness and openness. In 1962, Jacobsen became a professor at the Art Academy in Munich, where he remained for nearly twenty years, and he was professor at the academy in Copenhagen until 1985. He also produced an extensive painted and graphic oeuvre. His rank is testified by important commissions and museum acquisitions around the world.

---

4 JUNE

Jesús Rafael Soto

1923–2005 | Painter and sculptor | Venezuela

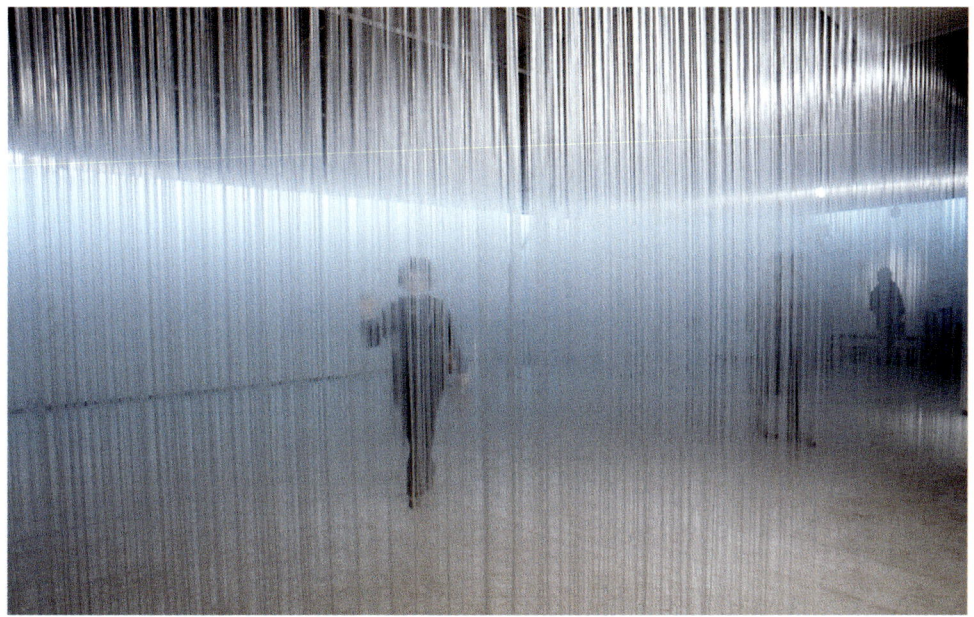

Pénétrable de Chicago, 1971

Since the 1960s, this Venezuelan painter and sculptor was one of the most renowned
protagonists of Op Art and Kinetic Art. Following initial studies in Caracas, he began
experimenting with optical illusions. In 1950, he moved to Paris, where he engaged in
serial art and, after 1960, created numerous kinetic objects and installations featuring
refined optical effects as well as murals. Soto's works were exhibited worldwide, and
his hometown, Ciudad Bolívar, dedicated a museum to him during his lifetime.

5 JUNE

Diego Velázquez

1599–1660 | Painter | Spain

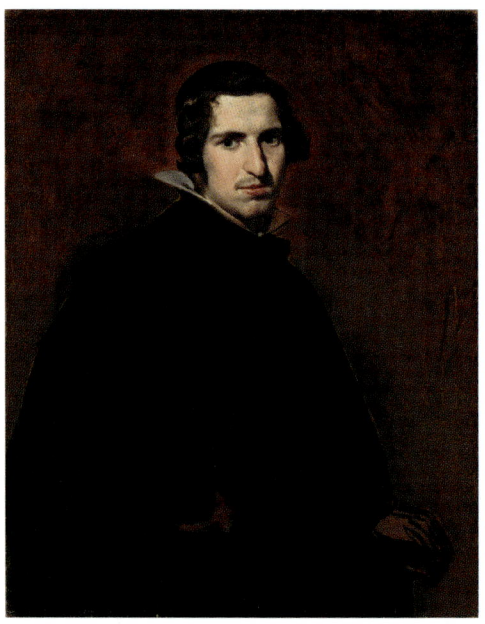

Young Spanish Nobleman, c. 1625–1627

Velázquez was one of the greats in the history of painting, who influenced numerous later artists, from Francisco de Goya through Manet into the twentieth century. As court painter to Philip IV, King of Spain, he created, starting in 1623, many notable portraits of figures in court society. In 1631, he spent time in Venice and. The portraits and equestrian portraits that he painted in the 1630s secured his reputation. On his return from an extensive tour through Italy in 1651, he painted, among other works, the world-famous masterpieces *Las Meninas* and *The Rokeby Venus*.

6 JUNE

Paul Gauguin

1848–1903 | Painter and graphic artist | France

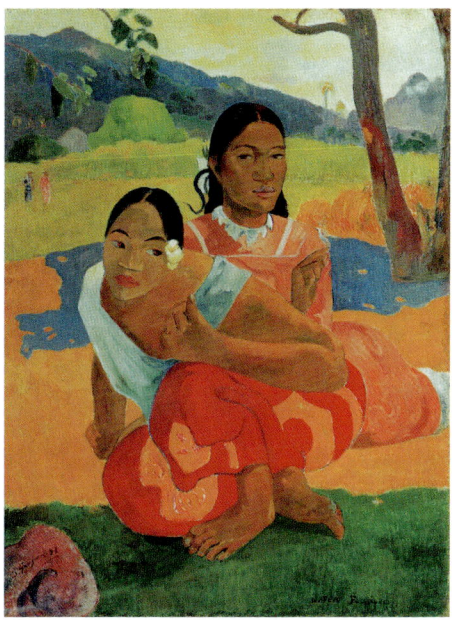

When Will You Marry?, 1892

As a painter and experimental graphic artist, Gauguin greatly influenced early twentieth-century European artists. Originally a bank employee by profession, he began painting in an Impressionist style. Constantly plagued by money worries, he lived in Normandy and Brittany, always in search of the simple life. This longing took him to Polynesia, where, living among the natives, his paradisical dreams of the primal found expression in pictures of colouristic and compositional brilliance. Before embarking on this journey, he spent two months with Van Gogh in Arles, in the South of France.

7 JUNE

John Everett Millais

1829–1896 | Painter | Great Britain

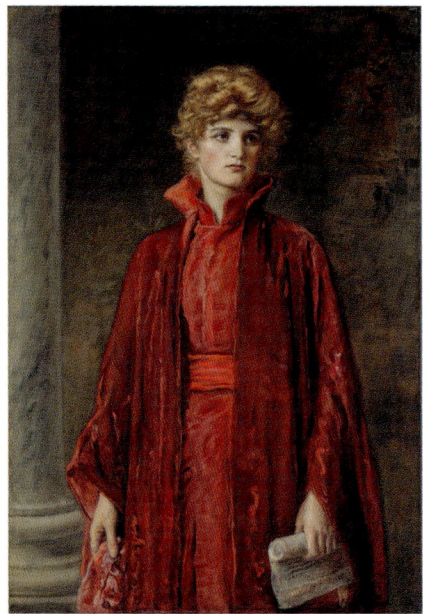

Portia, 1886

In 1840, eleven-year-old Millais became the youngest member of the Royal Academy of Arts in London, completing his training seven years later. He exhibited his first painting in the style of the Pre-Raphaelites in 1849. His became popular for his portraits, book illustrations, history and genre paintings, enjoying great success in the 1860s and 1870s. One of his best-known works, *Ophelia*, stands out for its faithfulness to detail and luminous colours. Knighted Ennobled by Queen Victoria, he was appointed president of the Royal Academy shortly before his death in 1896.

8 JUNE

Ethel Walker

1861–1951 | Painter | Great Britain

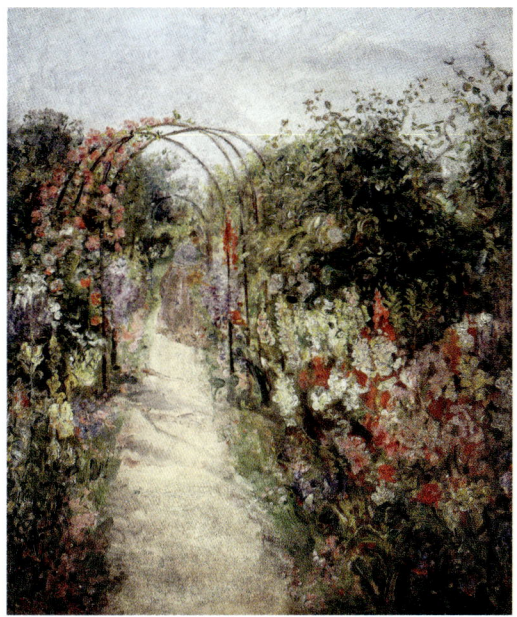

Watering the Garden, undated

This Scottish painter became known for her female nudes, portraits, floral paintings and seascapes in the style of Impressionism. She enjoyed considerable success with many exhibitions during her long career. She was represented at the Venice Biennale four times in the 1920s. A major retrospective was held at the Tate Gallery in London shortly after her death. As an openly lesbian artist who was highly regarded during her lifetime, she was presumably one of the first to explicitly portray the theme of female sexuality in her works.

9 JUNE

André Derain

1880–1954 | Painter, graphic artist and sculptor | France

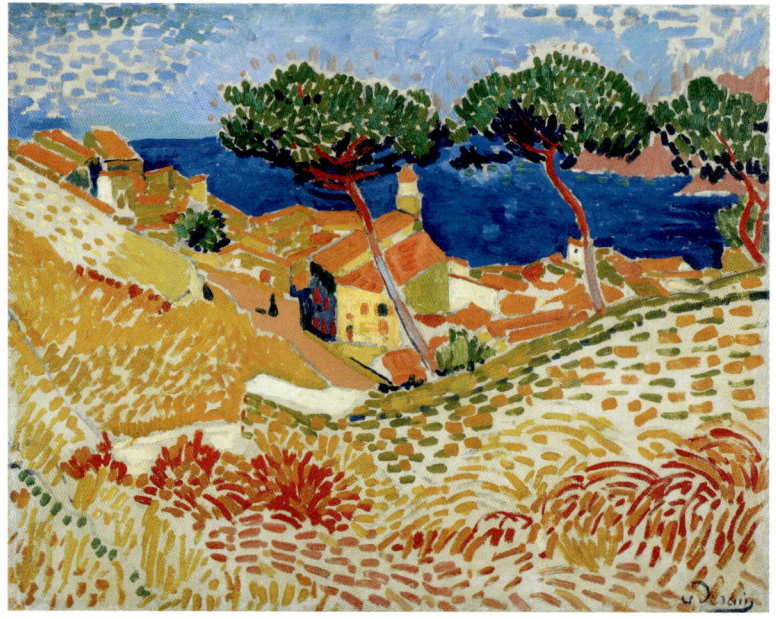

View of Collioure, 1905

With Henri Matisse, Derain was one of the leading painters of Fauvism by 1907, and he was in close contact with Pablo Picasso and Georges Braque. Even in his Cubist phase, he sought classical order and objective simplicity. Derain's style up until the First World War, in which he fought, was stringent and constructive. From the late 1920s, his works became more conventional and his stroke more elegant, bringing him success and criticism alike. He was held in contempt by many after his trip to Germany during the Nazi period. Of his friends, only Alberto Giacometti attended his funeral in 1954.

10 JUNE

Julia Margaret Cameron

1815–1879 | Photographer | Great Britain

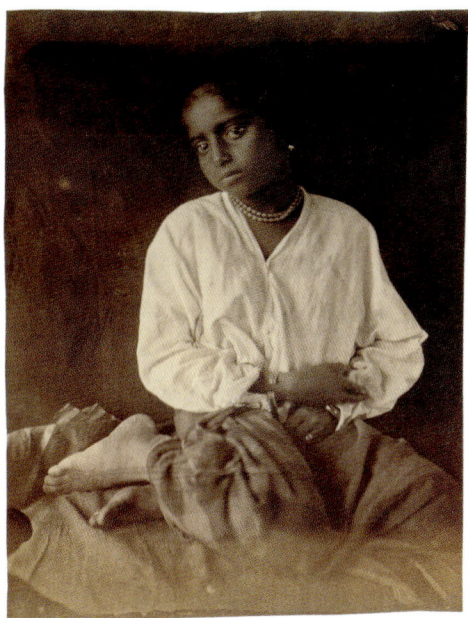

Girl, Ceylon, 1875–1879

After years of upper-middle-class life as a mother of six in India and England, Cameron only began taking photographs at the age of forty-eight. The family had relocated to Great Britain in 1848. Her estate on the Isle of Wight became the focus of her life as a photographer. She made portraits of celebrities and a range of religious tableaux. She moved to Ceylon in 1875, where she died, aged sixty-three, as one of the most important British photographers of the Victorian period.

11 JUNE

Anni Albers

1899–1994 | Textile artist and graphic artist | Germany, United States

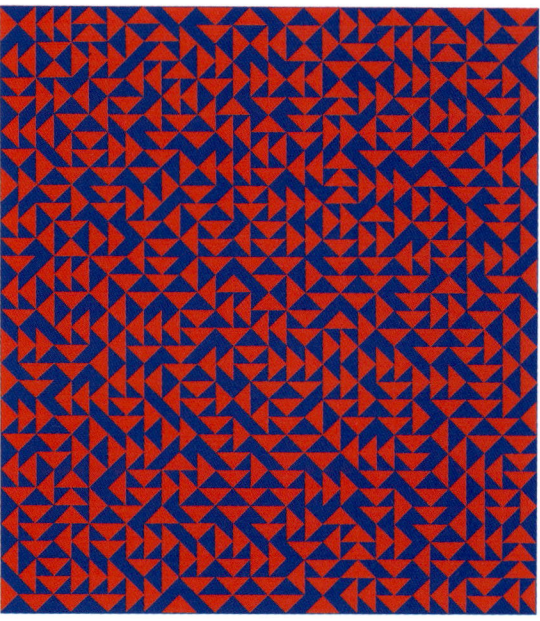

D (Blue-Red), 1969

In 1922, Anneliese Fleischmann began studying at the Bauhaus in Weimar, where she worked in the weaving workshop. In 1925, she married her fellow student Josef Albers and emigrated with him to the United States in 1933. She taught weaving at Black Mountain College in North Carolina. Albers was greatly influenced by joint trips in the 1930s to Mexico, with its ancient weaving traditions. She later worked as an independent artist, also making abstract prints. Although already honoured with an exhibition at the Museum of Modern Art in New York in 1949, she was not celebrated as a great artist in Europe until only recently.

12 JUNE

Christo and Jeanne-Claude

1935–2020/2009 | Artists | United States

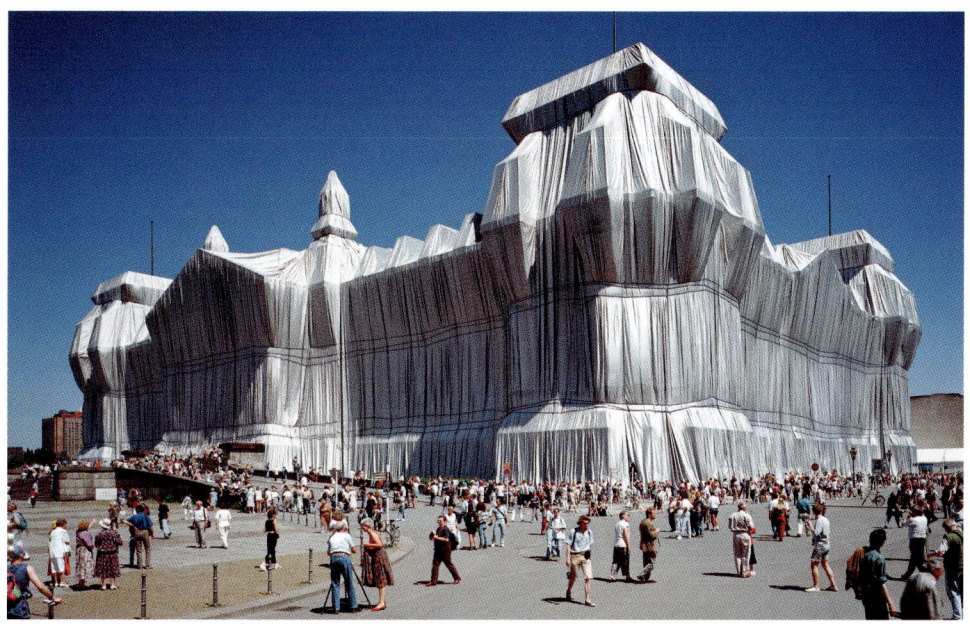

Wrapped Reichstag, Berlin, 1971–1995

These two artists, who shared a birthday, met in Paris and later married. They began their first joint piece in 1961. After moving to New York in 1964, they created nearly thirty large-scale projects over the decades, which they self-financed through sales of drawings and image rights. In their wrapped projects, they transformed landscapes and buildings into spectacular objects that were crowd-pleasing mega events. All projects were planned to be temporary, enduring only in documents and memories.

13 JUNE

Pan Yuliang

1895–1977 | Painter, graphic artist and sculptor | China

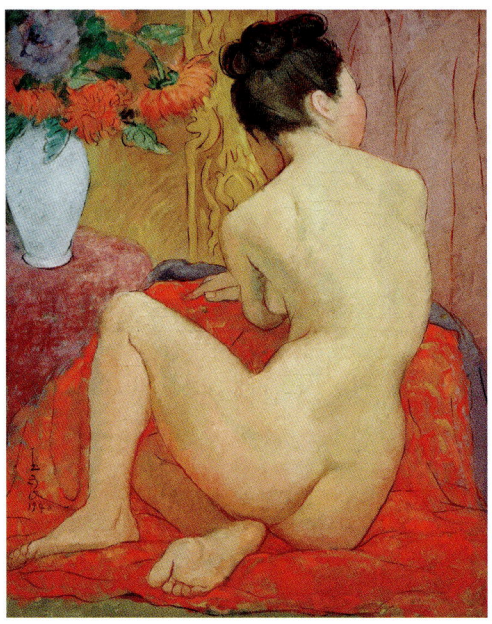

Chrysanthemum and Female Nude, 1948

At the age of fourteen, Pan, an orphan, was sold to a brothel by her uncle. A tax collector who was a customer there bought her freedom and married her. Pan began an apprenticeship in painting and, awarded a scholarship, went to Paris to continue her studies; after that, she lived in Rome, before returning to Shanghai. Owing to her past, her nude paintings caused an uproar in her homeland, and some of them were destroyed. That occasioned Pan to return to Paris, and political circumstances prevented her from ever travelling back to her home country.

14 JUNE

Nicolas Poussin

1594–1665 | Painter | France

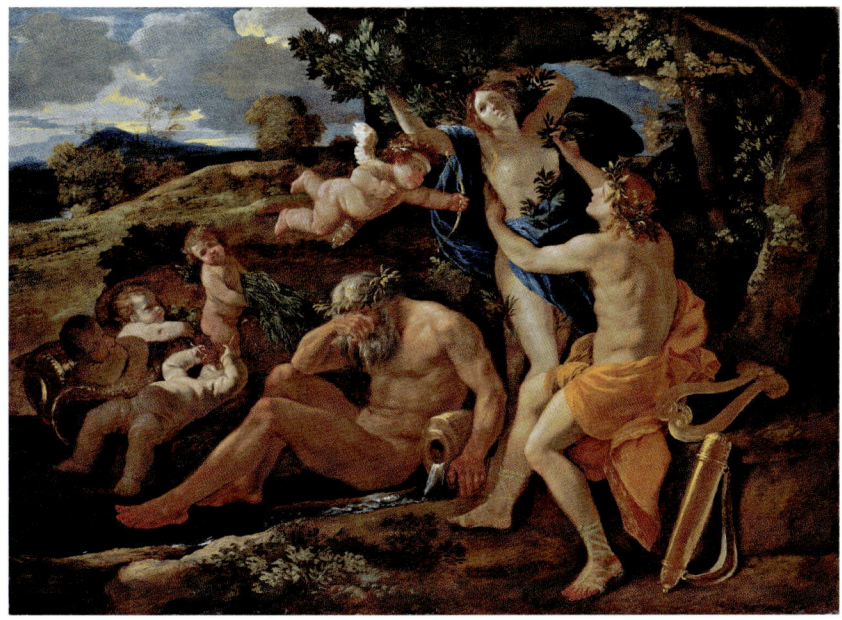

Apollo and Daphne, c. 1627

Poussin was the greatest French painter of the seventeenth century. From 1624,
he lived almost continuously in Rome until the end of his life. Raphael and antiquity
shaped his painting decisively. His depictions of events from history and mythology,
as well as landscapes, were in demand by erudite collectors and patrons in Rome
and Paris. Poussin's compositions are structured yet full of poetry and employ a very
specific colour palette of luminous golden tones. In the year of his death, he was
appointed First Painter to the King by Louis XIV.

15 JUNE

Henriette Browne

1829–1901 | Painter | France

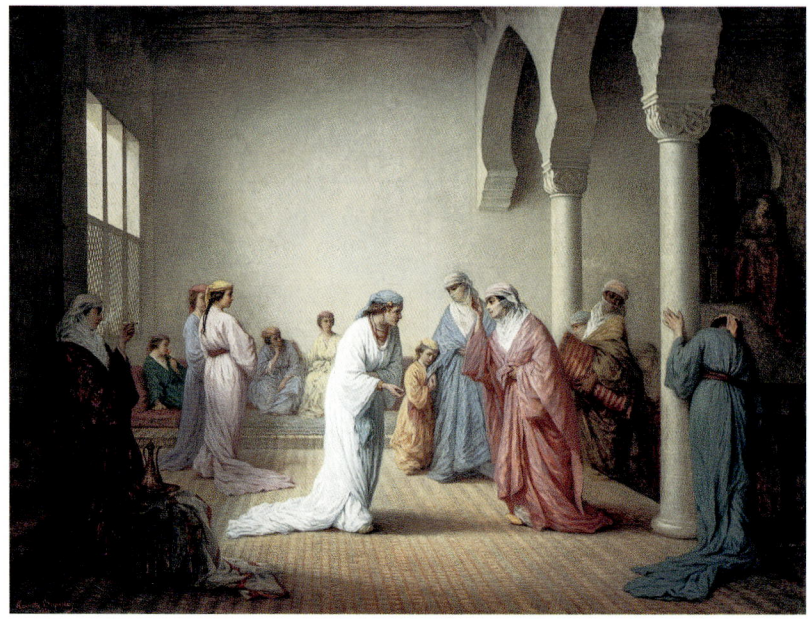

A Visit: A Harem Interior, 1861

As the privileged daughter of musical parents, Sophie de Bouteiller first studied under private tutors. In 1853, using her pseudonym Henriette Browne, she first participated in the Paris Salon, which she continued for more than twenty years. Following her marriage, she and her husband travelled to Holland, Italy and Constantinople. There, a visit to a harem proved influential for her later Orientalist pictures, created alongside genre and religious paintings. From the 1860s, her fame grew primarily through depictions of the Middle East that cast an explicitly female gaze onto the harem, ignoring male sexual fantasies.

16 JUNE

Charles Eames

1907–1978 | Designer and architect | United States

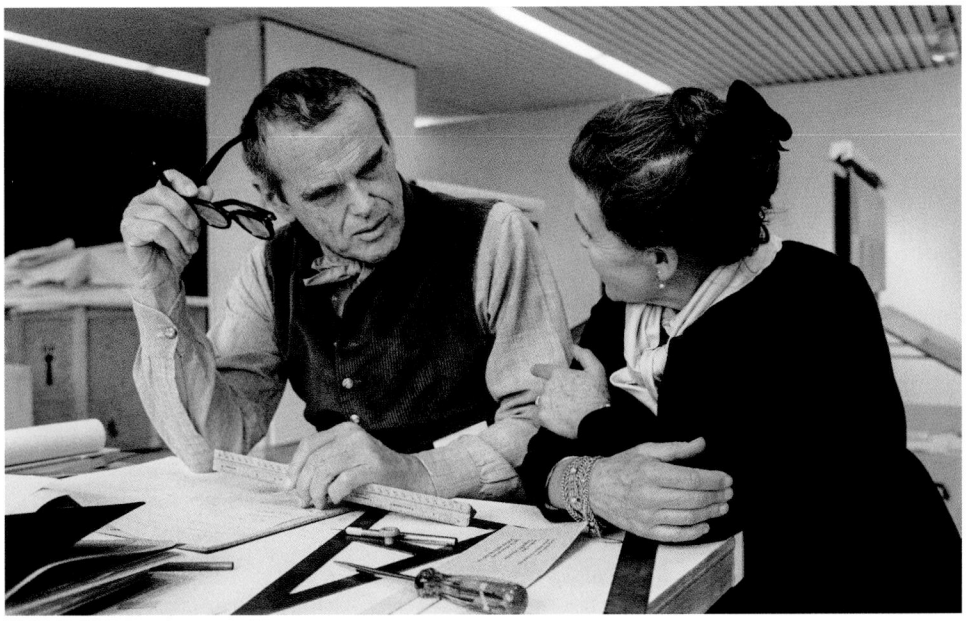

Charles Eames and his wife, Ray, working together, 1975

Together with his second wife, Ray, Eames is a legendary figure of twentieth-century design. The couple became world famous for their innovative chair designs. After studying architecture in St Louis, Eames set up his own studio in 1930. He worked with moulded plywood, fibreglass, plastic and aluminium to find the most effective three-dimensional form for the seat shell. One of their most famous creations is the *Lounge Chair and Ottoman* from 1956. Their furniture has never gone out of production and continues to be distributed in the United States and by Vitra in Germany.

17 JUNE

Bartolomeo Ammanati

1511–1592 | Architect and sculptor | Italy

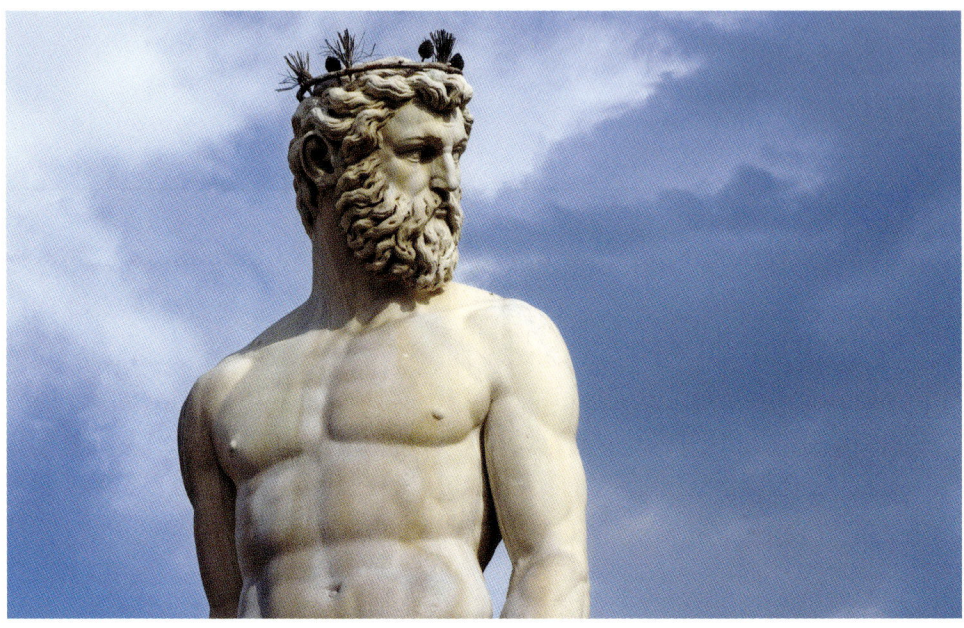

Neptune Fountain, 1563–1575

Under Michelangelo's influence, this sculptor and architect become one of the foremost representatives of Florentine Mannerism. He was the creator of a series of palaces in Florence and Rome as well as of statues and fountains. His most famous commission from the Medici was the fountain of Neptune on the Piazza della Signoria in Florence, with the giant figure of Neptune executed in white marble. Ammanati worked for twelve years on this project, begun in 1563. He and his wife, the poet Laura Battiferri, are buried together in a Florentine church that he designed.

18 JUNE

Cornelius Krieghoff

1815–1872 | Painter | The Netherlands, Canada

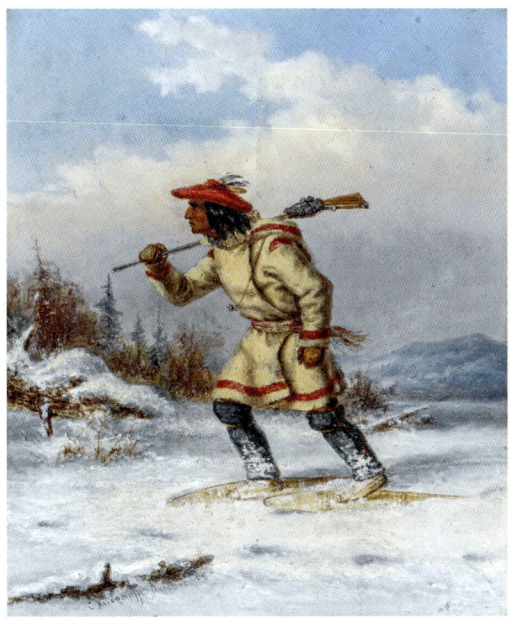

Following the Moose, c. 1860

Born in Amsterdam and trained in Düsseldorf, this Canadian artist was considered one of the leading Canadian painters of the nineteenth century for his pictures of French settlers and First Nations communities. In 1836, he moved to New York, and following his marriage in 1840, he moved to Montreal. He became known for his paintings of the Mohawks living on the Kahnawake reservation near Montreal. Following extensive travels in Europe, he moved back to the United States, where he died in Chicago.

19 JUNE

Magdalena Abakanowicz

1930–2017 | Textile artist and sculptor | Poland

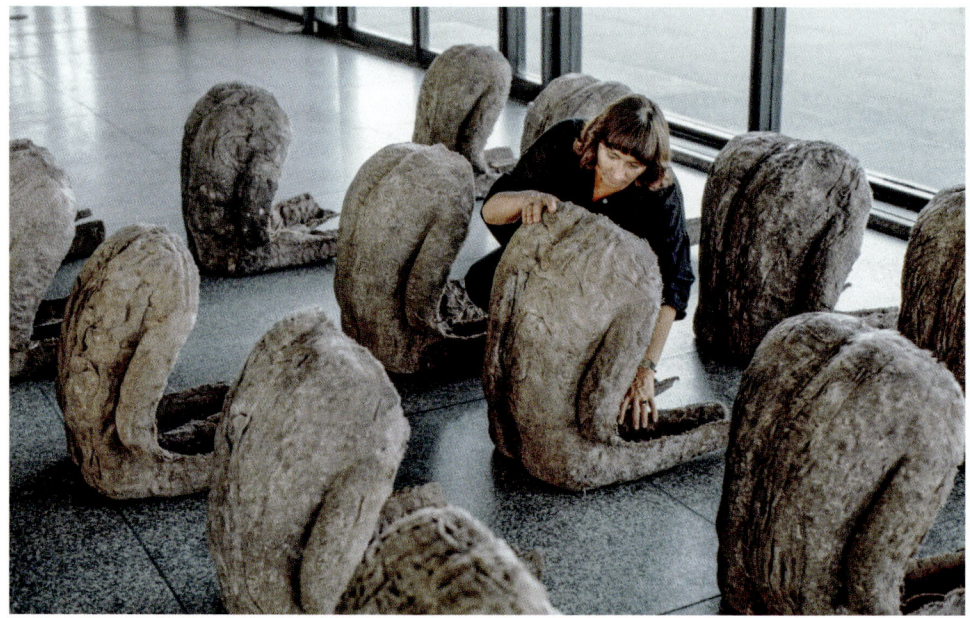

Magdalena Abakanowicz in the exhibition "Kunst wird Material", Berlin, 1982

This Polish artist became internationally famous in the 1960s with her large textile pieces, the *Abakans*. Later she created sculptural works such as heads, figures and animals – some using textiles that were moulded by means of dies – as well as environments in bronze, iron and stone. Her permanent outdoor installations are to be found on city squares around the globe. Many awards, honours and exhibitions have paid tribute to Abakanowicz's profound oeuvre, in which humanity's existential jeopardy dominates.

20 JUNE

Olga Rozanova

1886–1918 | Painter and book illustrator | Russia

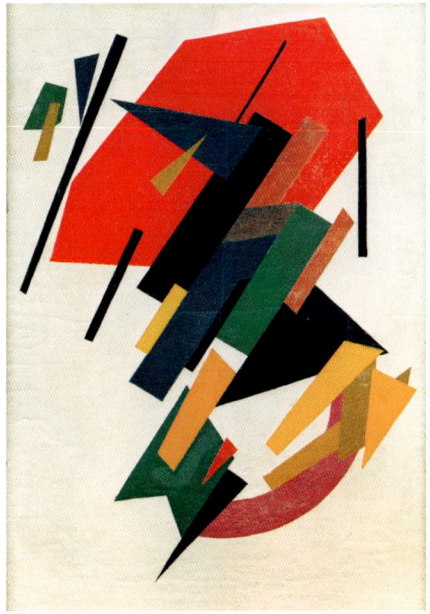

Suprematism, undated

After studying applied art in Moscow, Rozanova moved to St Petersburg, where she studied until 1913 and formed a friendship with artists including Kasimir Malevich. She took part in several avant-garde exhibitions up to 1917. A book project including her drawings for Filippo Tommaso Marinetti, the founder of Futurism, marked a renaissance of typography and book art along the lines of the avant-garde painting of those years. In 1914, she participated in the First Free Futurist Exhibition in Rome. Later, she created textile patterns and worked in design, fashion and book illustration.

21 JUNE

Gwen John

1876–1939 | Painter | Great Britain

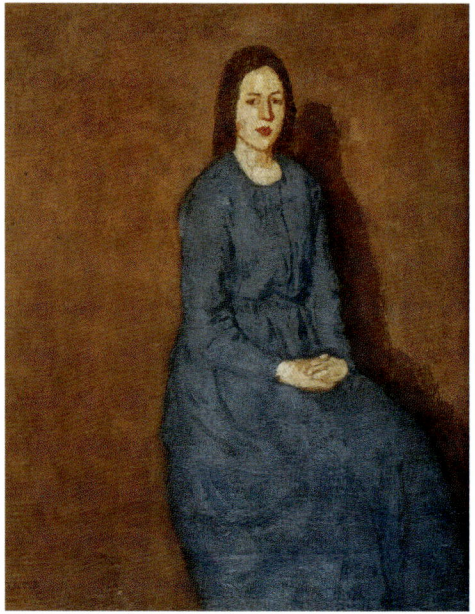

A Young Woman in Blue, c. 1914/1915

This Welsch artist studied painting in London and Paris. She modelled for Auguste Rodin; out of that grew an affair. In 1913, she converted to Catholicism, an experience which she declared inspiring. Her oeuvre consists predominantly of astutely drawn female portraits, which did not make her particularly famous. It was not until over twenty years after her death that her work became the subject of exhibitions and publications. Paintings by John can be found in major museums such as the Tate Gallery in London and the Metropolitan Museum of Art in New York.

22 JUNE

Louis de Silvestre

1675–1760 | Painter | France

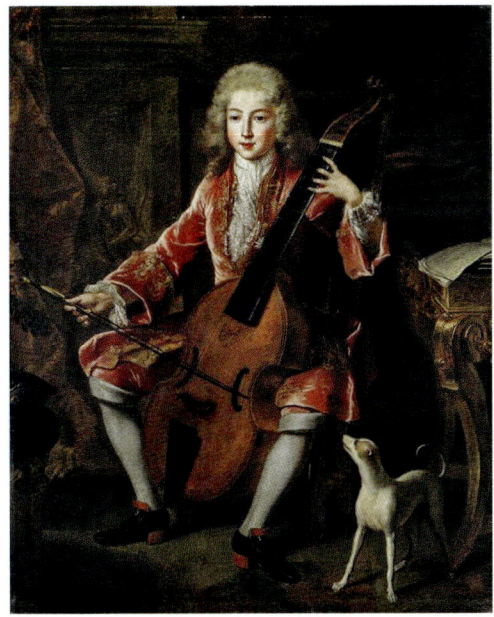

Chevalier de Bavière, 1707

Following studies at the Académie Royale in Paris under masters such as Charles Lebrun, Silvestre became its deputy director in 1712. At the invitation of Augustus II the Strong, in 1716, he went to Dresden, where he was active as court painter for more than thirty years. In addition to portraits, he made ceiling paintings in the Royal Palace, the ceremonial hall of Brühl Palace, the Japanese Palace and the Royal Cabinet of Mathematical and Physical Instruments at the Zwinger in Dresden. Upon his return to Paris, Silvestre became director of the Académie Royale in 1752.

23 JUNE

Lee Ufan

Born 1936 | Painter and sculptor | Korea

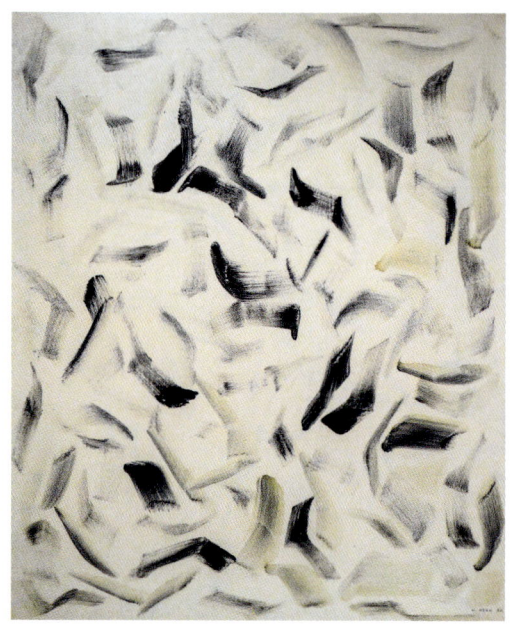

With Winds, 1982

After studying art in Seoul, Lee went to Japan in 1956 to explore East Asian and European philosophy. This is the foundation of his oeuvre. He has lived between Paris and Tokyo since the 1970s. Initially a member of an artists' collective that was opposed to Western modernism, Lee attempted to link elements of Minimalism and Land Art with traditional Asian concepts of space. He achieved international fame through numerous exhibitions, and a museum was dedicated to him in Japan in 2010.

24 JUNE

Antoni Gaudí

1852–1926 | Architect | Spain

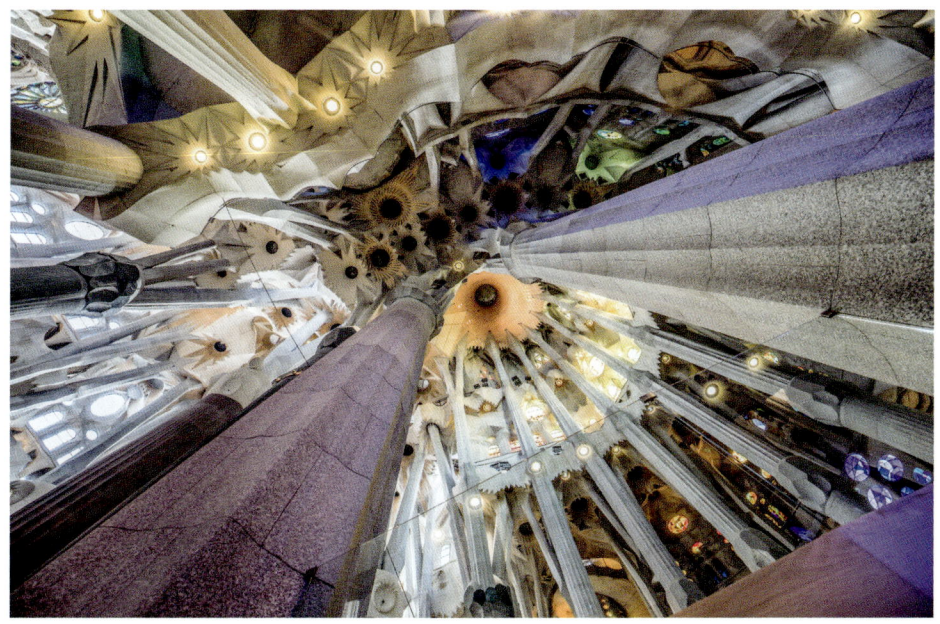

Sagrada Familia, Barcelona, from 1882

After breaking off his engagement, Gaudí led an ascetic life as a celibate layman, living from 1906 on in a house that is now a museum. He designed a number of buildings and pavilions in and around Barcelona. Gaudí's life's work was the now-famous church *Sagrada Familia*, a true *Gesamtkunstwerk*, or total work of art, and Barcelona's best-known landmark. His architectural style was *modernisme*, the Catalan interpretation of Art Nouveau. His idiosyncratic style is characterized by undulating, organic shapes with typical features such as curved lines, irregular floor plans, diagonal columns and floral motifs.

25 JUNE

Afi Ekong

1930–2009 | Painter | Nigeria

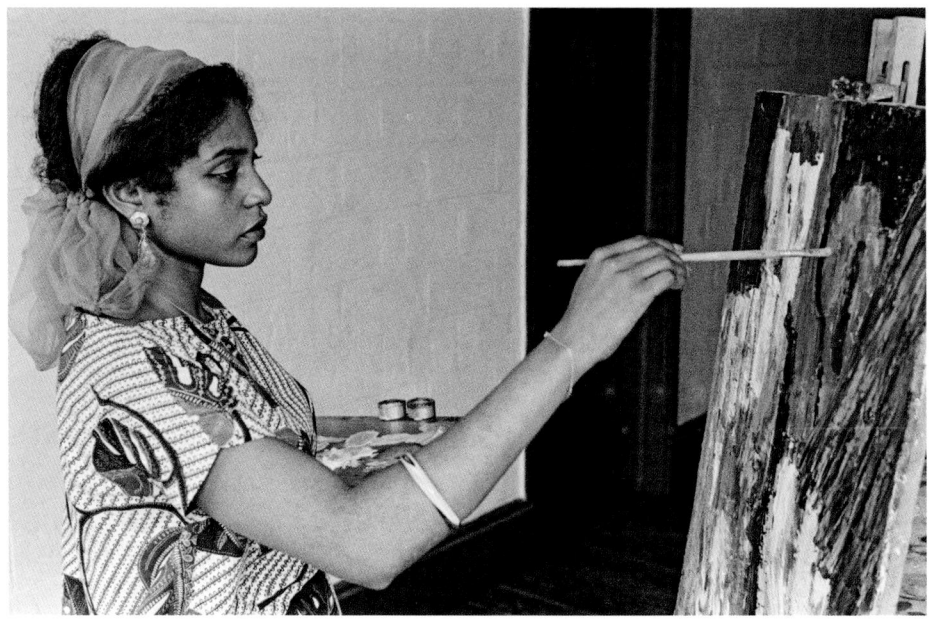

Afi Ekong al work, 1962

Ekong studied painting and fashion design in London in the 1950s, before returning to Lagos in 1957. She was the first woman to have a solo exhibition in Nigeria, and she subsequently had a gallery show in Buenos Aires. Besides being a painter, Ekong was a gallery owner as well as member, manager and chairwoman of various important institutions. In 1962, she was distinguished for her services to the arts and women's education in Western Africa. Her paintings can be found in the library of Lagos University, among other locations.

26 JUNE

Philip Guston

1913–1980 | Painter | United States

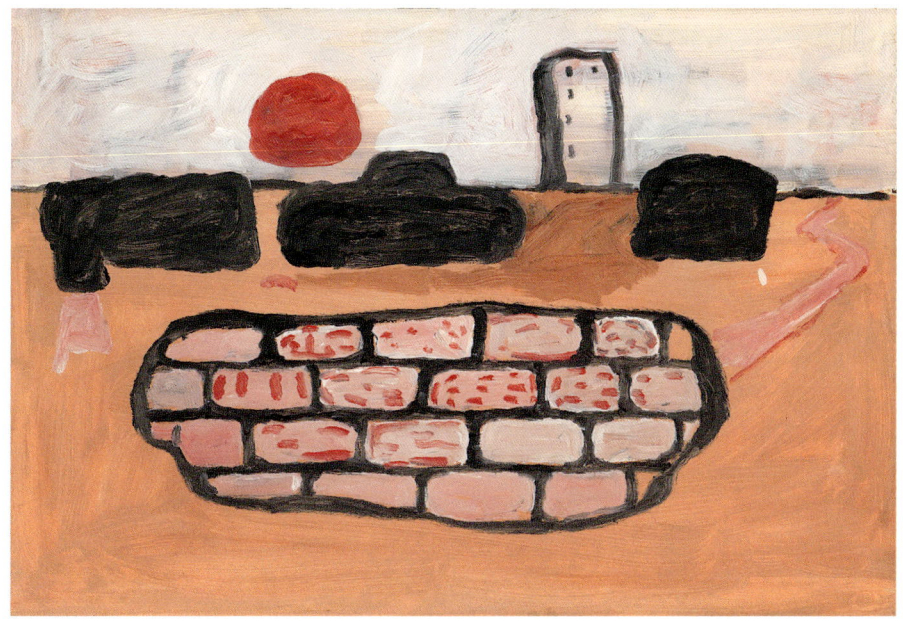

Untitled, 1971

The son of Jewish immigrants from Russia who settled in Los Angeles by way of Montreal, Guston was inspired by Mexican muralists. In 1940, he painted in a figurative style in Woodstock and discovered Italian Renaissance painting. After a sojourn in Rome, Guston developed a lyrically abstract style from 1950 but, in the mid-1960s, made a radical departure from abstraction and created works with symbol-laden realism. His global fame as one of the great American artists of the modern age grew after his death.

Peter Paul Rubens

1577–1640 | Painter | Flanders

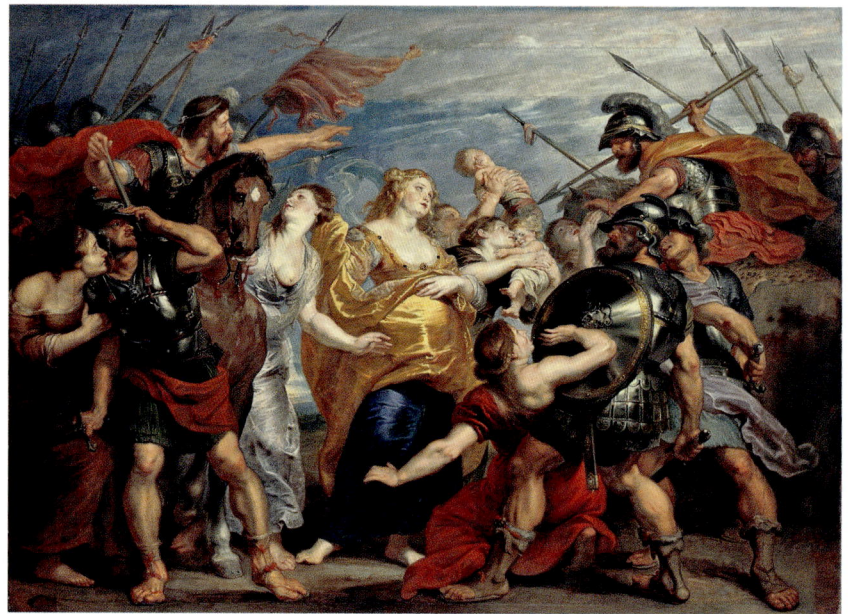

The Reconciliation of the Romans and Sabines, c. 1625

Rubens was one of Europe's greatest and most influential painters of the seventeenth century. In 1600, he went to Italy and became court painter in Mantua. When he returned to Antwerp, he married, enjoyed lucrative commissions and became the archdukes' court painter in 1610. Called to Paris by Marie de' Medici, he made a famous cycle of paintings. After that, Ruben took on diplomatic tasks in Madrid and London. His legacy, in his characteristic luminous, lush colours, is many hundreds of pictures of religious and mythological content, nudes, portraits and landscapes.

28 JUNE

Marie Eléonore Godefroid

1778–1849 | Painter | France

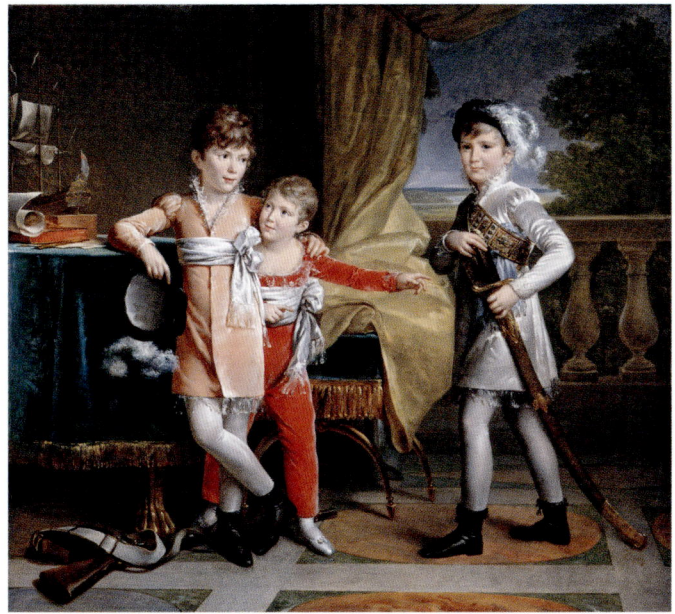

The Sons of Marshal Ney, 1810

Godefroid was taught by her father, who owned a studio in the Louvre, and by François Gérard. She took on portrait commissions in the style of Neoclassicism well into old age; her likenesses of children of the aristocracy, such as of the Duke of Orleans, were particularly highly esteemed. Her talent lay in empathically portraying the children's immediate charm as well as their social standing. Godefroid's works were exhibited in the Louvre many times, and the painter was honoured with medals.

_____

_____

_____

_____

29 JUNE

Sean Scully

Born 1945 | Painter | Ireland, United States

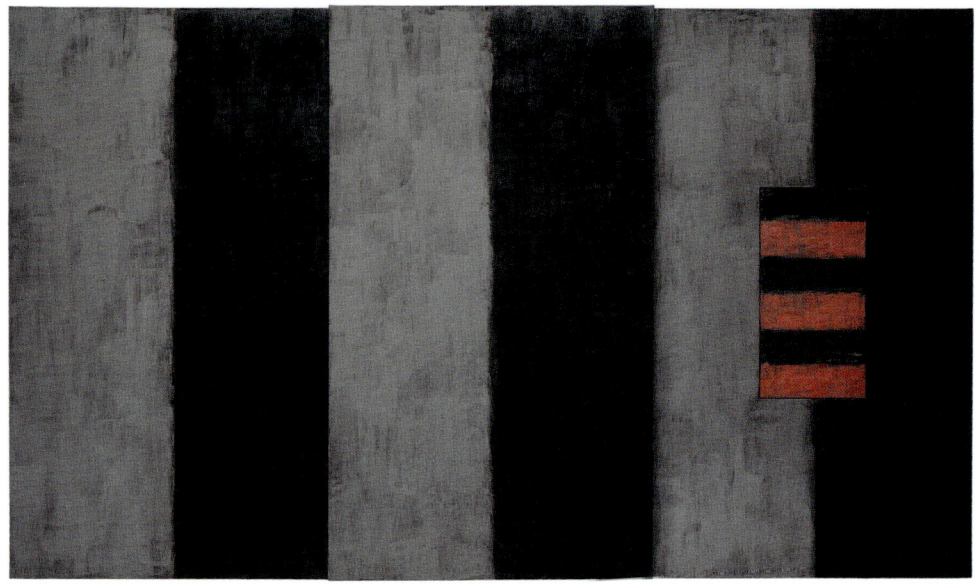

Red Star, 1990

Irish by birth, Scully is of the world's most successful abstract painters today. After figurative beginnings in London, he lived in New York from the mid-1970s, painting monochrome pictures until he found his own style. By juxtaposing colour planes, the painter transforms a stringent pictorial structure into a living, breathing whole. In this way, Scully creates countless variations on a never-changing formula using unique colour strategies. Scully has had many international exhibitions and teaching assignments.

30 JUNE

Anton Kolig

1886–1950 | Painter and draughtsman | Austria

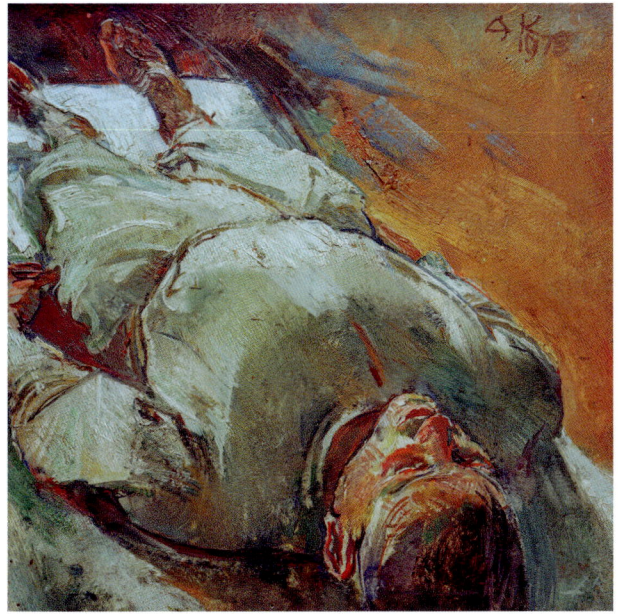

Recumbent Man, 1918

Kolig began his studies in Vienna in 1904 and spent the years after 1912 living in Paris on a fellowship. He was forced to flee France in 1914 on account of the war and arrived in a village in Carinthia. After various war deployments, he became a war painter. His murals in Salzburg and Klagenfurt were later destroyed by the Nazis. He became a professor in Stuttgart in 1928. Severely injured himself, he lost many of his works due to bombing. Kolig was a major late Expressionist painter and draughtsman who, on account of his homoerotic inclination, is particularly known for his male nudes.

1 JULY

Jacopo Sansovino

1486–1570 | Sculptor and architect | Italy

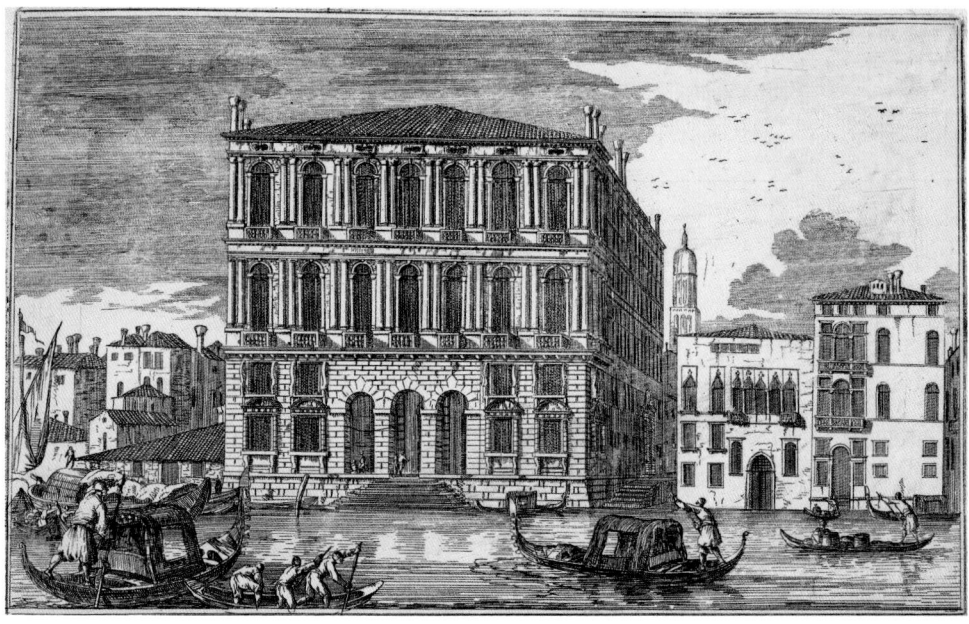

Palazzo Corner della Ca' Granda, Venice, engraving by Luca Carlevarijs, 1703

Starting in 1506, Sansovino spent twenty years working as a sculptor and architect in Florence and Rome, often in competition with Michelangelo. In 1527, he was commissioned by the doge of Venice to restore the dome of San Marco, an order that led to his appointment as chief architect. A succession of orders for important sculptures and construction projects in Venice followed, including the Palazzo Corner della Ca' Granda. Sansovino was friends with Titian, highly regarded in the Venetian patriciate and one of La Serenissima's most influential artists right up until his death.

2 JULY

Tracey Emin

Born 1963 | Artist | Great Britain

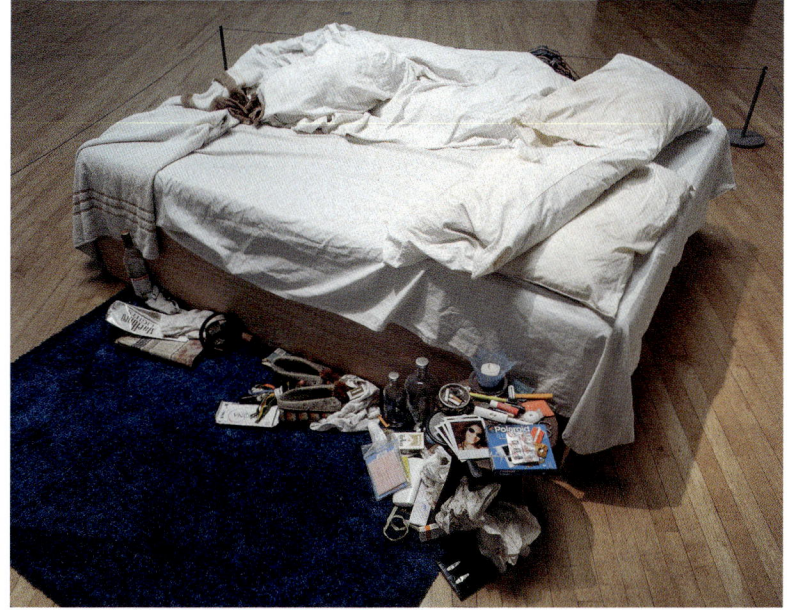

My Bed, 1998

Emin's unapologetic, autobiographically compromising art made her notorious within the circle of the Young British Artists. She caused an uproar in London and Berlin with the exhibition *Sensation* in 1997. One of her most popular works, *My Bed*, showing traces of a night of passion, was shown in the 1999 Turner Prize exhibition at the Tate Gallery in London. It was auctioned for 2.2 million pounds in 2014. Emin herself describes her work as "living autobiography" in which sexuality, abuse and the search for female identity are dominant themes. International exhibitions secured her fame.

3 JULY

Edmonia Lewis

1844–1907 | Sculptor | United States

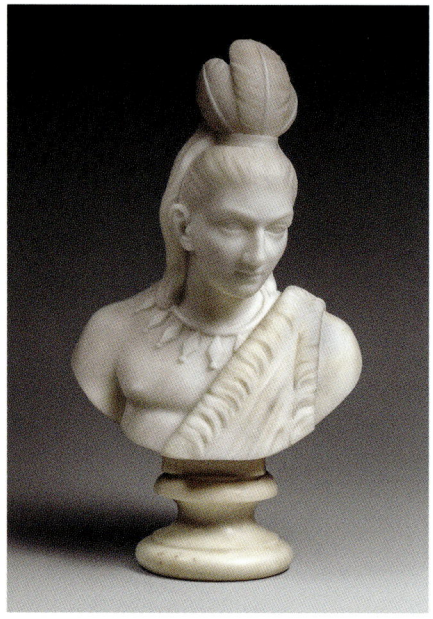

Hiawatha, 1868

The daughter of African American and Native American parents who died prematurely, Lewis studied at Oberlin College near Cleveland, Ohio, with her brother's assistance. In 1865, after making several sculptures in Boston, she moved to Rome, where she spent most of her active years. She secured high prices for her conservative, Neoclassicist sculptures. Numerous exhibitions in the 1870s in places such as Chicago, Rome and Philadelphia made her famous. Interest in her academic sculpture subsequently waned.

4 JULY

Jean Cocteau

1889–1963 | Writer, film director and painter | France

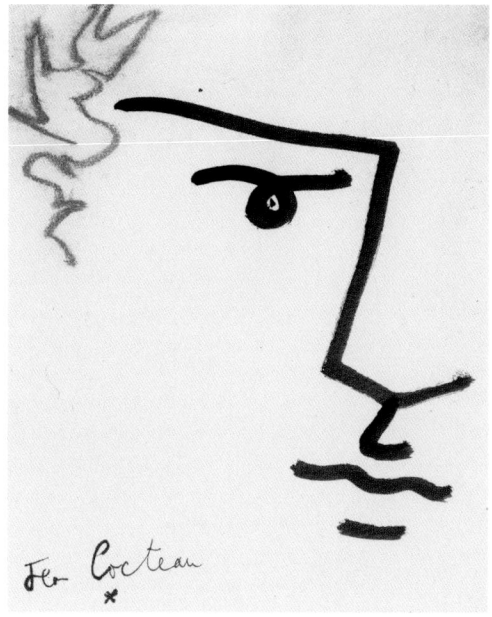

Self-Portrait, c. 1954/1955

Cocteau was a kind of universal artist and one of the most flamboyant figures on the French art scene in the first half of the twentieth century. He published his first poems at the age of seventeen and went on to write novels, plays and dramas. He directed more than a dozen films. He was in constant contact with prominent artists such as Pablo Picasso and Charlie Chaplin. A museum dedicated to him is located in Menton, and his tomb in the Chapelle Saint-Blaise-et-des-Simples is in Milly-la-Forêt.

5 JULY

Frida Kahlo

1907–1954 | Painter | Mexico

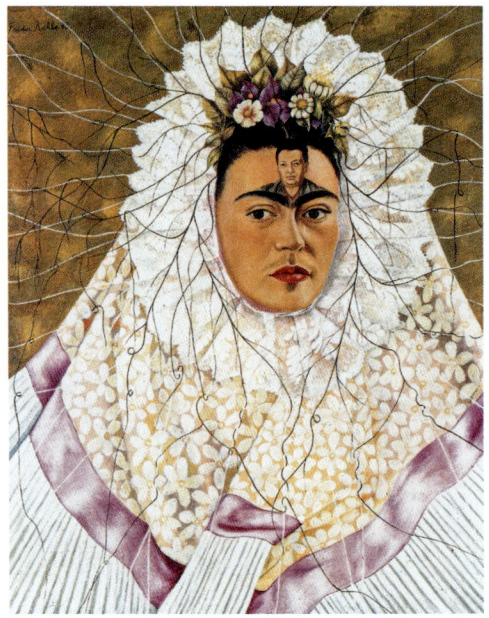

Diego on My Mind (Self-Portrait as Tehuana), 1943

Besides the magic of her paintings, Kahlo – one of the world's best-known and most highly priced painters today – owes her almost legendary fame primarily to her life story, which is dominated by illness, suffering, her marriage to the painter Diego Rivera, his unfaithfulness and her own affairs. She was a passionate Marxist and a close friend of Leo Trotsky. She was severely physically impaired throughout her life due to the consequences of polio and a serious bus crash. Long after her death, her popularity rose enormously amid the women's movement of the 1970s.

6 JULY

Hélène Sardeau

1899–1969 | Sculptor | United States

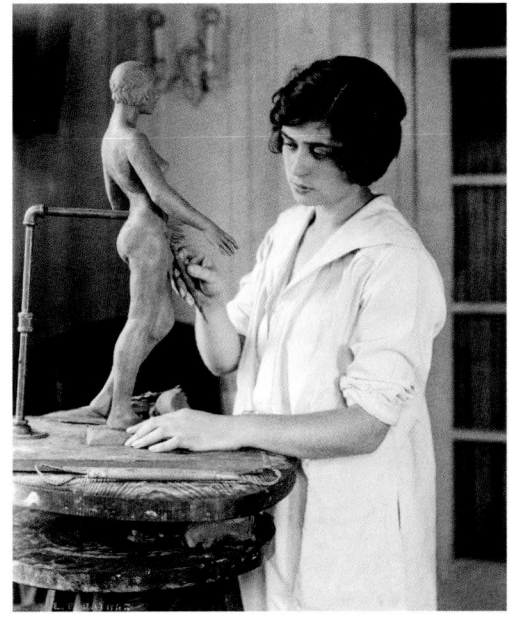

Hélène Sardeau models an American Venus, undated

Sardeau, who was born in Antwerp, arrived in New York with her family at the age of fourteen. She studied there at the School of American Sculpture, among other places. Her first major commission was the massive stone sculpture *The Slave*, created in 1940 for a memorial in Philadelphia. Sardeau's sculptures were exhibited many times at the Museum of Modern Art in New York, as well as at the Musée du Jeu de Paume in Paris and the Philadelphia Museum of Art. She made large reliefs for the National Library in Rio de Janeiro in 1942.

7 JULY

Käthe Kollwitz

1867–1945 | Graphic artist, painter and sculptor | Germany

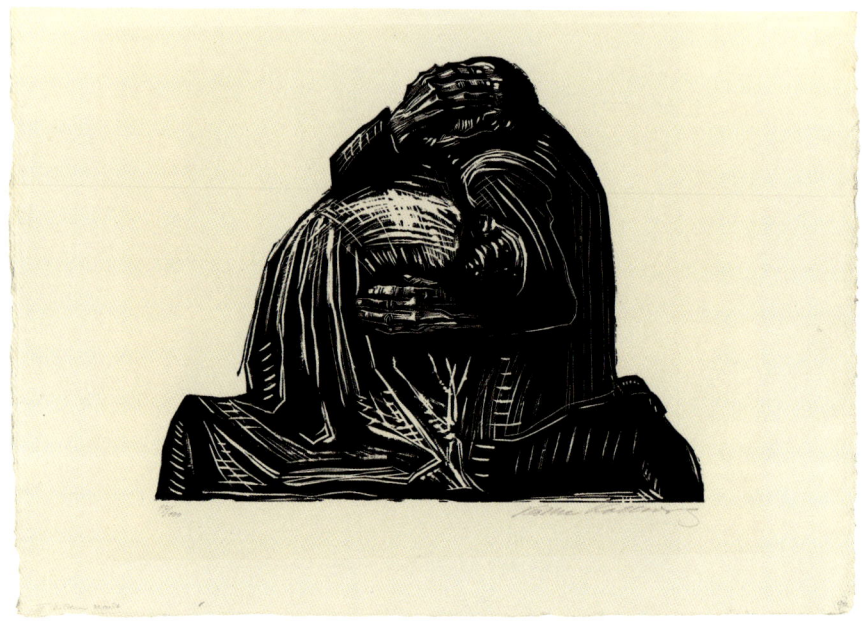

The Parents, sheet 3 from the series "War", 1921/1922

Following her studies and her marriage, Kollwitz moved to Berlin in 1891. She achieved her breakthrough as an artist there with her series of etchings titled *A Weavers' Revolt* in 1898. Kollwitz began sculpting in 1910. Her sons' deaths in the First World War lent strength to her pacifist conviction and her campaigning as a socialist, which occasioned the Nazis to confiscate many of her works in 1937. Her still rising fame is owed, above all, to her abundance of drawings, in which she addressed existential themes in an expressively realistic style.

8 JULY

David Hockney

Born 1937 | Painter, graphic artist, etc. | Great Britain

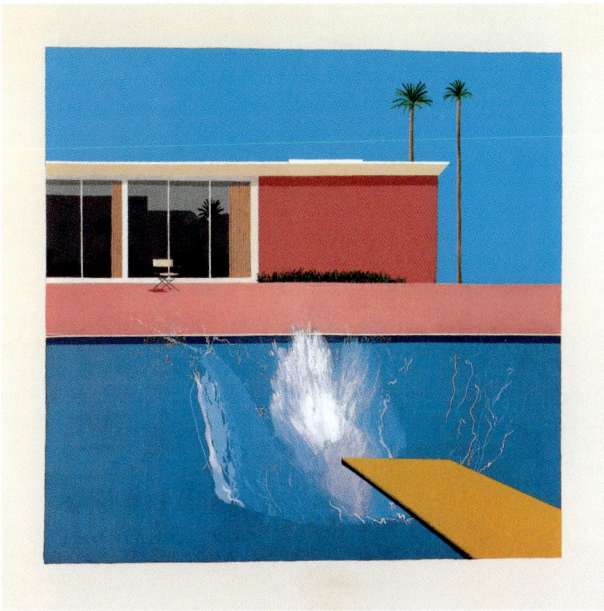

A Bigger Splash, 1967

Long one of Britain's most popular artists, Hockney also became one of the most highly priced in his advanced years. Works such as his homoerotically charged swimming pool pictures created in California brought him fame in the 1960s; he moved back and forth between the United States and Europe for decades. He explored seeing and perception by means of photographic experiments and by combining painting and photography. His late themes are expansive landscapes against natural backdrops. Hockney's inventive and experimental mind has kept his oeuvre evergreen.

9 JULY

Giorgio de Chirico

1888–1978 | Painter, sculptor and graphic artist | Italy

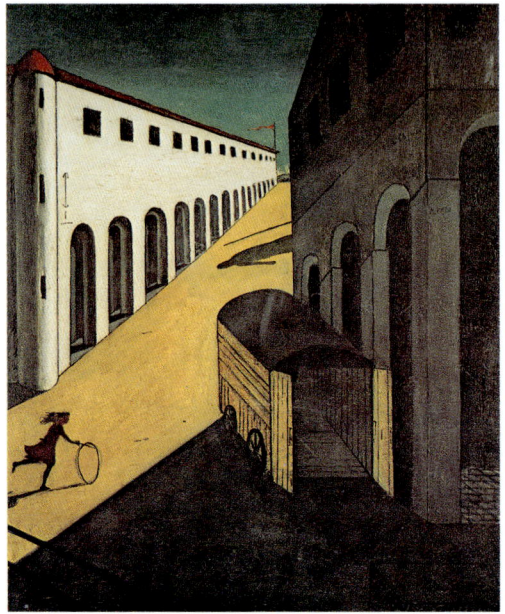

Mystery and Melancholy of a Street, 1914

Born in Greece to Italian parents, de Chirico was one of the famous painters of the twentieth century. Between 1906 and 1909, he attended the Art Academy in Munich, a city whose museums he was particularly impressed by Arnold Böcklin's pictures. De Chirico's reading of Friedrich Nietzsche was also formative. Having spent the years between 1911 and 1915 in Paris, he moved to Ferrara, where he was instrumental in establishing Metaphysical Painting with his pictures of cities, mannequins and interiors. His magical paintings of squares are unique contemplations on the deserted and enigmatic. His later work is characterized by a lofty Neo-Baroque style.

10 JULY

James McNeill Whistler

1834–1903 | Painter and graphic artist | United States

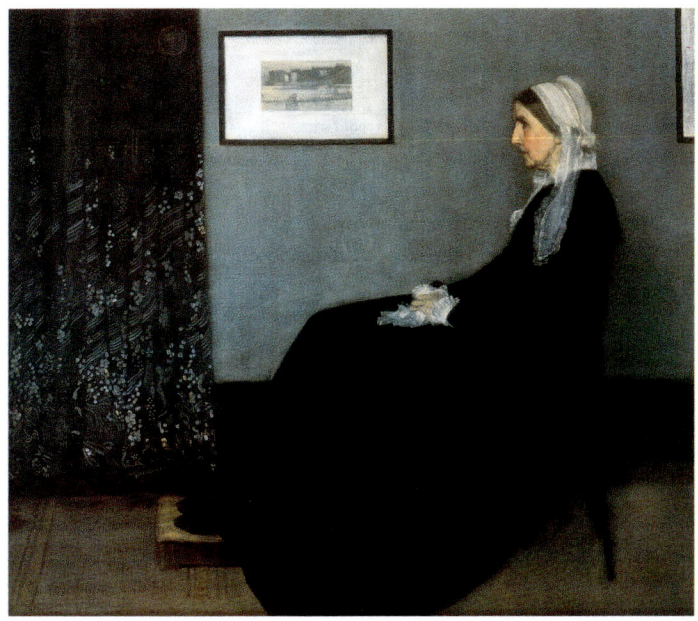

Arrangement in Grey and Black No. 1, Whistler's Mother, 1871

From 1855 until 1859, Whistler lived in Paris, where he led the eccentric life of a dandy, making friends with Gustave Courbet, Édouard Manet and Edgar Degas and admiring East Asian art and other genres. His movement between Paris and London was instrumental in bringing Impressionism to the attention of the English public. Whistler was particularly fond of Japanese motifs, made etchings and later lithographs and travelled extensively, including a trip to South America in 1866. In the 1880s, he exhibited in London in lavishly appointed rooms. When he died of heart failure in 1903, his oeuvre comprised more than one thousand works.

11 JULY

Amedeo Modigliani

1884–1920 | Draughtsman, painter and sculptor | Italy

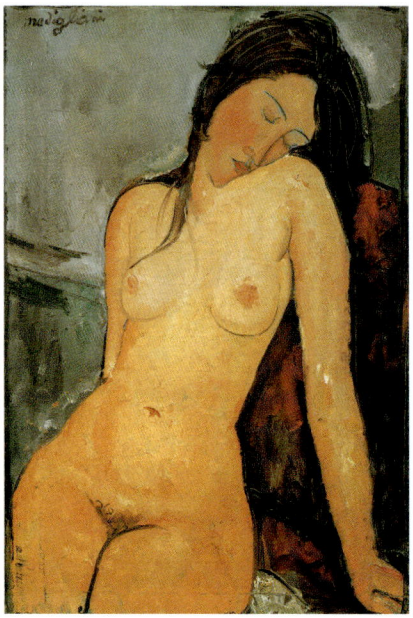

Female Nude, 1916

Modigliani is a true modern legend whose works fetch astronomical sums at auction. A charismatically sensual Mediterranean type, he was well aware of his Jewish heritage; the unparalleled melancholy lyricism of his pictures is founded in it. In 1906, he met Picasso in Paris, where the idolatrous force of African sculpture inspired him to make his own sculpture. Between 1914 and 1920, he arrived at his own style with his nudes and portraits. Marked by a lack of success in his lifetime, his oeuvre only first achieved greater popularity after his premature death.

12 JULY

Otto Wagner

1841–1918 | Architect, visionary and urban planner | Austria

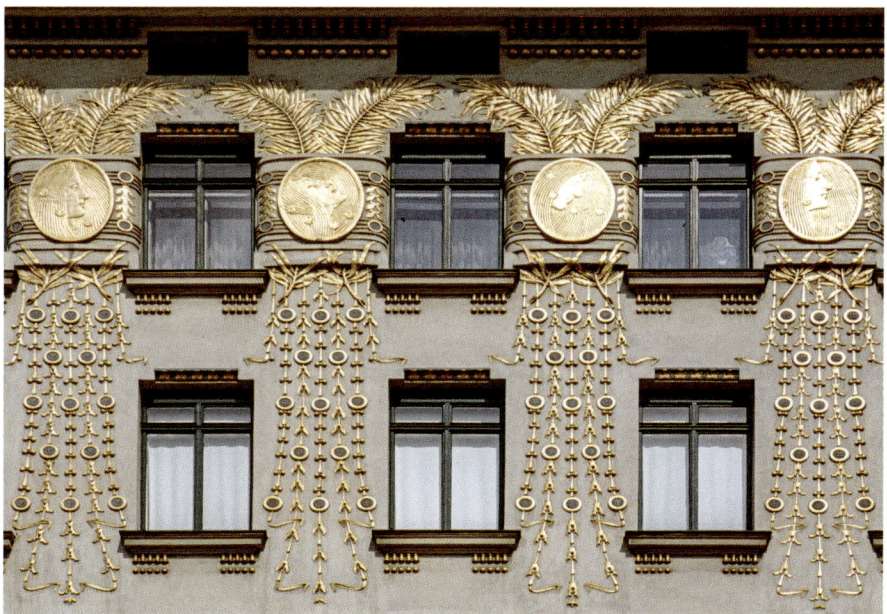

Building at Wienzeile 38, Vienna, 1898/1899

The Art Nouveau architect and urban planner Wagner was a key visionary of early modernism. He began building in the Historicist style in 1864. In Vienna, he designed numerous commercial and residential buildings – including two villas – and participated in international competitions. A professor at the Vienna Academy from 1894, Wagner also distinguished himself as an influential teacher and the author of seminal publications on architecture. His later buildings clearly anticipate Modernist principles. Wagner's apartment buildings on Wienzeile, built between 1898 and 1899, are significant examples of Viennese architecture of the time and mark his transition to Art Nouveau.

13 JULY

Gustav Klimt

1862–1918 | Painter and draughtsman | Austria

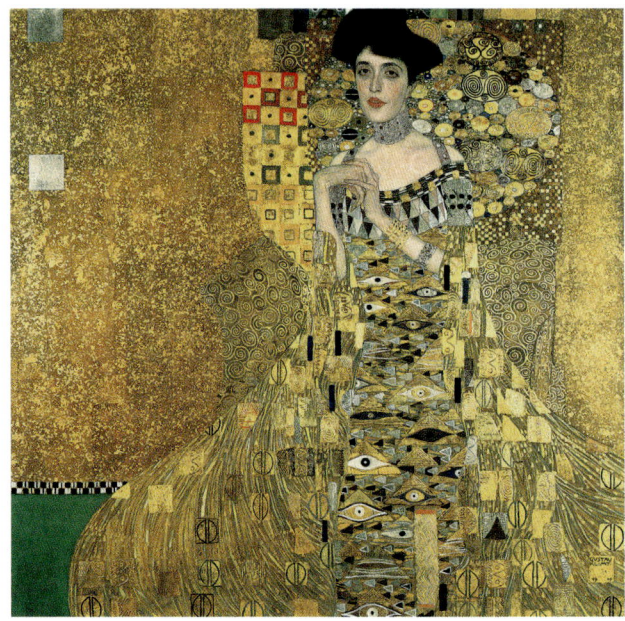

Portrait of Adele Bloch-Bauer I, 1907

Klimt, one of the best-known protagonists of Viennese Art Nouveau, became the first president of the Vienna Secession in 1897. His international reputation grew from 1900 onwards. The complex subject matter of his works between love and death is strongly defined by the eroticism of his female figures. Klimt painted *The Kiss*, his most famous painting, in 1907. His emphasis of planarity and ornamental abstraction of his paintings pointed the way for the modern era. Klimt was one of the finest draughtsmen of his day. Controversial during his lifetime, his idiosyncratic and emotionally stirring style had a major influence on twentieth century art.

14 JULY

Rembrandt van Rijn

1606–1669 | Painter, draughtsman and graphic artist | The Netherlands

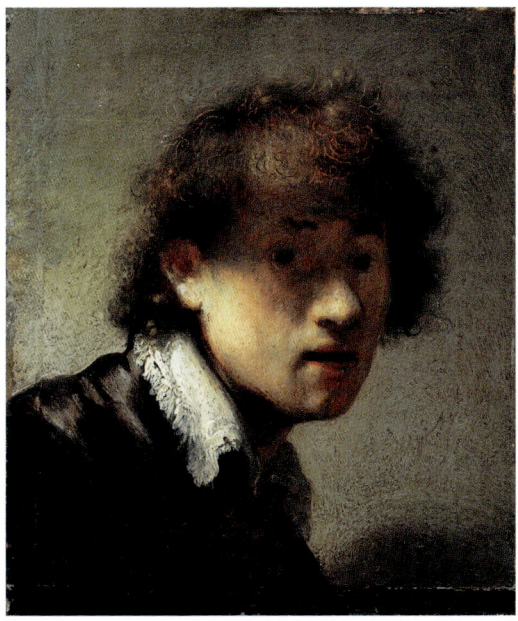

Self-Portrait as a Young Man, 1629

Rembrandt, one of art history's greatest painters and graphic artists, achieved early fame. Reception of his work was also very positive in the eighteenth and nineteenth century; only during the Neoclassical period was it rather more divided. His immense oeuvre chiefly covers biblical and mythological subjects, portraits and landscapes. The culmination of the genre of Dutch group portraits and pictures of civic guards, *The Night Watch*, his best-known work, is considered Rembrandt's masterpiece. Despite lucrative commissions, Rembrandt went bankrupt in 1656 and died in poverty in 1669.

15 JULY

Jean-Baptiste-Camille Corot

1796–1875 | Painter | France

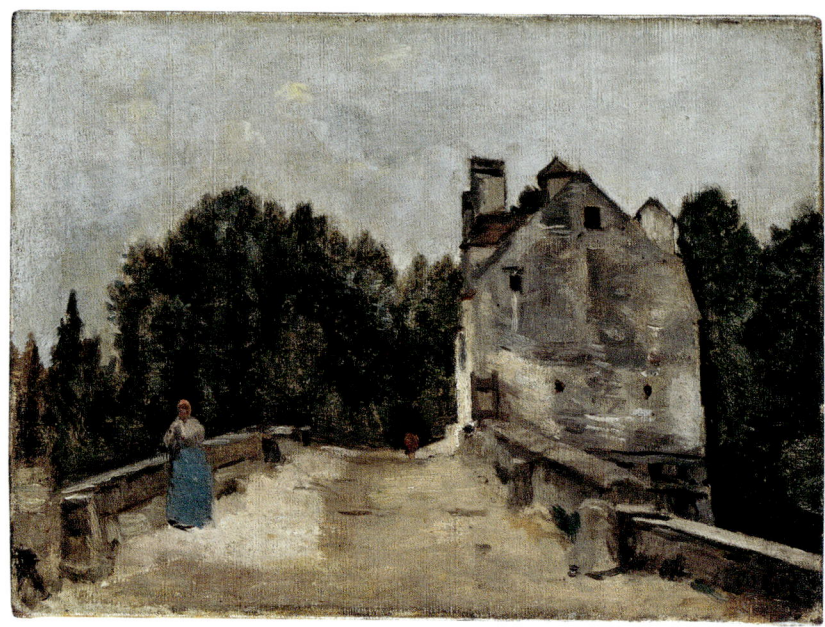

Bridge and Mill near Mantes, 1860–1865

Following an apprenticeship as a cloth trader, Corot devoted himself painting. In 1825, he went to Rome and spent three years painting in the Campagna. He later had a studio in Paris, where he exhibited regularly. His landscapes and portraits made him famous and secured him financial success. He was a generous donor to the poor and supported other artists. Among other reasons, his fame as the leading French landscape painter is founded on his incomparably atmospheric colours. Many later painters have referred to him.

16 JULY

Lyonel Feininger

1871–1956 | Painter, graphic artist, etc. | Germany, United States

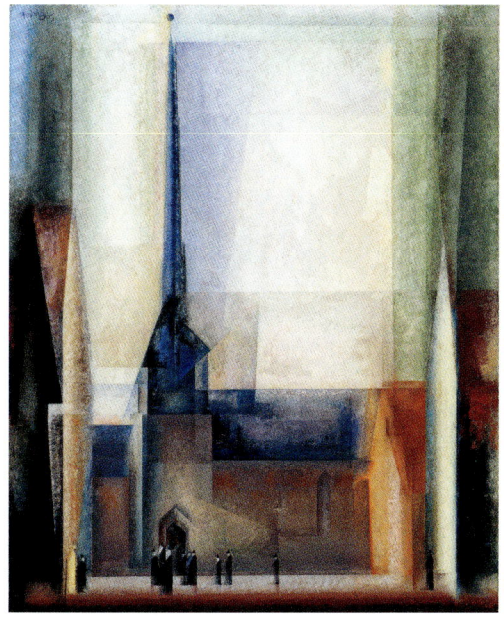

Gelmeroda IX, 1926

This son of German-American musicians was among the foremost artists of Classical Modernism. Following studies in Berlin and Paris, he began working as an independent illustrator and caricaturist in 1893. Starting in 1919, Feininger worked at the Bauhaus in Weimar and then, between 1926 and 1932, in Dessau. Designated "degenerate" by the Nazis, he moved to New York in 1937. His architecture pictures and seascapes are characterized by a prismatic, crystalline arrangement of transparent planes composed in strict counterpoint that is reminiscent of the work of Johann Sebastian Bach. In addition to paintings, Feininger created a significant oeuvre of works on paper.

Giacomo Balla

1871–1958 | Painter | Italy

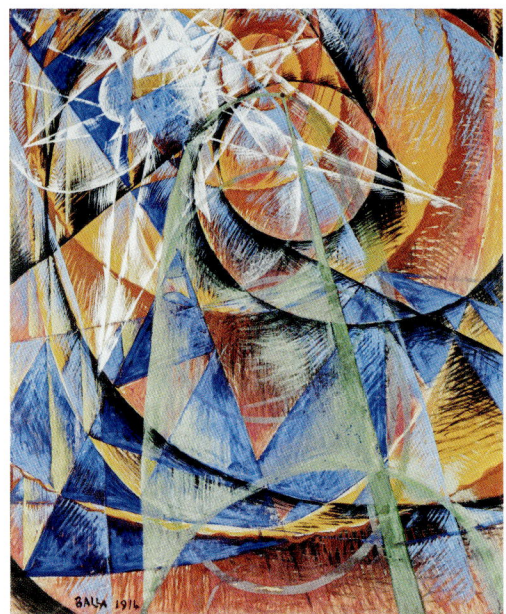

Mercury Passing Before the Sun, 1914

In 1900/1901, Balla sojourned in Paris, where he discovered Impressionism and Neo-Impressionism. He taught his friends – including Umberto Boccioni and Gino Severini – Divisionism, a painting technique in which an optical fusion of colours is achieved through the application of specific hues. This method was the perfect vehicle for Futurist ideas, which postulated the simultaneity of all sensory impressions. As a painter, Balla was interested in conveying movement and speed and visualizing the dynamism and rhythmicity of temporal sequences.

18 JULY

Edgar Degas

1834–1917 | Painter and sculptor | France

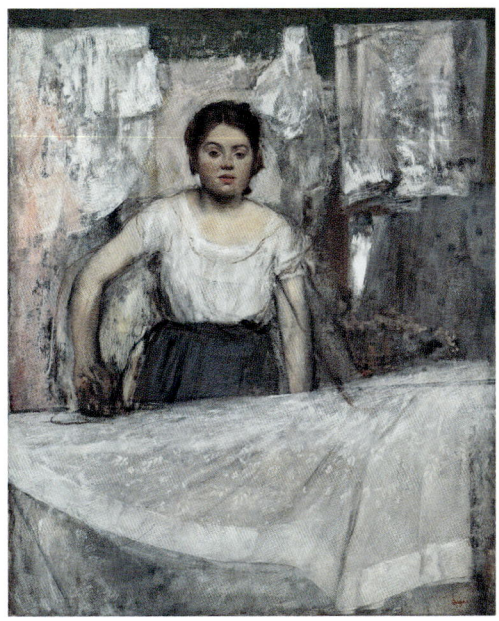

Woman Ironing, c. 1869

One of the nineteenth century's great French painters, Degas explored subject matter that includes portraits of people he knew as well as the city of Paris and its women. While he also made strikingly realistic pictures of female workers of the lower classes, his most famous topic was the ballet and ballerinas. Late pastels depict female nudes bathing and grooming themselves in different poses. Degas's fame is also founded on his drawings and experimental printed graphics. The Musée d'Orsay in Paris and the Metropolitan Museum of Art in New York have large collections of his work.

19 JULY

László Moholy-Nagy

1895–1946 | Painter, photographer, etc. | Hungary, United States

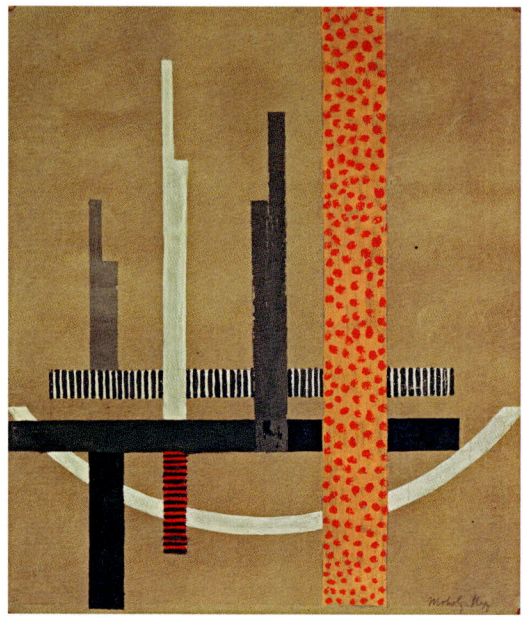

Glass Architecture, 1922

As a painter, Moholy-Nagy came under the influence of Constructivism in 1919 through Kazimir Malevich and El Lissitzky. Starting in 1923, as a distinguished teacher at the Bauhaus in Weimar, he directed the metal workshop, which seemed tailor-made for his adventuresome spirit. The abundance of his ideas and experiments with photography and photograms revealed a potential for application in the most diverse media – ranging from stage decoration and typography to industrial design – with which he worked in Berlin, Amsterdam and London after 1928. In 1937, he founded the New Bauhaus in Chicago and, in 1939, the School of Design.

20 JULY

Lovis Corinth

1858–1925 | Painter, draughtsman | Germany

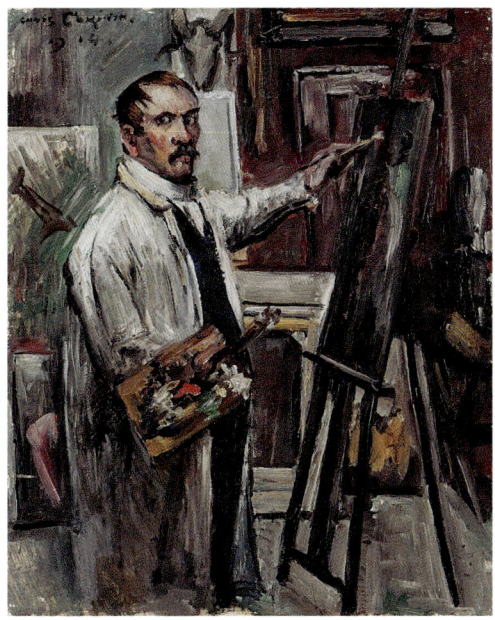

Self-Portrait at His Easel, 1914

Corinth lived intermittently in Berlin, spending the years between 1891 and 1900 in Munich. He became a member of the Berlin Secession in 1901. Alongside Max Liebermann and Max Slevogt, he was a prominent protagonist of German Impressionism. In 1911, after suffering a stroke that left him paralyzed on his left side, he nevertheless continued to paint numerous pictures. He moved to Lake Walchen in Bavaria after the First World War. There, in addition to self-portraits and still lifes, he created his famous landscapes in a visionary style that was inspired by Expressionism. Besides paintings, he produced a substantial oeuvre of works on paper.

21 JULY

Alexander Calder

1898–1976 | Sculptor | United States

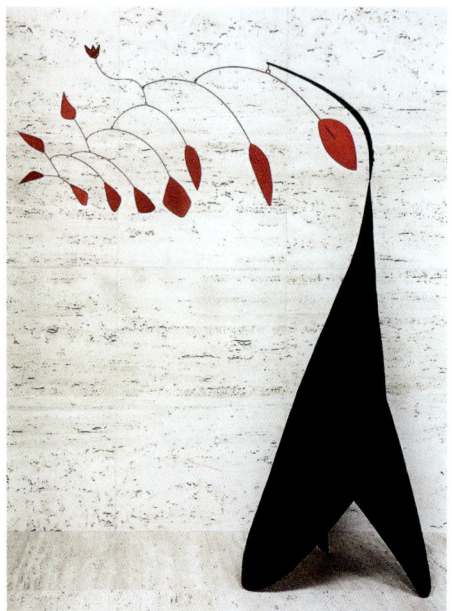

Red Petals, 1942

As the main representative of Kinetic sculpture and inventor of the mobile, Calder was one of the most popular sculptors of the twentieth century. The son and grandson of illustrious public sculptors, he moved to Paris in 1926, where he met Piet Mondrian, Fernand Léger and Joan Miró, among others. In the city on the Seine, he created his first moving wire constructions and mobiles, in which movement and abstraction are poetically combined. Living in Connecticut since 1933, he also created abstract monumental sculptures. Worldwide exhibitions and museum acquisitions underline Calder's fame.

_____

_____

_____

_____

22 JULY

Philipp Otto Runge

1777–1810 | Painter | Germany

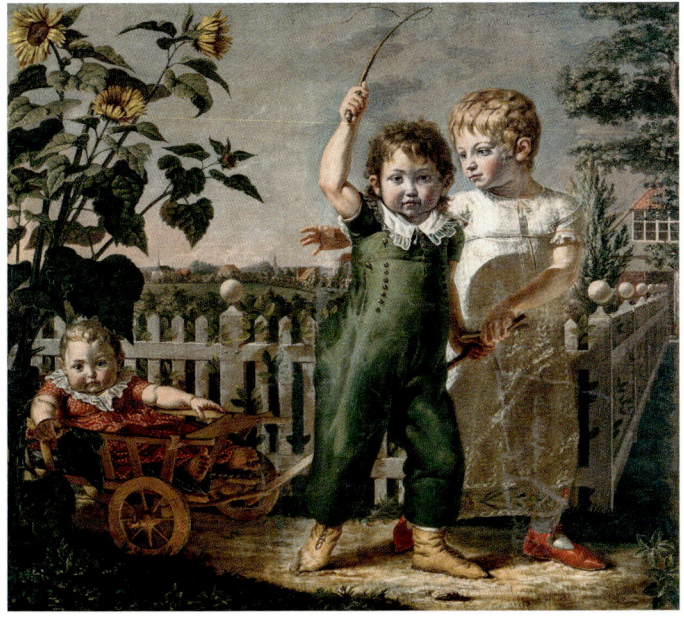

The Hülsenbeck Children, 1805/1806

Alongside Caspar David Friedrich, Runge was the foremost German painter of early Romanticism. After studying in Copenhagen, he encountered Romantic artists in Dresden, including Friedrich. In 1803, he met the writer Johann Wolfgang von Goethe, with whom he corresponded until his death. He made figure paintings and portraits as well as cut-out silhouettes and engravings. He is known chiefly for his masterly depictions of nature and profound portraits of an often mystical and symbolic quality. His revolutionary thinking – including his work on colour symbolism – makes him an intellectual pioneer of the *Gesamtkunstwerk*, or total work of art.

23 JULY

Sheila Hicks

Born 1934 | Artist | United States

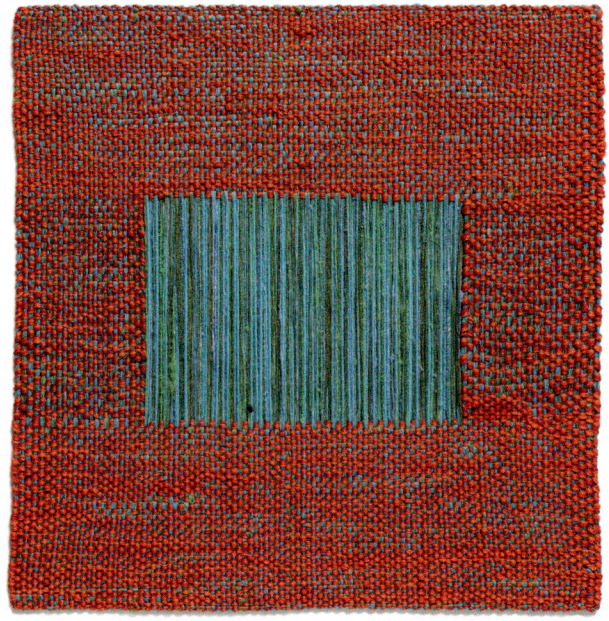

Window II, 2009

This internationally renowned textile artist studied at the Yale School of Art with Josef and Anni Albers. After spending several years in Mexico, she moved to Paris in the mid-1960s. Hicks studied the weaving practices of various Indigenous peoples on her travels across the continents of the world. She incorporates varied materials such as found objects from nature and everyday items in her works ranging from miniature formats to large installations. Exhibitions around the world, awards and museum acquisitions bear witness to her standing.

24 JULY

Thomas Eakins

1844–1916 | Painter | United States

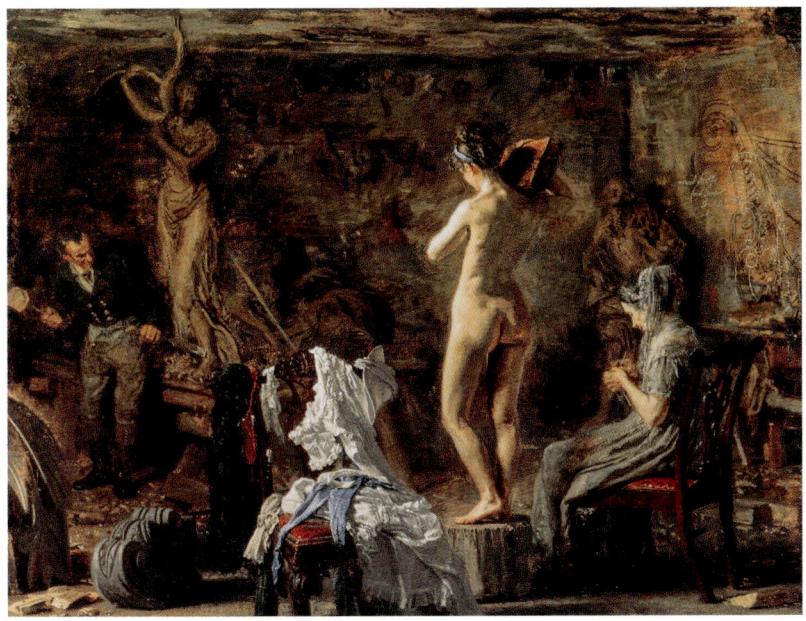

William Rush Carving His Allegorical Figure of the Schuylkill River, 1876/1877

Training in Paris between 1866 and 1870, Eakins never approximated Impressionism but was more interested in pursuing his own kind of Realism. When he returned to the United States in 1870, he made portraits and pictures of rowers, which have become famous. His models were often his students posing in the nude. Eakins's fascination with the naked body also involved homoerotic fantasies. Although he was only able to sell a few of his works during his lifetime, they are much in demand today.

25 JULY

George Grosz

1893–1959 | Painter, graphic artist, etc. | Germany, United States

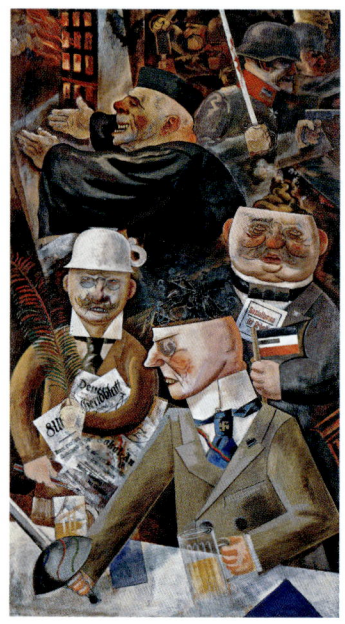

The Pillars of Society, 1926

Alongside Otto Dix, Grosz was the foremost protagonist of socially critical verism in Germany. As a pacifist, he was one of the founders of Berlin Dada group, which was characterized by anarchy and targeted political provocation. A series of major paintings and especially the relentless bite of his graphic style helped establish his fame. His typical subjects include political opponents and life in the metropolis with its whores, pimps and hoodlums. In 1933, Grosz emigrated to the United States, where he enjoyed success as an artist and was a teacher at the Art Students League of New York.

26 JULY

Erwin Wurm

Born 1954 | Artist | Austria

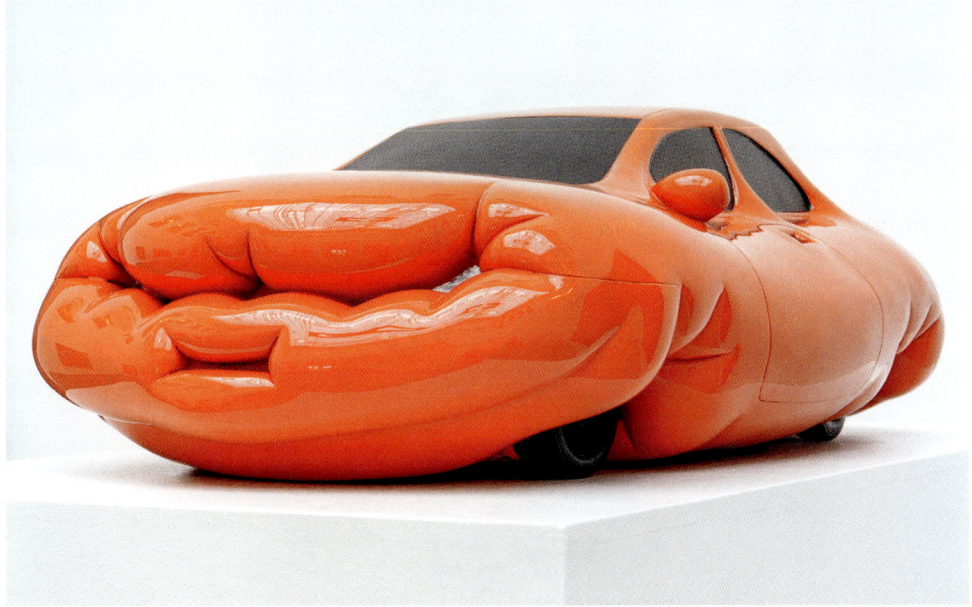

Fat Car, 2005

Wurm is one of the most successful contemporary artists in Austria. Consisting of material sculptures, actions, videos, drawings and more, his works frequently involve satirical, bizarre humour. Wurm is known for his *One Minute Sculptures* in which people pose with everyday objects in surprising configurations and are photographed by the artist. In his *Fat* sculptures, he alienates middle-class status symbols by inflating them. In the words of the artist, he is interested in "showing the everyday from a different perspective".

Marcel Duchamp

1887–1968 | Painter and object artist | France, United States

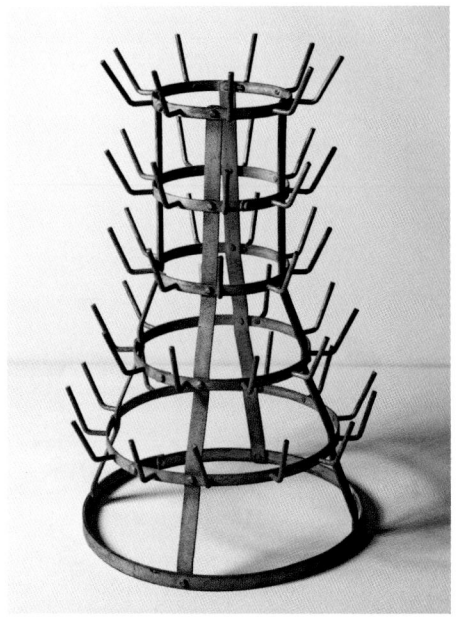

Bottle Rack, 1914/1964

A speculative mind of anarchic genius, Duchamp was one of the most revolutionary and influential artists of the twentieth century. In 1913, working between Paris and New York, he abandoned conventional painting and as an anti-artist playfully and ironically devoted himself to experiments involving randomness within the context of machines and mechanisms. His most famous readymades, with which he radically challenged common concepts of art, are *Bottle Rack* and *Fountain*, prefabricated objects that he declared art by adding his signature to them. With this gesture, Duchamp introduced Conceptualism.

28 JULY

Jenny Holzer

Born 1950 | Conceptual and installation artist | United States

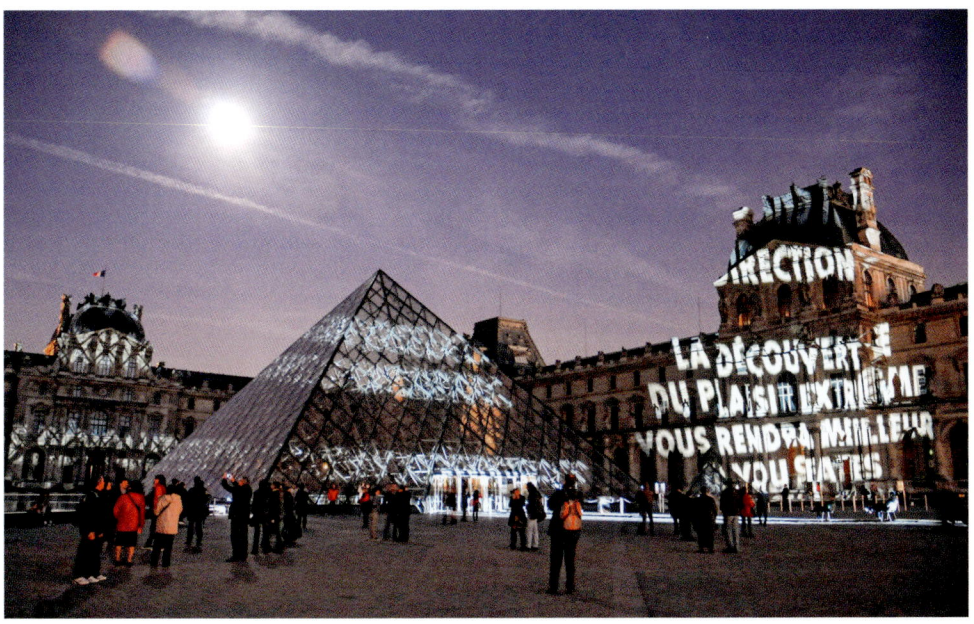

France – Paris (75) 1st Arrondissement: The Louvre Pyramid (04–09), 2009

After working as an abstract painter and experimenting with diagrams and words, Holzer became an internationally acclaimed Conceptual and installation artist. In her text art she focuses on political power structures and topics such as sexualized violence, AIDS and feminism. Her famous *Truisms*, a series of pithy one-liners, have been shown using various media, including LED signs and projections. Holzer received the Golden Lion in 1990 for her installation at the Venice Biennale.

29 JULY

Henry Moore

1898–1986 | Sculptor and graphic artist | Great Britain

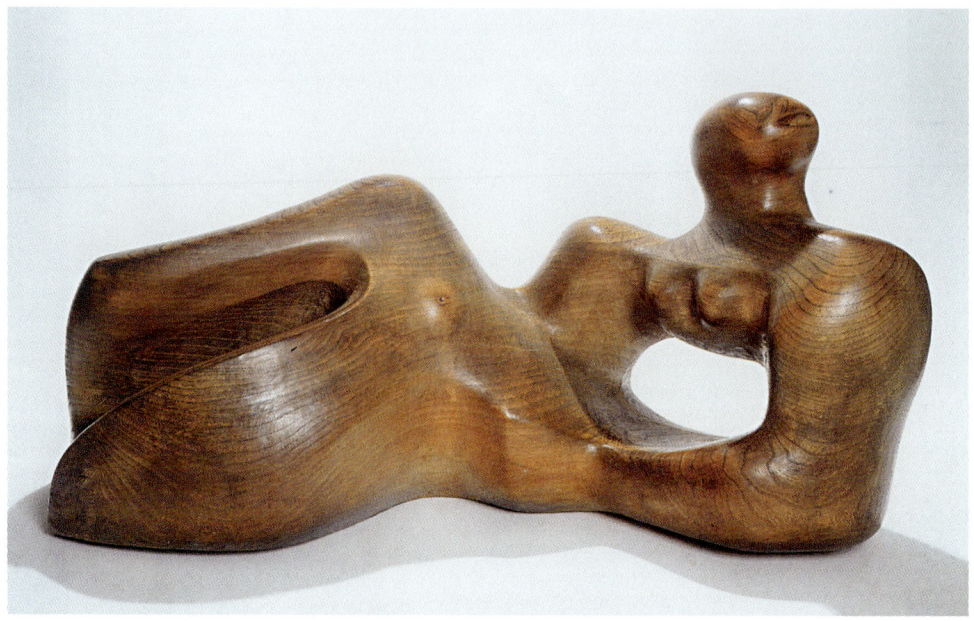

Recumbent Figure, 1935/1936

Moore is one of the world's best-known sculptors of the twentieth century. In the 1920s, his imagination was fired by African and Mexican sculpture. In the ensuing decade, he created his *Transformation Drawings*, which made found objects such as bones or shells the object of transformations reaching to the figuratively abstract. His speciality was the recumbent female figure. The Second World War saw the creation of his famous *Shelter Drawings* in the tunnels of the London Tube. In the post-war period, Moore's sculptures brought him fame all around the globe.

_____

_____

_____

_____

30 JULY

Jean Dubuffet

1901–1985 | Painter, sculptor and action artist | France

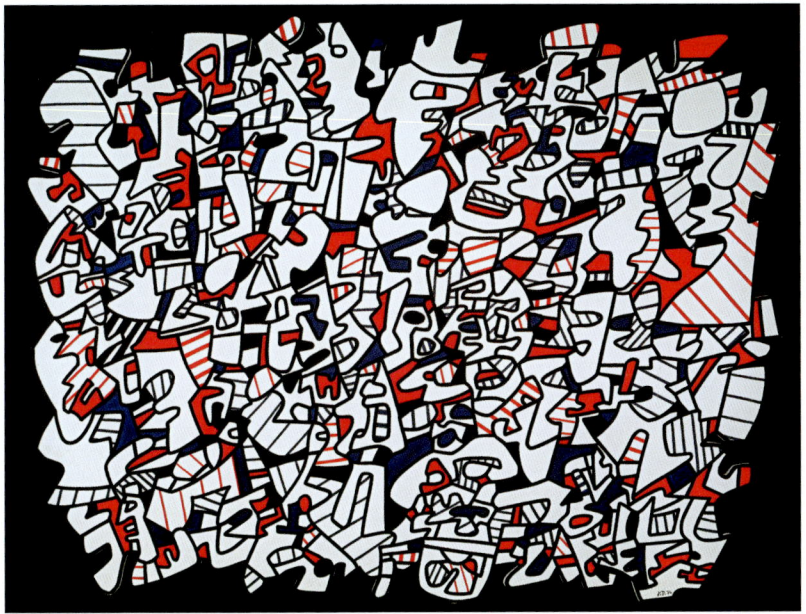

Ontogenesis, 1975

Dubuffet began his career making figurative paintings in the circle of the Surrealists in Paris. However, he soon gave up art, worked as a wine trader and did not return to paintings until the 1940s. Exhibitions in galleries quickly followed. He found inspiration for his paintings, drawings and experimental prints in art by "naive" painters and the mentally ill. His murals featuring scratched graffiti became famous; these paintings employing unorthodox materials are the epitome of Art Brut. Dubuffet was one of the most inspiring painters and sculptors after 1945.

31 JULY

Gego

1912–1994 | Sculptor, installation artist, etc. | Germany, Venezuela

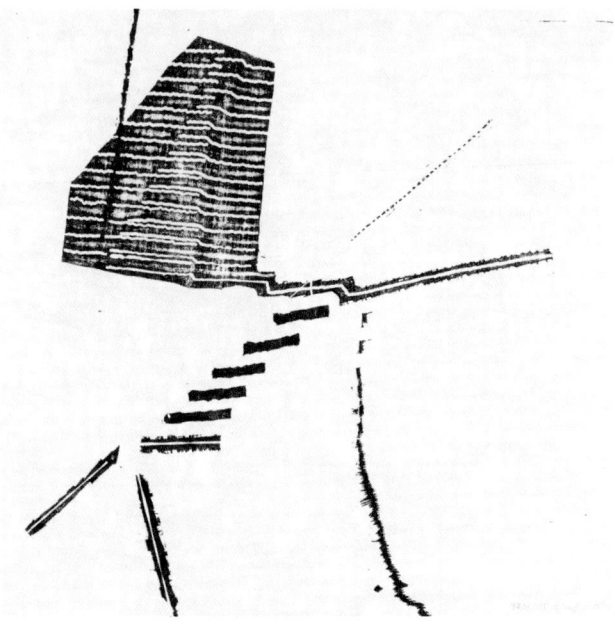

Sin título (Tamarind 1893), 1966

Gego, who was born in Hamburg as Gertrud Louise Goldschmidt, studied architecture and engineering in the 1930s at the Technical University in Stuttgart. In 1933, she moved to Caracas, where she was active as an eclectic artist. In the 1960s and 1970s, she came to the fore with her subtle graphic abstractions combined with net-like immersive installations, which made her one of the best-known artists in Latin America. Large collections of works by Gego can be seen at the Museum of Modern Art in New York, the Museum of Fine Arts in Houston, the Museu d'Art Contemporani de Barcelona and the Kunstmuseum Stuttgart.

1 AUGUST

Ida Gerhardi

1862–1927 | Painter | Germany

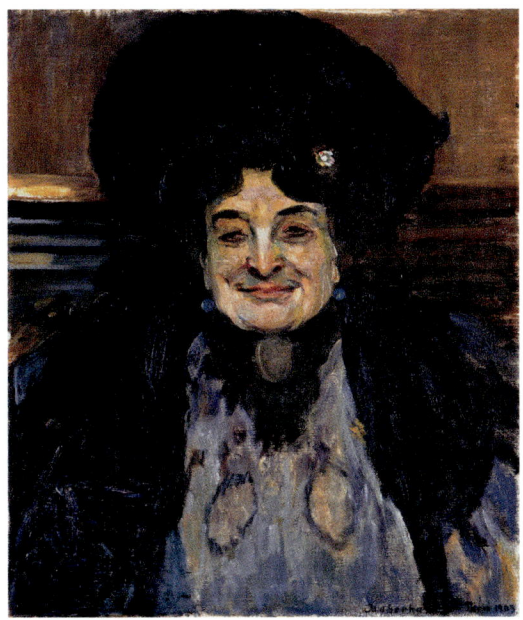

The Singer (Madame de Riau), 1903

Between 1891 and 1913, Ida Gerhardi lived mainly in Paris, where she studied and socialized with artists such as Auguste Rodin. Besides painting, she taught art and curated. For health reasons, she spent the years between 1913 and her death living in the family home in Lüdenscheid. Her early work includes atmospheric landscapes, and she later became increasingly interested in painting portraits and pictures of dancers in Parisian nightclubs, some of which she visited with her friend Käthe Kollwitz. Her works are part of museum collections in Essen, Düsseldorf and Münster.

2 AUGUST

Maria Wiik

1853–1928 | Painter | Finland

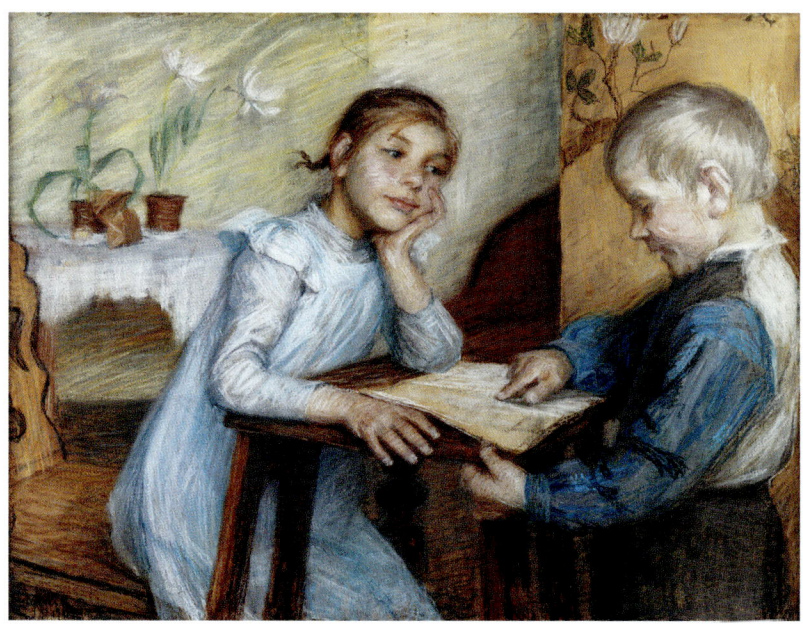

An Interior with a Boy Reading to a Girl, 1912

In 1875, after studying in Helsinki, Maria Wiik moved to Paris, where she attended the Académie Julian. In the mid-1880s, she engaged in *plein-air* painting in Brittany. She also made portraits, some of them of celebrities. Depictions with social and symbolic content later dominated. A visit to Norway in 1911 awakened her interest in the art of Edvard Munch, which is evident in her works. Due to an eye condition, she largely withdrew from active life until her death. In 1916, an art dealer bought her works, which are now split among several Scandinavian museums.

3 AUGUST

Hedda Sterne

1910–2011 | Artist | Romania, United States

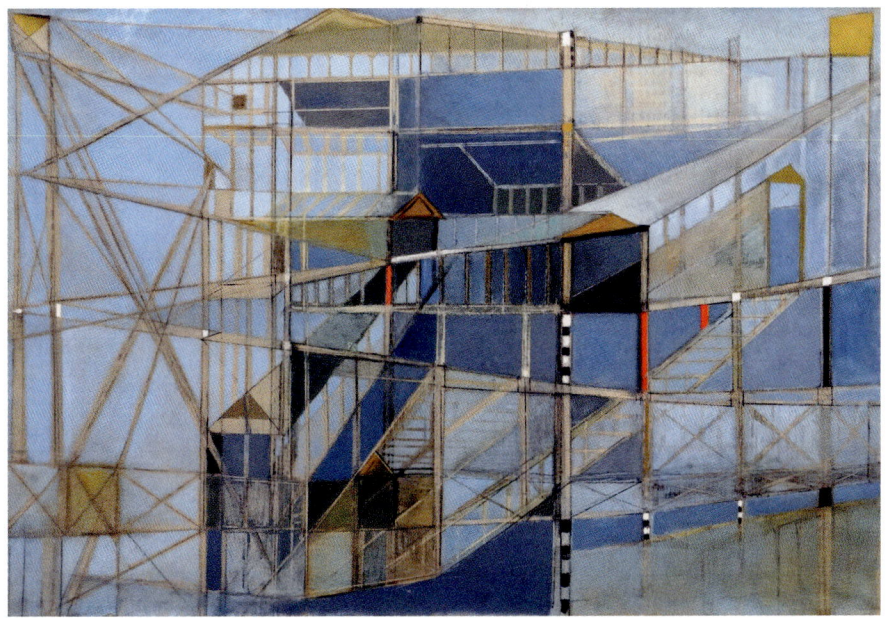

NY, NY No. X, 1948

Before moving to Paris, where she continued to develop as a painter and sculptor, Sterne studied in Vienna and Bucharest. In 1941, she fled from the Nazis to New York, where Peggy Guggenheim introduced her to the local art scene. Her second marriage was to the well-known Romanian-born American caricaturist and illustrator Saul Steinberg. She worked and exhibited extensively into old age. Her figurative and abstract works are in the collections of various American museums, including the Museum of Modern Art and the Whitney Museum of American Art in New York.

4 AUGUST

Naum Gabo

1890–1977 | Sculptor, painter, architect, etc. | Russia, United States

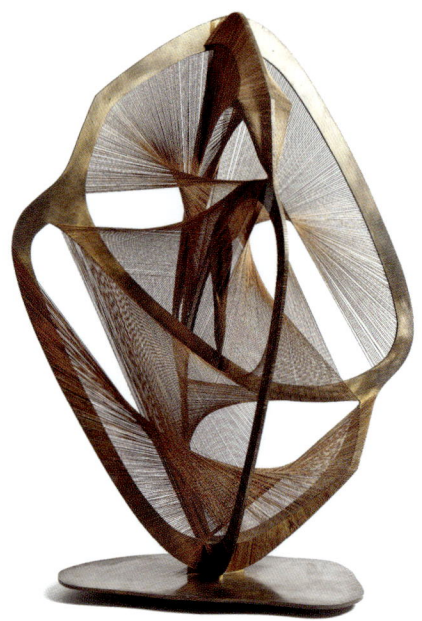

Linear Construction in Space No. 4, 1958/1959

Between 1910 and 1914, Gabo studied structural engineering at the Technical University in Munich, where he encountered Wassily Kandinsky. At the outbreak of the First World War he fled to Denmark and Oslo. His first sculptural structures were made during that period. Following the October Revolution in Russia, he published the art-historically important *Realistic Manifesto* with Antoine Pevsner, his brother, in 1920. He taught architecture in Boston in 1953/1954. Gabo rejected solid volume in his sculptures, instead creating spatial structures balanced between stasis and dynamism.

_____

_____

_____

_____

5 AUGUST

Andy Warhol

1928–1987 | Painter, graphic artist and filmmaker | United States

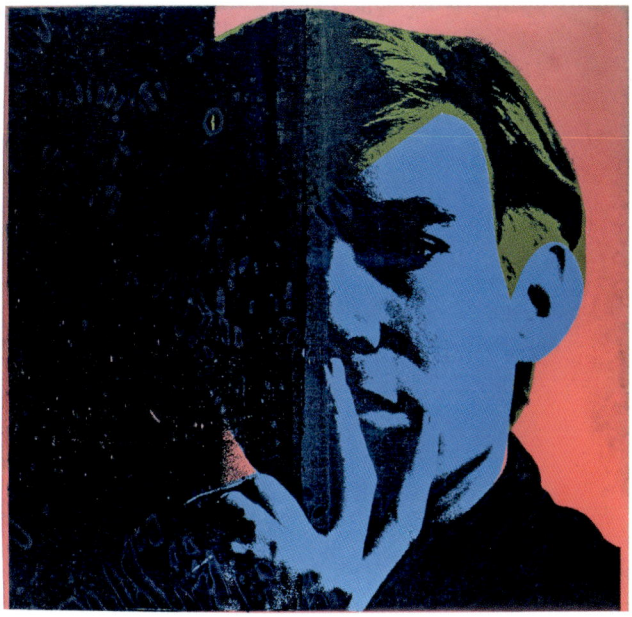

Self-Portrait, 1967

As the most famous protagonist of American Pop Art, Warhol was one of the most influential artists in the second half of the twentieth century. Active in the 1950s as an industrial and advertising graphic artist, he familiarized himself with screen printing a short while later. He sold serial reproductions of trivial subjects, including consumer society, comic motifs and pictures of Hollywood stars, worldwide. Warhol's boundless creativity was also reflected in his drawings, photographs and films, with which he created his own legend between art and commerce.

6 AUGUST

Emil Nolde

1867–1956 | Painter | Germany

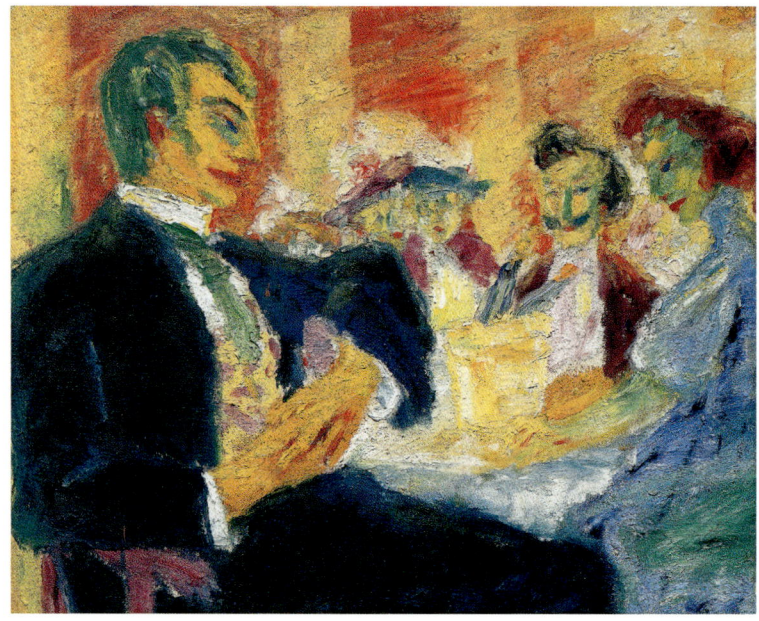

In the Café, 1911

As a great painter and watercolourist, as well as an expressive graphic artist, Nolde is the epitome of German Expressionism. Around 1905, he found his way to his characteristic language of colours while painting floral and garden pictures. In the ensuing years, he painted religious works, and in 1913/1914, he discovered the art of Indigenous people on a trip to New Guinea. After the First World War, Nolde lived both in Berlin and at his country house in Seebüll on the North Sea. Landscape painting became more dominant from the 1920s. His role in the Nazi era was ambivalent.

7 AUGUST

Louis Valtat

1869–1952 | Painter | France

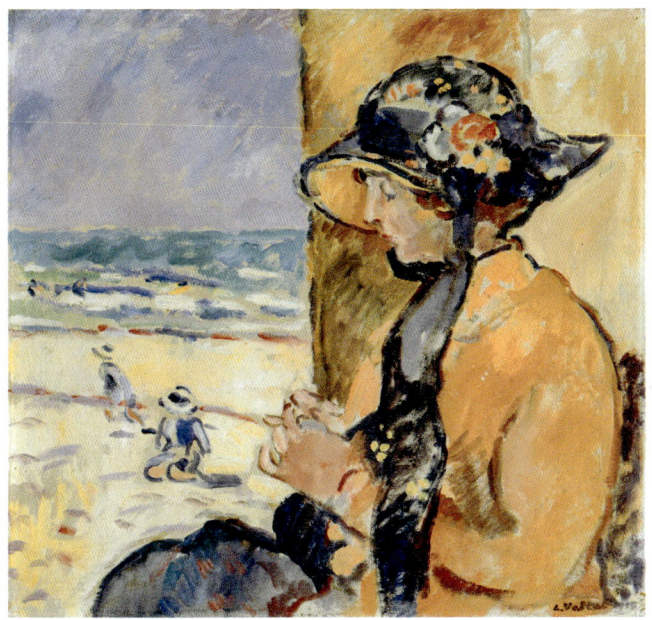

Woman and Children at the Beach, 1916

Having attended the Académie Julian in Paris in 1888, Valtat worked jointly with Henri de Toulouse-Lautrec on set designs several years later. Starting in 1903, he regularly exhibited his Fauvist-inspired paintings at the Paris Salon d'Automne, where they caused an uproar. In 1914, he began to painting pictures of both his wife and son. A contract with the influential art dealer Ambroise Vollard made it possible for several of his works to enter major collections, including that of the Russian collector Ivan Morosov. Due to his increasing blindness, Valtat was forced to give up painting in 1948.

8 AUGUST

Yinka Shonibare

Born 1962 | Artist | Great Britain

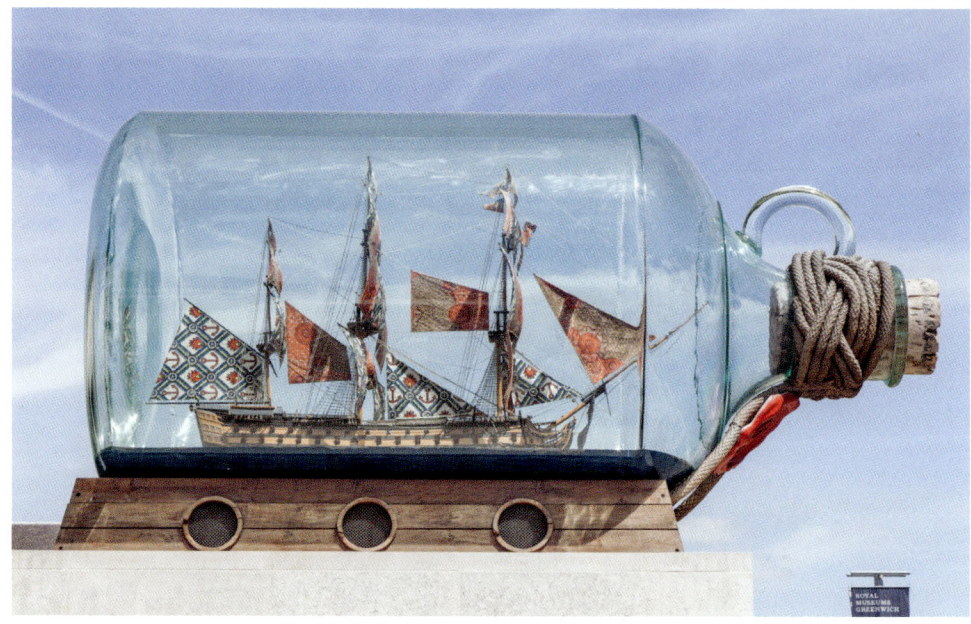

Nelson's Ship in a Bottle, 2010

This British installation and conceptual artist was nominated for the Turner Prize in 2004 as one of the Young British Artists. Following an illness, Shonibare has been paralyzed on one side since the age of eighteen. His breakthrough occurred when Okwui Enwezor invited him to participate in documenta 11. His artistic means of expression are sculpture, photography, installation, painting and film, which he employs to engage critically with colonialism and Victorian values, which he describes as "values of oppression". Many exhibitions and honours testify to his international standing.

9 AUGUST

Thomas Bewick

1753–1828 | Graphic artist | Great Britain

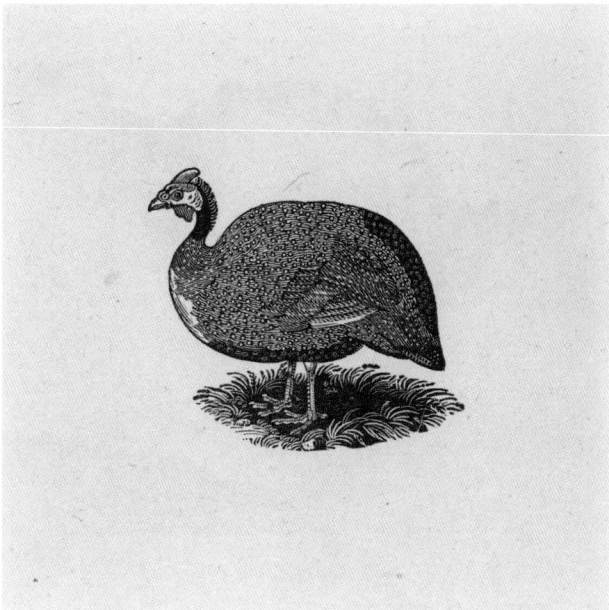

Guinea Hen, c. 1800

Bewick was completing an apprenticeship as an engraver when he made his first piece on wood in the early 1870s. He is regarded as the inventor of wood engraving, in which hard beechwood is engraved with tools used for metal engraving, although recent research shows that the history of this medium in England may be older. In the ensuing decades, Bewick created a series of publications using the wood engraving technique, which was highly valued throughout the nineteenth century after his death in 1828.

10 AUGUST

André Thomkins

1930–1985 | Painter and draughtsman | Switzerland

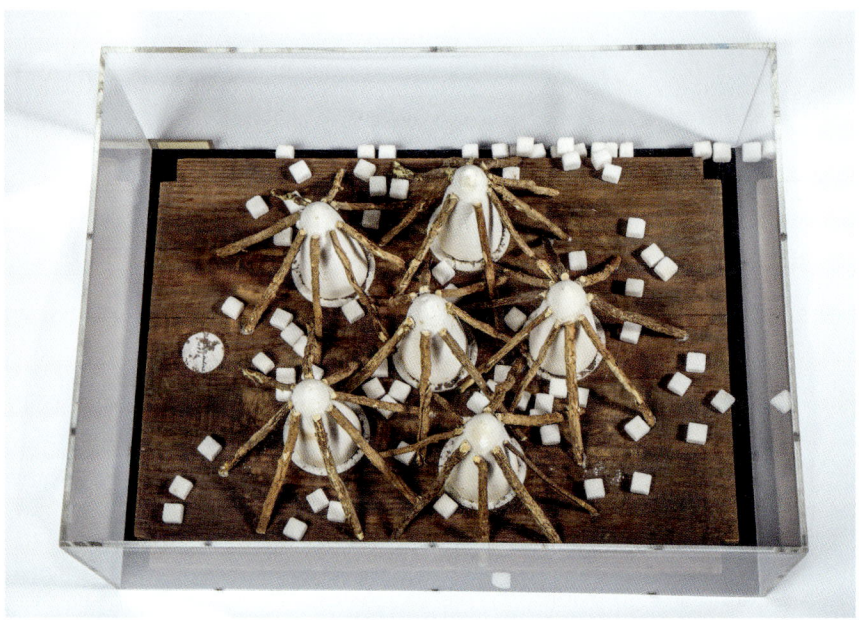

Sugarloaves, 1971

The Swiss artist André Thomkins studied in Lucerne and Paris, where he met his future wife, the artist Eva Schnell. His later works were shaped by his exploration of Surrealism. He frequently collaborated with the Fluxus artists Dieter Roth and Daniel Spoerri on joint exhibitions. Thomkins experimented with various techniques and media, making paintings, sculptures, drawings, stained-glass windows and set designs for theatres in Cologne and Düsseldorf. His inventive, poetic work earned him international fame.

11 AUGUST

Walter Bodmer

1903–1973 | Painter and sculptor | Switzerland

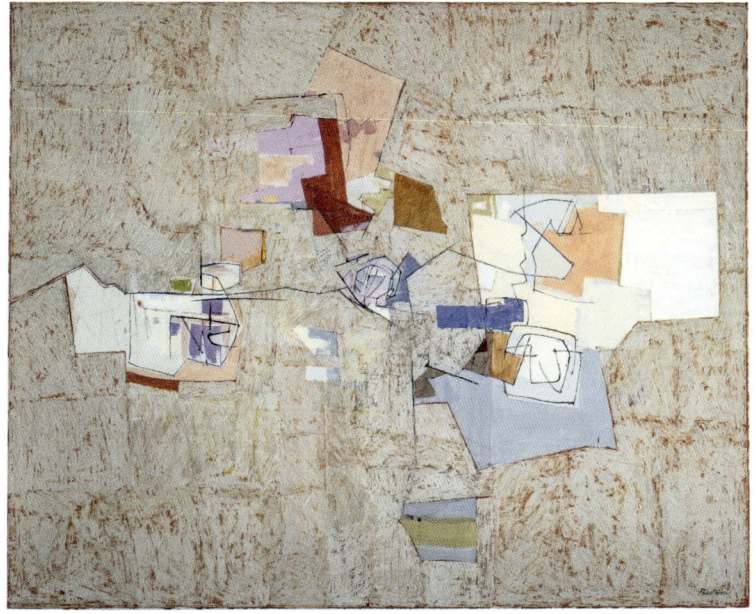

Without Beginning or End, 1972

Bodmer is regarded as a pioneer of Abstract art in Switzerland. In 1933, with artist friends in Basel, he initiated the anti-fascist Gruppe 33 to counteract conservative trends in art. Through his exploration of Cubism, Bodmer developed his personal style in wire pictures, sculptures, reliefs and drawings. Starting in 1936, he began to focus on reliefs and wire sculptures. He also worked as a saxophonist and drummer during that period. In the 1950s, Bodmer received international recognition due to his participation in the Venice Biennale and documenta in Kassel.

12 AUGUST

James Gillray

1757–1815 | Caricaturist and etcher | Great Britain

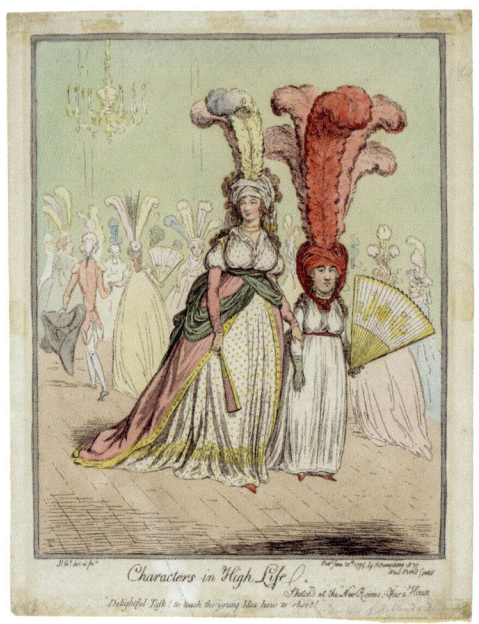

Characters in High Life, 1795

As the most prolific English caricaturist of the eighteenth century, Gillray's fame is founded on his satirical etchings and engravings lampooning current politics as well as universal human foibles. Acerbity, a sure-fire aim and humour are the main criteria of his caricatures, which in addition to social conditions in England and France also focus on individuals such as King George III and his family or Napoleon Bonaparte. More than works on paper are known to be by Gillray, who died, suffering from mental illness, in 1815.

13 AUGUST

Claude Joseph Vernet

1714–1789 | Painter | France

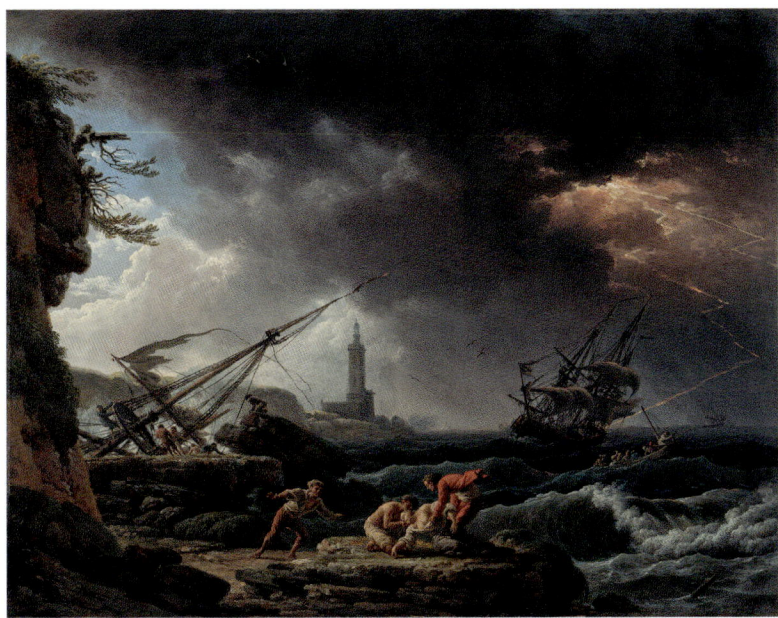

A Shipwreck in Stormy Seas, 1772

A grant enabled Vernet to travel to Rome in 1734 at the age of twenty and spend several years studying under two well-known marine painters. He later married the daughter of a captain in the Papal Navy. In 1753, Vernet was summoned to the French court by King Louis XV, where he was to depict France's maritime power in twenty-four harbour views. Vernet created new, panorama-like views prospects with staffage figures. He became famous for his dramatic scenes of storms and shipwrecks.

14 AUGUST

Richard Deacon

Born 1949 | Sculptor | Great Britain

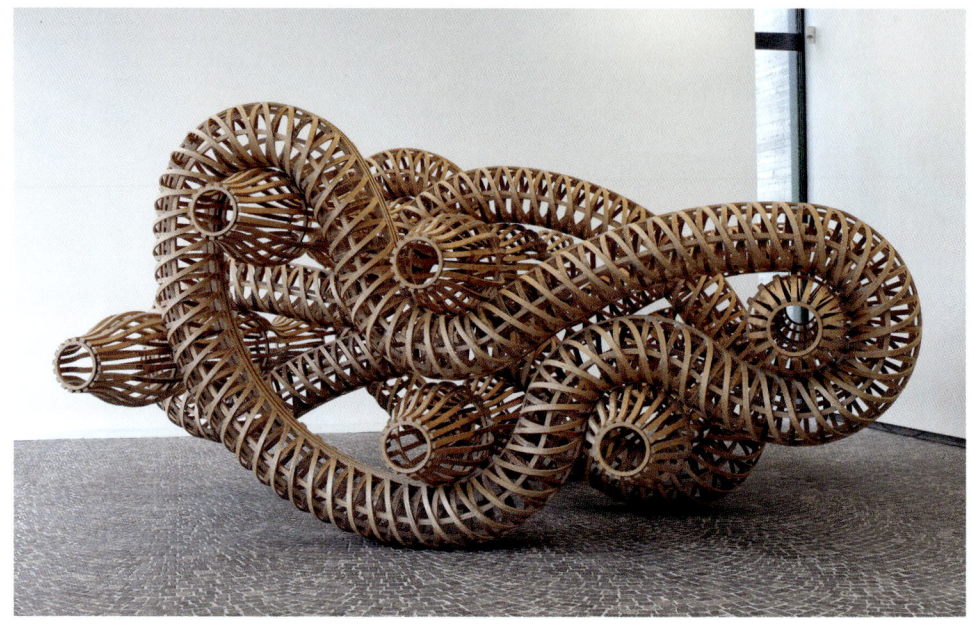

What Could Make Me Feel This Way (A), 1993

Deacon is a leading figure in contemporary sculpture. Following his studies in London, he held various international visiting professorships starting in 1978 and, in 2009, became a professor at the Düsseldorf Academy. Since the 1980s, he has produced countless objects and installations. In formal terms, his work is characterized by richly varied, dynamic abstraction; he demonstrates utmost experimental versatility in handling materials such as wood, metal, ceramic and plastic. Numerous exhibitions and honours testify to his international fame.

15 AUGUST

Agostino Carracci

1557–1602 | Painter and engraver | Italy

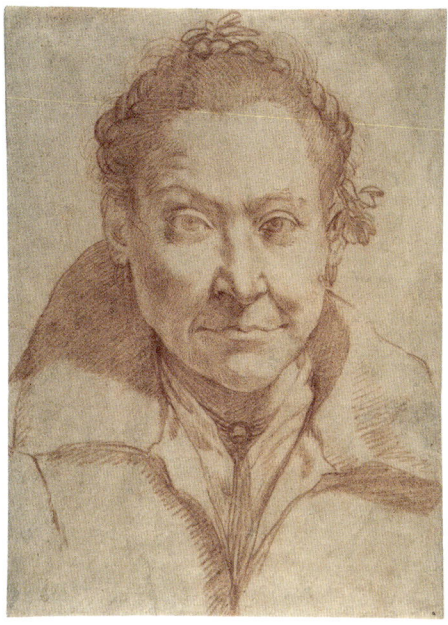

Portrait of a Woman, undated

A major Italian painter and engraver of the sixteenth century, Carracci came to the fore as an engraver soon after completing his painting apprenticeship. In 1583, he made frescoes in a palace in Bologna with his brothers Annibale and Lodovico. In the 1590s, he accompanied Annibale to Rome, where they collaborated on the frescoes in Palazzo Farnese. In 1600, the brothers fell out, and Agostino was called to the court in Parma. His frescoes there remain unfinished. In addition to painting, his posthumous fame is assured by around 270 engravings.

16 AUGUST

Larry Rivers

1923–2002 | Musician and artist | United States

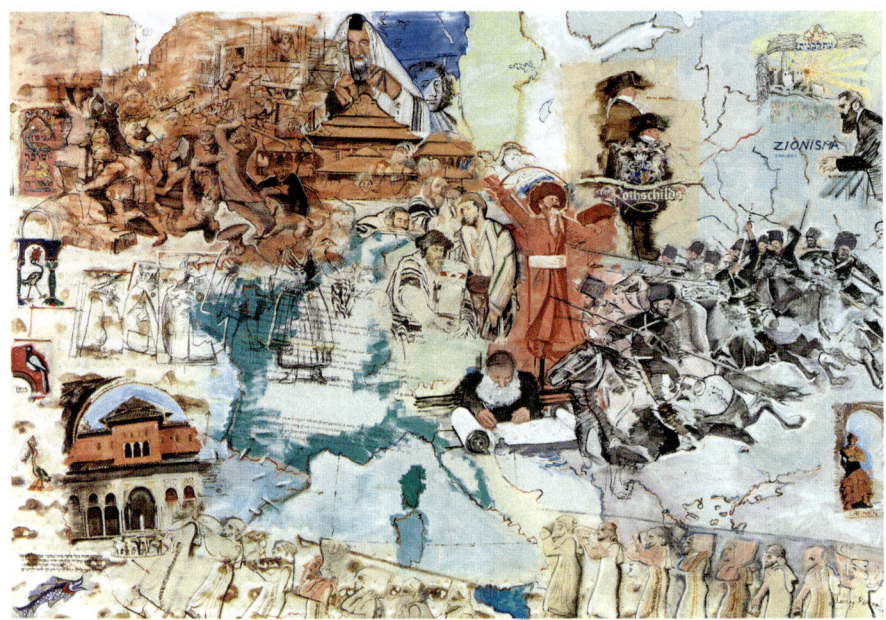

History of Matzah: The History of the Jews, 1982–84, 1984

Between 1940 and 1945, Rivers was a jazz saxophonist in New York and studied at the Julliard School of Music until 1946. He became interested in painting in 1945, which he subsequently studied in New York until 1951. He had an affinity for Abstract Expressionism early on and later also made sculptures. In the 1960s and 1970s, he produced works in various materials in Paris and London, also making videos and films. In 1964 and 1968, Rivers achieved international renown due to his participation in documenta.

17 AUGUST

Anna Ancher

1859–1935 | Painter | Denmark

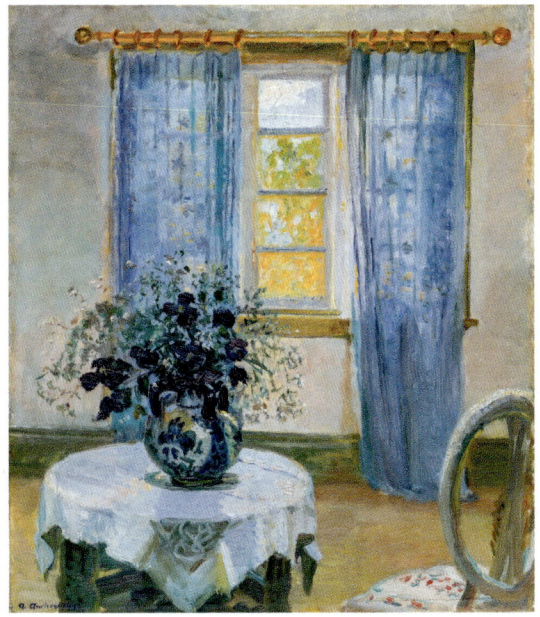

Interior with Clematis, 1913

After her apprenticeship in Copenhagen, Ancher retreated to the quiet and picturesque idyll of her birthplace in Skagen, where she married and lived until her death. Other painters working alongside her in the Skagen artist colony introduced *plein-air* painting to Danish art history. Ancher preferred interiors, which reflect her subtle sense of colour and use of lighting. She also made portraits and pictures depicting scenes of rural labour. Departing from French Impressionism, Ancher brought Danish painting into the modern era.

18 AUGUST

Gustave Caillebotte

1848–1894 | Painter | France

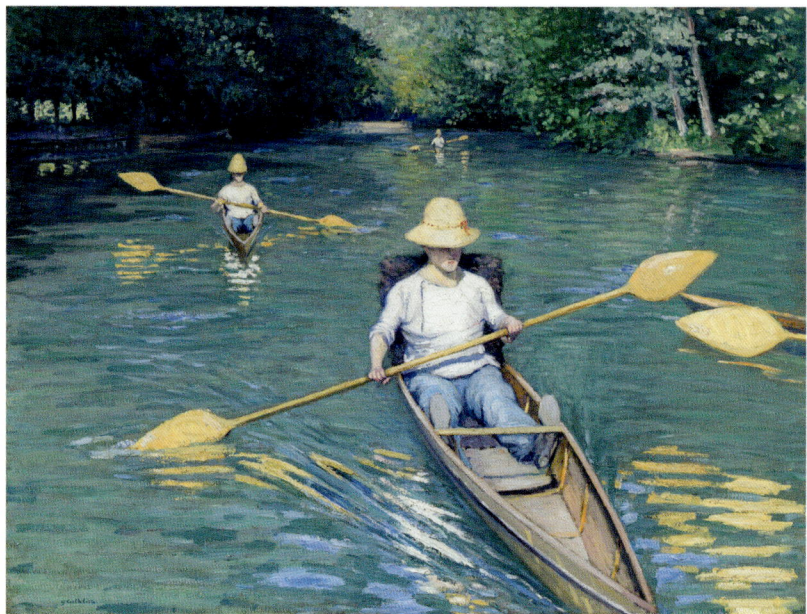

Skiffs, 1877

The scion of a prosperous family, Caillebotte studied in Paris and inherited an estate from his father. Working there until 1879, he painted around eighty works, including street scenes, landscapes and portraits in the style of Impressionism. Due to his financial independence, the painter became an important patron of the Impressionists, whose works he collected. He was also a passionate sailor and began building boats professionally in the 1880s. A large part of his significant collection is now part of the Musée d'Orsay in Paris.

Bernd Becher

1931–2007 | Photographer | Germany

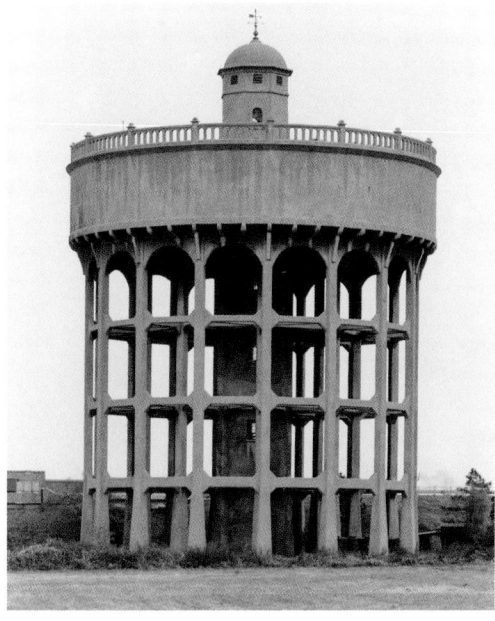

Water Tower, Newton le Willows, GB, 1966

Together with his wife, Hilla, Becher created an extensive body of black-and-white photographs, focusing on subjects such as half-timbered houses and industrial buildings, some of which would soon be lost to time. The Bechers' typological approach and their intensive search for subjects created a culturally important body of documentary photographs that earned them international recognition and numerous awards. From 1976, Bernd Becher was professor of photography at the Art Academy in Düsseldorf, where he influenced later generations of leading photographers including Andreas Gursky, Thomas Struth and Candida Höfer.

20 AUGUST

Jean-Baptiste Greuze

1725–1805 | Painter | France

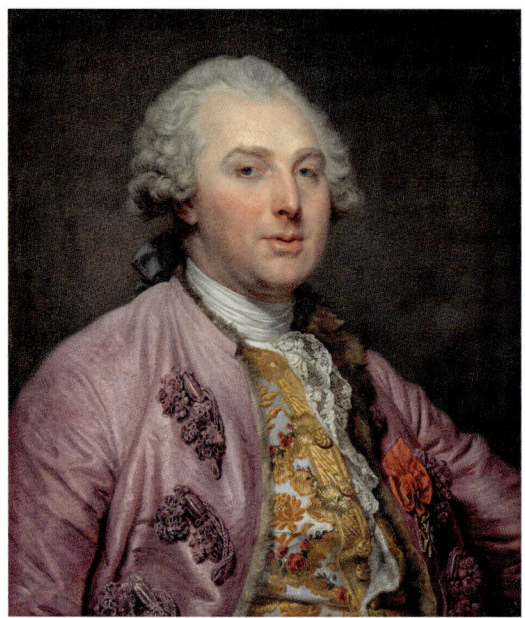

Charles Claude de Flahaut (1730–1809), Comte d'Angiviller, 1763

Greuze began studying in Paris in 1750, spending two years in Italy and returning to the city on the Seine to work as a painter in 1757. For his contemporaries, however, his art soon went out of style due to its strong affinity to the Rococo. His pictures primarily feature bourgeois scenes and depictions of young women. On account of his speculation with assignats and in the wake of the French Revolution, the painter lost everything he owned and died in bitter poverty in Paris.

21 AUGUST

Jacques Lipchitz

1891–1973 | Sculptor | Lithuania, France, United States

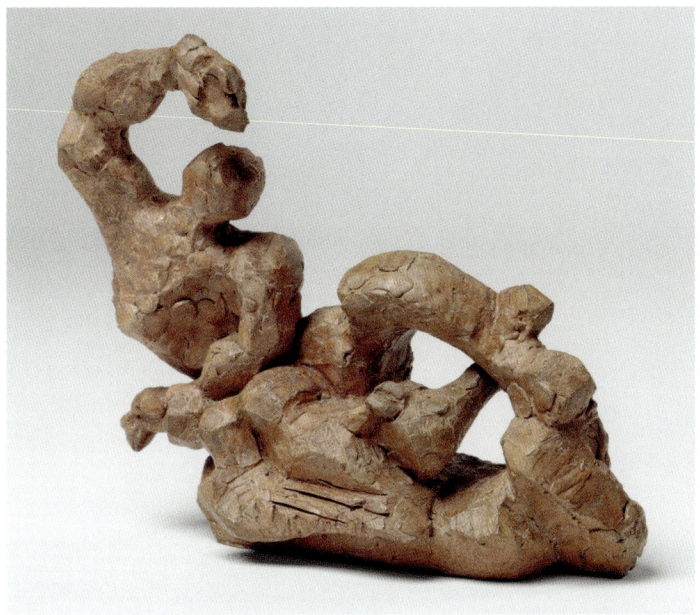

Study for Prometheus, 1936

One of the great protagonists of twentieth-century sculpture, Lipchitz was also one of the major sculpting draughtsmen. In 1909, he went to study art in Paris, where he became friends with artists such as Pablo Picasso and Amedeo Modigliani. Through 1920, he created significant Cubist sculptures. Later, his style became more organic and dynamically Baroque. One of his commissions was a monumental work for the Paris World's Fair. In 1941, he emigrated to New York, where a studio fire in 1952 destroyed many of his works. Exhibitions and honours testify to his global fame.

22 AUGUST

Allan Kaprow

1927–2006 | Artist | United States

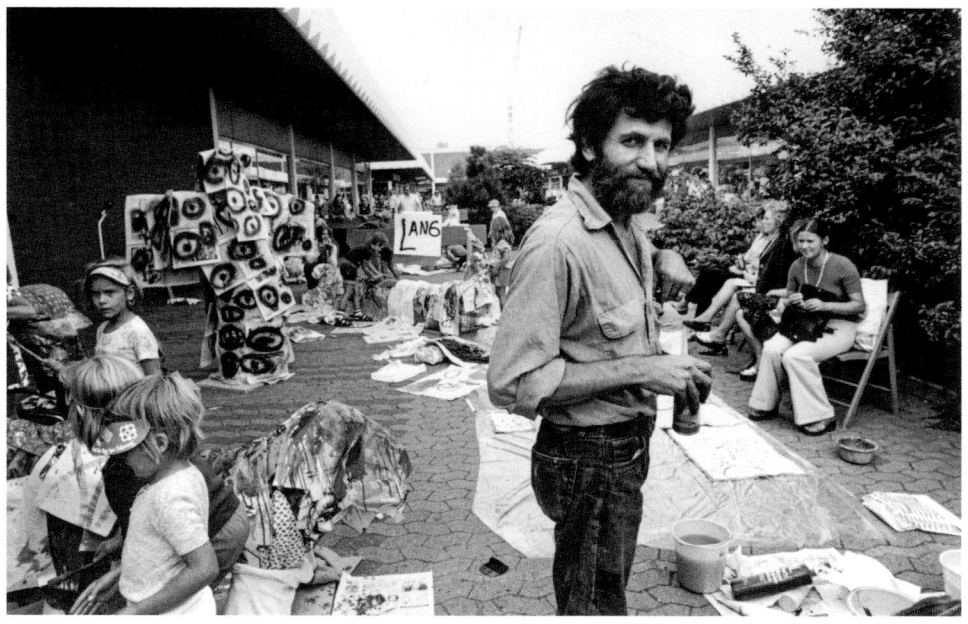

Portrait of Allan Kaprow, 1971

As a student in New York, Kaprow studied composition, among other things, with John Cage, and in 1958 he coined the art term *Happening*, which he also expounded in art-theoretical texts. His action art was open to temporal processes, randomness and improvisation, and assembled heterogeneous materials in a collage-like way. Starting in 1958, Kaprow staged more than 250 Happenings at important institutions around the globe.

23 AUGUST

Graham Sutherland

1903–1980 | Painter | Great Britain

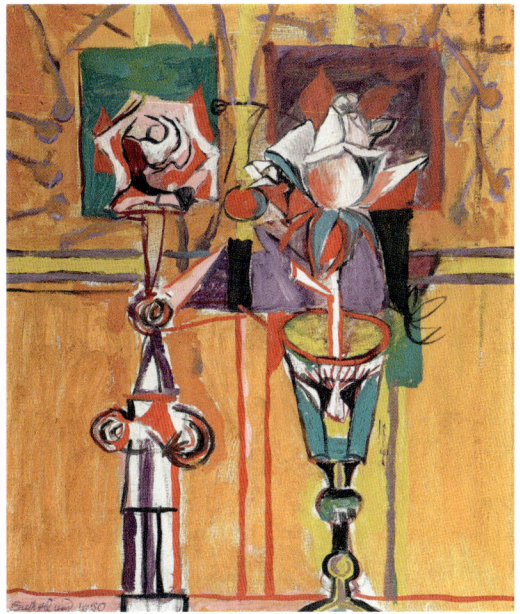

Roses, 1950

Trained in London in graphic techniques, Sutherland began painting in 1935. He primarily produced landscapes in an abstract Surrealist style that is simultaneously poetic and magical. After the Second World War, he became friends with Francis Bacon, who influenced him, and made pictures with thorn patterns of fantastic malignancy. He later lived in the South of France, where he painted brighter pictures that nevertheless always have something uncanny about them. Portraits, including some of celebrities, and many exhibitions made Sutherland internationally famous.

24 AUGUST

Dorothea Tanning

1910–2012 | Painter, sculptor and writer | United States

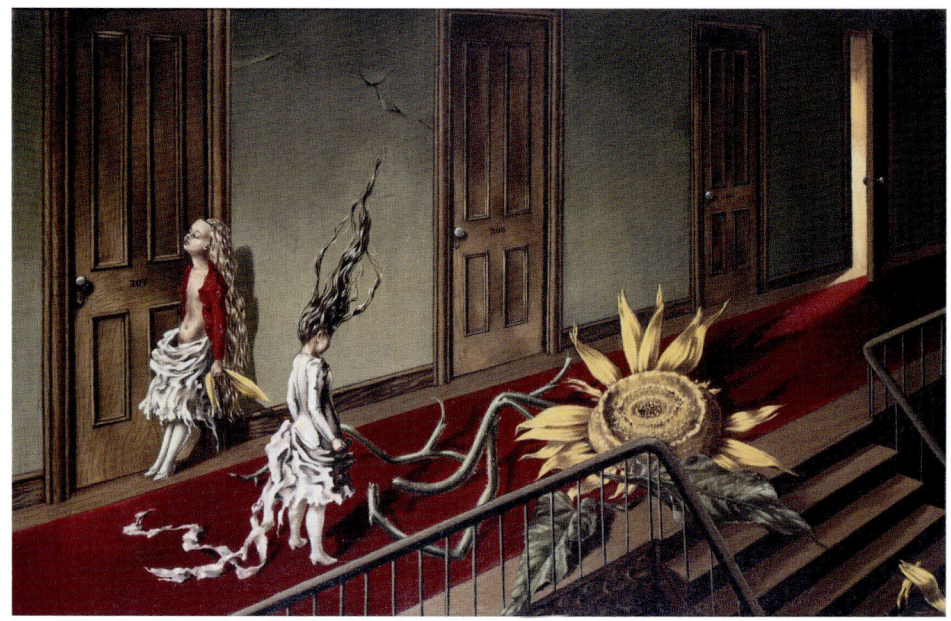

A Little Night Music, 1943

This self-taught artist first experienced the art of Dada and Surrealism in New York in 1936. In 1946, she married the famous painter Max Ernst, with whom she lived in Arizona until 1953. After that, the couple moved to Paris and, in 1963, to the South of France. Tanning returned to New York after Ernst's death. She published poems, several books and created stage sets for ballet and theatre. Tanning painted Surrealist works for many years before she shifted to a new style, which is described as "prismatic", in 1955. Her paintings were included in international exhibitions early on.

25 AUGUST

Rufino Tamayo

1899–1991 | Painter | Mexico

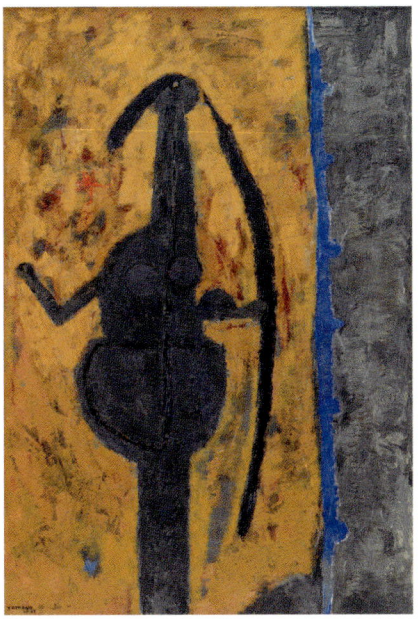

Woman in Grey, 1959

Tamayo attended the Art Academy in Mexico City in 1917. His symbolic, figurative style of painting was greatly influenced by French modernism, pre-Columbian art and traditions of Mexican folk art. He created important murals in Mexico City, even though he rejected the political themes of his famous fellow painters, the Mexican Muralists. He moved to New York in 1938, travelling to Europe in 1950, where he paid an extended visit to Paris, before returning to Mexico in 1959. International exhibitions secured the renown of this painter, to whom a museum has been devoted since 1981.

26 AUGUST

Man Ray

1890–1976 | Photographer, film director, etc. | United States

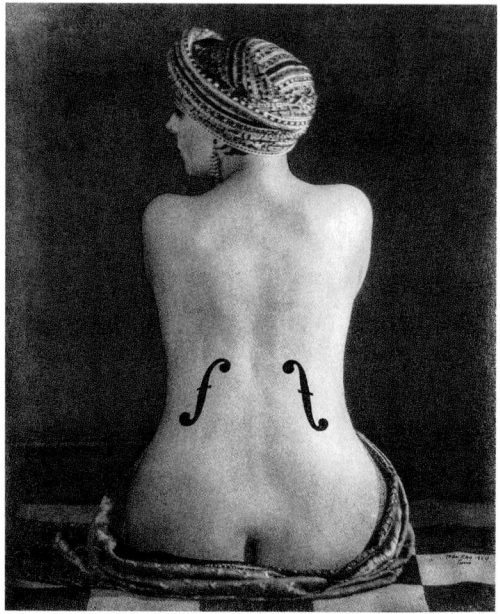

Le Violon d'Ingres, 1924

With his vast oeuvre of photographs, films, paintings and objects, Man Ray was one of the twentieth century's most versatile artists. His friendship with Marcel Duchamp was decisive for him in 1915. Under Duchamp's influence, he began doing technical experiments and making sculptural assemblages using photography and film. He was the only major American artist to take up the ideas of Dada. One of his most famous and most sensual photos is *Le Violon d'Ingres*, featuring the naked back of a woman to which he has added two *f*-holes of a stringed instrument.

27 AUGUST

Edward Burne-Jones

1833–1898 | Painter | Great Britain

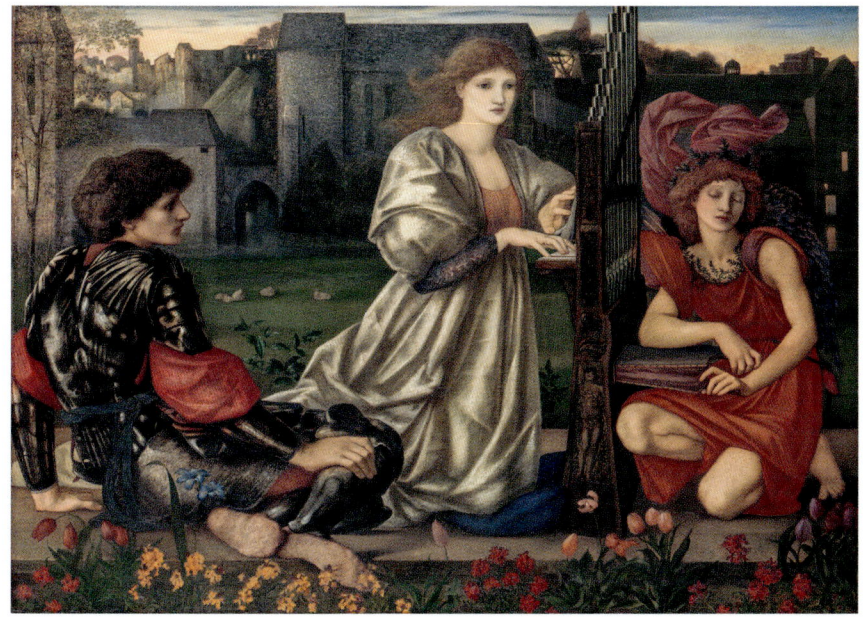

The Love Song, 1868–1877

This British painter was one of the foremost representatives of the Pre-Raphaelites and a close friend of the influential all-round artist William Morris. In 1861, he was appointed designer for glass painting in the Morris workshops and later designed tapestries. In addition to painting, ceramic and book illumination were included in his artistic spectrum. Burne-Jones influenced both French Symbolism and Art Nouveau. His paintings and works on paper are in the collections of numerous international museums.

_____

_____

_____

_____

28 AUGUST

Jean-Auguste Ingres

1780–1867 | Painter and draughtsman | France

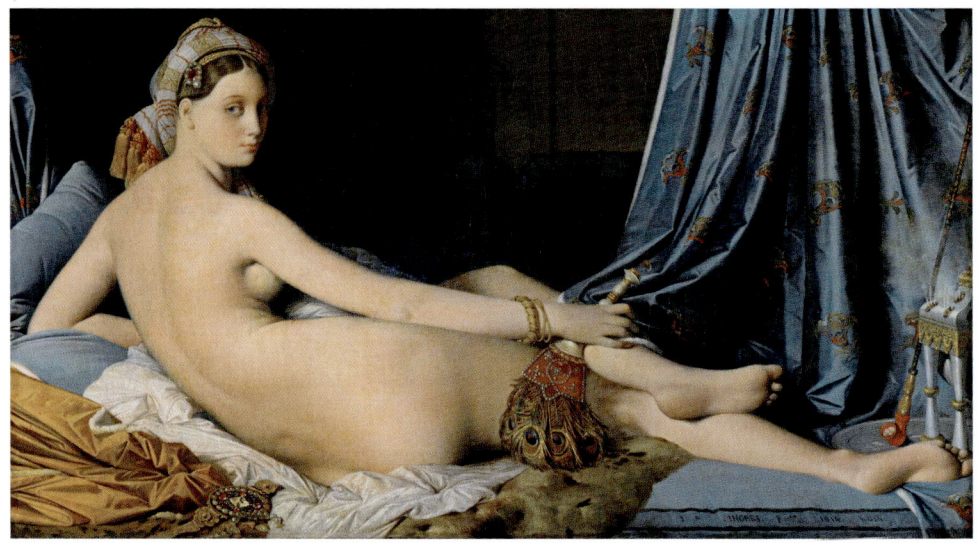

La Grande Odalisque, 1814

In 1806, the foremost painter and draughtsman of French Neoclassicism went to Rome, where he lived for nearly twenty years. He enjoyed wide acclaim in France after 1824. Having returned to Rome in the meantime, he later became the director of the Art Academy in Paris. His specialties were history paintings, portraits and nudes. One of his most famous paintings is the tondo *The Turkish Bath*. Ingres exercised a great influence on many artists both contemporary and later. One of the great draughtsmen of the nineteenth century, he founded a museum in Montauban that is dedicated to his work.

29 AUGUST

Jacques-Louis David

1748–1825 | History painter | France

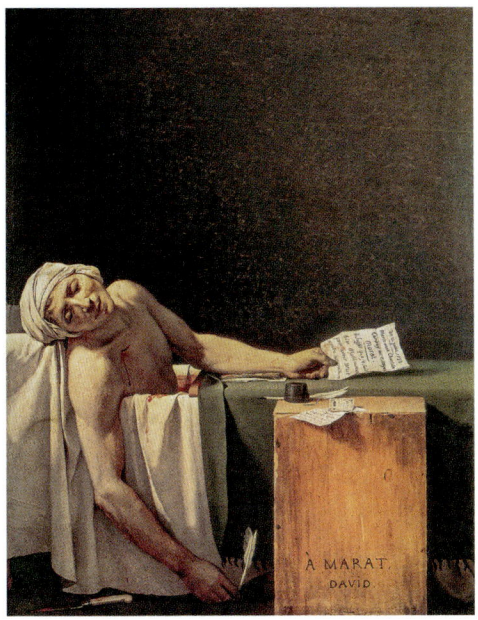

The Death of Marat, 1793

David was the greatest and most influential French history painter of Neoclassicism. In 1774, he travelled to Italy, where, during a years-long sojourn in Rome, he studied antiquity and the Italian Renaissance masters. He painted his famous *Oath of the Horatii* in 1784. David later took part in the French Revolution as a resolute republican. In 1793, he painted one of his most famous pictures, *The Death of Marat*, showing the subject as a political martyr. He produced many portraits and battle paintings under Napoleon. After the latter's downfall, David moved to Brussels, where he died in 1825.

30 AUGUST

Helen Levitt

1913–2009 | Photographer and filmmaker | United States

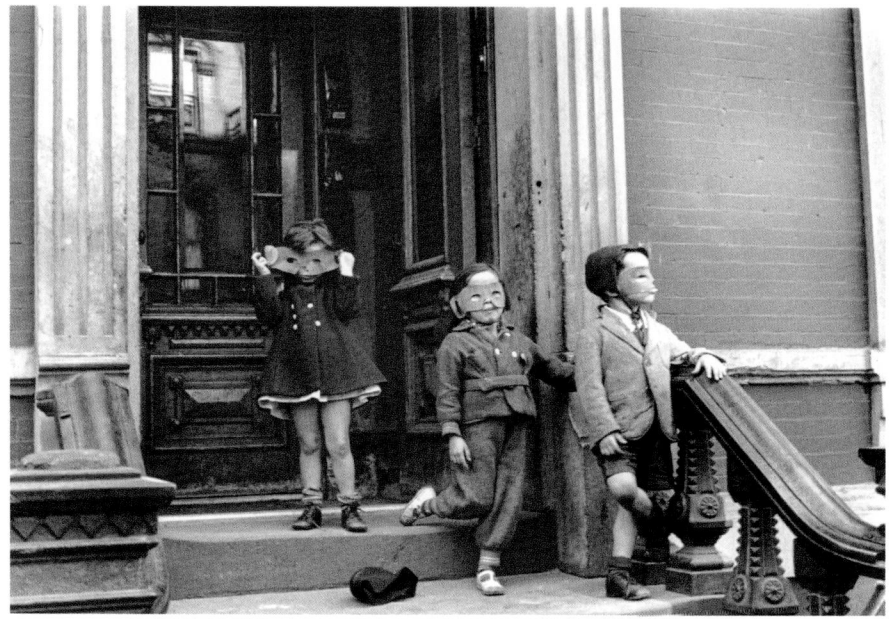

New York City, 1940

As a major American photographer, Levitt was one of the most important protagonists of New York street photography. Her preferred subjects were children playing in the street and everyday life in poorer city neighbourhoods. In 1938, she became Walker Evans's assistant. In 1941, following a trip to Mexico, she began to work as a film editor under Luis Buñuel. Levitt later made Oscar-nominated documentaries and movie scripts. She had exhibitions around the globe during her lifetime and died aged ninety-five in New York.

31 AUGUST

Max Peiffer Watenphul

1896–1976 | Painter | Germany

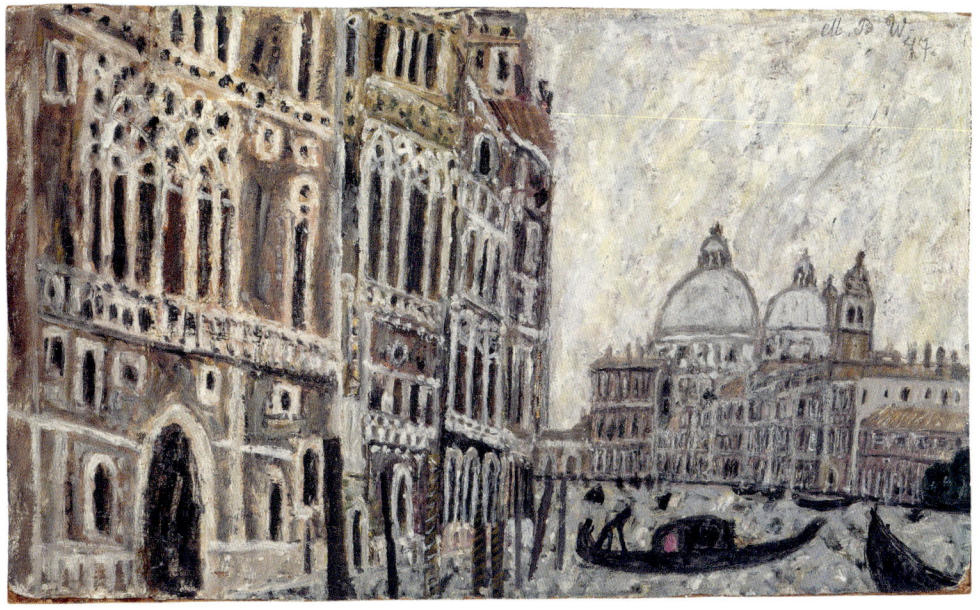

Grand Canal with View of Santa Maria della Salute in Venice, 1947

In 1919, after studying law, Peiffer Watenphul decided to become a painter. He joined the Bauhaus in Weimar, where he became friends with the likes of Oskar Schlemmer and Wassily Kandinsky. His life was shaped by extensive travels to places such as Italy and Mexico. For political reasons, he relocated to Italy in 1937. He later returned to Germany for a period, before moving to Vienna and Salzburg, spending twelve years in Venice and settling in Rome in 1958. His Italian landscapes, views of Venice and still lifes became well known through many exhibitions. He was a maverick with a distinctive style.

1 SEPTEMBER

Séraphine Louis

1864–1942 | Painter | France

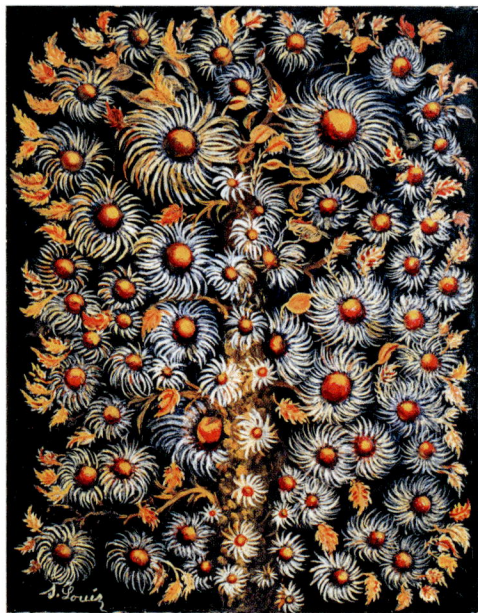

Daisies, c. 1925–1927

Following the early deaths of her parents, Louis was obliged to earn her living as a shepherd and cleaner in Senlis, which is why she was often called "Séraphine de Senlis". She painted mystical, religious pictures and was discovered in 1912 by the German critic Wilhelm Uhde, who supported her. Her "naive" paintings, mostly of which feature abstract floral patterns, made her one of the best-known French artists of this genre. Delusions – presumably provoked by toxic painting materials – forced her into an institution in 1932. Works by Louis can be seen in both French and German museums.

2 SEPTEMBER

Helene Funke

1869–1957 | Painter and graphic artist | Germany, Austria

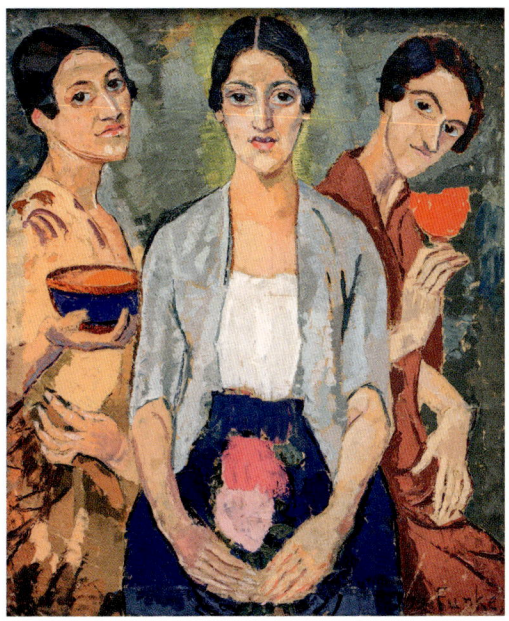

Three Girls, 1915

In 1899, Funke moved from Chemnitz to Munich, where she studied at the Ladies' Academy. From 1904, she spent a few years living in Paris, discovering an enthusiasm for the Fauves Henri Matisse and André Derain. From then on, her pictures portraying women burst with colour and were shown in many exhibitions from 1909. In 1913, Funke moved to Vienna, where she celebrated successes as an avant-gardist. In 1928, she was the second woman in history to receive the Austrian State Prize. Largely forgotten after the war, Funke died in 1957. She was rediscovered in the late 1990s.

3 SEPTEMBER

Oskar Schlemmer

1888–1943 | Painter, sculptor and set designer | Germany

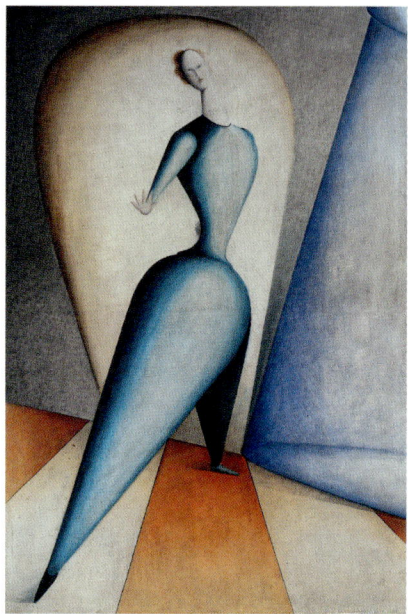

The Dancer (The Gesture), 1922

A master at the Bauhaus in Weimar from 1920, Schlemmer was among the influential German artists of the first half of the twentieth century. All his efforts were directed at figural painting, with the human figure as the measure of all things. He valued working on the Bauhaus Theatre, which he conceived of as an art space. From the spatial experience of a dancer – which he himself was – he understood the figure in relation to space. In the 1920s, he completed his *Triadic Ballet*, designed sets and costumes and had major exhibitions. His emotional suffering increased during the Nazi period.

4 SEPTEMBER

Caspar David Friedrich

1774–1840 | Painter and draughtsman | Germany

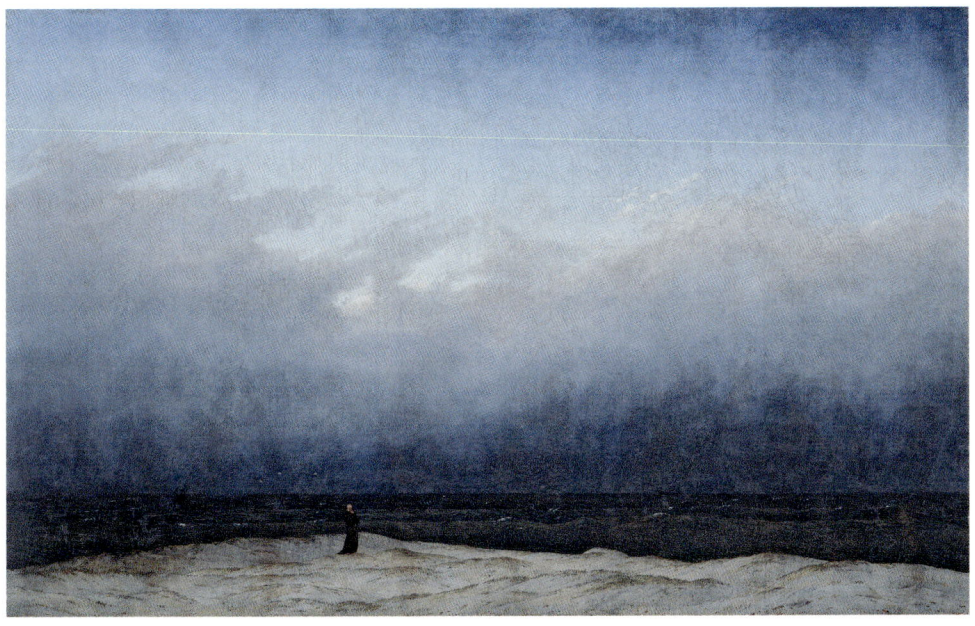

Monk by the Sea, c. 1808–1810

Friedrich was one of the great artists of early Romanticism, fascinating many generations and, particularly due to international exhibitions in recent times, becoming Germany's second best-known painter after Albrecht Dürer. With its complex contrasts, interpreting his art is a contentious matter; themes of nature and religion are central. Friedrich broke with the traditions of landscape painting and instead made "constructed" paintings, which can be read as allegories of loneliness and death, and an expression of his hope for redemption.

5 SEPTEMBER

Christian Boltanski

1944–2021 | Artist | France

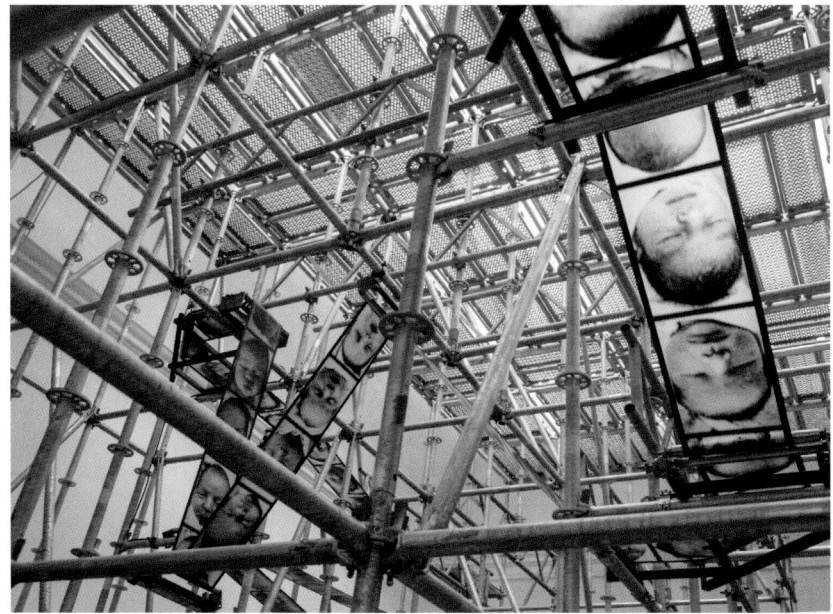

Chance, 2011

For Boltanski, whose father was a Jewish Ukrainian, the memory of the Holocaust was formative. Memory, alongside transience and death, is one of the key themes of his oeuvre. He created vitrines containing objects to reconstruct his own past in the 1960s. Later, photography became important in his work, and he made inventory installations containing personal items owned by other people. Many international presentations earned Boltanski worldwide fame and distinctions.

6 SEPTEMBER

Grandma Moses

1860–1961 | Painter and illustrator | United States

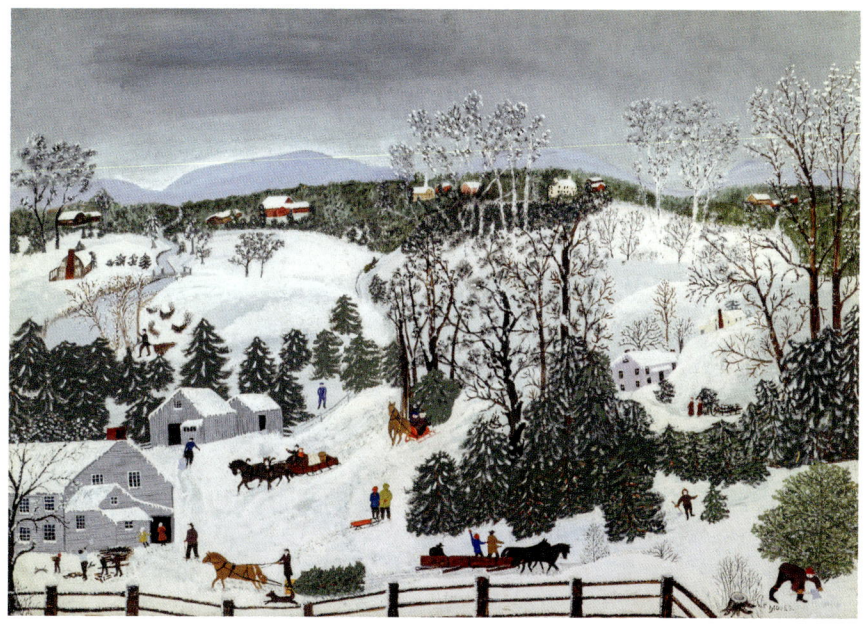

Out for Christmas Trees, 1946

Anna Mary Robertson, alias Grandma Moses, left her parents' farm at the age of twelve and worked as a maid. Since long daily chores were the focal point of her life, she used her talent solely for decorating the family home. She did not begin painting scenes of rural North American life in her "naive" style until the age of seventy-five. With the aid of a collector, three of her pictures were exhibited at the Museum of Modern Art in New York. After 1940, her fame began to grow. She died at the age of 101, after Nelson Rockefeller had declared her one hundredth birthday Grandma Moses Day.

7 SEPTEMBER

Maria Lassnig

1919–2014 | Painter, graphic artist and media artist | Austria

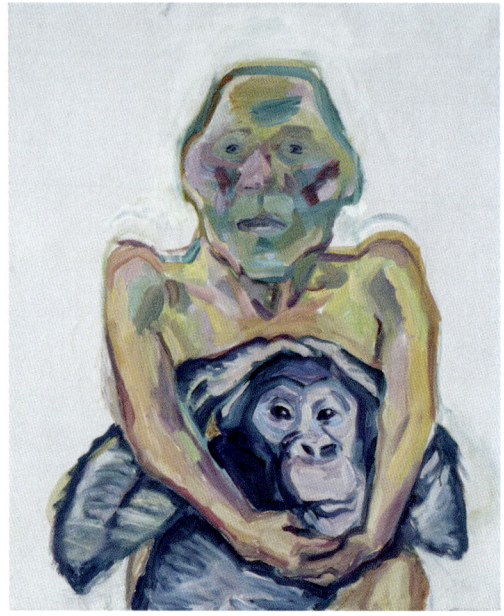

Self-Portrait with Monkey (Beloved Forefathers), 2001

Lassnig only first came to international notice through exhibitions and awards in the 1980s. After Surrealistic beginnings, she co-established Art Informel in Austria with her friend Arnulf Rainer. In the 1960s, Lassnig lived in Paris, and between 1968 and 1980, she was in New York, where she made her first films. She was subsequently a professor in Vienna. Her subject was the portrayal of corporeality, its perceptions and sensations. With her concept of "body awareness", she was a precursor to feminist body art and Viennese Actionism.

8 SEPTEMBER

Sol LeWitt

1928–2007 | Artist | United States

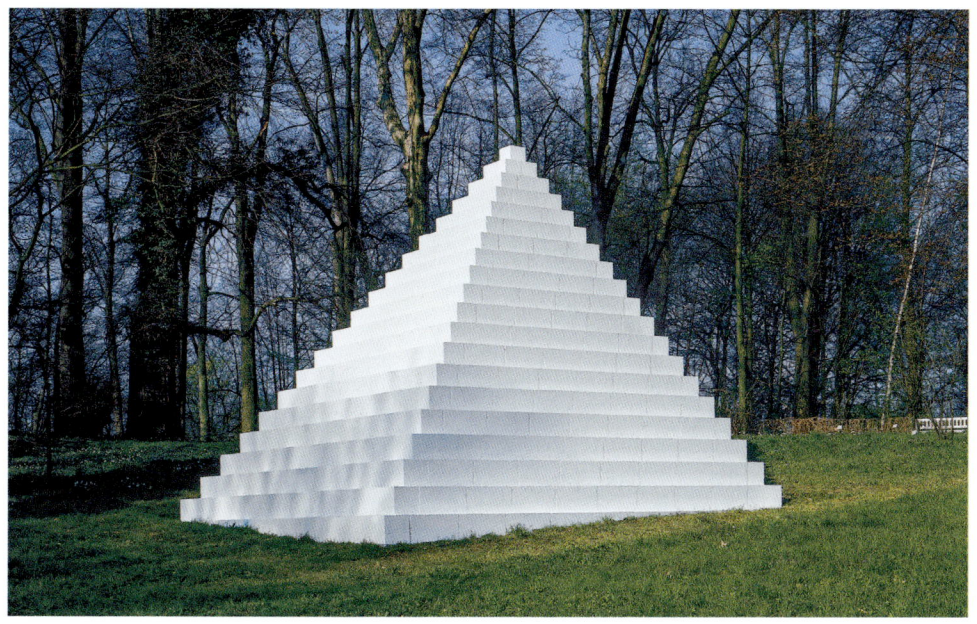

White Pyramid, Münster, Germany, 1987/1988

One of the most internationally important artists of Minimalism, LeWitt also shaped Conceptual Art. In the 1960s, he worked at the Museum of Modern Art in New York, where he encountered many leading artists. Publishing his theory in 1967, he defined his concept as "notional", as opposed to "perceptual art". Taking inspiration from Constructivism and concepts of Dutch De Stijl, he experimented with grid structures, patterns of bars and stringent architectonic structures in wood and metal. He made large, colourful wall drawings from 1968.

9 SEPTEMBER

Marianne von Werefkin

1860–1938 | Painter | Russia

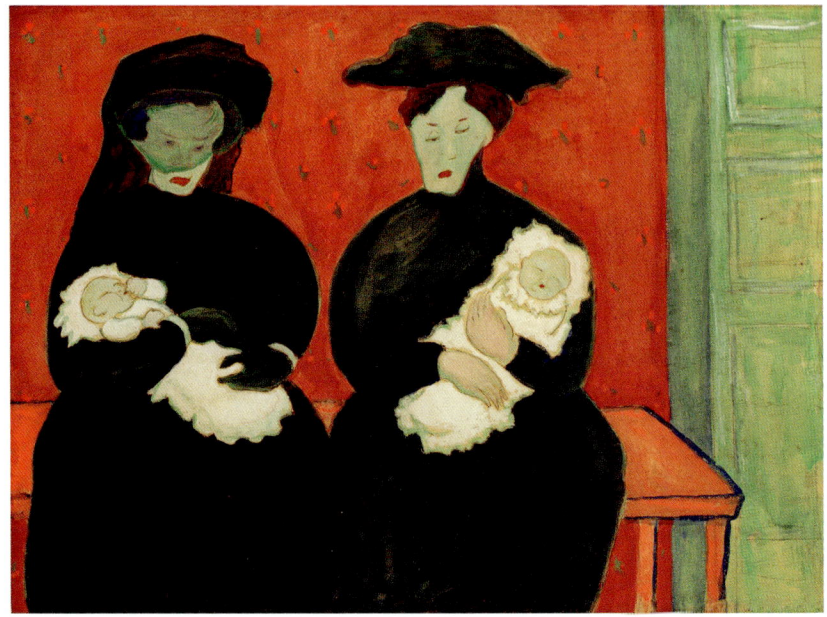

Twins, 1909

At age twenty, Werefkin became a private student under the prominent Russian Realist Ilya Repin. She met Alexej von Jawlensky, whom she lived with for many years, first in Moscow and later in Munich. She made her first Expressionistic paintings in 1907, and kept company with Wassily Kandinsky, Gabriele Münter and Franz Marc. Shortly before the outbreak of the First World War, Werefkin and Jawlensky moved to Switzerland. After they separated, she lived in Ascona from 1921. Her estate is managed by the Fondazione Marianne Werefkin in Ascona.

10 SEPTEMBER

Manina Tischler

1918–2010 | Painter | Austria

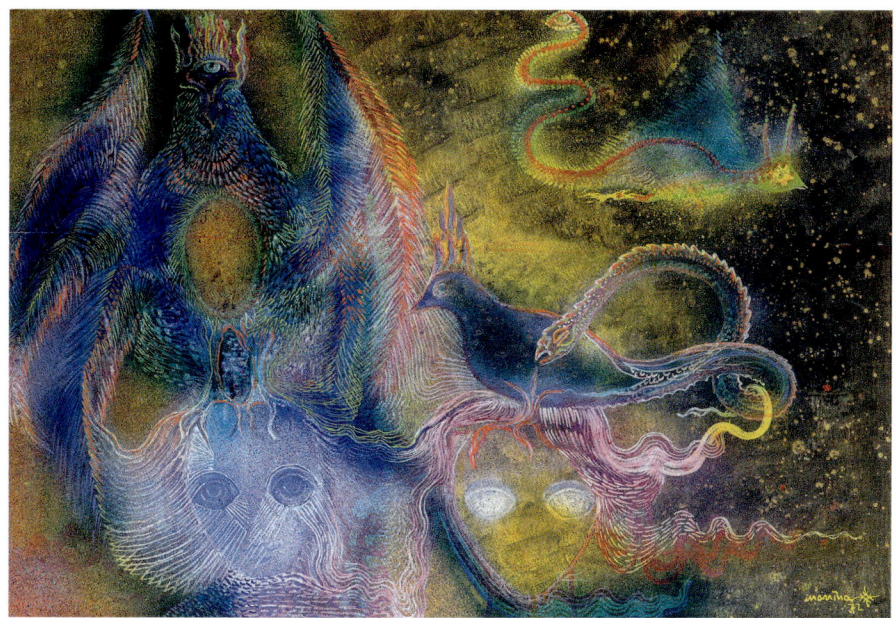

Phoenix, 1972

When she was ten, Tischler and her parents moved from Vienna to Paris, where she frequented artist circles. She married, and the couple emigrated to the United States in 1938. In the 1940s, after training as a sculptor, Tischler devoted herself to painting and drawing. Following her divorce, she lived in New York; she subsequently moved to London and then Venice. Her poetic, magically Surrealist pictures earned her renown through numerous international exhibitions. Her late work includes collages as well as jewellery pieces made of copper and colourful stones.

11 SEPTEMBER

Nan Goldin

Born 1953 | Photographer | United States

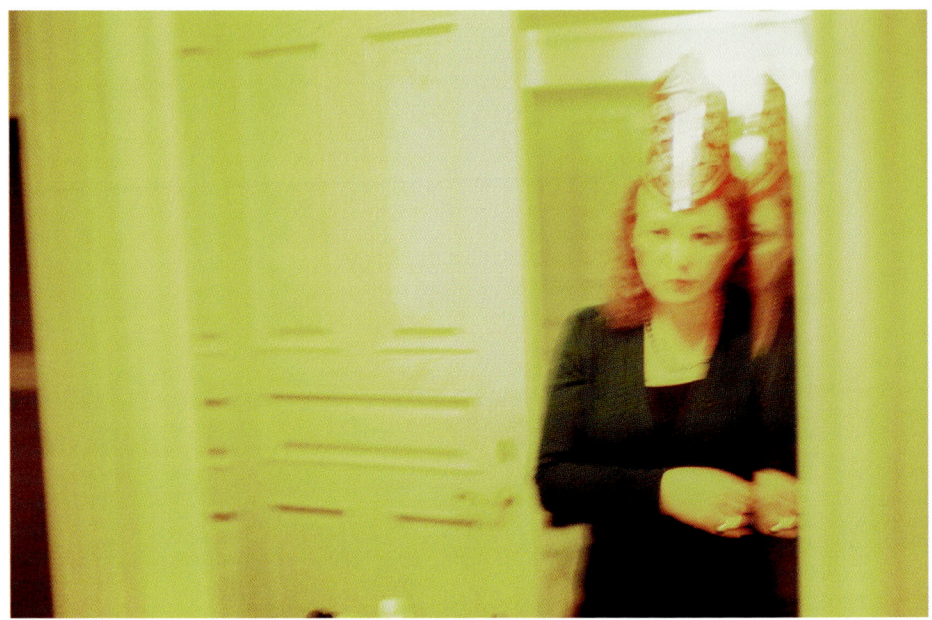

Self-Portrait on New Year's Eve, Malibu, California, 2006

One of the most important and influential artists of her generation, Goldin has revolutionized the art of photography through her frank and deeply personal portraiture.
Over the last forty-five years, Goldin has created some of the most indelible images
of the twentieth and twenty-first centuries. Since the 1970s, her work has explored
notions of gender and definitions of normality. By documenting her life and the lives
of the friends who surround her, Goldin gives a voice and visibility to her communities.
In the 1980s these images of her "extended family" became the subject of her seminal
slide show and first book *The Ballad of Sexual Dependency*.

12 SEPTEMBER

Richard Paul Lohse

1902–1988 | Painter and graphic artist | Switzerland

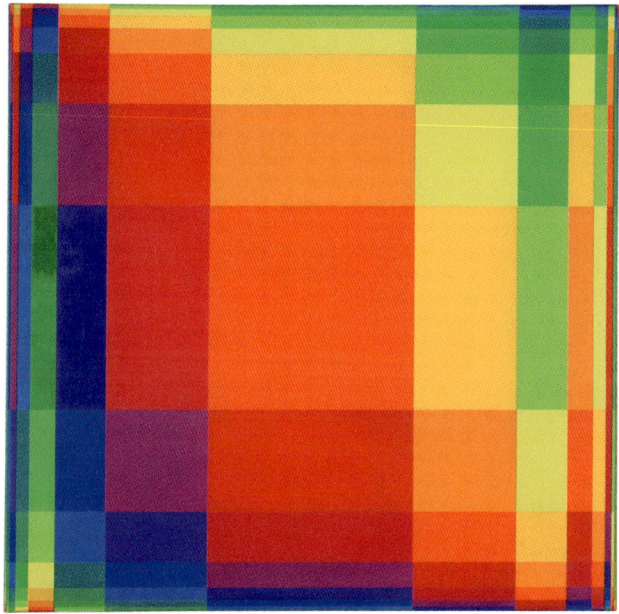

15 Systematic Colour Rows with Red Centre, 1950–1967

Lohse was the co-founder of an avant-gardist union of Swiss modern artists. Politically engaged as an anti-Fascist during the Second World War, Lohse began to explore Concrete Art as an autodidact in the 1940s. His pictures feature stringently structured horizontal and vertical colour fields based on a mathematical, constructivist principle of arrangement. Lohse achieved international fame through his twofold participation in documenta. His oeuvre is part of the collections of many Swiss museums, and the Lohse Foundation in Zürich has promoted and documented it since 1988.

13 SEPTEMBER

Peter Lely

1618–1680 | Painter | Germany, Great Britain

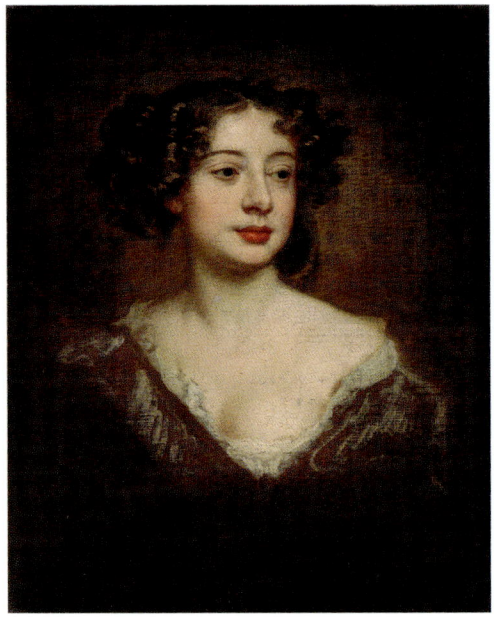

Study for a Portrait of a Woman, 1670s

Lely – who was based in London from 1647 – quickly became known for his portraits in the style of the famous Dutch painter Anthony van Dyck. He advanced to one of the leading portrait painters during the era of Oliver Cromwell and his successors. King Charles II appointed him court painter in 1661. During that period he made series of likenesses, including of various court ladies under the title *The Windsor Beauties*. Lely was dubbed a knight bachelor one year before his death in 1680.

14 SEPTEMBER

Jacob Philipp Hackert

1737–1807 | Landscape painter | Germany

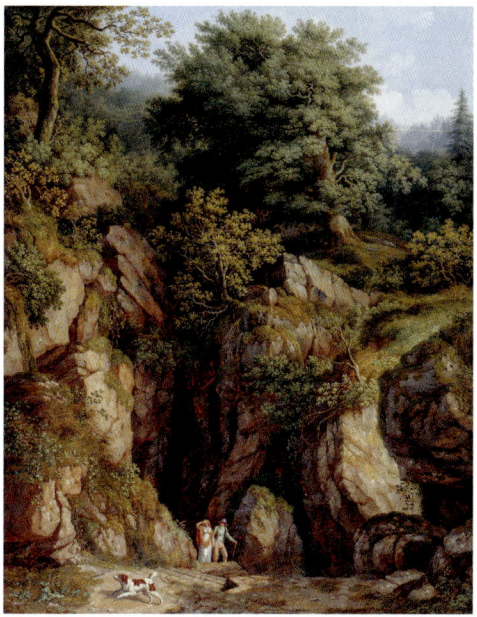

Cave of St Francis, 1801

From 1765, Hackert lived in Paris, where he was influenced by painters such as Joseph Vernet. In 1768, he went to Rome and Naples, travelling throughout Italy, where he soon became known as a landscape painter and received many commissions from European aristocracy. As court painter to the king of Naples, he met Johann Wolfgang von Goethe in 1786; he gave drawing lessons to the German poet, who wrote his biography in 1811. Hackert later lived in Florence. With his true-to-detail *vedute* and paintings depicting volcano eruptions of Vesuvius and Etna, he was the most famous landscape painter of early Neoclassicism.

15 SEPTEMBER

Jean Arp

1886–1966 | Painter, graphic artist and sculptor | Germany, France

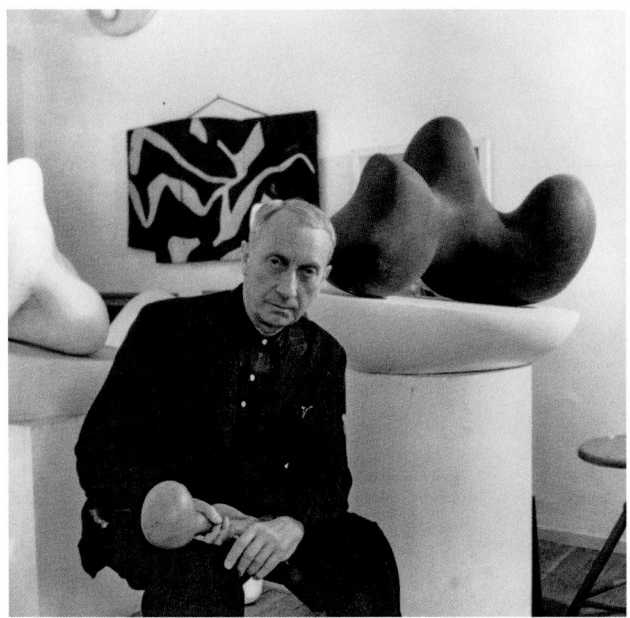

Jean Arp (in His Studio in Meudon, 1948), 1948

Arp was one of the leading figures of the artistic and literary movement Dada, which he co-founded in Zürich in 1916. That marked the start of his friendship with the artist Sophie Taeuber, whom he married in 1922 and with whom he moved to the Paris region in 1926, and after that to Grasse, where he produced poems and works on paper. In 1942, Arp and his wife fled from the German *Wehrmacht* to Switzerland. Arp's international fame grew from the 1950s: the biomorphic shapes of his sculptures, reliefs and drawings are distinctive.

16 SEPTEMBER

Maqbool Fida Husain

1915–2011 | Painter | India

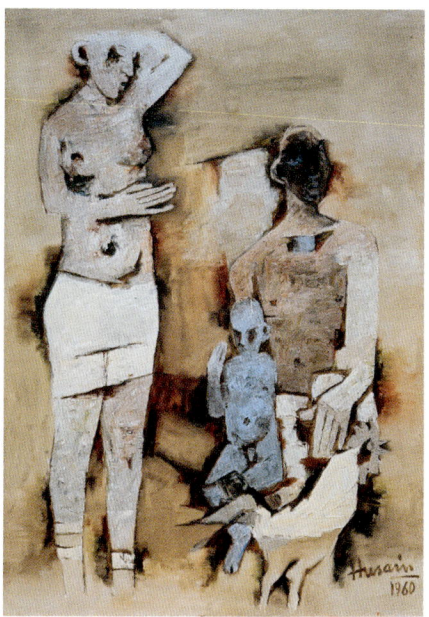

Couple with Small Child, 1960

Husain emerged in the 1940s as one of the internationally best-known and highest-earning Indian painters of the twentieth century and subsequently had exhibitions in Europe and America. In a modified Cubist style, he explored subject matter including British colonial rule and motifs from Indian life. He won the Golden Bear for a filmed documentary at the Berlinale in Berlin in 1967. A controversy steered by nationalists escalated around early pictures of naked Hindu divinities, prompting Husain to move to London and later to Dubai.

17 SEPTEMBER

Anton Mauve

1838–1888 | Landscape painter | The Netherlands

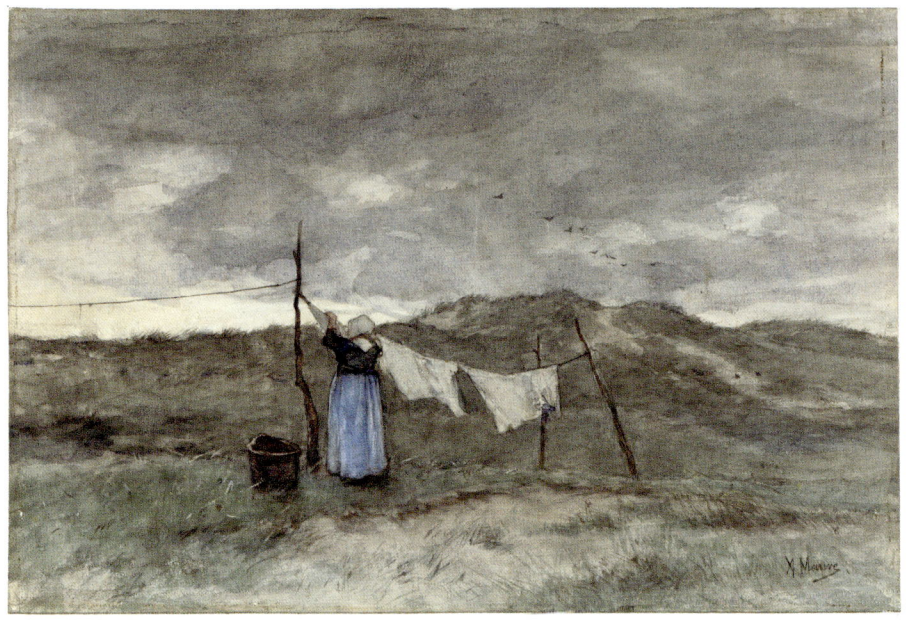

Clothesline in the Dunes, 1876

Mauve trained under an animal painter, who inspired his topical preference for sheep, cows and horses. He married a cousin of Vincent van Gogh and, in 1885, moved to Laren, where he co-founded the Laren School. Mauve was also successful in the United States with the landscapes he made there, featuring flocks of sheep. Later, he painted people at work and in the landscape. He was also an outstanding watercolourist. He gave van Gogh lessons in watercolour technique for a brief period in 1881. Mauve's works can be found in private and museum collections in the Netherlands and the United States.

18 SEPTEMBER

Augustin Pajou

1730–1809 | Sculptor | France

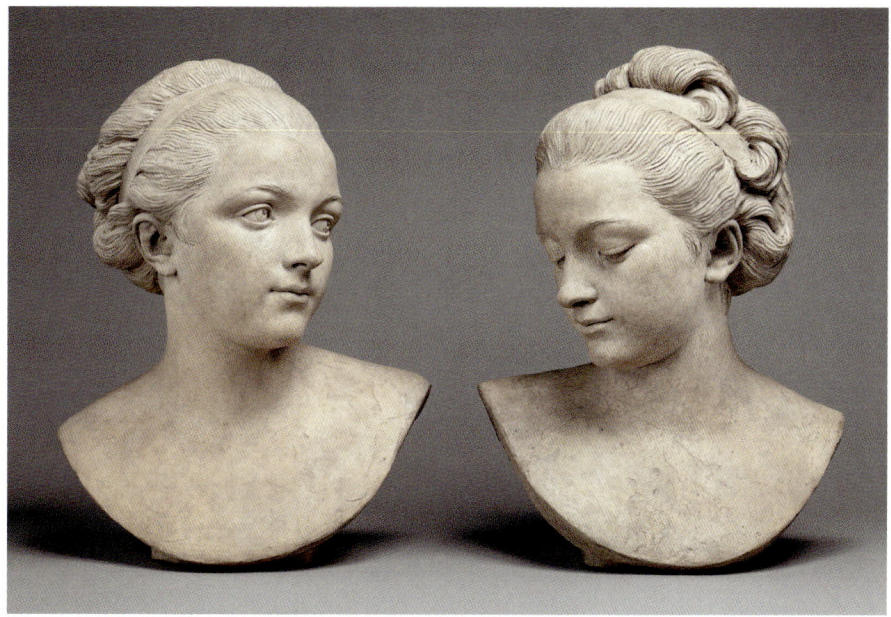

Ideal Female Heads, undated

As a youth, Pajou attended the Académie Royale in Paris and won the Prix de Rome at the age of eighteen. For several years, he lived in Italy, particularly in Rome, and spent the 1760s working on the façades of important public buildings in Paris, notably the Palais Royal and the Palais de Justice. In 1803, he was commissioned by Napoleon make copies of the two Medici lions that had stood on the steps to the Villa Medici in Rome until 1789. A prominent sculptor of French Neoclassicism, Pajou's works are located in major museums worldwide.

19 SEPTEMBER

Théodore Chassériau

1819–1856 | Painter | France

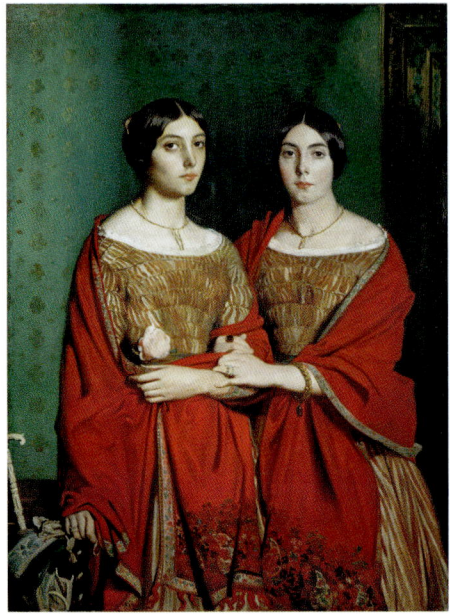

The Two Sisters, 1843

Chassériau was a major French Romantic and Neoclassicist painter, who had a considerable influence on painters of the subsequent generation. At the age of eleven he began studying under Jean-Auguste-Dominique Ingres, who inspired him as a painter of portraits and nudes. Chassériau's portraits were widely known at the time they were made. Later, the painter – especially with his painting featuring historical and exotic subjects – was influenced by Eugène Delacroix. Chassériau died prematurely at the age of thirty-seven. Recent international exhibitions have contributed to his posthumous renown.

20 SEPTEMBER

Julio González

1876–1942 | Sculptor | Spain

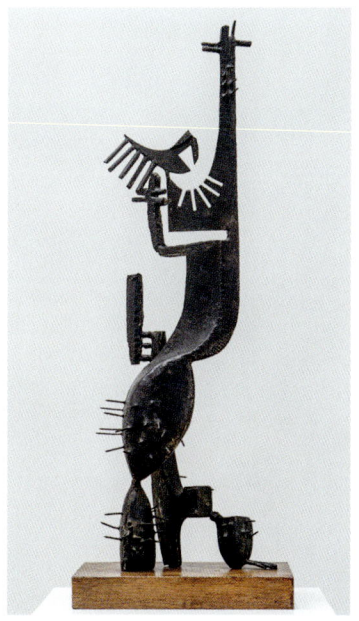

Homme cactus II (Cactus Woman), 1939/1940

Among the European sculptors, this Spanish iron sculptor was a protagonist of abstraction. Following a goldsmith apprenticeship under his father, he met major artists such as Pablo Picasso and Constantin Brâncuși in Paris in around 1900. In 1918, he learned welding at the car manufacturer Renault. With these manual skills, he embarked on his path as the "first master of the torch", initially still figurative and later increasingly abstract. A mutually fruitful artistic relationship arose with Picasso. In the 1930s and 1940s, Gonzales made his most important works, including *The Angel* or his *Cactus Man* series. Global exhibitions testify to his fame.

21 SEPTEMBER

Joseph Duplessis

1725–1802 | Painter | France

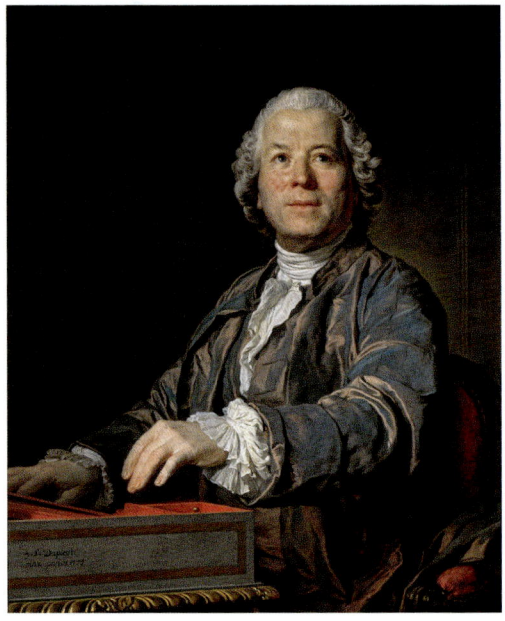

Christoph Willibald Gluck at the Spinet, 1775

After an apprenticeship, Duplessis spent four years in Rome, starting in 1744. He then went to Lyons and, from 1752, lived in Paris, where he decided to make his name as a portrait painter. Exhibitions ensued, and he was accepted in the Académie Royale in 1769. After his breakthrough in the Salon, he had many public commissions for portraits until the Revolution started, when the orders stopped. From 1796 until his death in 1802, he was the curator of the museum at the Palace of Versailles.

22 SEPTEMBER

Suzanne Valadon

1865–1938 | Painter | France

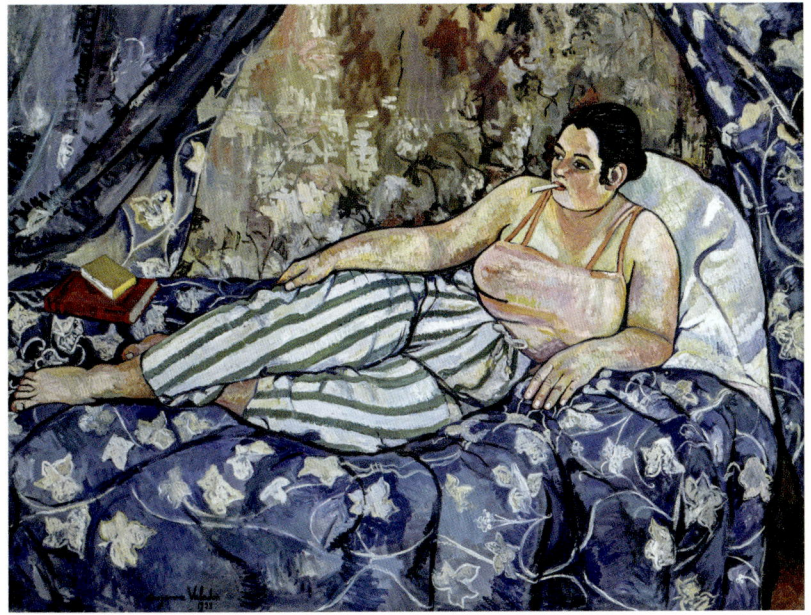

The Blue Room, 1923

Marie-Clémentine Valadon initially wanted to be a trapeze artist in the circus, but an accident prevented that. Instead, she modelled for famous painters such as Pierre-Auguste Renoir and Henri de Toulouse-Lautrec, who gave her the artist's name Suzanne. Valadon was self-taught as a draughtswoman and painter, creating works including nudes, portraits and floral paintings. She developed a striking formal language, in which various influences of the period merge: dark outlines and vibrant colours are characteristic of her pictures. Valadon produced an extensive oeuvre of paintings and drawings; many of her works are in the collections of international museums.

23 SEPTEMBER

Antoine-Louis Barye

1795–1875 | Sculptor | France

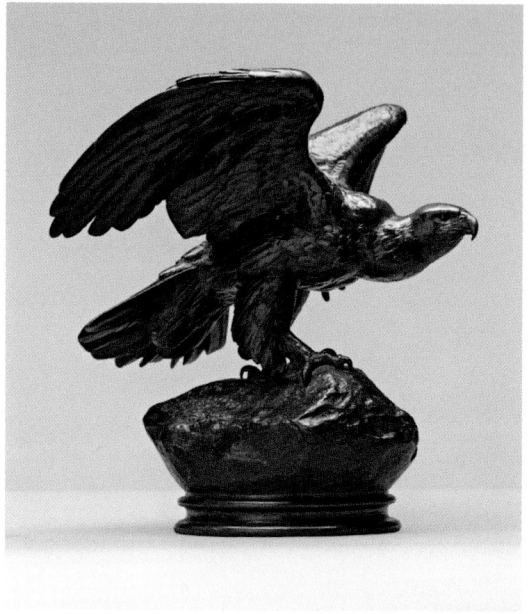

Eagle with Wings Outspread, c. 1847

In his youth, Barye learned metal engraving, chasing and artistic modelling; after successes in the Paris Salon, he was employed by a goldsmith and began animal studies. In 1831, his reputation as an animal sculptor was founded on his sculpture *Tiger Devouring a Gavial*. He made table settings featuring animal groups for the duke of Orléans. Both larger statues in bronze and smaller statuettes followed, alongside paintings and works on paper. Barye combined the realism of his portrayals, which were preceded by thorough studies in nature, with freedom and vigour of expression.

---

24 SEPTEMBER

Mark Rothko

1903–1970 | Painter | Russia, United States

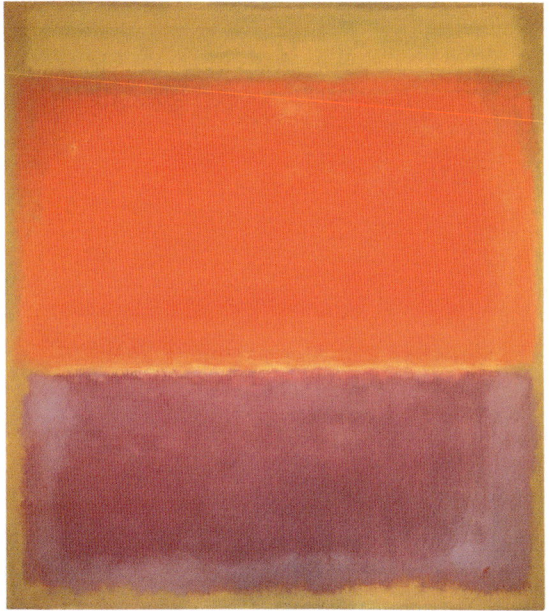

Untitled, 1960

Rothko is one of the most famous and highly priced American painters of the twentieth century. His Jewish family emigrated from Russia to America in 1913. Rothko lived in New York from 1923, had his first solo exhibition in 1933 and became increasingly successful from the 1950s onwards. Initially influenced by Surrealism, he developed his own style in 1950, in which colour fields that "breathe" together to create a magical, meditative aura. These are large-format oil paintings with stacked, monochrome colour planes, seeping into each other, which can be up to three metres in height.

25 SEPTEMBER

Théodore Géricault

1791–1824 | Painter, sculptor, draughtsman and lithographer | France

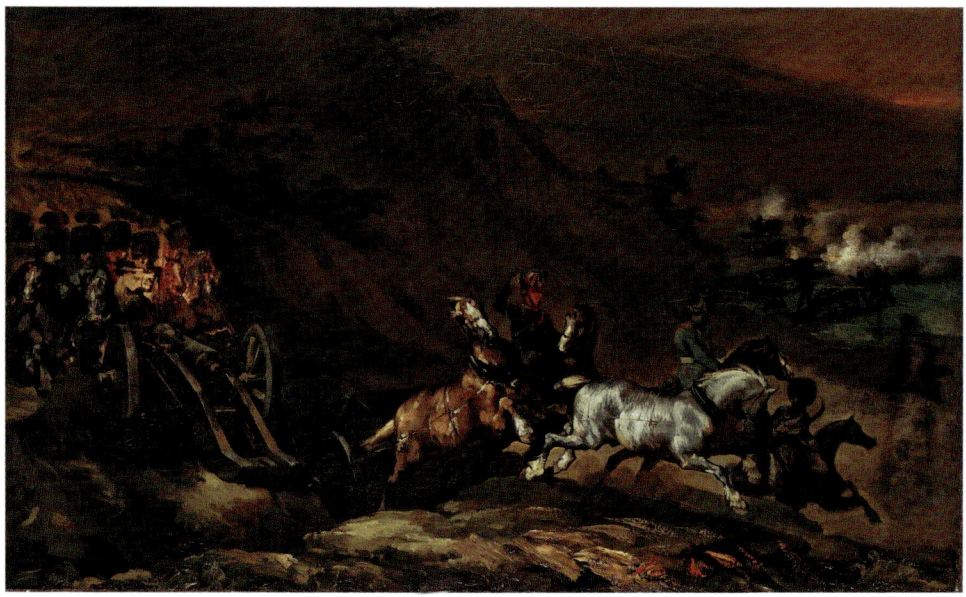

Irascible Artillery, c. 1814

Géricault became famous with *The Raft of the Medusa*, his painting shown in the Paris Salon in 1819. That *Scene of a Shipwreck* – its exhibition title – takes up a disturbing incident in 1816 that took the lives of many more than one hundred sailors. In spite of the Romantic character of the technique, a realistic precision dominates in the portrayal of the figures, which were based on many studies of injured and dead people in Parisian hospitals. Géricault's other subjects were equestrian scenes, landscapes and portraits. He died aged just thirty-three following a riding accident.

26 SEPTEMBER

Joel Shapiro

Born 1941 | Sculptor and draughtsman | United States

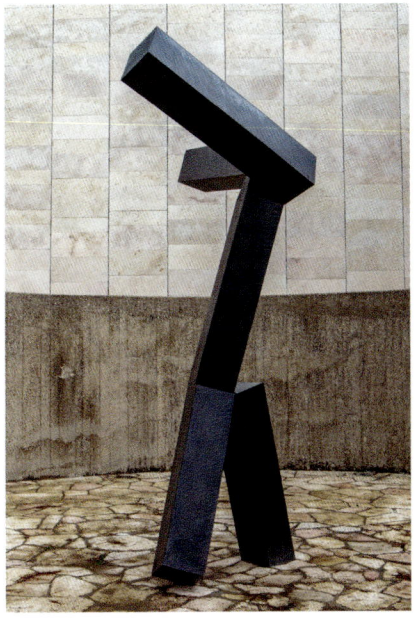

Untitled, undated

Shapiro, who grew up in New York and still lives there, became famous around the world from the 1970s through exhibitions and permanent presentations of his works on public squares. At first still influenced by Minimalism, his later sculptures in bronze and wood dominate space: perfectly composed beam structures in whose gestural vitality, anthropomorphic basic structures and abstraction hold themselves in playful balance. From the 1980s, the human figure became the focus of his work, which – in strongly stylized form – he portrays mostly in motion or in a pose.

27 SEPTEMBER

Hellen van Meene

Born 1972 | Photo artist | The Netherlands

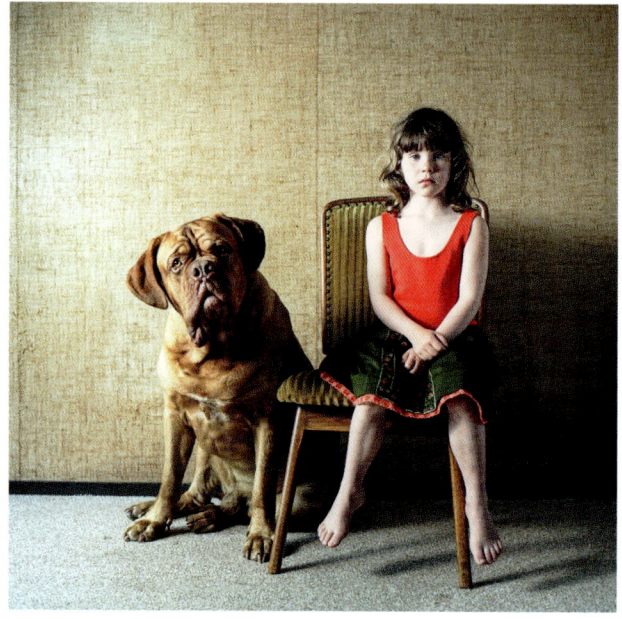

Untitled (#0389), 2012

Van Meene began photographing at an early age and studied in Edinburgh, among other places, in the 1990s. She has become known for her portraits of young girls growing into adulthood. Van Meene stages her portrayals very precisely as concerns her young models' clothes and gestures, as well as location and lighting of the respective scene. The sexuality shown in her photographs may seem provocative to some viewers, since they raise the question of whether the subjects are already aware of their sexuality and its effect. International exhibitions and museum acquisitions testify to van Meene's renown.

28 SEPTEMBER

Caravaggio

1571–1610 | Painter | Italy

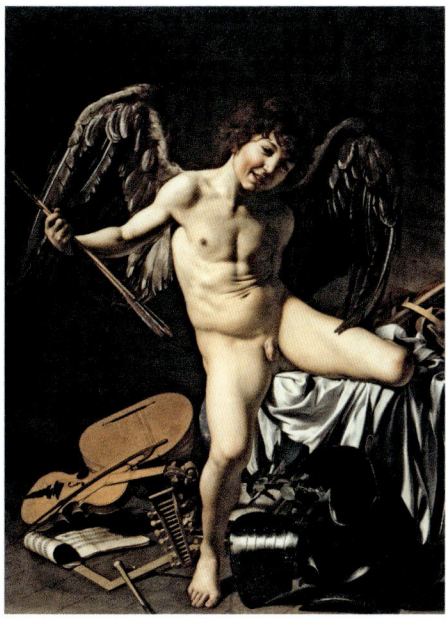

Cupid as Victor, 1601/1602

Caravaggio has become a legend, not least owing to his eventful life. He was banished from Rome and subsequently worked in Naples and on Malta. His innovative naturalism is founded on sharp light and dark contrasts: by means of dramatic lighting, he managed to delineate his figures in a true-to-life way. His models were androgynous boys and whores, which only added fuel to the legend of the disreputable, bisexual painting genius. Caravaggio had a lasting influence on early Baroque painting in Europe. Although his career lasted only twenty years and his oeuvre comprised only sixty-seven works by his own hand, he displayed a trailblazing resilience.

_____

_____

_____

_____

29 SEPTEMBER

Ilya Kabakov

1933–2023 | Painter and conceptual artist | Russia, United States

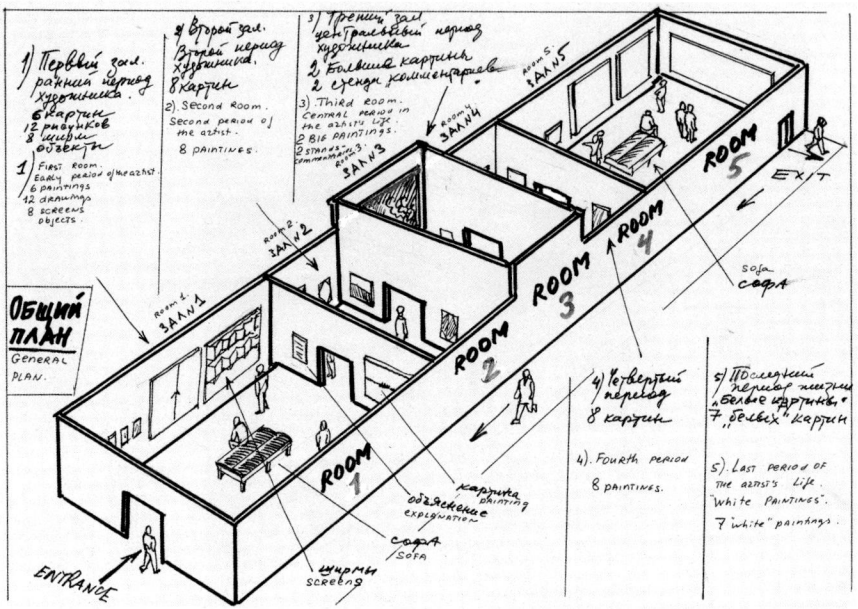

Life and Work of Charles Rosenthal, 1999

This Russian-American painter and Conceptual artist was an important representative of Moscow Conceptualism in Russia. Having emigrated in 1988, he and his wife Emilia lived as an artist couple in New York. In the 1980s, he presented his drawings and pictures in Europe and subsequently worldwide. His Conceptual works, in which the subjects are social conditions in the USSR and, later, fundamental societal utopias, had a great influence on the contemporary art scene. Many exhibitions and awards brought him international fame.

30 SEPTEMBER

Walter De Maria

1935–2013 | Minimalist, conceptualist and land artist | United States

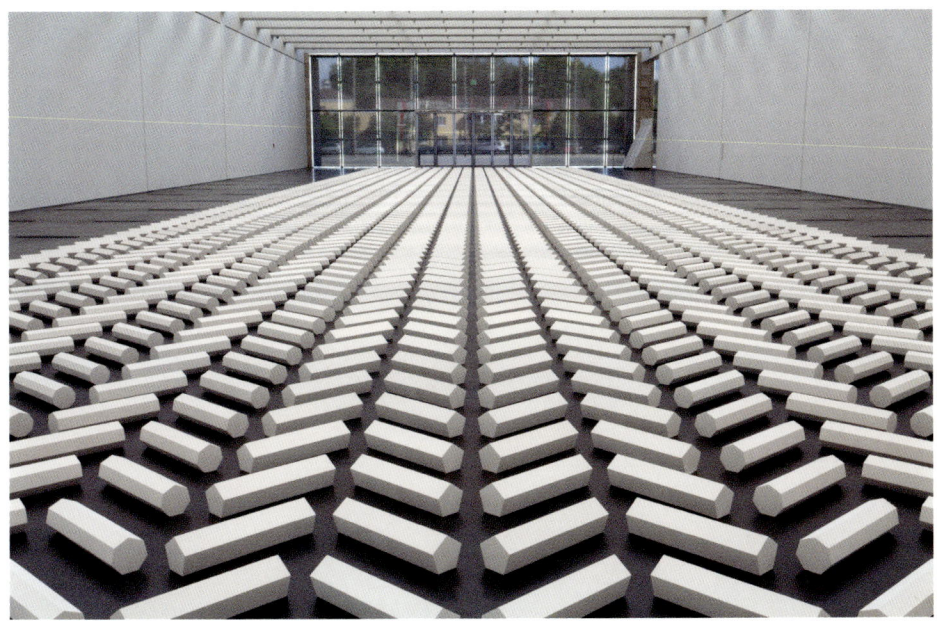

Installation of Walter De Maria's "The 2000 Sculpture", 1992

A world-renowned practitioner of Conceptual and Land Art, De Maria was best known for his monumental installations. Guided by a spirit of creativity and experimentation, he sought to create immersive art that endures. Among his most famous works are *The Earth Room* and *The Lightning Field*. In the latter, four hundred steel rods are arranged with mathematical precision across a vast expanse of land; when lightning strikes, the landscape is transformed into a site of transcendent experience within a realm of infinite space. By elevating a natural phenomenon to the status of artistic medium, De Maria expanded the boundaries of artistic expression.

1 OCTOBER

Jacob van Strij

1756–1815 | Painter | The Netherlands

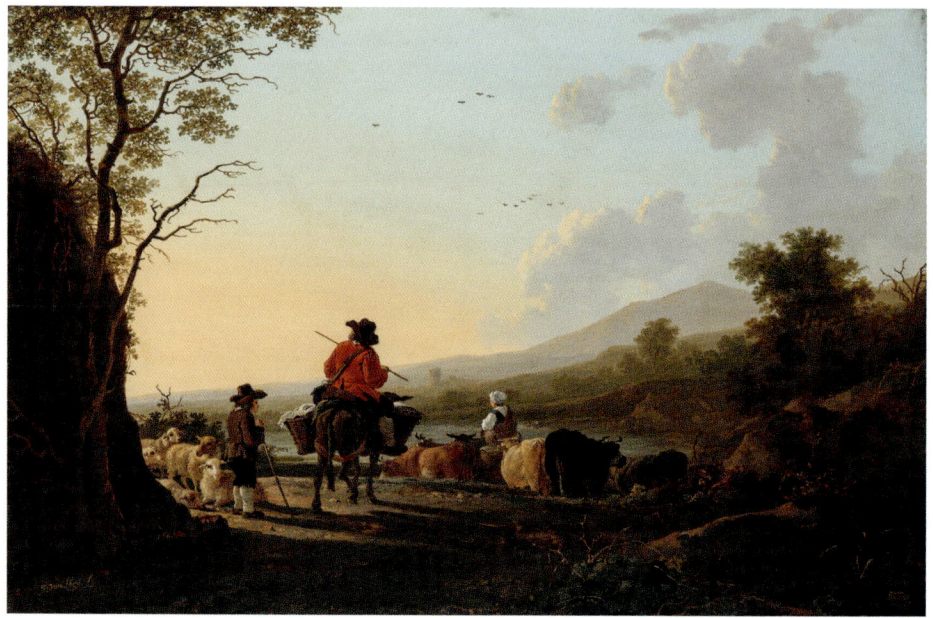

Landscape with Cattle Driver and Shepherd, c. 1780–1785

After studying at the Royal Academy in Antwerp, Van Strij worked on interior decoration, including large-scale tapestries depicting idyllic Italianate landscapes. An important artistic influence on his work was Aelbert Cuyp. Later, with his pastoral idylls – characterized by his brilliant treatment of light – he played a significant role in the eighteenth-century revival of pastoral painting in the tradition of the Dutch Golden Age, which brought him international fame and made his work highly prized by collectors.

2 OCTOBER

Pierre Bonnard

1867–1947 | Painter | France

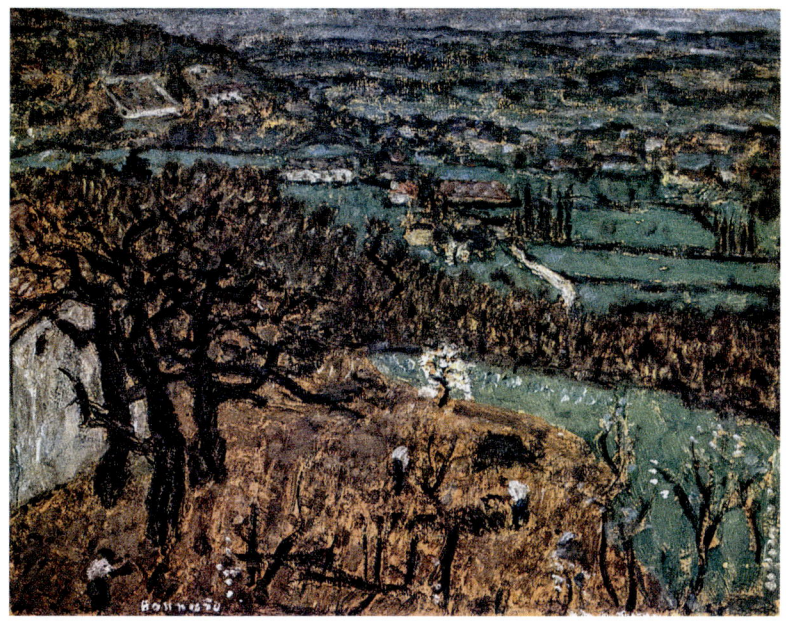

Dauphiné Landscape, c. 1899

After co-founding the Nabis group in 1888, Bonnard embarked on his own distinctive artistic path. His works are a celebration of painting itself – landscapes, flowering gardens, portraits and female nudes all radiate with subtle, vibrant colour. A true maverick, Bonnard became one of the great colourists of modern European painting, known for the exceptional lyricism of his painting. Although he did not revolutionize the medium, he enriched it in a way few others have. His international renown continues to this day.

3 OCTOBER

Jean-François Millet

1814–1875 | Painter | France

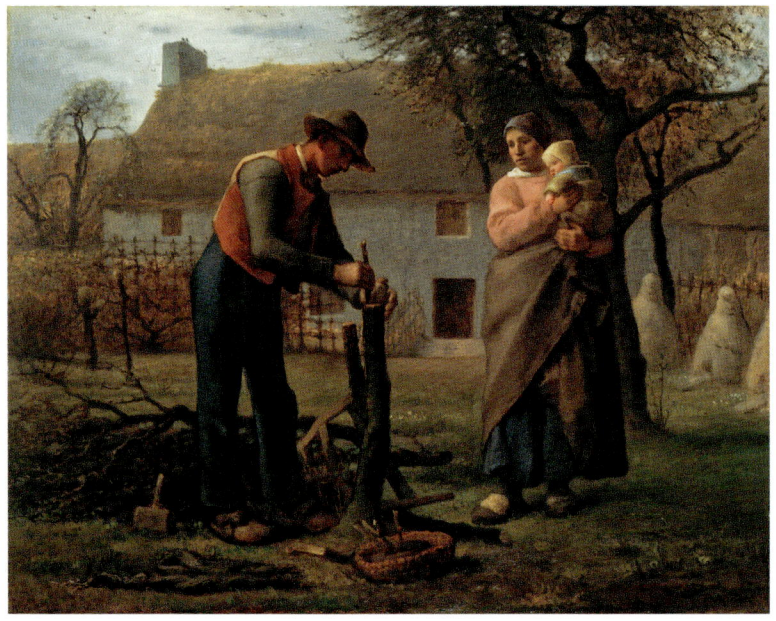

A Farmer Grafting a Tree, 1855

Along with Camille Corot, Millet was one of the leading artists of the Barbizon School. After studying in Cherbourg and Paris and making his debut as a painter, Millet started off painting in a Realist style from 1848, focusing on the hardships of peasant life. From the 1850s, his work attracted increasing attention and success. Paintings such as *The Gleaners* eventually gained international fame and were widely copied. His later landscapes anticipated stylistic elements of Impressionism and Symbolism. Today his paintings, etchings and drawings are held in major museums around the world.

4 OCTOBER

Francesco Guardi

1712–1793 | Veduta and landscape painter | Italy

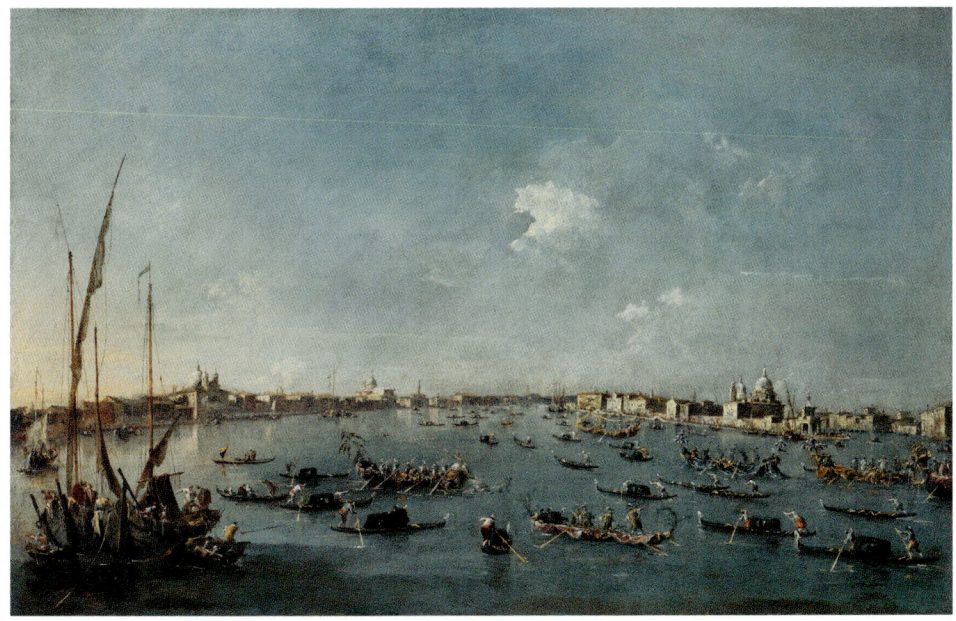

Regatta on the Giudecca Canal, c. 1784–1789

Born into a family of artists, Guardi focused on painting views of Venice since about 1760 under the influence of the famous Canaletto. His style was less topographically precise and, with its heightened use of light and colour, far freer. He painted both real and imagined subjects. His depictions of contemporary events such as festivals and ceremonies also made Guardi a chronicler of Venetian life. Today his paintings and drawings can be seen in major museums around the world.

5 OCTOBER

Meret Oppenheim

1913–1985 | Artist and poet | Germany, Switzerland

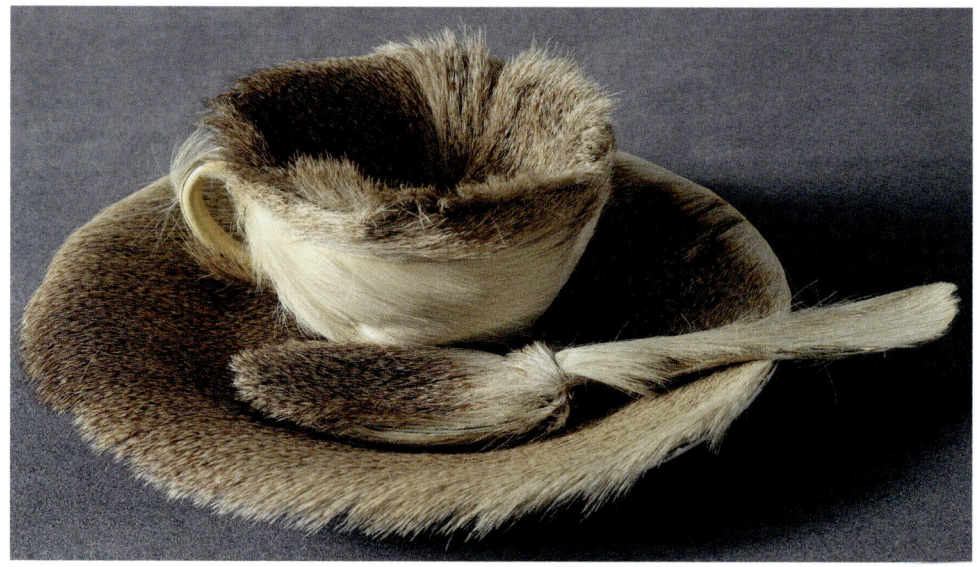

Object (Breakfast in Fur), 1936

Born in Berlin, the artist met Alberto Giacometti and Max Ernst in Paris in the early 1930s, having a brief liaison with Ernst. As the "muse of the Surrealists" she moved within their circles. In 1936, she created her famous *Object*, a fur-covered coffee cup with saucer and spoon, which was featured in the *London International Surrealist Exhibition* shortly afterwards. Following a creative crisis, she revisited ideas from her Paris years. She also gained recognition as a sculptor and poet. International exhibitions brought her widespread acclaim.

6 OCTOBER

Rosalba Carriera

1675–1757 | Pastellist | Italy

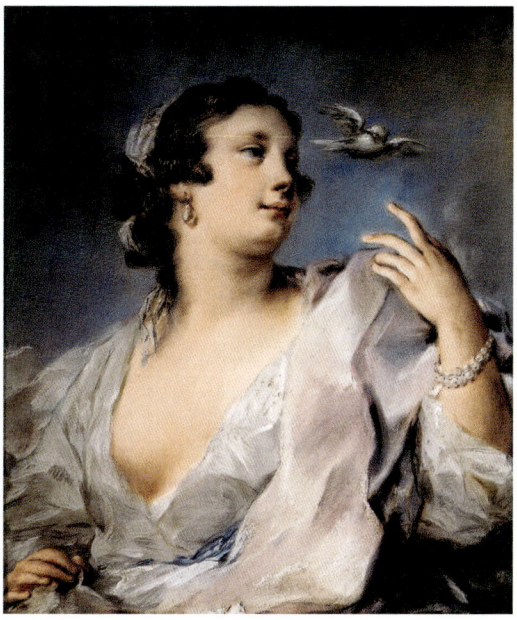

Air, from the series "Allegory of the Four Elements", 1746

Rosalba Carriera became a celebrated artist throughout Europe, renowned for her work in pastel. She began her career as a miniaturist before turning to pastels. From the 1720s, she was a frequent guest at the courts of Paris, Modena and Vienna and received many commissions. Family bereavement and a progressive eye condition limited her output from 1737. She went blind in 1746 and, after suffering from depression, died in Venice. Many of her virtuoso pastels are held in the Picture Gallery in Dresden.

7 OCTOBER

Max Slevogt

1868–1932 | Painter, graphic artist and stage designer | Germany

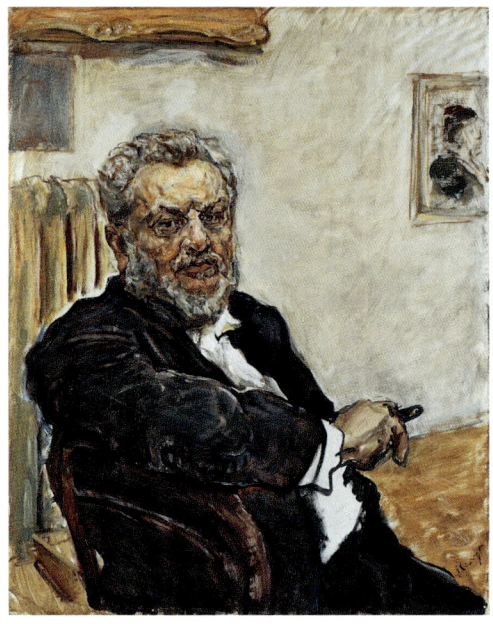

Self-Portrait, c. 1929/1930

Along with Lovis Corinth and Max Liebermann, Slevogt is considered the third figure
in the triumvirate of German Impressionists. His oeuvre includes paintings, book illustrations and works on paper. Among his most famous works is *Francisco d'Andrade as
Don Giovanni (The Champagne Aria)* from 1902, which portrays the famous baritone
in Mozart's opera. In 1906, Slevogt designed sets for Max Reinhardt in Berlin, and
during a trip to Egypt in 1914, he painted numerous works. He served as an official war
artist during the First World War, an experience that deeply affected him. Esteemed
during his lifetime, Slevogt remains a fixture in German museums.

8 OCTOBER

Sophie Calle

Born 1953 | Conceptual artist | France

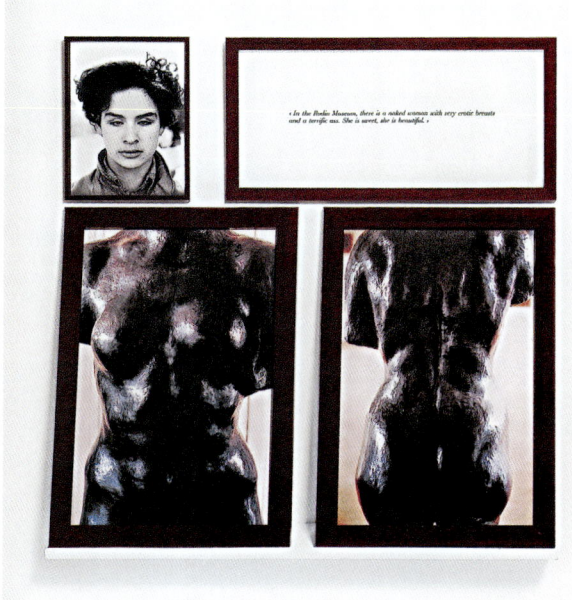

Blind #14, from the series "The Blind", 1986

Calle is an acclaimed Conceptual artist whose practice encompasses photography, text, video and installation. She took up photography in 1978 during a stay in California. Upon her return to Paris, she began Conceptual projects using investigative and often provocative methods to explore themes of intimacy, identity and the boundaries between public and private life. In 1983, she sparked controversy with *L'Homme au carnet*, in which she constructed a portrait of a stranger by interviewing the contacts listed in his lost address book and publishing the results in a daily newspaper. Calle has gained worldwide recognition through numerous exhibitions and prestigious awards.

Alberto Giacometti

1901–1966 | Sculptor, painter and printmaker | Switzerland

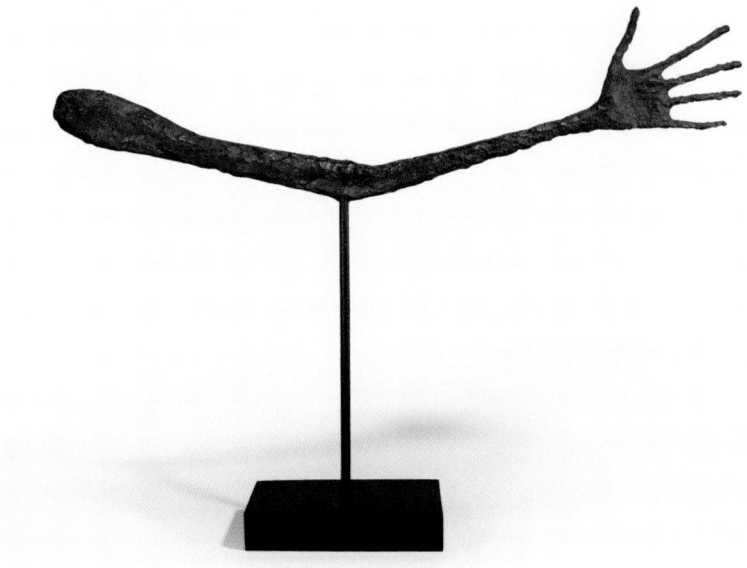

The Hand, 1947/1948

Giacometti is considered one of the most important and renowned sculptors, painters and draughtsmen of the twentieth century. His oeuvre is a unique reflection on the *condition humaine*, addressing themes that shape human existence. Moving from post-Cubist influences in the 1920s to Surrealism in the 1930s, he increasingly focused on the human figure within the vastness of surrounding space. During this period he began to radically pare down his figures, culminating in the elongated, slender forms characteristic of his work in the 1950s. The existential dimension of his life and art – his tiny Parisian studio, his models and his love affairs – contributed to his enduring myth.

_____

_____

_____

_____

10 OCTOBER

Gazbia Sirry

1925–2012 | Painter | Egypt

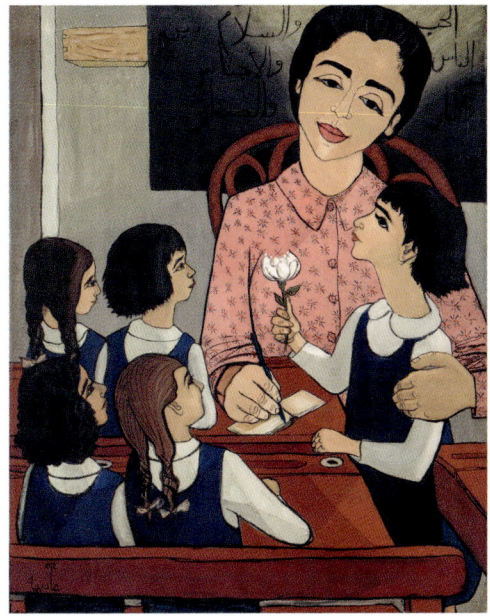

The Teacher, 1954

Gazbia Sirry was one of the icons of modern and contemporary Egyptian art and participated in numerous international exhibitions. After studying at art schools in Paris, Rome and London, she joined the Modern Art Group in Cairo. Political and social themes, such as women's emancipation, inform Sirry's paintings, which were initially figurative and later shifted towards Abstract Expressionism. Her paintings of Egyptian women brought her widespread recognition and reflected her humanist beliefs and rejection of all forms of inequality, as exemplified by the inscription in *The Teacher*: "Love and peace between people and races, old and young."

11 OCTOBER

Rudi Tröger

Born 1929 | Painter and draughtsman | Germany

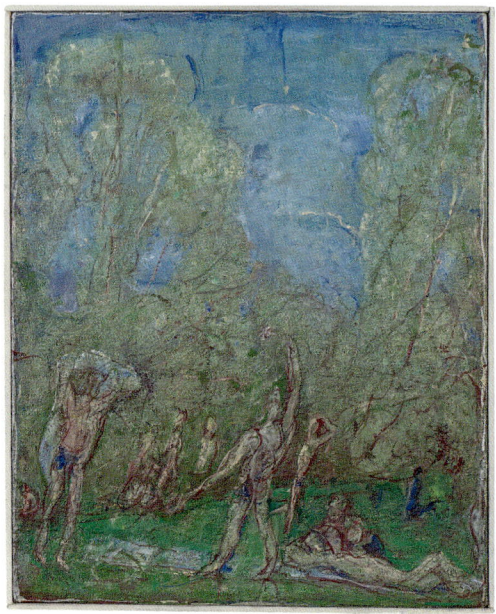

Untitled (Painting of Bathers), 2003

Tröger was one of the quiet loners of German painting in his day. He painted land-scapes, portraits and still lifes. After the early influence of painters such as Lovis Corinth and Oskar Kokoschka, he developed a particular affinity for French painting. His contemporaneity is rooted in his lengthy painting process, which encompasses fragility, restlessness and doubt. This is how he transforms the given elements of nature and brings them to life. As a professor at the Munich Academy, he inspired many students, who still revere him today.

12 OCTOBER

Eduardo Sívori

1847–1918 | Painter | Argentina

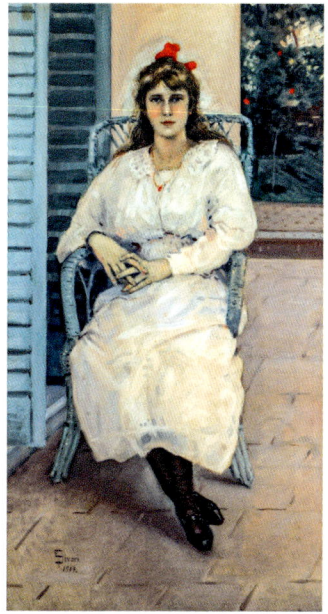

Spring, 1914

The son of Italian immigrants, Sívori was born and studied in Buenos Aires and gained recognition in Argentina, France and the United States from the 1880s onwards. He painted realistic portraits and landscapes, including commissions for prominent, wealthy collectors. In 1910, Sívori was appointed president of the National University of Arts in his home city. Twenty years after his death, the Museo Sívori in Buenos Aires was inaugurated to honour his legacy.

13 OCTOBER

Adolphe Monticelli

1824–1886 | Painter | France

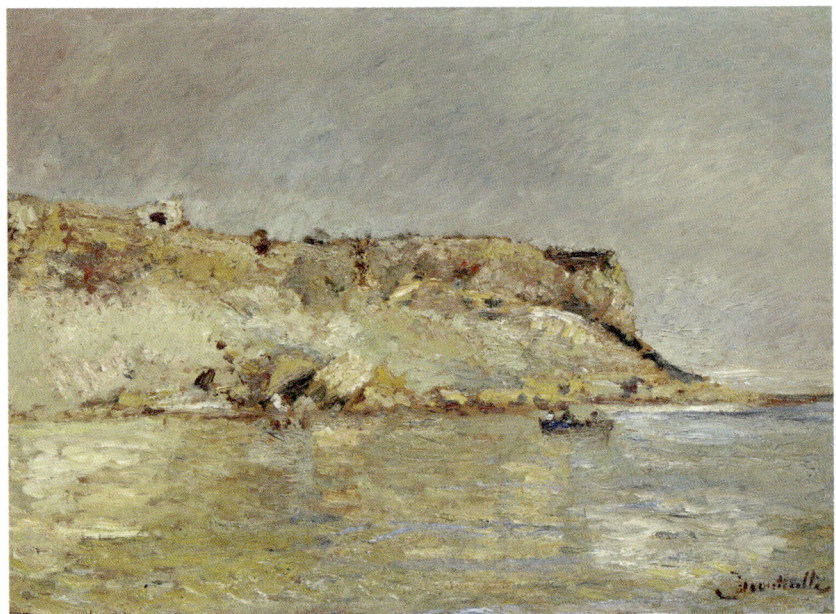

Coastal Mountains, 1870–1880

After studying in Marseille and Paris, Monticelli developed a distinctive style character-ized by a heavy, almost relief-like application of paint and bold, expressive brushwork. In the 1860s, he met the young Paul Cézanne, who would later be inspired by him, as was Vincent van Gogh. Monticelli's favourite subjects were figurative scenes, portraits, landscapes and floral compositions. The modernity of his style influenced many later artists. A museum bearing his name opened in Marseille in 2010.

14 OCTOBER

Brice Marden

1938–2023 | Painter, draughtsman and graphic artist | United States

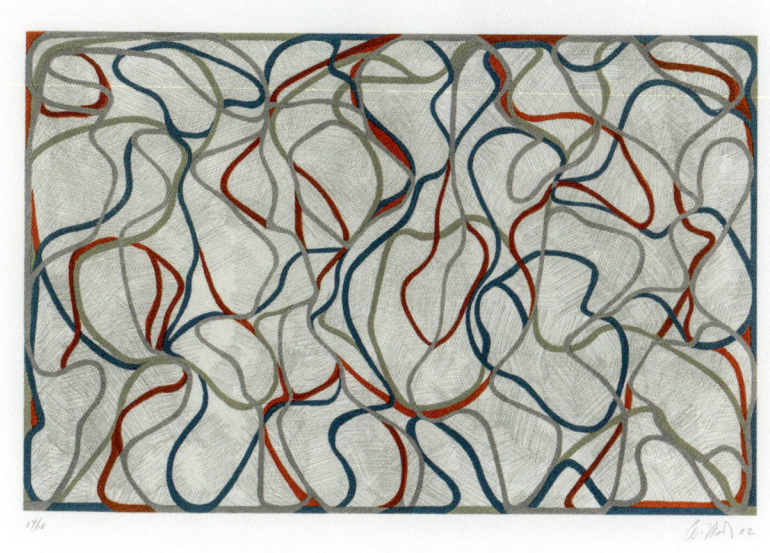

Eagles Mere Muses, 2001

Marden was a major proponent of American abstract painting in the second half of the twentieth century. After immersing himself in the work of Jasper Johns, he produced his first monochrome paintings. In 1964, he encountered the work of Alberto Giacometti in Paris. Shortly afterwards, Marden became Robert Rauschenberg's assistant. In his *Work Books* of the 1970s, the dual themes of construction and nature emerged as opposing forces in his art. From 1971, the Greek island of Hydra became his second home, and the impressions he gathered there informed his work. His later paintings were influenced by Japanese calligraphy.

15 OCTOBER

Paul Strand

1890–1976 | Photographer | United States

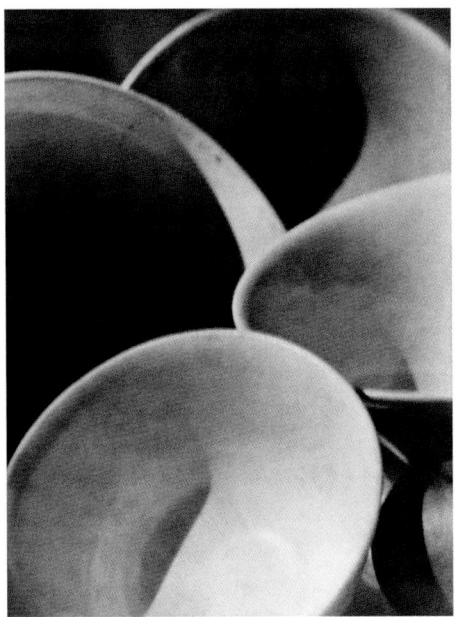

Abstraction, Bowls, 1916

Alongside Alfred Stieglitz and Edward Steichen, Strand was one of the most influential American photographers of the early twentieth century. Stieglitz played a pivotal role in his life as a mentor. In the 1920s, he produced close-up nature studies and films, and later travelled throughout the United States and Canada, where he became interested in rural communities and social issues. From 1932 to 1934, he lived in Mexico. Strand helped establish the Photo League, an organisation dedicated to social documentary photography. During the McCarthy era, political persecution of his left-wing beliefs led him to move to France in the early 1950s.

16 OCTOBER

Childe Hassam

1859–1935 | Painter | United States

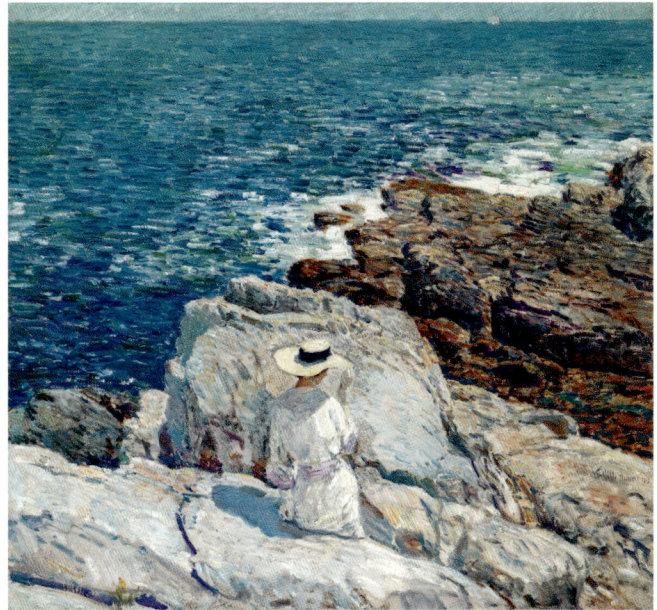

The South Ledges, Appledore, 1913

Hassam was one of the leading figures of American Impressionism. In 1883, he first travelled to Europe, where he was influenced by artists such as William Turner. On his return home, he exhibited watercolours inspired by this trip. From 1886 to 1889, Hassam lived in Paris, where he gained critical recognition by winning a medal at the Exposition Universelle. Back in the US, he won acclaim for his luminous landscapes and cityscapes of New York. He continued to travel throughout Europe and the United States. In 1898 Hassam and nine other artists formed the group Ten American Painters. In 1909, the Metropolitan Museum of Art in New York made its first acquisition of his work.

17 OCTOBER

Luca Giordano

1634–1705 | Painter and etcher | Italy

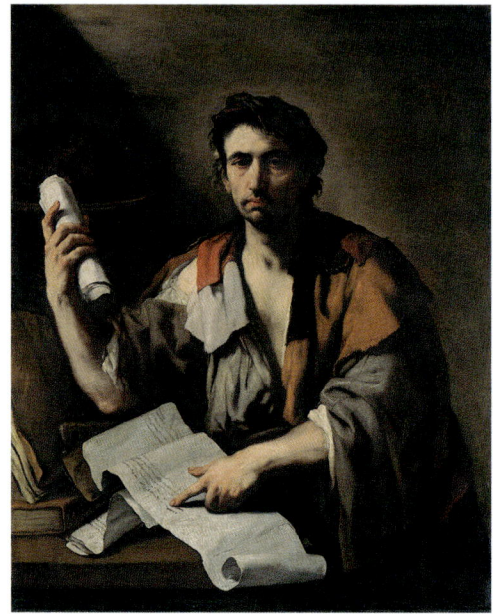

A Cynical Philosopher, c. 1650–1653

Giordano was one of the most prolific Neapolitan painters of the seventeenth century. Although best known for his frescoes, he also produced numerous oil paintings depicting religious, historical and mythological subjects. Giordano lived and worked in Naples, Rome and Venice, and later in Florence and northern Italy. In 1692, he went to Spain, where he worked at El Escorial and in Toledo. He left behind a large and varied oeuvre, much of it featuring a markedly lighter palette, which in his later work becomes delicate and airy, anticipating the Rococo style. Giordano was a major influence on eighteenth-century painters.

18 OCTOBER

Umberto Boccioni

1882–1916 | Painter and sculptor | Italy

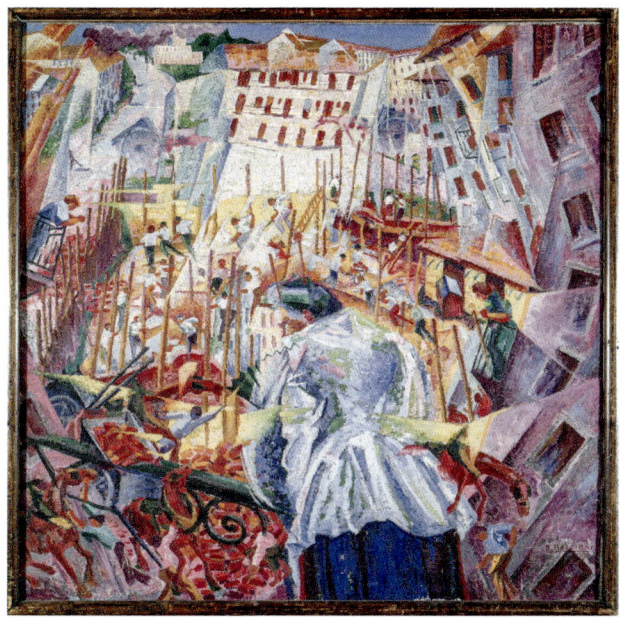

The Street Enters the House, 1911

Born in southern Italy, Boccioni became one of the leading figures of Futurism. In 1910, he signed *The Manifesto of Futurism* with other key members of the movement. Between 1911 and 1913, he visited Paris where he met Pablo Picasso and participated in important exhibitions. In his sculptural work, Boccioni rejected traditional materials and the classical concept of sculpture in favour of dynamic forms that extended into space and embodied movement. He died in Verona after falling from his horse after voluntarily signing up for military service.

19 OCTOBER

Jennie Cell

1905–1988 | Painter | United States

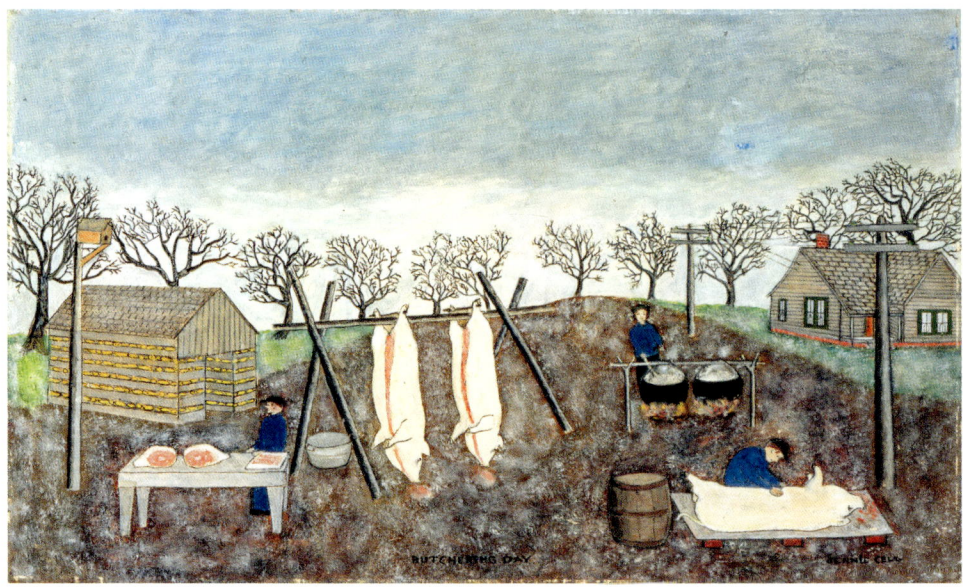

Butchering Day, c. 1955

Cell lived on a farm near Charleston and did not take up painting until she was about fifty. Unable to afford a camera, she used shoe polish to paint a picture of the house of a relative that appealed to her as a subject. Her uncle, an enthusiastic amateur painter, bought her oil paints and from then on they worked together in the farmhouse sitting room, next to the stove. Cell mainly painted rural scenes, such as the pruning of trees and butchering days. Some of her "naive" paintings are now in the collection of the Smithsonian Institution in Washington, DC.

20 OCTOBER

Domenichino

1581–1641 | Painter and fresco artist | Italy

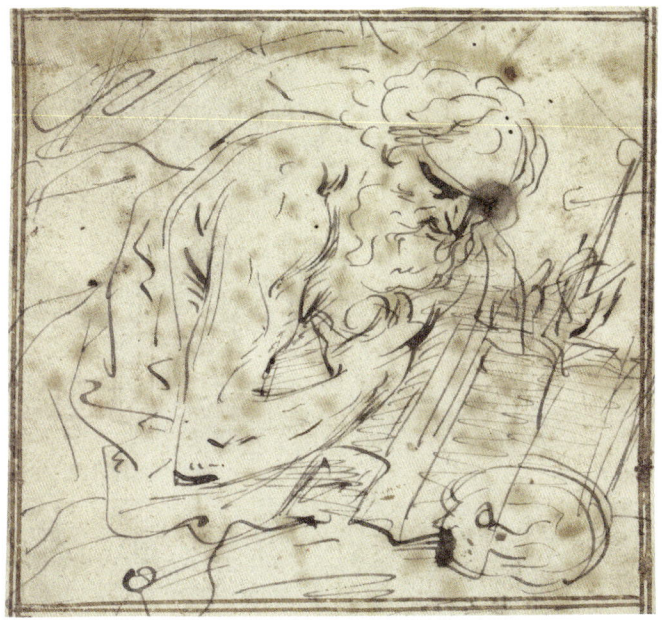

Penitent St Jerome, seventeenth century

Domenichino lived and worked mainly in Rome until 1630, then in Naples until his death. He received numerous commissions for frescoes in churches and palaces. To meet the demand, it was often essential to divide the labour within his workshop. His classically elegant style was inspired by Raphael among others. Domenichino's landscapes in particular had a profound influence on later painters such as Claude Lorrain and Nicolas Poussin. He was one of the most significant Italian painters of the first half of the seventeenth century, and today his works are in museums across the world.

21 OCTOBER

Robert Rauschenberg

1925–2008 | Painter, printmaker and object artist | United States

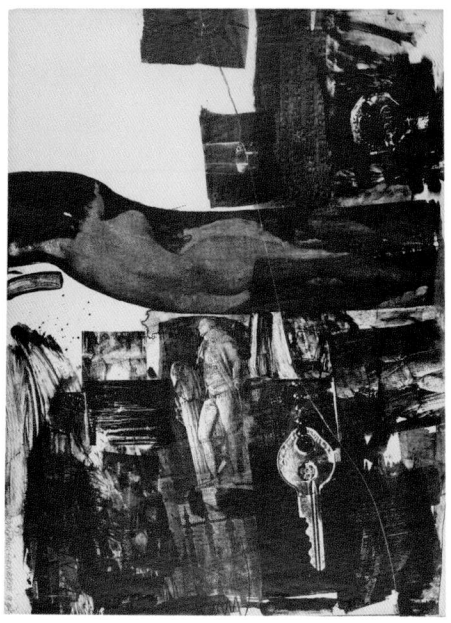

Breakthrough I, 1964

Rauschenberg's highly inventive works not only established him as a precursor of Pop Art but also positioned him as one of the most innovative artists of the second half of the twentieth century, continually pushing the boundaries of genre and style. Determined to challenge the dominance of Abstract Expressionism, he created his series of monochrome paintings in the 1950s. In his later *Combine Paintings*, he created assemblages that combined painting with found objects, exploring the boundary between art and the everyday world. Numerous exhibitions and prestigious awards have secured his international reputation.

22 OCTOBER

Erwin Pfrang

Born 1951 | Painter and draughtsman | Germany

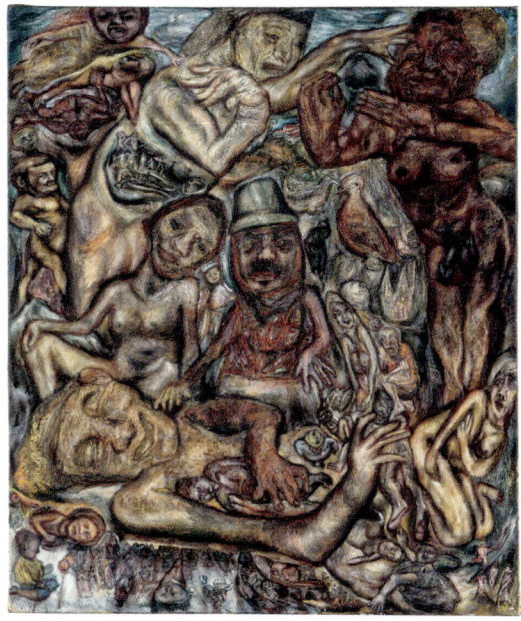

Untitled, 1990

For decades, Pfrang has worked against the grain of the German art scene. Drawing on a wealth of visual experience, he gathers diverse impressions and weaves them into intricate worlds of drawing and painting. "Thought through my eyes" – a quotation from James Joyce's *Ulysses* – serves as a leitmotif throughout his work. He has produced extensive cycles inspired by Joyce's novel, in which quasi-literary narrative structures emerge within his compositions. Pfrang, who spent many years in Italy and now lives in Berlin, has only gradually gained international recognition.

23 OCTOBER

Richard Cockle Lucas

1800–1883 | Sculptor and photographer | Great Britain

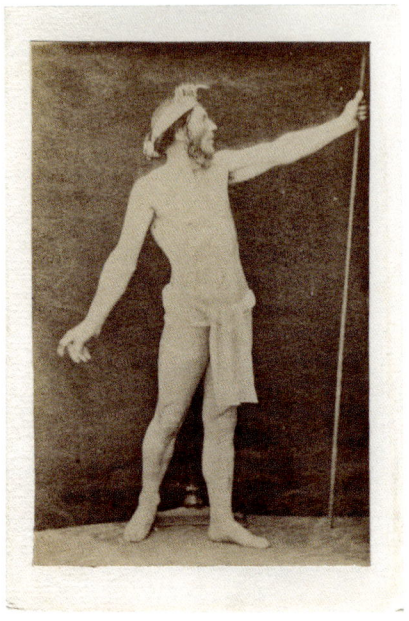

Richard Cockle Lucas as Apollo, 1858

This highly eccentric British sculptor and photographer, whose works are in several British museums, remains one of the lesser-known artists of the nineteenth century. He studied at the Royal Academy in London in the 1820s and exhibited there regularly. His work includes classically styled busts, medallions and sculptures in marble, wax and ivory. In his photographs, he recreated some his own works in theatrical poses. The *Flora* bust in the Bode Museum in Berlin has been the subject of controversy for over a century: is it the work of Leonardo da Vinci or Richard Cockle Lucas?

24 OCTOBER

Claude Cahun

1894–1954 | Photographer | France

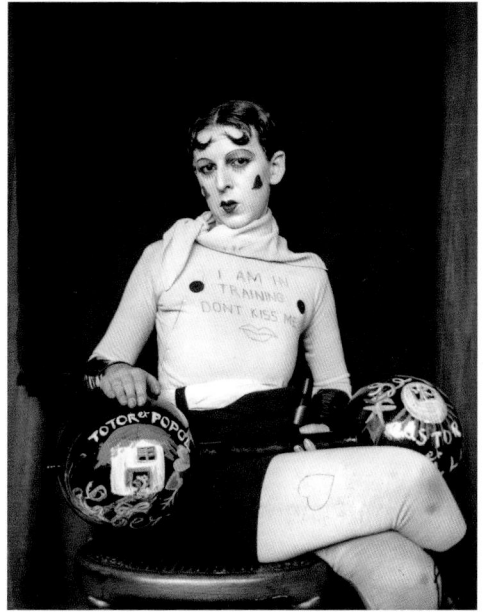

Self-Portrait, from the series "I am in training, don't kiss me", 1927

As a writer and photographer, Cahun has only recently gained international recognition, particularly within the context of feminist and queer theory. With her partner, she hosted an art salon in Paris, was associated with the Surrealist movement and was a committed anti-fascist. The lesbian couple moved to the Channel Island of Jersey in 1937 and were sentenced to death in 1944 during the Nazi occupation but were later pardoned. Their home was ransacked by the Gestapo and much of their work was lost. One of the few surviving published self-portraits shows Cahun with a shaved head.

25 OCTOBER

Hilma af Klint

1862–1944 | Painter | Sweden

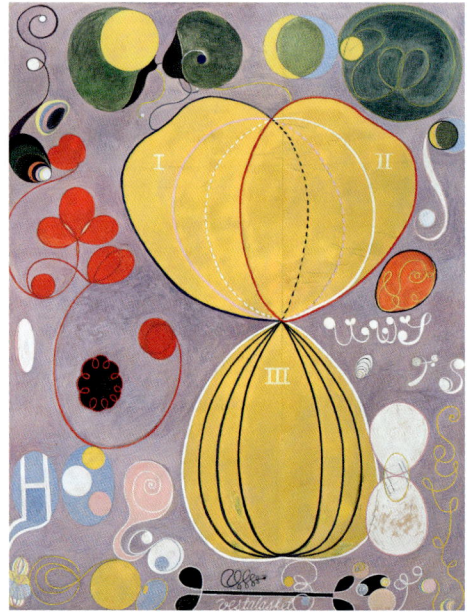

The Ten Largest, No. 7, Adult, Group IV, 1907

Since her rediscovery in the 1980s, the art of this Swedish painter has been featured in exhibitions around the world. She became interested in spiritualism and theosophy at seventeen. In 1906, she produced her first small-format abstract works. In 1912, after meeting Rudolf Steiner, she began the boldly geometric large-scale series *Paintings for the Temple*. She later embraced anthroposophy and forbade exhibitions of her work during her lifetime. She stipulated in his will that her work was not to be exhibited until twenty years after her death. She is now viewed as a pioneer of abstract art, having explored non-representational forms prior to Wassily Kandinsky.

26 OCTOBER

Roy Lichtenstein

1923–1997 | Painter | United States

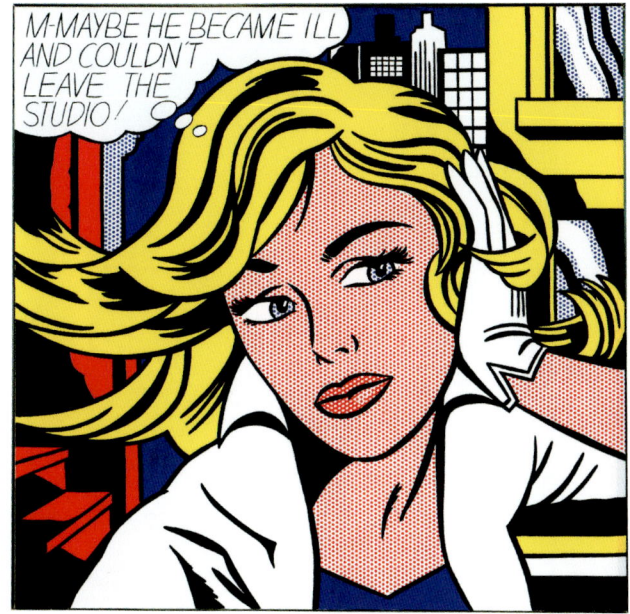

M-Maybe, 1965

Lichtenstein was the most famous American Pop artist after Andy Warhol. After success eluded him for years, his breakthrough came in 1961 with the painting *Look Mickey*. This was followed by a series of works in the style of printed comic strips, which achieved great commercial success. He went on to create comic-inspired abstractions and re-interpretations of works by other artists. Embracing industrial techniques, Lichtenstein developed a stencil technique for the dots that soon became his trademark. His fusion of art and commerce served as a conscious critique of the elitist discourse surrounding high-brow art.

27 OCTOBER

Francis Bacon

1909–1992 | Painter | Great Britain

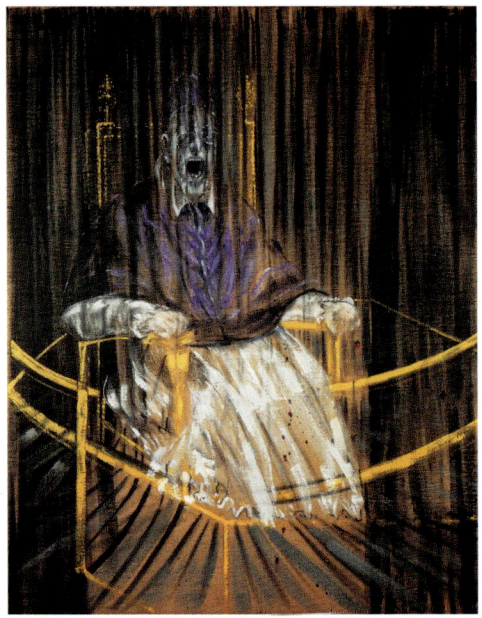

Study After Velázquez's Portrait of Pope Innocent X, 1953

A cultured autodidact and avid reader – with Friedrich Nietzsche among his influences – Bacon is one of the greatest and most highly valued figurative painters of twentieth-century art. Known for his openly homosexual and bohemian lifestyle, his career was marked by a serious addiction to alcohol and gambling. Bacon painted with relentless, obsessive intensity, often working in series. His iconic, Velázquez-inspired depictions of popes, mouths agape in a silent scream, became famous. His works are hallucinatory metaphors for the human condition. With his distorted figures trapped in claustrophobic spaces, Bacon conjured haunting visions of the darkest recesses of the mind.

28 OCTOBER

Niki de Saint Phalle

1930–2002 | Painter and sculptor | France, Switzerland

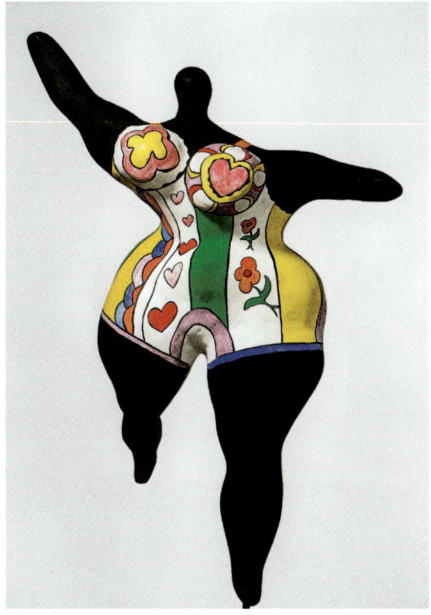

Black Dancing Nana (Big Black Dancer), c. 1968

The artist grew up in the United States before moving back to Europe in 1952. In 1971, she married her second husband, the famous Swiss sculptor Jean Tinguely. From 1965, she began to create her first "Nanas" – voluptuous, colourful female figures in polyester – which became her signature works and brought her international acclaim. These figures symbolize vitality, femininity and freedom of expression, free from inhibition and convention. From the 1960s on, she had numerous international exhibitions. Later, in Tuscany, she created a *Gesamtkunstwerk* in the form of a fantastical sculpture garden. Saint Phalle's art is defined by a consistently positive, bold, playful and humorous spirit.

_____

_____

_____

_____

29 OCTOBER

Angelika Kauffmann

1741–1807 | Painter | Switzerland, Austria

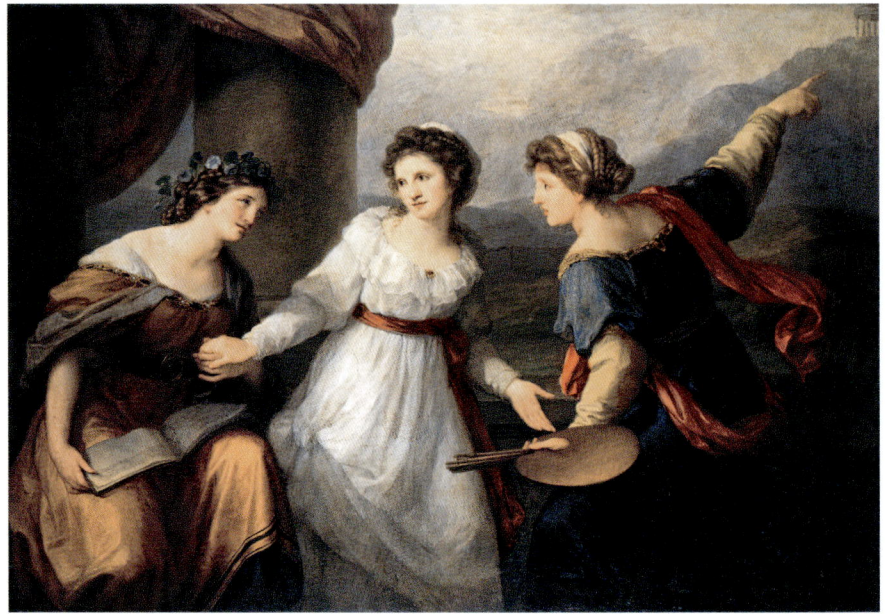

Self-Portrait of the Artist Hesitating between the Arts of Music and Painting, 1792

Even in her infancy Kauffmann was recognized for her artistic talent. After her mother's death, she developed a close relationship with her father, a painter, and accompanied him on many journeys. In 1766, after spending time in Rome, she moved to London, where she became famous and later married for the second time. Her Neoclassical history paintings and her portraits in particular brought her recognition across Europe and made her wealthy. She moved in prominent circles and was friends with many luminaries including Goethe, who greatly admired her. In 1782, she returned to Rome, where she died in 1807 after a long illness.

30 OCTOBER

Jan Vermeer

1632 (baptism)–1675 | Painter | The Netherlands

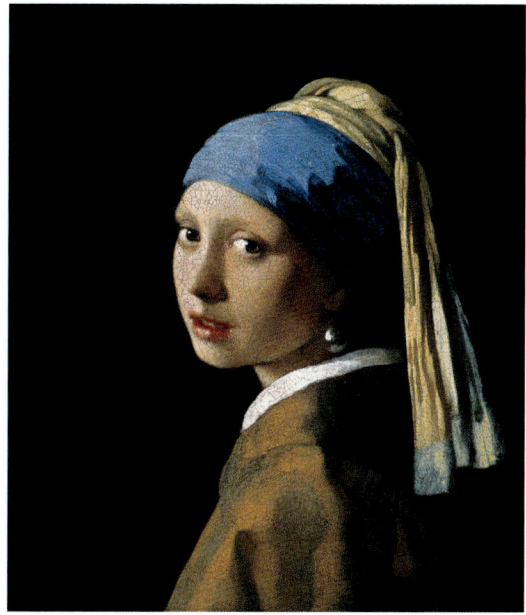

Girl with a Pearl Earring, c. 1665

Vermeer is one of the great masters in the history of painting. While recent exhibitions around the world have made him the most popular painter of the Dutch Golden Age, he remains one of its most elusive and enigmatic figures, as little is known about his life and his oeuvre is small, with only three dozen works to his name. He is best known for his depictions of women. Geometry and light take on a new role in his paintings, establishing innovative compositional practices through simple structures and a minimal use of pictorial elements. Vermeer suffuses materiality with colour, and it is the incomparable richness of this colouration that makes his paintings "breathe".

31 OCTOBER

Hannah Höch

1889–1978 | Painter, graphic artist and collage artist | Germany

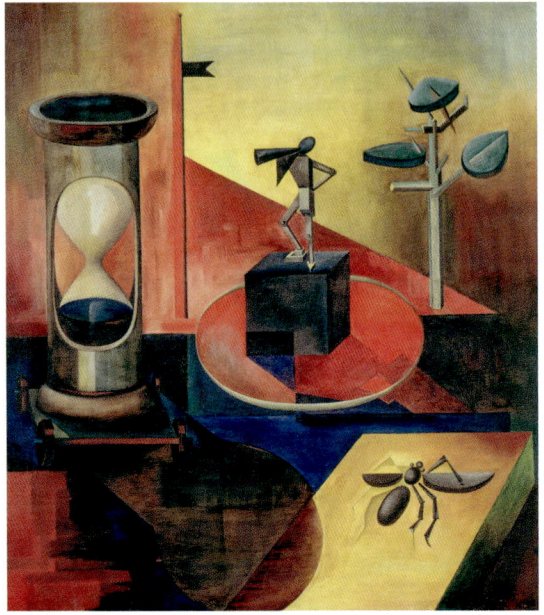

The Mosquito Is Dead, 1922

Living in Berlin from 1912, Höch met the Dadaist Raoul Hausmann in 1915, with whom she had a seven-year relationship. Through him, she became the only woman active in Berlin's Dada circle and developed photomontage as a central technique in her work. In 1926, she met the Dutch writer Til Brugman, with whom she lived until 1936. Under the Nazis her art was labelled "degenerate". Höch created paintings, montages and collages that expressed her political views as an opponent of war and of authoritarian structures.

1 NOVEMBER

Richard Serra

1938–2024 | Sculptor | United States

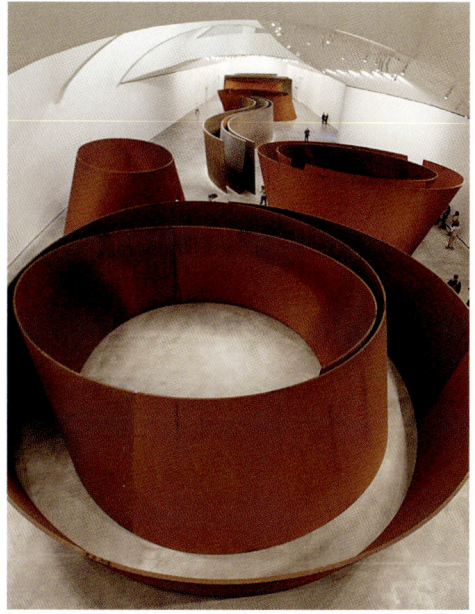

The Matter of Time, 1994–2005

Serra was one of the most important sculptors of his generation. While his early works in the 1960s explored materials such as rubber and lead, he later turned his attention to metal, particularly Corten steel. Known for his uncompromising and often confrontational approach, the artist often found himself at the centre of controversy. His international reputation rests on monumental sculptures weighing several tonnes that dominate public spaces and squares. With their striking interplay of aesthetic presence and latent menace, many of these works have become landmarks. Serra's large-scale etchings complement his sculptural work.

2 NOVEMBER

Benvenuto Cellini

1500–1571 | Goldsmith and sculptor | Italy

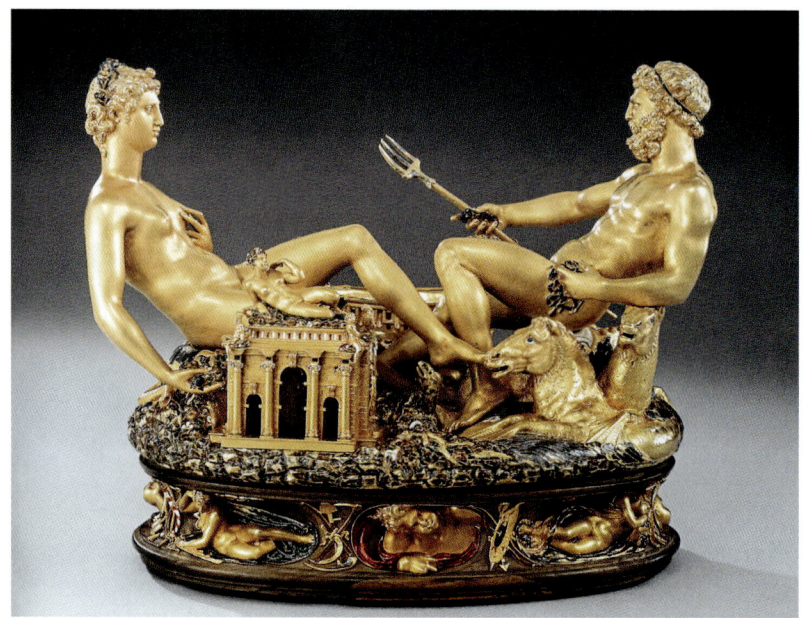

Salt Cellar, 1540–1543

The Florentine goldsmith and sculptor was one of the most famous artists of the sixteenth century, active in the transition between the High Renaissance and Mannerism. Quarrelsome and pugnacious to the point of violence, he led a turbulent life marked by constant strife. In the 1520s, he secured various commissions in Rome, where he set up a workshop. One of his medals earned praise from Michelangelo. At the French court, he was commissioned to create the famed salt cellar. Returning to Florence in 1545, he completed his masterpiece, *Perseus with the Head of Medusa*. He also wrote an autobiography, later translated into German by Johann Wolfgang von Goethe.

3 NOVEMBER

Guido Reni

1575–1642 | Painter, fresco artist and etcher | Italy

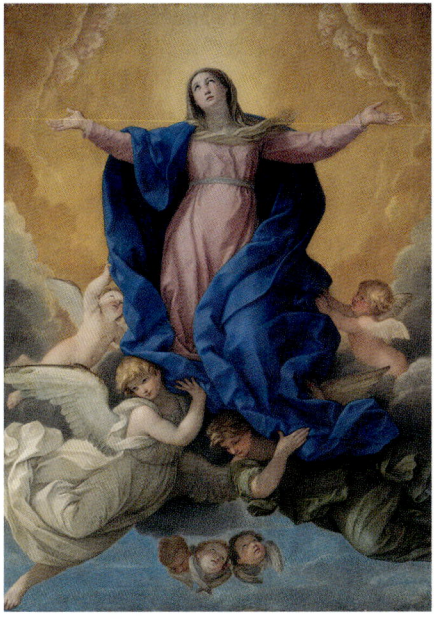

Assumption of the Virgin, c. 1638/1639

Reni was one of the most revered painters of his time. His style, initially in the Baroque tradition, developed into a more classical idiom after 1620. He was a major influence on both his contemporaries and subsequent generations of artists. Financial difficulties, caused by his lifestyle and excessive gambling, led his workshop to produce many replicas of his compositions. Reni worked mainly in Bologna and Rome, producing numerous frescoes and altarpieces for commissions throughout Europe. His paintings are now held in major museums around the world.

4 NOVEMBER

Pietro Longhi

1702–1785 | Painter | Italy

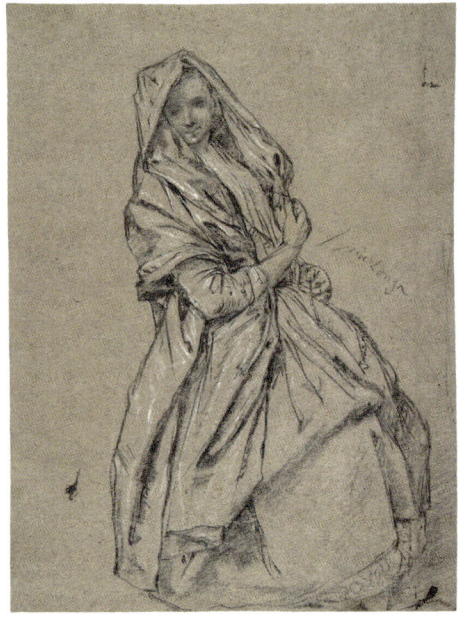

Study of a Seated Woman, undated

In 1756, Longhi was admitted to the Academy of Fine Arts in Venice, where he taught for over twenty years. His patrons were mainly Venetian noble families. He painted altarpieces, portraits and genre scenes. These mostly small-scale, colourful works capture the charm of contemporary Venetian life and serve as delightful conversation pieces in the Rococo style. With humour and subtle irony, Longhi depicted the everyday world of Venetian society, and in this he shared the same vision as his close friend, the playwright Carlo Goldoni, an admirer of Molière and famous for his comedies.

5 NOVEMBER

Alois Senefelder

1771–1834 | Inventor of lithography | Germany

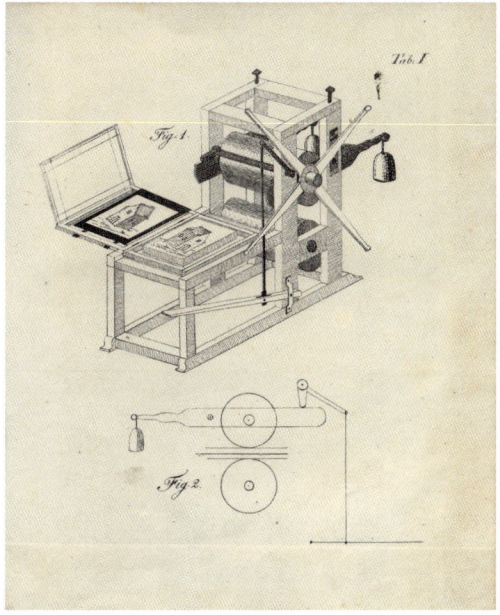

Printing Press / Stone Printing, Lithography, 1818

Senefelder's invention of lithography is said to have been inspired by a rainy day
in Munich in 1796 when he noticed a leaf imprinted on a piece of limestone. This
observation sparked the idea of printing from stone. In 1797, he built a press for this
new planographic printing process, which was initially used to produce sheet music
and soon attracted interest both in Germany and abroad. Senefelder's invention had
far-reaching consequences, paving the way for reproductions after Albrecht Dürer.
By 1826, he had succeeded in printing in colour, and his later experiments with printing
on metal plates anticipated the development of offset printing.

6 NOVEMBER

Francisco de Zurbarán

1598 (baptism)–1664 | Painter | Spain

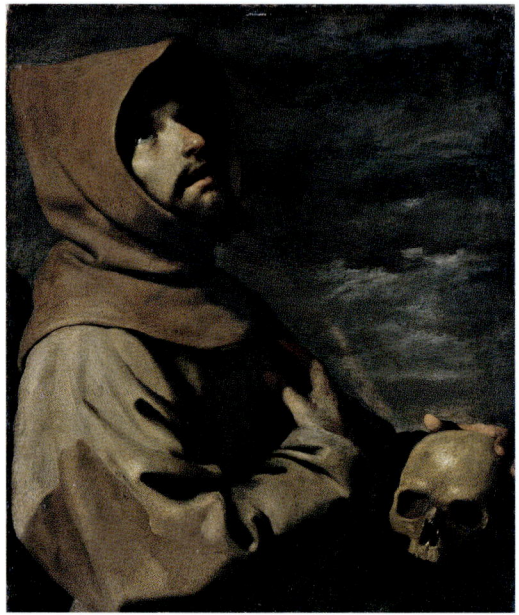

St Francis in Ecstasy, c. 1660

Zurbarán was one of the great masters of Spanish Baroque painting. He gained renown for his austere, often darkly coloured religious works, most of which were commissioned by ecclesiastical patrons. He received his first major commissions in Seville, where he settled permanently in 1629. Throughout the 1630s and 1640s, he produced numerous devotional paintings alongside several notable still lifes. Following a period of work for the royal court, he relocated to Madrid in 1658. The sculptural, monumental presence of his figures combined with his subtle mastery of colour and chiaroscuro, left a lasting impression on generations of artists to come.

7 NOVEMBER

Elizabeth Sparhawk-Jones

1885–1968 | Painter | United States

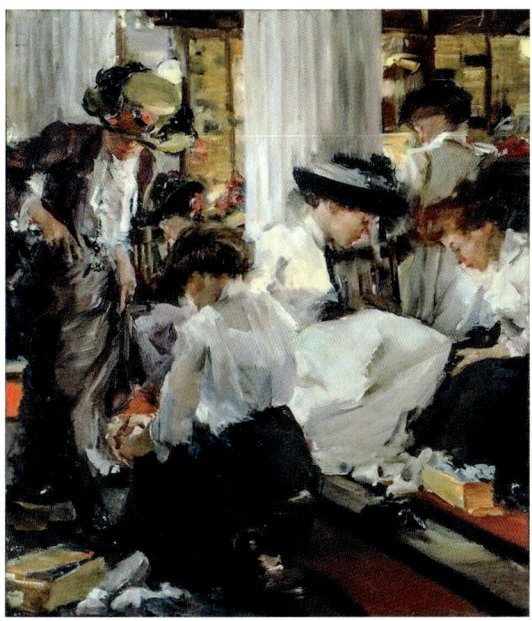

The Shoe Shop, 1911

The painter studied at the Pennsylvania Academy of the Fine Arts in Philadelphia, which commissioned *The Market*, a vivid panorama of women shopping, when she was only twenty. Early on, she was able to support herself through the sale of her impressionistic paintings. Her evocative work *The Shoe Shop* – depicting female employees and their customers engaged in everyday activity, a distinctly modern subject rendered with contemporary techniques – was acquired by the Art Institute of Chicago. Following a nervous breakdown in 1913, she did not return to painting until the 1930s, when she increasingly favoured watercolour.

8 NOVEMBER

Gigo Gabashvili

1862–1936 | Painter | Georgia

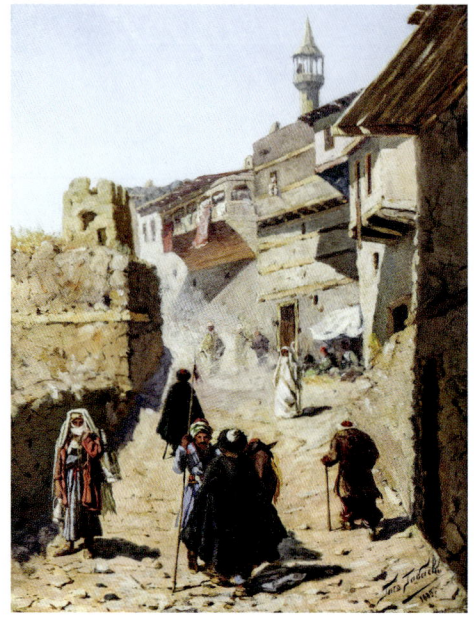

Old Tbilisi, 1885

After studying at the academies in St Petersburg and Munich between 1886 and 1897, Gabashvili held his first exhibition in Tbilisi, where he taught until 1920. There he became one of the founding professors of the State Academy of Arts. Gabashvili became famous for his realistic style, painting landscapes, portraits of peasants and townspeople and everyday scenes with an Orientalist flavour. In 1894, he travelled to Central Asia and produced many atmospheric sketches. His painting *The Bazaar in Samarkand* sold for 1.36 million dollars at Christie's in 2006.

Lisette Model

1901–1983 | Photographer | Austria, United States

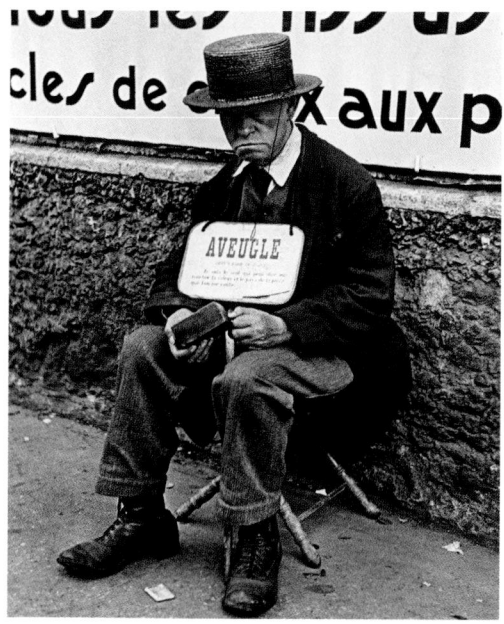

Paris, Blind Man in Front of Bilboards, 1933–1938

Born in Vienna, Model became a leading figure in American photography. She initially studied music under Arnold Schönberg and, following her father's death, moved to France with her mother. In 1933, she shifted her focus to photography, later marrying and emigrating to the United States in 1938. Her breakthrough came in 1935 with a series capturing wealthy holidaymakers in Nice. In New York, she photographed scenes in hotels, bars and nightclubs as well as portraits of celebrities such as Frank Sinatra. Model was also an influential teacher, counting Diane Arbus and Bruce Weber among her students.

10 NOVEMBER

Édouard Vuillard

1868–1940 | Painter | France

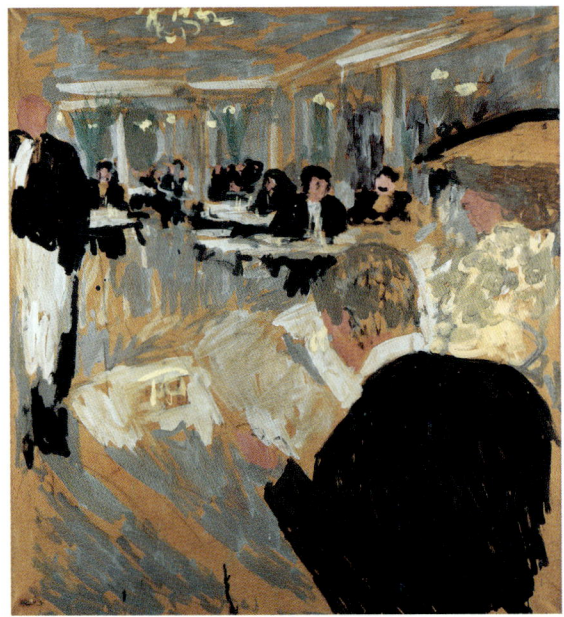

Café Scene, c. 1908–1910

Vuillard's international fame rests largely on his early work of the 1890s. As a member of the Nabis, he produced paintings and print masterpieces that established him as the "intimiste de la belle époque". His two-dimensional compositional approach, influenced by his study of Japanese woodblock prints, combined bold cropping and overlapping with a disciplined pictorial structure, while his exquisite, warm colour harmonies appear woven into a tapestry-like surface. Vuillard was a keenly observant poet of the intimate.

11 NOVEMBER

Auguste Rodin

1840–1917 | Sculptor and draughtsman | France

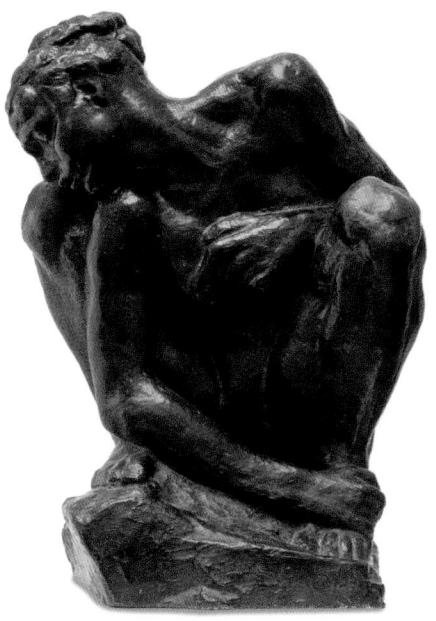

Crouching Woman, 1880–1882

One of the greatest and most influential sculptors and draughtsmen of his time, Rodin set the standard for generations of artists to follow. Drawing inspiration from antiquity and Michelangelo, he nevertheless developed a distinctly modern approach to form. For Rodin, the fragmentary became an original and authentic means of expression. Among his most important works is *The Burghers of Calais*, a monument commemorating a historic event of the fourteenth century. This figure group portrays individuals united as a collective in a common destiny. Rodin's sculptures and famous drawings are in major museum collections around the world.

_____

_____

_____

_____

12 NOVEMBER

Rosemarie Trockel

Born 1952 | Conceptual artist | Germany

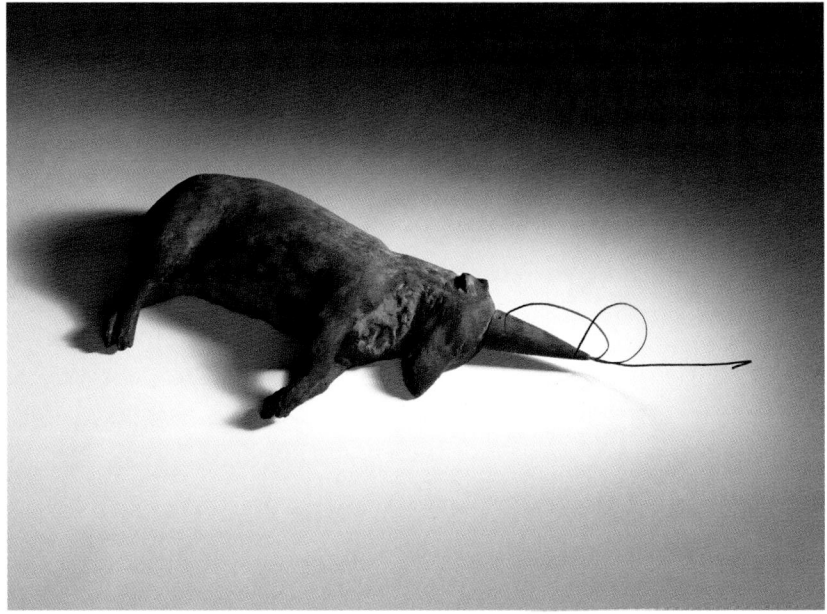

Creature of Habit 1 (Drunken Dog), 1990

An internationally renowned Conceptual artist, Trockel's practice spans a wide range of media including painting, drawing, sculpture, video and installation. Her enigmatic and intellectually complex works engage with themes such as feminism and sexuality. Some of her ambiguous objects and many delicate drawings – at times evocative of Joseph Beuys – convey a sense of the surreal and the grotesque. She became particularly well known for her *Strickbilder* (knitted pictures) and for works exploring the domestic motif of the oven. Major museum exhibitions and acquisitions and prestigious awards attest to her international standing.

13 NOVEMBER

Claude Monet

1840–1926 | Painter | France

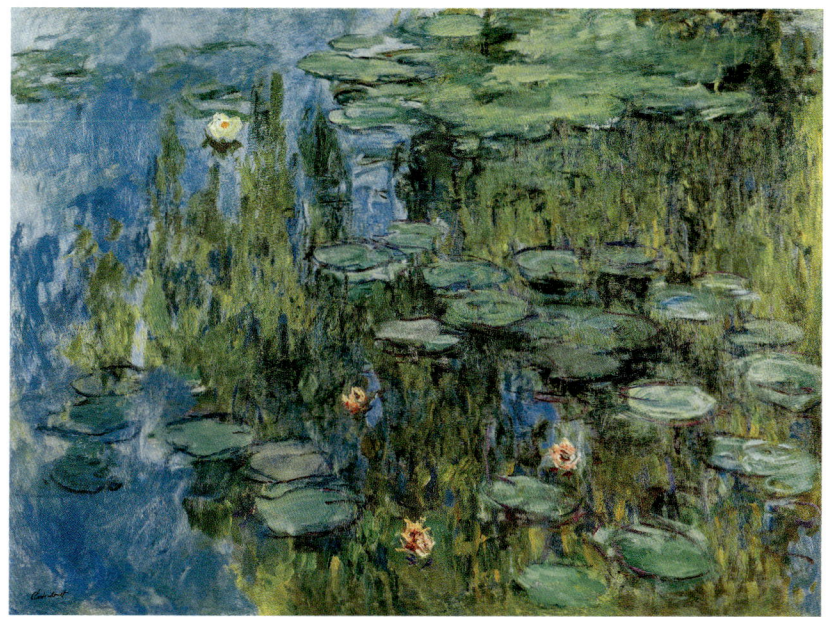

Water Lilies, c. 1915

Monet was one of the best-known French painters of his day and his fame shows no sign of abating. Not only do we have him to thank for the term *Impressionism* itself, named after his 1872 painting *Impression, Sunrise*, but he was also a major influence on Modernism by producing works in series: painting grainstacks and cathedrals in the 1890s to capture shifting light conditions, and, later, water lilies in ever-increasing degrees of abstraction. Spanning the last three decades of his life, the latter series was inspired by his garden in Giverny and includes many canvases painted to a monumental scale.

14 NOVEMBER

Georgia O'Keeffe

1887–1986 | Painter | United States

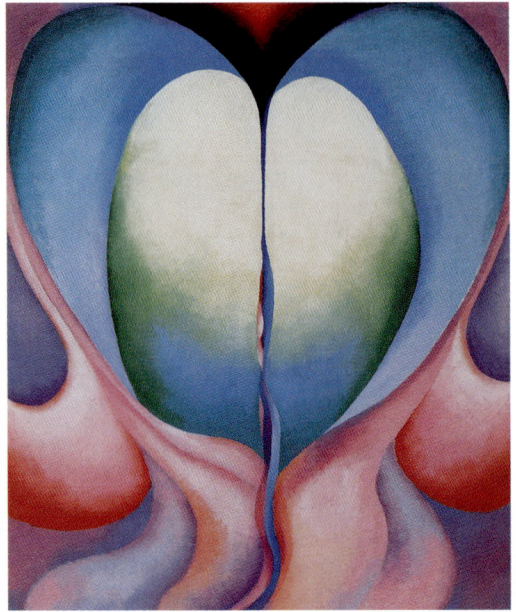

Series I, No. 8, 1919

O'Keeffe is a true icon of twentieth-century American painting. After struggling to make a name for herself, she met the photographer and gallery owner Alfred Stieglitz, who gave her a show and, in 1924, his hand in marriage as well as taking numerous photographs of her. A pioneer of abstraction, O'Keeffe gradually shifted to figuration. She explored the extreme close-up view of floral forms, in which the metaphysical and the erotic cojoined. From 1933, she often stayed in New Mexico to paint landscape and bones, moving there permanently after Stieglitz's death. She died at ninety-eight after returning from an around-the-world trip in search of new subjects.

---

15 NOVEMBER

Katharina Sieverding

Born 1941 | Artist | Germany

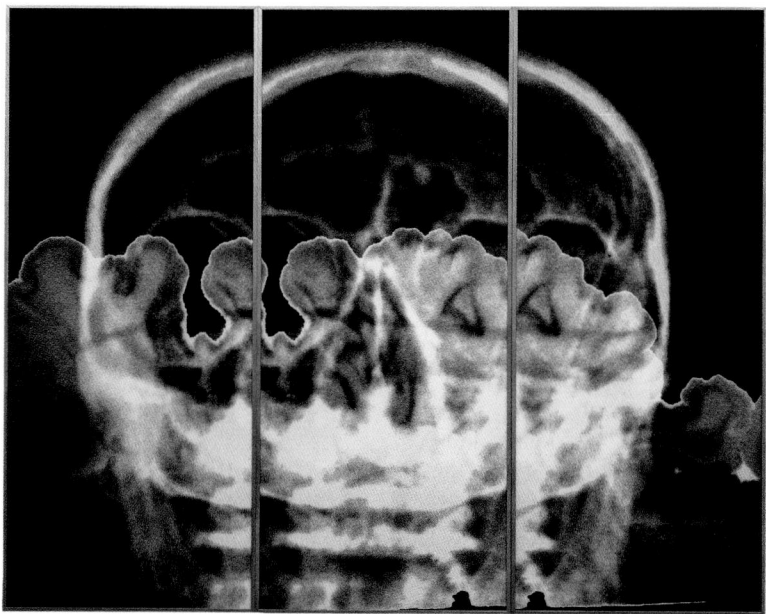

Capillary Dynamolysis III, 1997

As an internationally renowned artist, Sieverding expanded the visual vernacular of art photography, in particular by working in unprecedently large formats. In Hamburg, she met the legendary Austrian theatre director Fritz Kortner, whom she subsequently followed to Vienna to work in costume design. From 1967, she studied under Joseph Beuys in Düsseldorf. In the mid-1970s, she became known for her close-ups of her own face and her political statements on the Nazi period, German identity, power and violence. Her work has been honoured through exhibitions, museum acquisitions and prizes around the world.

16 NOVEMBER

Agnolo Bronzino

1503–1572 | Painter | Italy

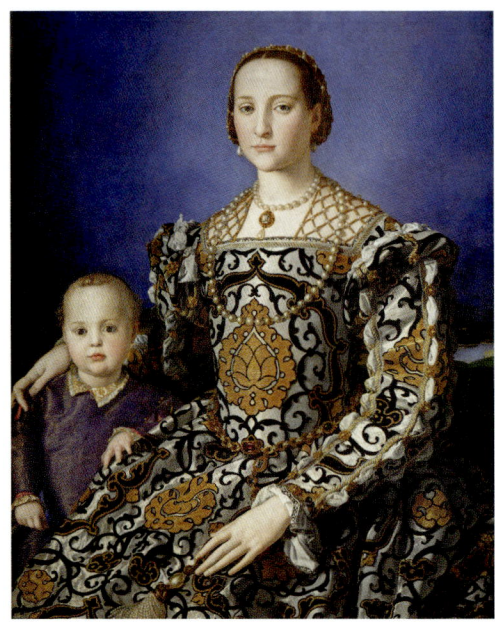

Eleonora di Toledo with Son Giovanni de' Medici, c. 1545

A native of Florence, Bronzino was an important painter and draughtsman of the sixteenth century and a key figure in Mannerism. In the 1530s, he became court painter to the Medici, responsible for festive decorations, among other things. He spent nearly his entire life in Florence, where, in addition to frescoes and altarpieces, he painted outstanding portraits of members of the Medici family and the Florentine nobility, as well as poets and musicians, thereby cementing his fame. Many of his portraits are characterized by a noble, even haughty, reserve. Bronzino's works are found in major museum collections around the globe.

Louis Daguerre

1787–1851 | Painter and inventor of the daguerreotype | France

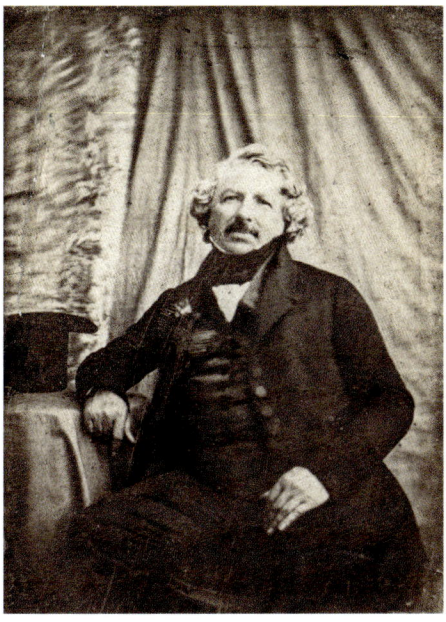

Louis-Jacques-Mandé Daguerre (1787–1851), c. 1844

The invention of the daguerreotype, the first commercially viable photographic process, heralded the dawn of the modern photographic age. Daguerre, a busy panorama painter, made a name for himself in the mid-1810s as a set painter for a popular theatre in Paris. Thanks to its many multimedia effects, his Parisian diorama was a run-away success. In 1839, he first demonstrated to the public his photographic process of fixing images on light-sensitive materials. The French government acquired the rights, and Daguerre, who was honoured many times over, received a pension for life.

18 NOVEMBER

Bertel Thorvaldsen

1770–1844 | Sculptor | Denmark

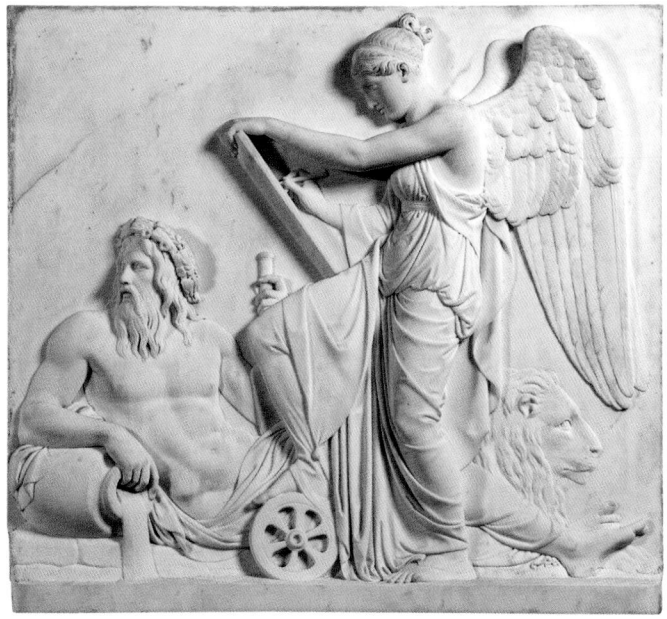

Epitaph for Johann Philipp von Bethmann-Hollweg, Rome, 1813–1832

This sculptor was the most important artist of Danish Neoclassicism, reviving something of the spirit of antiquity in his idealized mythological figures. He started working in Rome in 1797. In 1805, he joined the ranks of the Royal Danish Academy in Copenhagen and the Academy in Bologna, and soon received commissions from no less than Napoleon himself. In the 1820s and 1830s, he maintained a studio in both Copenhagen and Rome, where he was commissioned by the Vatican to make the sepulchral monument to Pope Pius VII in St Peter's Basilica. The Thorvaldsen Museum opened in his hometown in 1846, just two years after his death.

19 NOVEMBER

Rachel Khedoori

Born 1964 | Artist | Australia

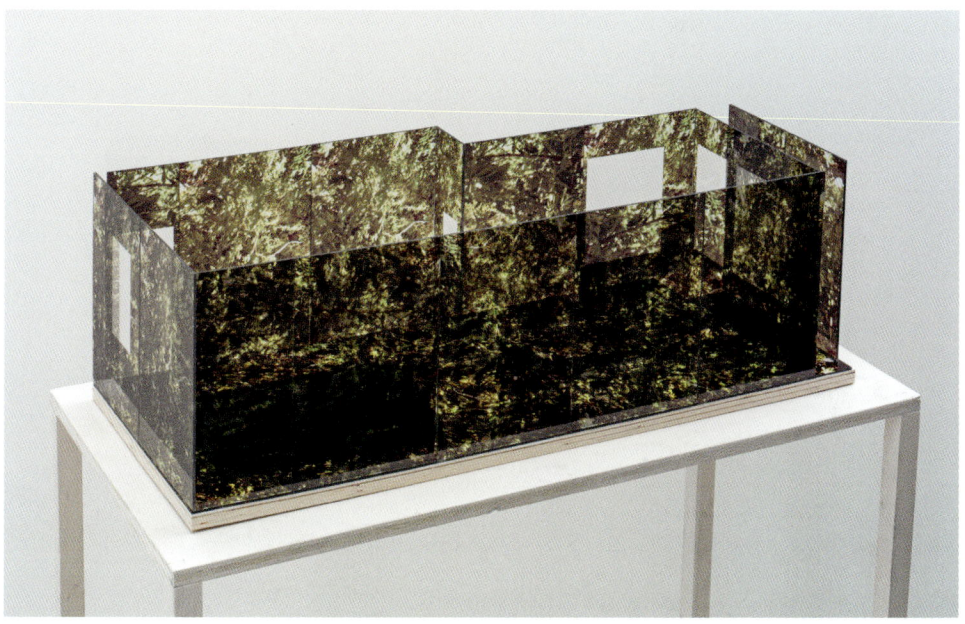

Untitled, 2005

Rachel Khedoori first exhibited in a joint show with her twin sister, Toba, in 1994. In 2001, the Kunsthalle Basel gave the artist her first European solo show, which brought her work to the attention of the international art world. Khedoori presented films that were projected onto two- and three-dimensional objects, allowing video, sculpture and architecture to correspond to the viewer's movements through the space. In this way, her art links the two- and three-dimensional, the experienced and dreamed, seen and heard, and makes the gallery visitor part of the work.

20 NOVEMBER

René Magritte

1898–1967 | Painter | Belgium

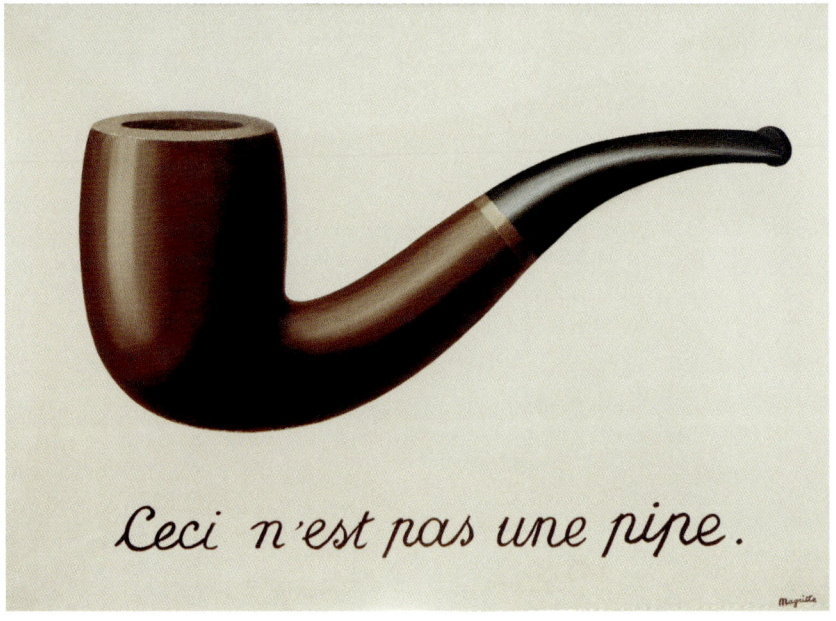

The Treachery of Images, 1929

The Belgian painter and master of Surrealism left a lasting legacy to future generations of Pop and Conceptual artists. Based in Paris and Brussels, he was friends with
Surrealists such as André Breton and Salvador Dalí. In his paintings, he recurringly
made use of quotidian motifs, such as an apple, pipe, curtains, a house, table and
forest, which he defamiliarized. In diagrammatic assemblages that could be described
as "thought pictures", Magritte highlights the gap between an object's image and its
linguistic term. In *The Treachery of Images*, for example, he shows a painted pipe,
while pointing out in the caption: "Ceci n'est pas une pipe."

21 NOVEMBER

Ignaz Günther

1725–1775 | Sculptor | Germany

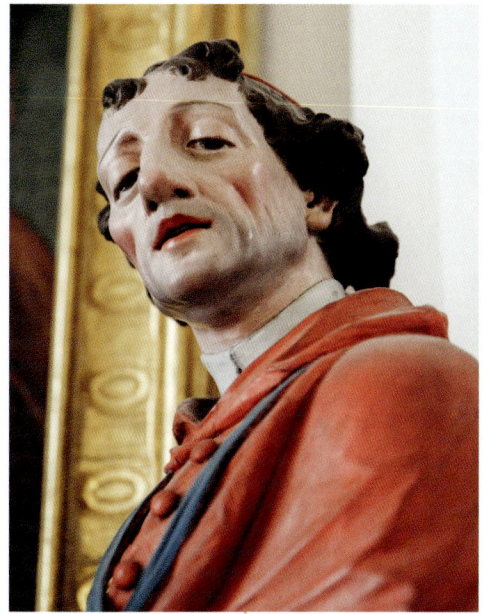

St Peter Damian, c. 1762/1763

Günther is the perfect embodiment of the Bavarian Rococo. A pupil of Johann Baptist Straub in Munich in the 1740s, after his journeyman years he attended the Vienna Academy in 1753, whereupon he set up his own workshop in Munich the following year. He created church furnishings, altarpieces, individual figures and figural groups that rank among the finest sculptures produced in the eighteenth century. His depictions of the Pietà are particularly poignant. Besides his work as a sculptor, he also produced important drawings.

22 NOVEMBER

Marie Bashkirtseff

1858/60 – 1884 | Painter | Russia

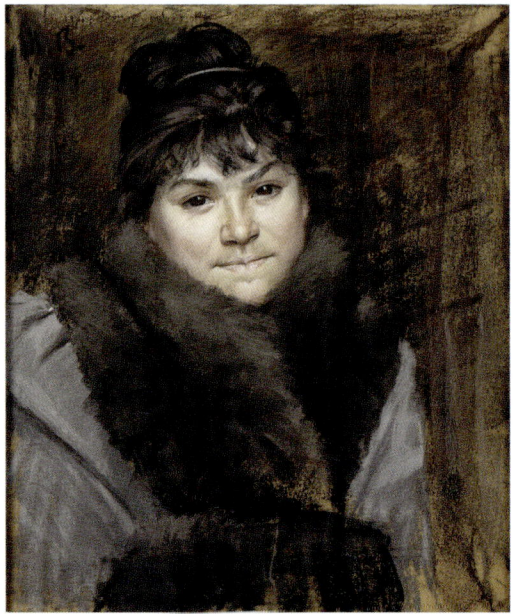

Portrait of Madame X, c. 1883/1884

Scion of a wealthy Russian aristocratic family, Bashkirtseff grew up with her mother and grandparents. The family sojourned in style on the French Riviera from 1870 to 1872, when Bashkirtseff started keeping a diary. In 1877, she commenced studying painting in Paris and subsequently opened her own studio, where she made portraits and naturalistic multi-figure paintings. She died of tuberculosis at an early age. Her diary, a cult book for women of her generation, was published in three languages from 1887 and sold well. Her life, from aristocratic beginnings to studio owner, was the subject of many books.

23 NOVEMBER

Henri de Toulouse-Lautrec

1864–1901 | Painter and printmaker | France

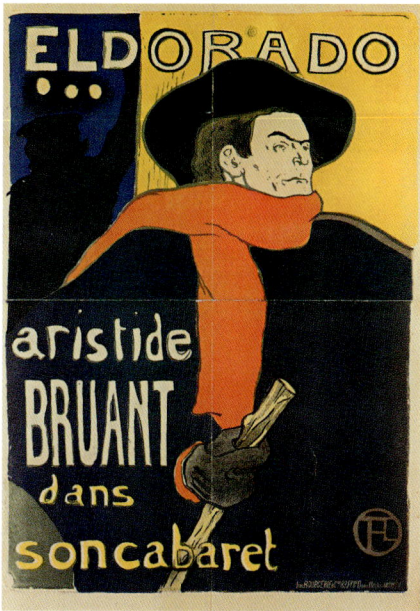

Eldorado: Aristide Bruant, 1892

The French painter and graphic artist is world-renowned primarily for his posters. The son of an aristocratic family, he suffered from a hereditary disease resulting in stunted growth. The highly talented artist studied under various teachers from 1882 and soon arrived at his unique signature style. His recurring subject was the denizens of Montmartre, where he lived the life of a bohemian, drawing inspiration from the demimonde that frequented the night cafés and appeared, most notably, in his lithographic posters such as the one for the Moulin Rouge.

24 NOVEMBER

Maurice Denis

1870–1943 | Painter| France

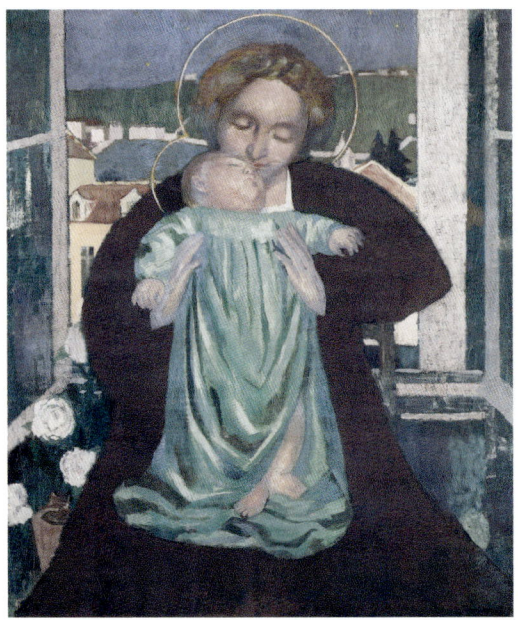

Madonna and Child (The Kiss), 1902

A founding member of the Nabis, Denis was widely seen as the group's ideological leader thanks to his theoretical writings. Between 1890 and 1927, he travelled around Italy and later much of the globe. He created frescoes, paintings, prints and book illustrations in the Symbolist style, with gently undulating contours and pastel-coloured surfaces. An advocate of a "naive simplicity of execution", as he called it, Denis strove for stark simplification of form. In 1919, the devout Catholic founded the Ateliers d'Art Sacré, an artists' collective that would soon have a strong influence on religious art in Europe.

25 NOVEMBER

Kara Walker

Born 1969 | Artist | United States

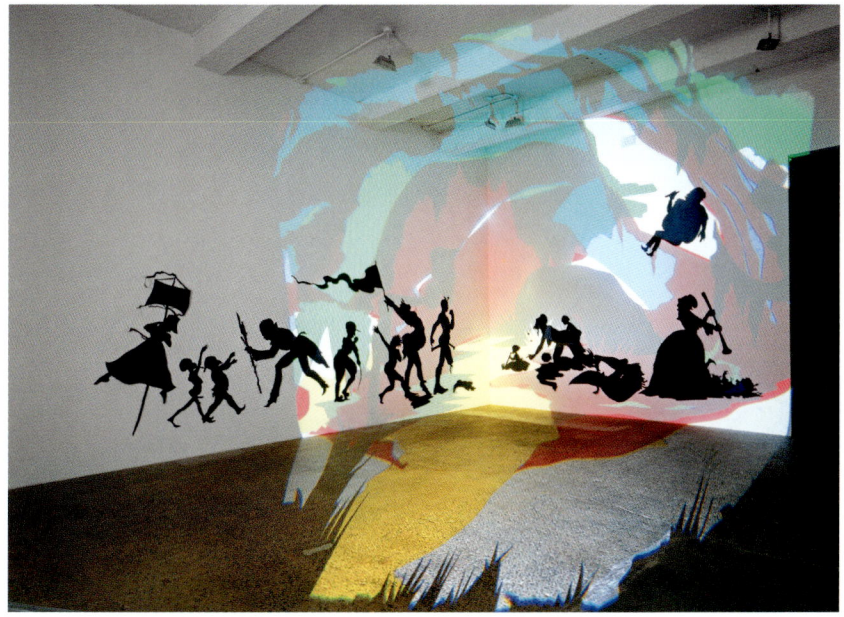

Darkytown Rebellion, 2001

This American is one of the most internationally recognized Black artists active today. Her fame is based above all on her monumental black cut-paper silhouettes mounted on the gallery wall. Working in this medium, she creates seemingly playful multifigure panoramas, whose dark underlying themes such as racism, violent sexuality and oppression make them profound existential statements. Numerous accolades, international exhibitions and museum acquisitions of her art bear witness to Walker's exceptional place in contemporary art production.

26 NOVEMBER

Léonard Tsuguharu Foujita

1886–1968 | Painter and printmaker | Japan, France

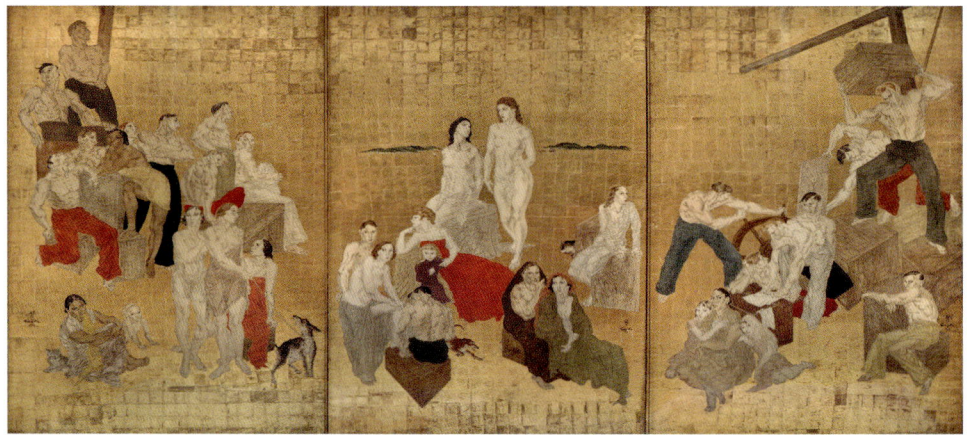

The Arrival of Westerners in Japan, 1929

After studying in Tokyo, Foujita moved to Paris in 1913, where he met important artists and befriended Amedeo Modigliani, among others. His art is the interfusion of traditional Japanese and modern European art and first went on view in Europe in 1917. In the mid-1920s, he started featuring in major international exhibitions. His career led him to New York, back to Japan, where he was much celebrated, and finally back to France, where he is best remembered for his frescoes for a chapel in Reims. His eccentric life was peppered by a string of affairs and marriages, for example, with the painter Fernande Barrey.

27 NOVEMBER

Lotte Laserstein

1898–1993 | Painter | Germany, Sweden

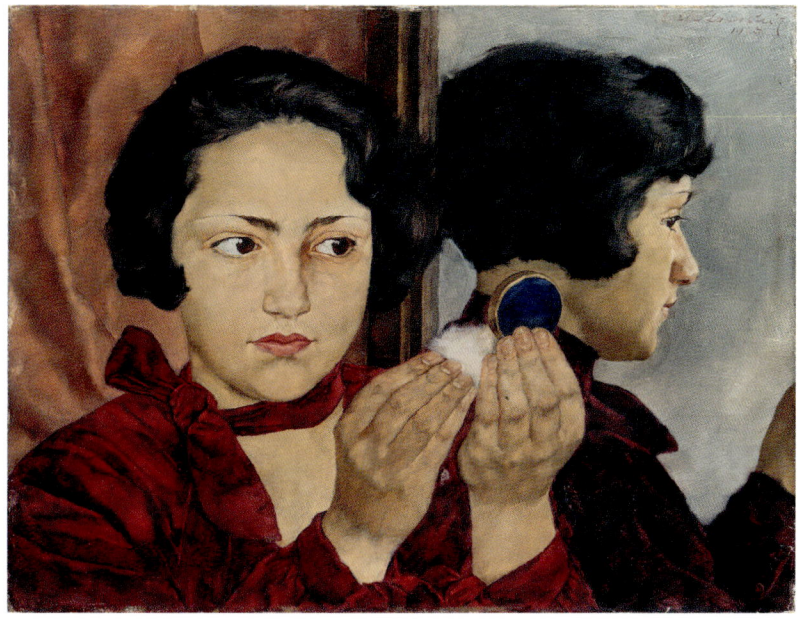

Russian Girl with Compact, 1928

Laserstein was an important German-Swedish painter who was only plucked from obscurity after her art was featured in exhibitions in England and Germany in the 1980s, shortly before her death. She enjoyed her critical and commercial heyday between 1927 and 1933; during this period she painted *Evening over Potsdam*, which was acquired by the Nationalgalerie in Berlin in 2010. Central to her work were her portraits, whose objective style epitomized the "new woman" of the 1920s. Declared "three-quarter Jewish" by the Nazis and banned from exhibiting, she emigrated to Sweden in 1937, remaining artistically active into old age.

28 NOVEMBER

Guillaume Coustou the Elder

1677–1746 | Sculptor | France

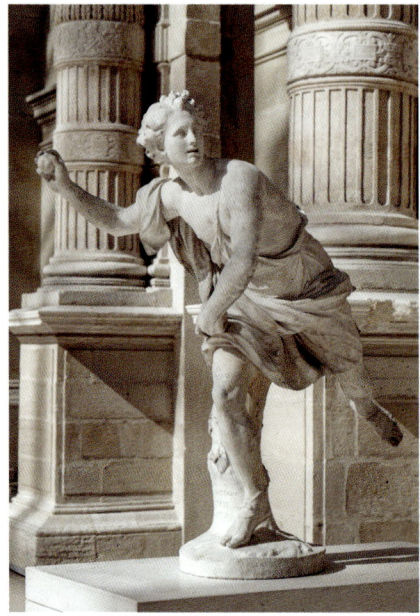

Hippomenes, 1711/1712

This French sculptor, who came from a family of artists, went to Paris at the age of eighteen and won the Académie Royale's Prix de Rome just two years later. However, unlike his elder brother, he did not stay at the Académie de France in Rome, but soon entered the Roman workshop of Pierre Le Gros, who had a strong influence on him. When he returned to Paris, Coustou held several prestigious posts until 1733. He carved numerous marble sculptures of horses and mythological figures, now preserved in Versailles and at the Louvre.

29 NOVEMBER

Marina Abramović

Born 1946 | Performance and conceptual artist | Serbia

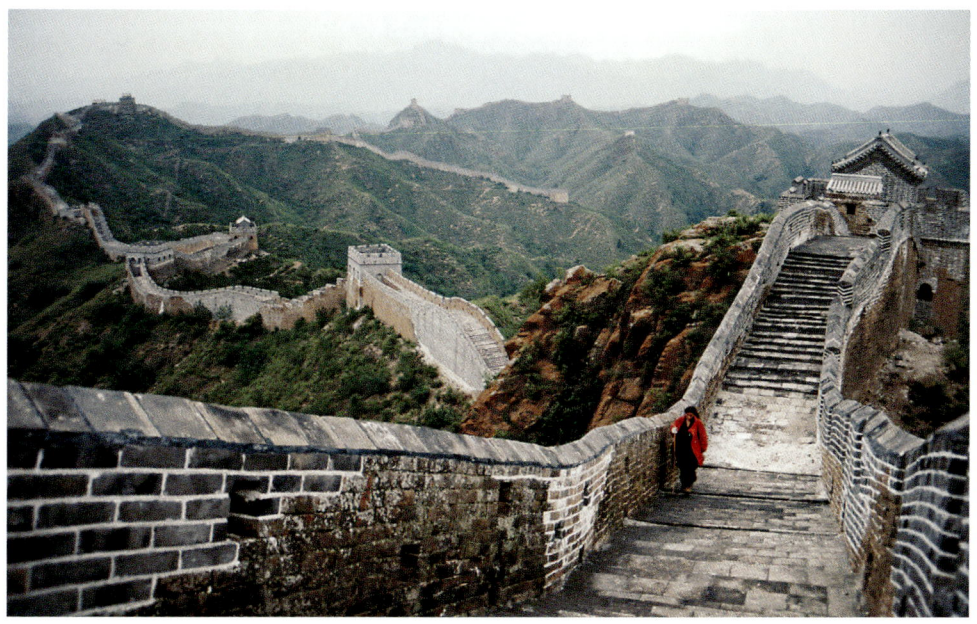

The Lovers – The Great Wall Walk (with Ulay), 1988

The world-famous Conceptual and body artist revolutionized contemporary art with performances marked by a degree of physical risk. Her oeuvre, which could be paraphrased as endurance in the name of art, was only possible due to the uncompromising radicalism of her vision and her severity towards her own body. She collaborated with her partner, Ulay, from 1976 to 1988. Her performance *The Artist Is Present*, in which she sat on a chair for three months looking thousands of visitors to the Museum of Modern Art in New York directly in the eye, made her a household name. International professorships, prizes and exhibitions testify to her critical acclaim.

30 NOVEMBER

Marie Tussaud

1761–1850 | Wax sculptor | France

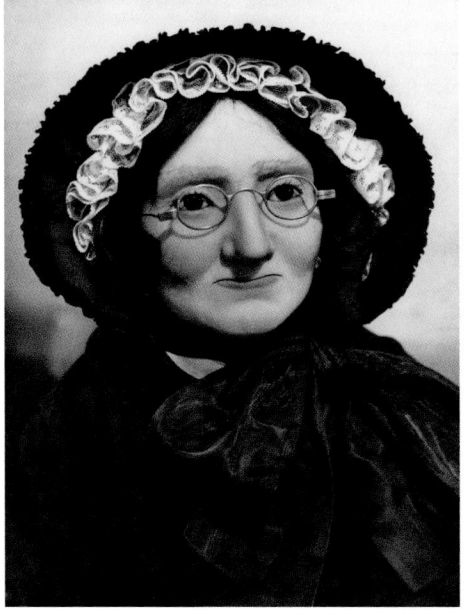

Madame (Marie) Tussaud, undated

Tussaud was born shortly after her father's death. Her mother was taken in by a man called Philippe Curtius, whom she followed to Paris in 1767. There, Curtius set up a waxworks cabinet. Marie quickly learned the modelling technique from him. At seventeen, she created the first life-size portrait of Voltaire and later heads of other luminaries of the age. After Curtius's death in 1794, she inherited his collection and soon got married. Having survived the Reign of Terror, she made Great Britain her home in 1802. In London in 1835, the French wax sculptor opened the museum named after her, subsequently passing the business on to her two sons.

1 DECEMBER

Georges Seurat

1859–1891 | Painter and draughtsman | France

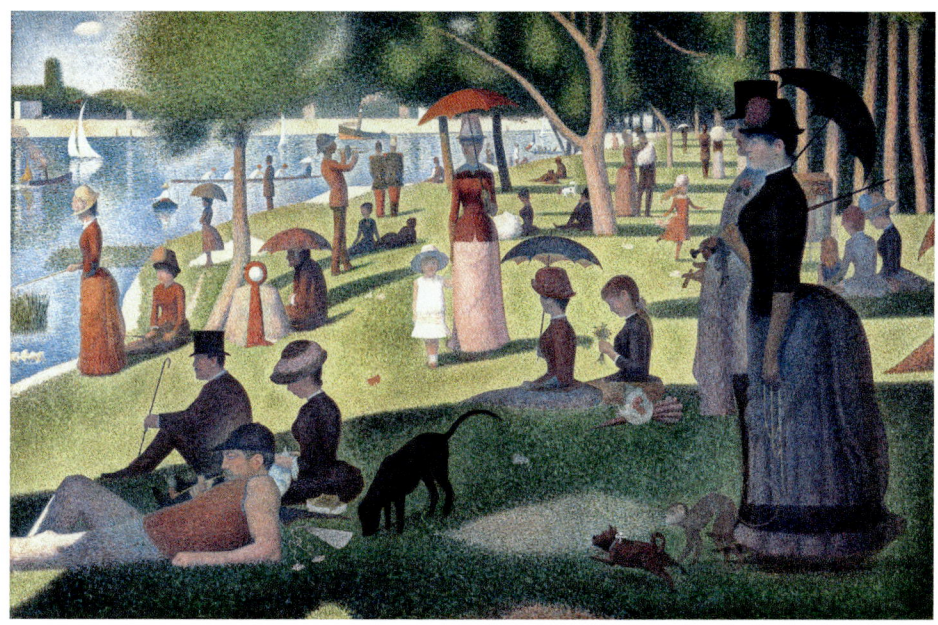

A Sunday on La Grande Jatte, 1884–1886

This French artist was one of the great methodical minds who, distancing himself from the Impressionist temperament, sought discipline and regularity in composition. Surface construction and geometry, as well as a new understanding of colour, led to him achieving absolute harmony in his images. Largely the product of scientific study, his Pointillist technique marked the optical combination of colour values and light values. Seurat's paintings and drawings occupied a singular place in the art production of his time and were an inspiration to many later artists.

2 DECEMBER

Constantin Guys

1802–1892 | Painter and draughtsman | The Netherlands, France

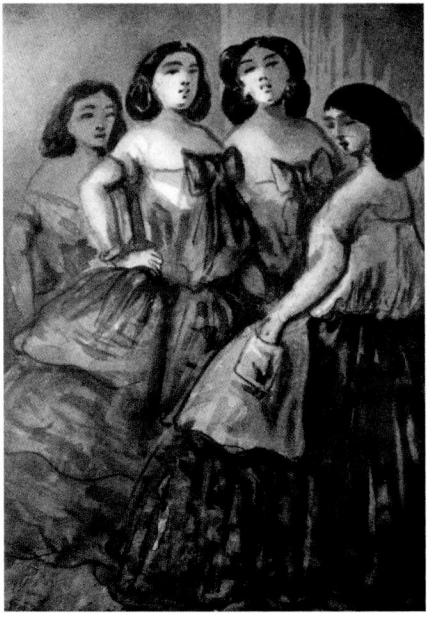

Four Girls, nineteenth century

The Dutch-French artist fought in the Greek War of Independence as a young man.
He later taught himself how to watercolour and draw by studying works by Rembrandt
van Rijn, Francisco de Goya and others. In 1830, he had his first major success with
drawings and lithographs and travelled to places in the Ottoman Empire and London
and Paris, where in 1860 he decided to settle, becoming friends with Charles Baudelaire
and Honoré Daumier. He was a critically astute chronicler of the society of his time.
His choice of subject was, above all, the life of the bourgeoisie during the Second
French Empire, their pleasures – and their vices.

3 DECEMBER

Felice Casorati

1883–1963 | Painter | Italy

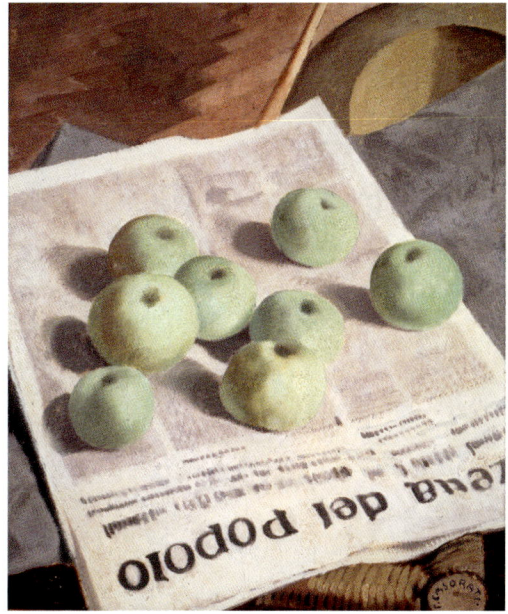

Apples, 1930

This Italian was an important figurative painter in the first half of the twentieth century. Casorati was initially indebted to Symbolism and Viennese Art Nouveau, before the Metaphysical Painting of Giorgio de Chirico and the imagery of Paul Gauguin took his art in a new direction. Often imbued with a cool classicism, Casorati's figure paintings adhere to a strict compositional scheme that echoes the traditions of the Early Renaissance. Based in Turin from 1918, Casorati taught at the Turin Academy from the 1920s onwards and was highly regarded for his nudes, portraits and still lifes.

_____

_____

_____

_____

4 DECEMBER

Alexander Rodchenko

1891–1956 | Painter, printmaker, photographer and architect | Russia

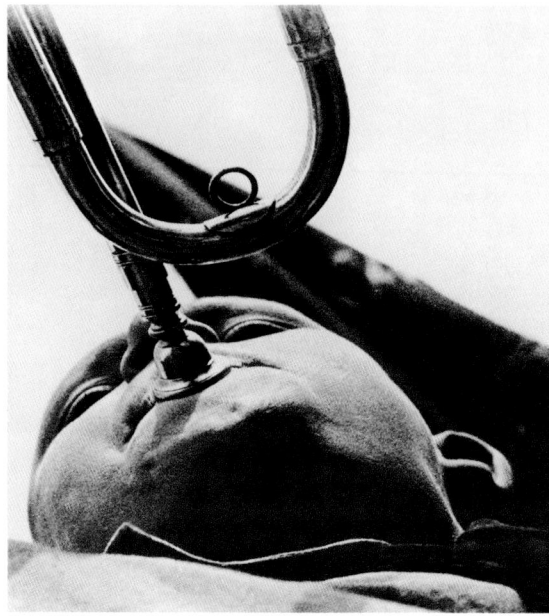

Pioneer with Horn, 1930

In 1914, Rodchenko moved to Moscow, where he studied sculpture and architecture. With his abstract paintings and drawings, he staked his place as a foremost member of the avant-garde. In the early 1920s, he created experimental Constructivist sculptures and declared that painting was dead. Rodchenko saw art as an organic part of life, with the artist called upon to help forge modern society. He worked with his wife on the production of industrially manufactured objects of the everyday. Also prolific in the areas of book design and photography, Rodchenko took part in many international exhibitions.

5 DECEMBER

Frédéric Bazille

1841–1870 | Painter | France

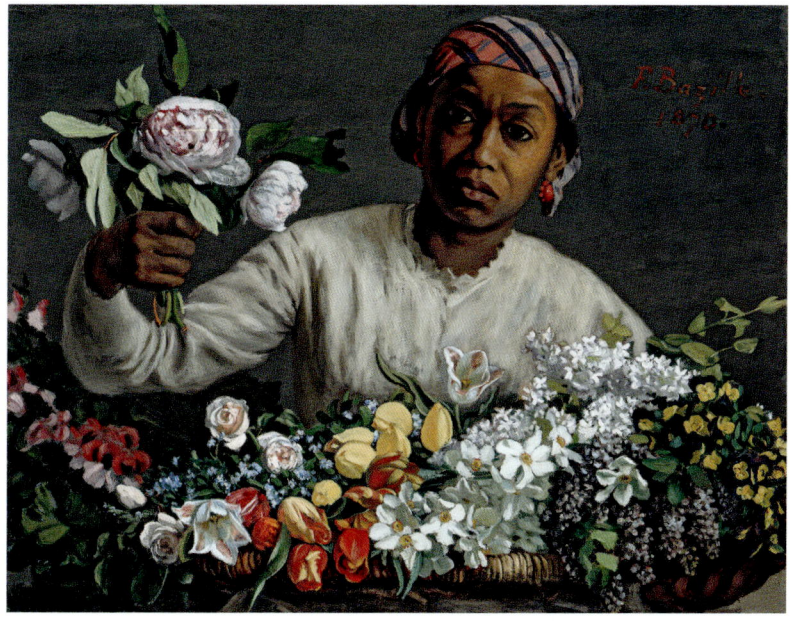

Young Woman with Peonies, 1870

The son of a wealthy family, Bazille moved to the French capital in 1862. He produced some sixty pictures – portraits and figural scenes with landscape backdrops – in the mere space of eight years, managing to exhibit just a handful and selling none, before his early death in 1870 fighting in the Franco-Prussian War. In Paris, he shared his studio with Pierre-Auguste Renoir. He often had painting sessions with his Impressionist friends, such as Claude Monet, and even offered some of them financial and material support by tapping into the family fortune. Found in museum collections in France and the United States, his canvases now fetch high prices.

6 DECEMBER

Gian Lorenzo Bernini

1598–1680 | Sculptor | Italy

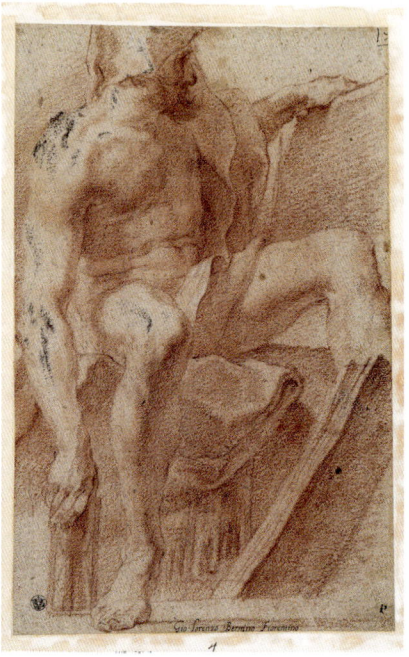

Kronos, undated

One of the greatest and most influential Italian sculptors of the Baroque, Bernini also left his mark as an architect. He came to Rome from his birthplace of Naples in 1606. Bernini's early work included iconographically inventive mythological sculptural groups. His patron Pope Urban VIII commissioned him to create the canopy over the tomb of St Peter in the Basilica of St Peter. He later designed the colonnade lining St Peter's Square and made the famous Fountain of the Four Rivers in the Piazza Navona. Works of his, including portrait busts and drawings, are preserved in museums across the globe.

7 DECEMBER

Lucian Freud

1922–2011 | Painter | Great Britain

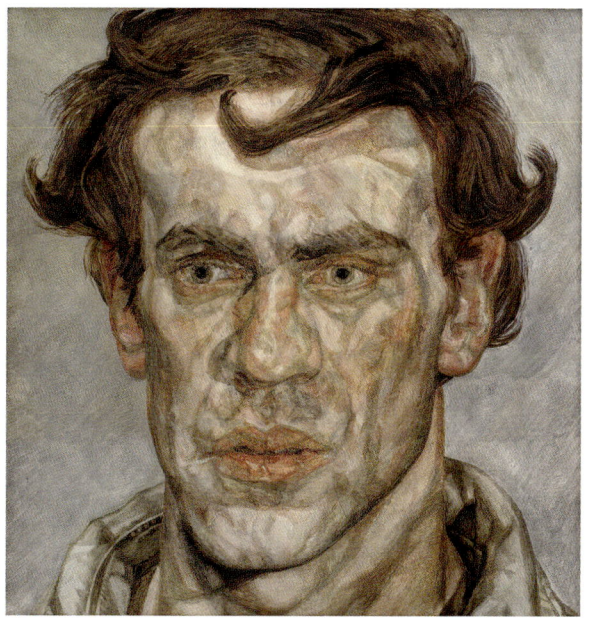

A Young Painter, 1957/1958

Freud was one of the greatest figurative painters and etchers in twentieth-century European art. The grandson of Sigmund Freud, he was born in Berlin and emigrated with his family to England in 1933. At the age of nineteen, he took a flat in London that he would occupy for the next thirty years. Freud's worldwide fame rests on his haunting portraits, often large-scale nudes, which present the female and male body with unflinching candour. His models were mostly drawn from his personal circle, and he would spend months studying them – in motion, at rest, even asleep. Of his unsparing pictures he once said, "I don't paint nudes, I paint naked portraits."

8 DECEMBER

John McCracken

1934–2011 | Sculptor | United States

Untitled, 1981

A born and bred Californian, McCracken became known in the mid-1960s for his Minimalist objects – monochrome, smooth of surface and reduced to the simplest geometric form. After starting out as a painter, he began producing objects from industrial materials, often with reflective surfaces, in which the concise, pure form chimes perfectly with the material's luminous shine. Numerous exhibitions in Europe and the United States have garnered him an international reputation.

9 DECEMBER

Adriaen van Ostade

1610 (baptism)–1685 | Painter and etcher | The Netherlands

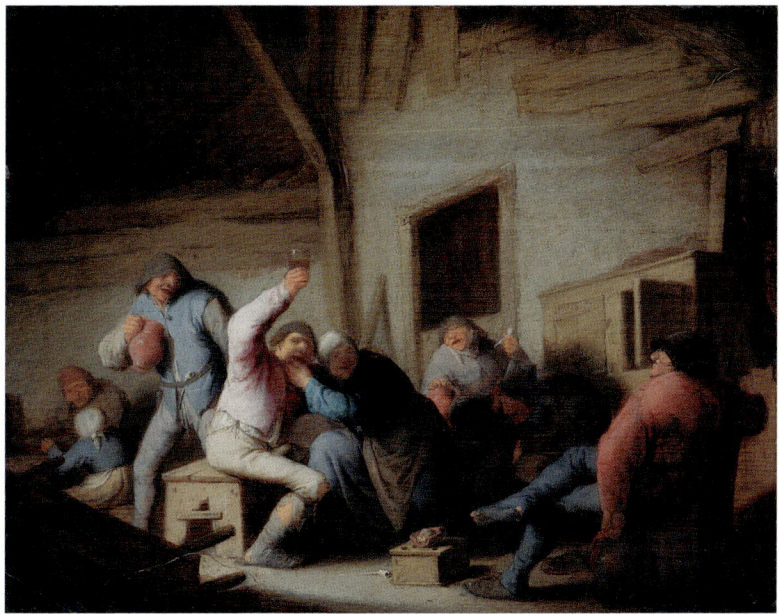

Carousing Peasants in a Tavern, c. 1635

Apprenticed to Frans Hals in 1627 or thereabouts, the Dutch painter and etcher was the author of a number of small-format genre scenes depicting the burgher and peasant classes and rendered in the style of his teacher. With biting humour, his images feature smokers, drinkers, gamblers and brawling men. Ostade later borrowed from Rembrandt's style of painting, especially his use of chiaroscuro. Ostade had numerous pupils, and his paintings fetched high prices during his lifetime. Ostade's works can be found in many major European museum collections.

10 DECEMBER

Mark Tobey

1890–1976 | Painter | United States

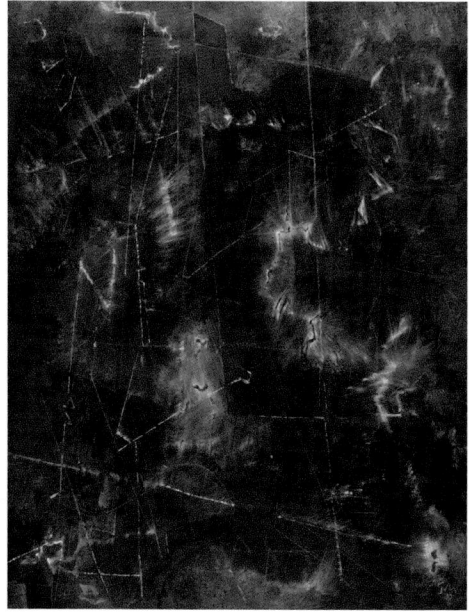

Above the Earth, 1953

After moving to Seattle in 1922, the painter was introduced to Chinese painting by a Chinese artist. Tobey subsequently lived in Paris before travelling to Mexico and Asia, including Japan, where he spent some time in a Zen monastery and studied East Asian calligraphy. In 1935, he produced his first painting with delicate calligraphic marks that he called "white writing". His canvases vibrate with a humming network of lines and signs, in a technique that predated the Abstract Expressionism of Jackson Pollock. Tobey received the highest accolade in 1958, when he was awarded the Golden Lion at the Venice Biennale.

11 DECEMBER

Edvard Munch

1863–1944 | Painter and printmaker | Norway

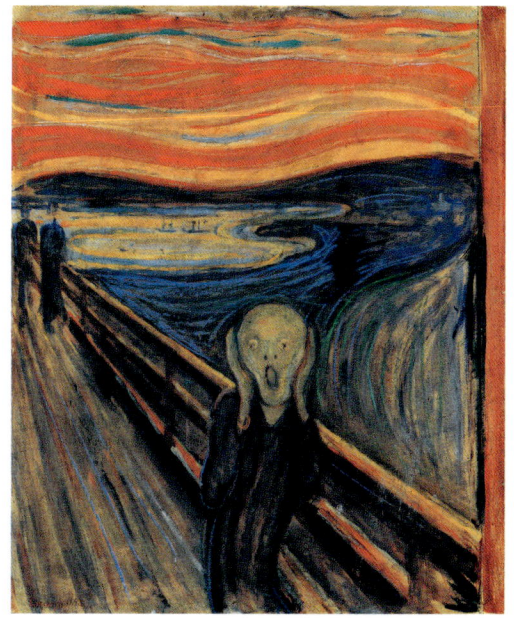

The Scream, 1893

The psychological depth and wilful style of the Norwegian's art soon guaranteed his place as one of the great artists of his day. Mournful childhood memories and the experience of abandonment and death flowed into his – often dark – art, while prolonged illness and alcoholism gradually took their toll on his nerves. His career took him to Paris, Berlin and back to Norway, where he lived from 1909 until his death. Munch succeeded in turning underlying states of panic and a nervous sensibility into a unique visual vernacular. His expressive and overtly emotional paintings and wood-cuts had a lasting impact on subsequent generations of artists.

12 DECEMBER

Emily Carr

1871–1945 | Painter | Canada

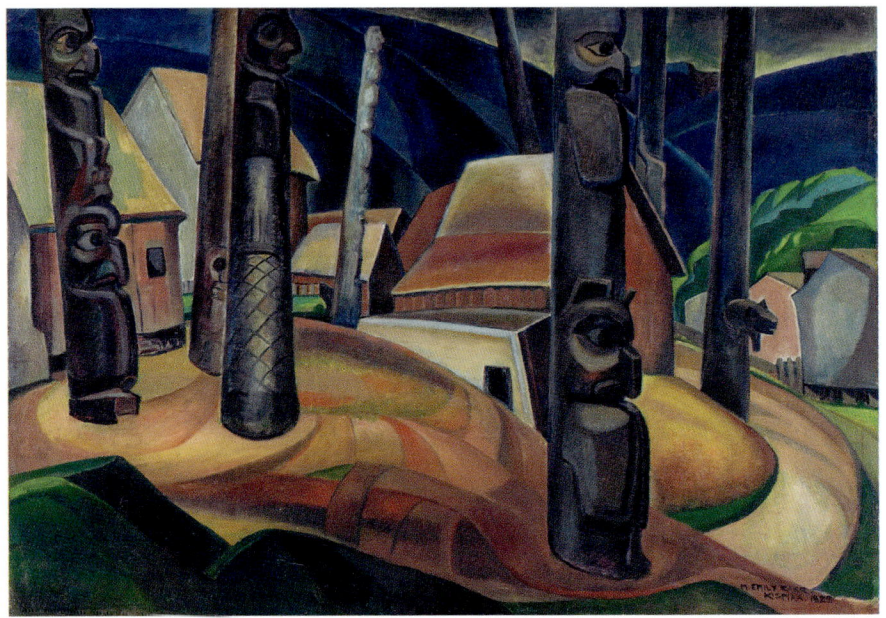

Kispiox Village, 1929

This Canadian painter and writer went to San Francisco and later to London to study art. In 1905, she returned to her homeland, living with the Indigenous peoples to visually document the lives of the First Nations. She also started painting totem poles. In 1910, she came into contact with the art of Henri Matisse and Pablo Picasso in Paris, but this did not draw her away from her chosen path of painting native Canadian subjects. As an author, she wrote popular travel accounts. In the 1930s, she had a series of successful exhibitions and remains a household name in Canada.

13 DECEMBER

Pierre Puvis de Chavannes

1824–1898 | Painter | France

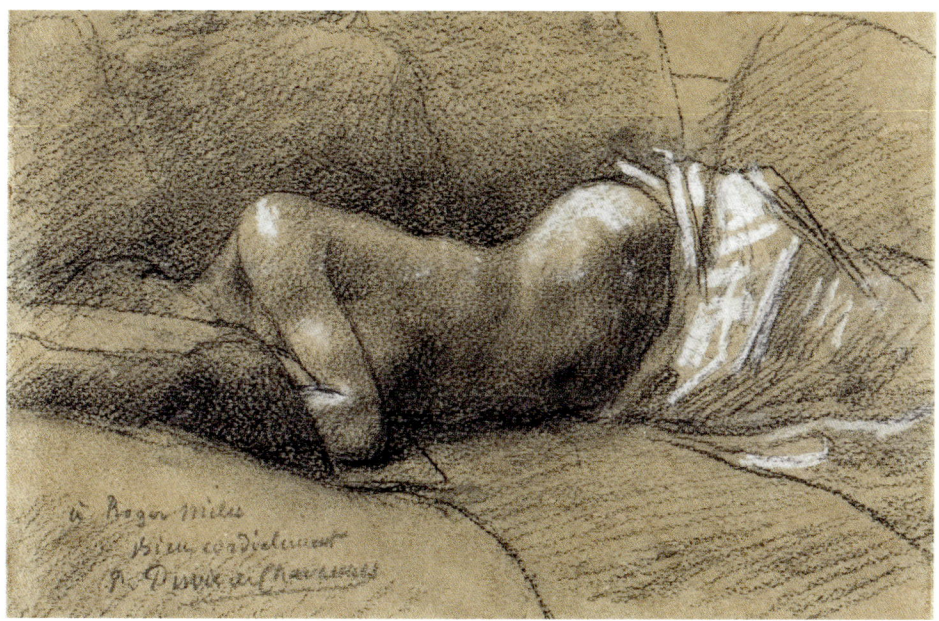

Study of a Sleeping Woman, c. 1867

The formative years of de Chavannes, who was a member of the haute bourgeoisie, were marked by two trips to Italy and contact with Eugène Delacroix, resulting in a brief spell as the latter's pupil. In 1852, he set up his own studio in Paris, working from the life model. His breakthrough came late. He made numerous paintings and drawings in the Symbolist style but is best known for his large murals in public buildings, such as those in Paris and Boston. In terms of the style of his figures and his choice of colours, some of his paintings seem to anticipate Pablo Picasso's Neoclassical period.

14 DECEMBER

David Teniers the Younger

1610–1690 | Painter, draughtsman and curator | Flanders

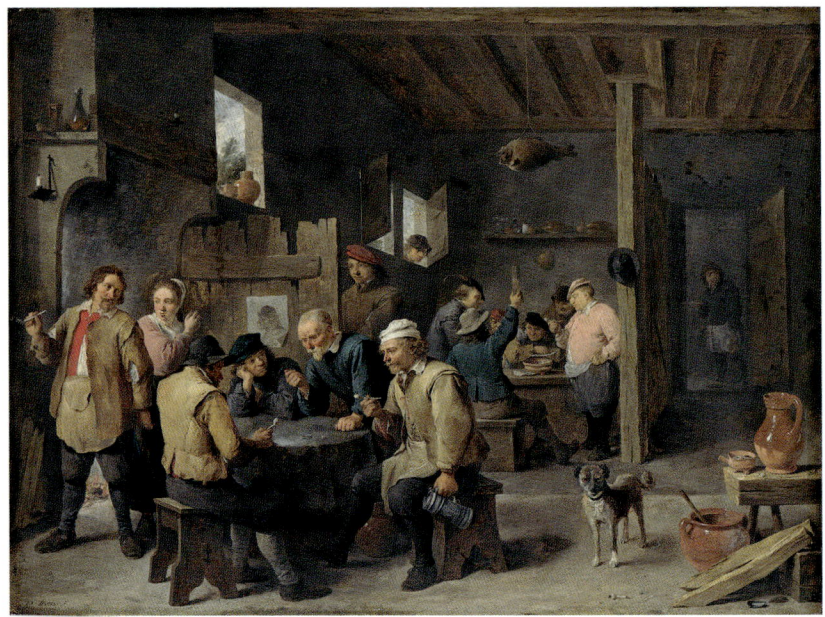

Tavern Scene, 1643

The astonishingly prolific Flemish painter and printmaker was one of the most important genre painters of the seventeenth century. Principally influenced by Peter Paul Rubens, he also created history paintings, landscapes, portraits and still lifes. He was famous for his numerous peasant scenes of revellers, smokers and card players. In 1664, he founded the Antwerp Academy as a place to train young artists. Shortly before this, he was the custodian of Archduke Leopold Wilhelm's painting collection in Brussels, for whom he compiled an inventory catalogue. His works are scattered across museum collections all over the world.

15 DECEMBER

Wassily Kandinsky

1866–1944 | Painter and printmaker | Russia, Germany, France

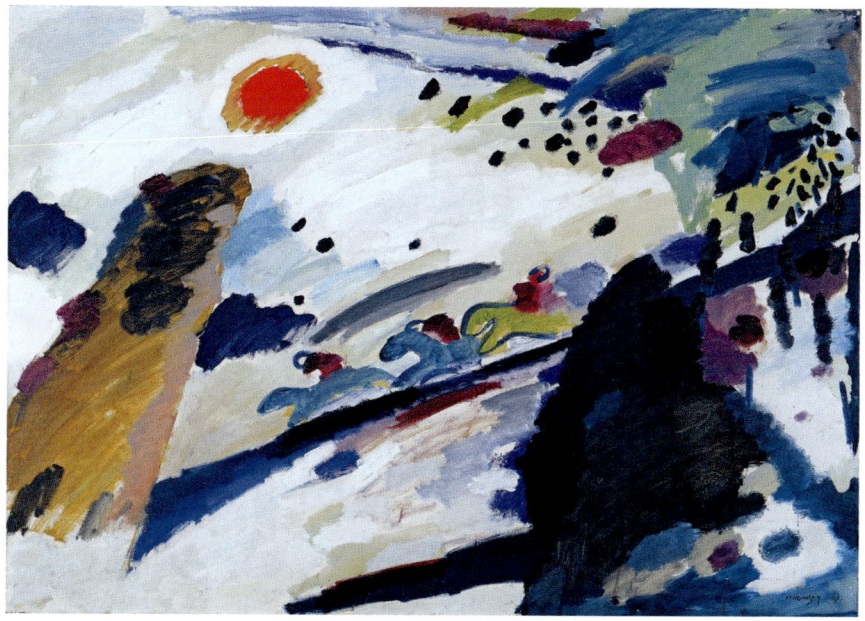

Romantic Landscape, 1911

This Russian artist revolutionized painting in the first decades of the twentieth century. He began his studies in Munich in 1900, creating his first abstract watercolour in 1910. Together with Franz Marc, he participated in the inaugural exhibition of the legendary group Der Blaue Reiter. After spending 1914 to 1921 in Moscow, he taught at the Bauhaus for over ten years, first in Weimar and then in Dessau, becoming one of its longest-serving instructors. After its dissolution in 1933, he emigrated to France, living just outside Paris. A master colourist, the painter's keenly felt synaesthesia led him on a quest for what he called "the inner sound".

16 DECEMBER

François-Marius Granet

1775–1849 | Landscape, genre and history painter| France

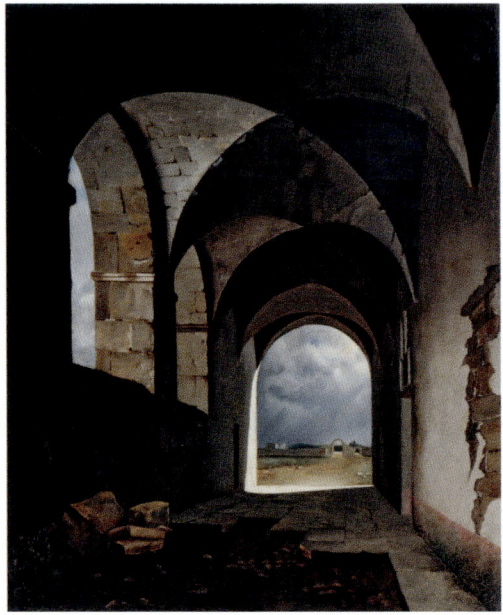

Light Effect in Ruins, c. 1820

In 1796, Granet moved to Paris, where he met the great Neoclassical painters Jacques-Louis David and Jean-Auguste-Dominique Ingres, who had a profound influence on his art. He initially painted interior scenes of monasteries and churches. In 1802, he moved to Rome, where he spent the next twenty years, broadening his repertoire from scenes in religious settings to include landscapes. The light and atmosphere in these pictures would later have a great influence on French *plein-air* painting. He was appointed curator of the Musée du Louvre in 1826, and in 1830, he became director of the picture gallery in Versailles. His artist estate is preserved in the Musée Granet in Aix-en-Provence.

17 DECEMBER

Paul Klee

1879–1940 | Painter and printmaker | Germany

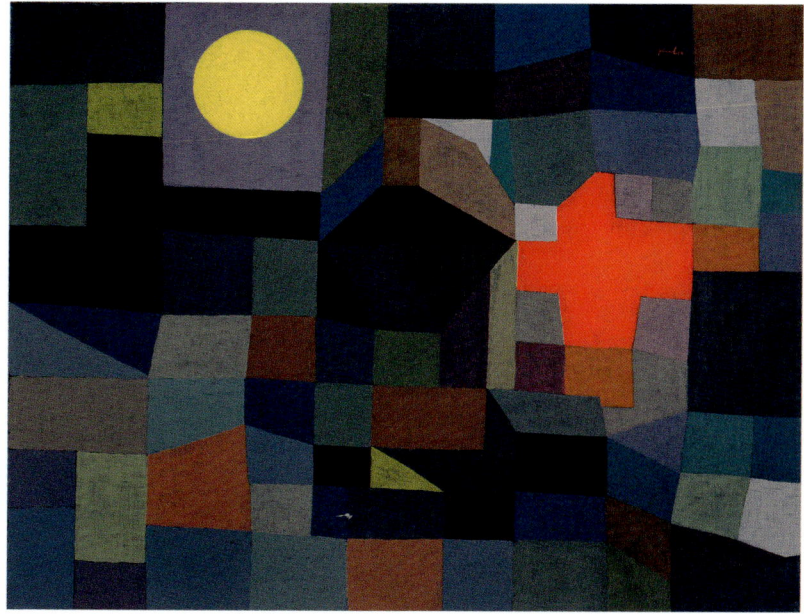

Fire at Full Moon, 1933

One of the pivotal figures of modern art, Klee was first active as a printmaker in Munich. His trip to Tunis in 1914 marked a turning point and, according to Klee himself, made him into a painter. After the First World War, he came to critical attention with his quietly abstract works and joined the Bauhaus as a teacher in 1920, where his style took a Constructivist turn. Fleeing Nazi Germany, Klee moved to Bern in 1933, marking the start of his late period. His images became increasingly hieroglyphic in nature, as he strove to give unifying visual expression to both the cosmic and the worldly. He also penned works of art theory.

18 DECEMBER

Lucie Cousturier

1876–1925 | Painter and writer | France

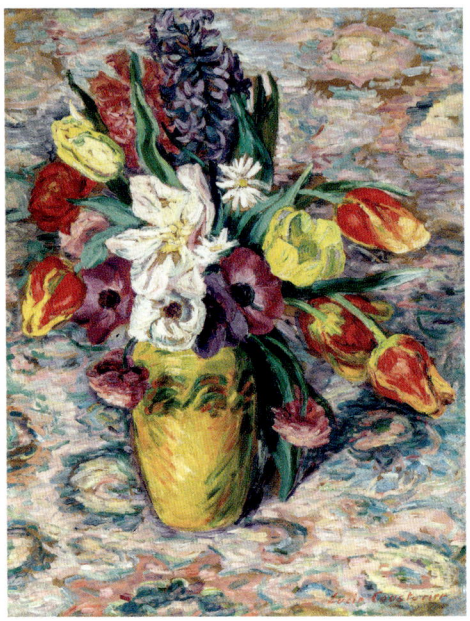

Still Life, undated

Cousturier was a pupil of the late Impressionist Paul Signac, and her oeuvre spanned landscape, still life and portrait painting in the Pointillist style. As art critic and author, she advocated for the art of her teacher and that of Seurat, whose major work, *A Sunday on La Grande Jatte*, was acquired by her father, a wealthy business owner. After her marriage, Cousturier had a series of exhibitions across Europe. From 1913, she lived in the South of France, taking in and caring for Senegalese soldiers during the First World War. These experiences would later flow into her book on those years.

19 DECEMBER

Jan Toorop

1858–1928 | Painter | The Netherlands

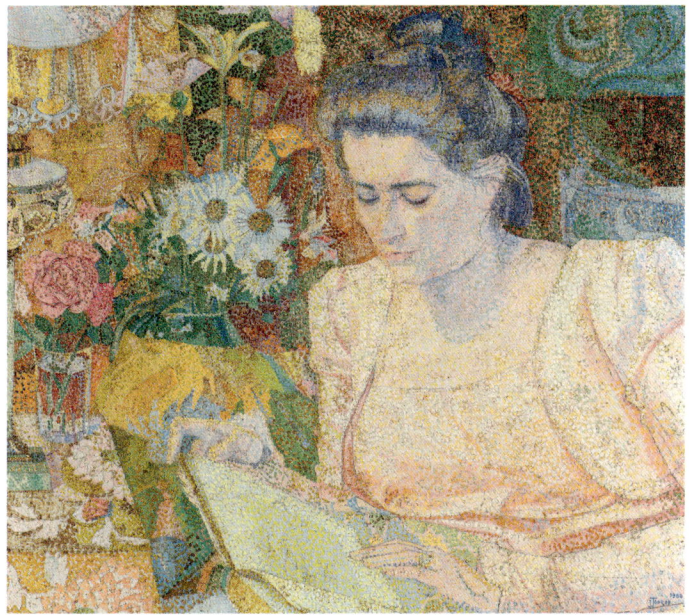

Portrait of Marie Jeanette de Lange, 1900

Born in Java, the painter lived in the Netherlands from 1869 and later studied in Amsterdam and Brussels. This was followed by study trips to Paris and England, where he also met James McNeill Whistler. Toorop's Pointillist paintings mainly depicted social subjects. He later produced graphic works in the style of the Art Nouveau and developed his own, highly individual, symbolic idiom in his works on canvas. After converting to Catholicism in 1905, he devoted himself to religious art. Seriously ill, he was confined to a wheelchair from 1920 but remained active as an artist until his death in 1928.

20 DECEMBER

Anne Vallayer-Coster

1744–1818 | Painter | France

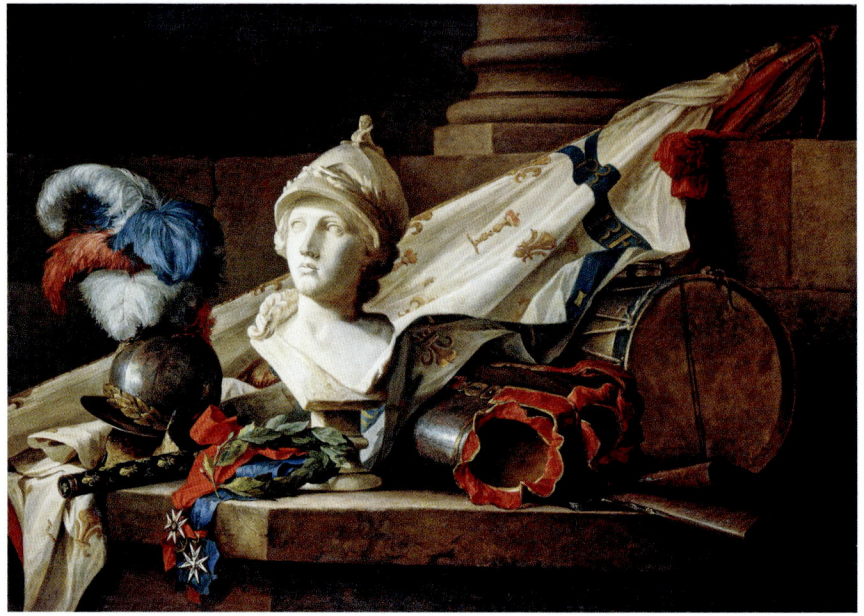

Bust of Minerva with Armour and Weapons on a Stone Ledge, 1777

The earliest documented works by this French artist date from 1762. Her pictures did well at the Paris Salon, opening doors to clients that desired her still lifes of flowers, fruit and game. From 1772, she enjoyed the royal patronage of future Queen Marie-Antoinette and was commissioned to paint the portraits of several members of the royal family. Her works on paper were also highly prized by collectors. Her exquisitely composed still lifes were so similar in style to those of the great Jean Siméon Chardin that many required reattribution at a later date. Works by this successful woman painter have found their way into many museum collections around the world.

21 DECEMBER

Max Bill

1908–1994 | Architect, painter and designer | Switzerland

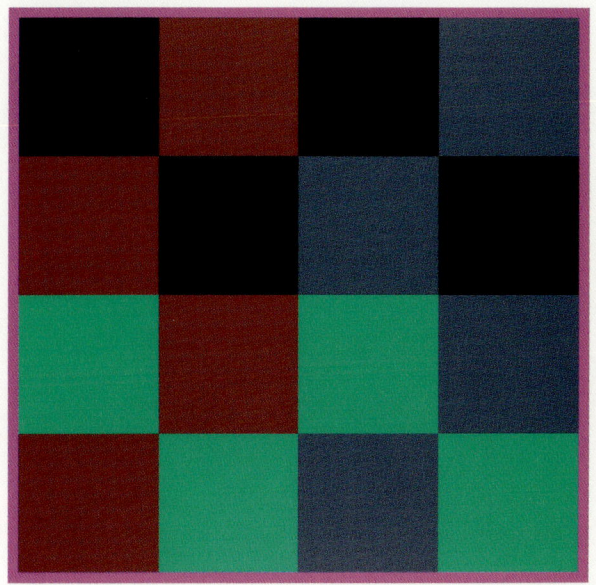

Plate X, from 11 × 4: 4, 1970

After studying at the design school in Zurich and the Bauhaus in Dessau, Max Bill began working in 1929 as an architect, sculptor, graphic designer and painter. He became a leading figure in the Zurich-based Concrete Art movement, was a lecturer and published numerous writings. From 1951 to 1953, he co-founded the Ulm School of Design, designing its building and serving as its first rector until 1956. There, he created the Ulm stool, a multifunctional object that serves as a seat, side table, lectern, shelf, tray and carrying aid. Bill achieved international acclaim across disciplines and was honoured with many exhibitions and awards.

22 DECEMBER

John Marin

1870–1953 | Painter | United States

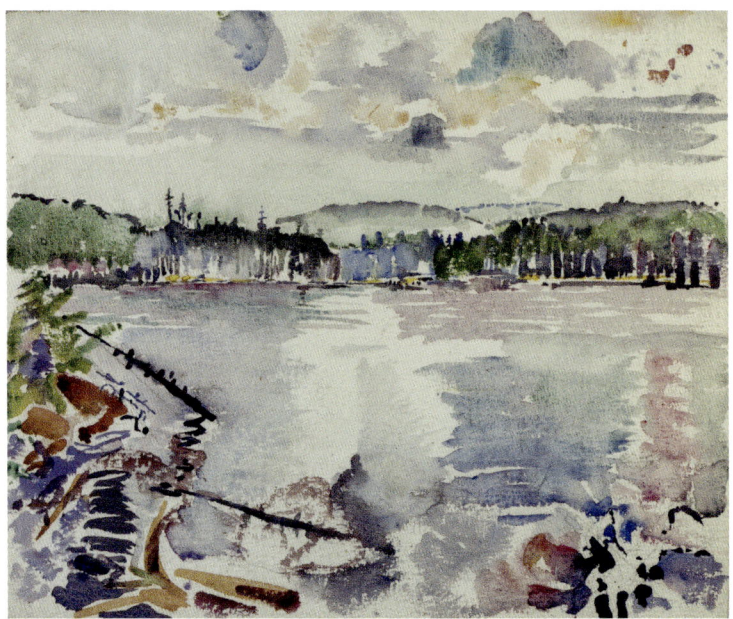

Earth's Forms, Delaware River, before 1920

While studying art in Philadelphia and New York, Marin began to paint. As one of the first American artists to work in abstraction, he lived in Paris from 1905 to 1909, where he met the photographer Edward Steichen, who introduced him to Alfred Stieglitz. From 1909, his works were repeatedly shown in Stieglitz's 291 gallery. Upon his return from Europe, he made the city of New York, with its futuristic views and dynamism, his principal subject. A visionary, expressive pathos resonates in his many crystalline, radiant watercolours. In 1936, he had a solo exhibition at the Museum of Modern Art in New York.

23 DECEMBER

Ad Reinhardt

1913–1967 | Painter, caricaturist and art theorist | United States

Abstract Painting, Number 33, 1963

Reinhardt was one of the most radical opponents of traditional painting, as laid out in his "Twelve Technical Rules" of 1957. He saw painting as a process of reduction, in which the colour black represented the extreme end point. Well versed in literature and art history, he was also a notable theorist. In 1946, he started making cartoons that were often stinging parodies of the art world. The art of Piet Mondrian and Mark Rothko shaped his own, as did Josef Albers's colour theory. After several series of red and blue pictures, from 1953 the only canvases he painted were his meditative *Black Paintings*.

24 DECEMBER

Louise Bourgeois

1911–2010 | Sculptor and graphic artist | France, United States

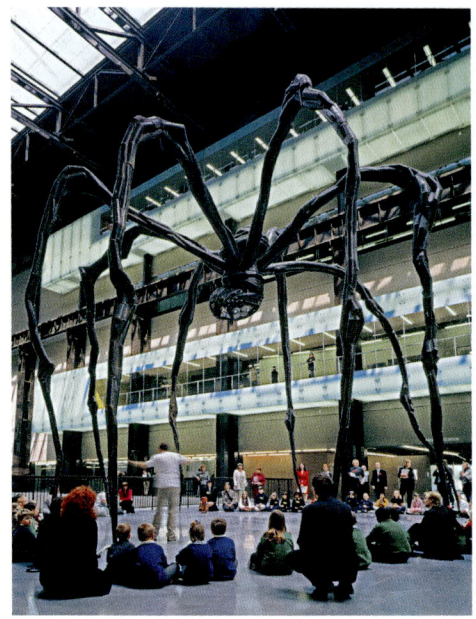

Maman, 1999

As a sculptor, Bourgeois was a living legend, but her fame only came late in life. Her main themes were sexuality, femininity and the patriarchy, following traumatic experiences with her father in her early youth. After studying in Paris, she moved to New York with her husband in 1938. Works on paper created in the 1940s foreshadow her later sculptures. The last phase of her work saw the creation of whole-room installations with autobiographical underpinnings and her iconic, giant spider sculptures. Worldwide exhibitions were followed by exorbitant prices on the art market.

25 DECEMBER

Maurice Utrillo

1883–1955 | Painter | France

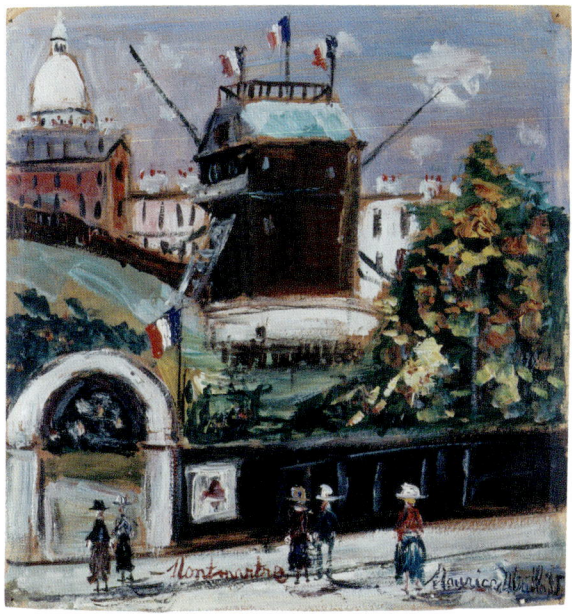

The Windmill in Montmartre, undated

The son of Suzanne Valadon, herself a painter and famous model for artists such as Pierre-Auguste Renoir, Utrillo never knew his father and already had a drinking problem by the age of seventeen. With therapeutic intent, his mother encouraged him to try his hand at painting. Largely self-taught, he enjoyed commercial success in the 1920s with his views of Montmartre, which display his distinctive brand of lyrical yet realistic Impressionism. The charm of his paintings rests in his wilfully "naive" definition of reality. Between 1910 and 1914, his palette lightened, characterized by whites and greys, before becoming richer again and including more colours from 1927 onwards.

26 DECEMBER

René Georges Hermann-Paul

1864–1940 | Painter and illustrator | France

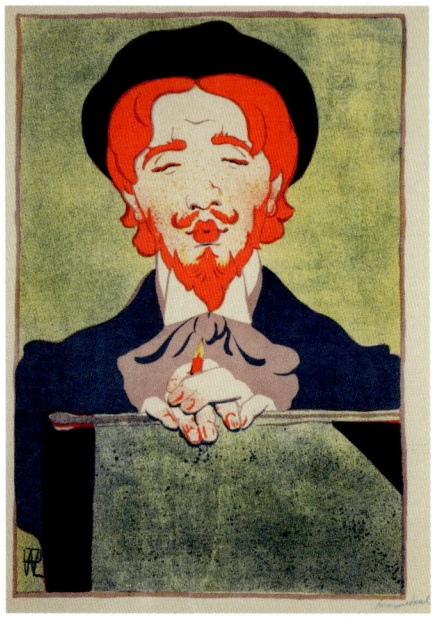

Salon of the One Hundred, 1895

Hermann-Paul was a respected painter of the Belle Époque in Paris. His fame as an often satirical illustrator is based on his work for numerous literary publications. In addition to paintings, he also created drawings, pastels and watercolours in which he captured Parisian society with his subtle powers of observation. His "intimist" interiors were exhibited in 1905 alongside works by Édouard Vuillard and Henri Matisse. He documented the First World War in many watercolours and drawings. Hermann-Paul was also an inventive creator of woodcuts, book illustrations and lithographs.

27 DECEMBER

Vladimir Tatlin

1885–1953 | Sculptor | Russia

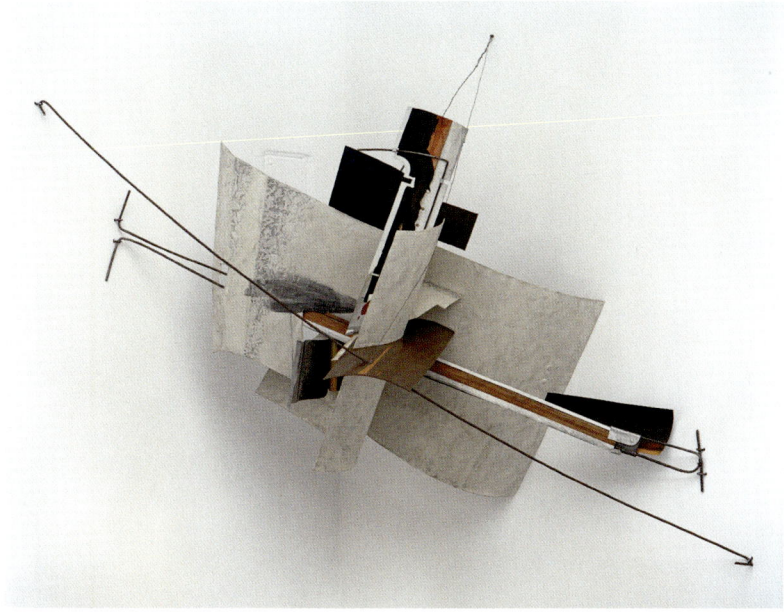

Counter Relief, 1915, reconstruction of 2008

The son of an engineer, Tatlin ran away from home at fourteen to be a sailor on a steamship. After studying in Moscow, he met Kazimir Malevich in 1911 and later Pablo Picasso in Paris. He first came to public attention for his abstract reliefs around 1915. In 1919/1920, he created his iconic design for the *Monument to the Third International*, a four-hundred-metre-high construction that, while never built, made history as a utopian statement. His work is characterized by an expressive revolutionary spirit, with which he propagated a new, aesthetically meaningful machine art. Tatlin was a leading artist of the avant-garde, a teacher and co-publisher of an art magazine.

28 DECEMBER

Elizabeth Armstrong Forbes

1859–1912 | Painter | Canada

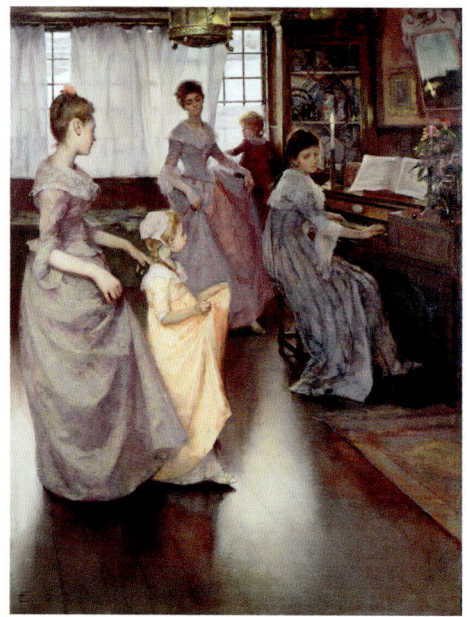

The Minuet, 1892

After studying in London and New York, where she was a member of the Art Students League, Armstrong Forbes travelled to Brittany in 1882 and visited the artist colony in Pont-Aven. In the west of France, she began to paint pictures of the rural population. When she returned to London, Armstrong Forbes learnt the technique of drypoint etching. Shortly afterwards, she met her future husband in Cornwall, with whom she founded the Newlyn School in 1899, where they both taught. She was particularly well known for her watercolours and pastels, and her many activities made her the centre of Newlyn's artistic life.

29 DECEMBER

François-André Vincent

1746–1816 | Painter and draughtsman | France

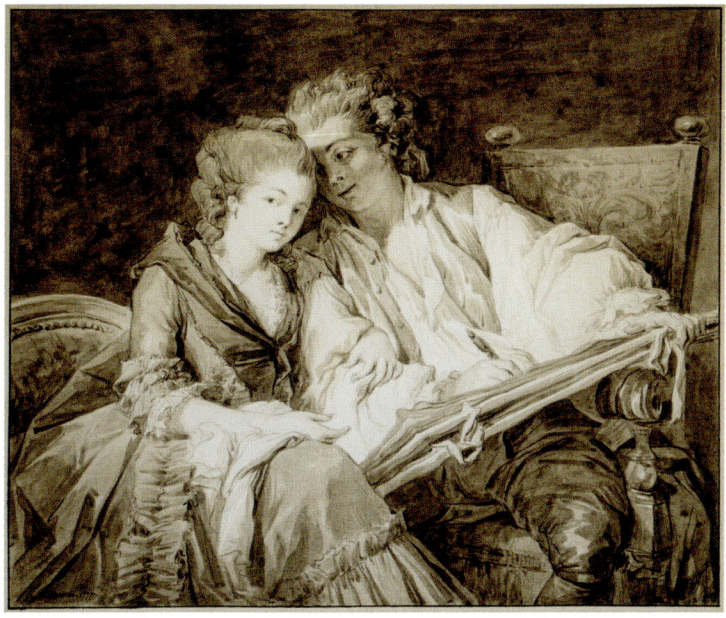

The Drawing Lesson, 1777

The French painter and draughtsman won the Prix de Rome in 1768 as a pupil of
Joseph-Marie Vien, then studied under Charles-Joseph Natoire before going to Italy
for a sojourn in Rome. In 1790, Vincent became court painter to Louis XVI and two years
later professor at the Académie Royale. In the French history and portrait painting of
his time, he was considered a representative of the Neoclassical movement alongside
his more famous colleagues, the young Jacques-Louis David and the late Jean-Honoré
Fragonard. Due to health problems, Vincent's output was severely restricted in his
later years.

30 DECEMBER

Henri Matisse

1869–1954 | Painter, draughtsman, printmaker and sculptor | France

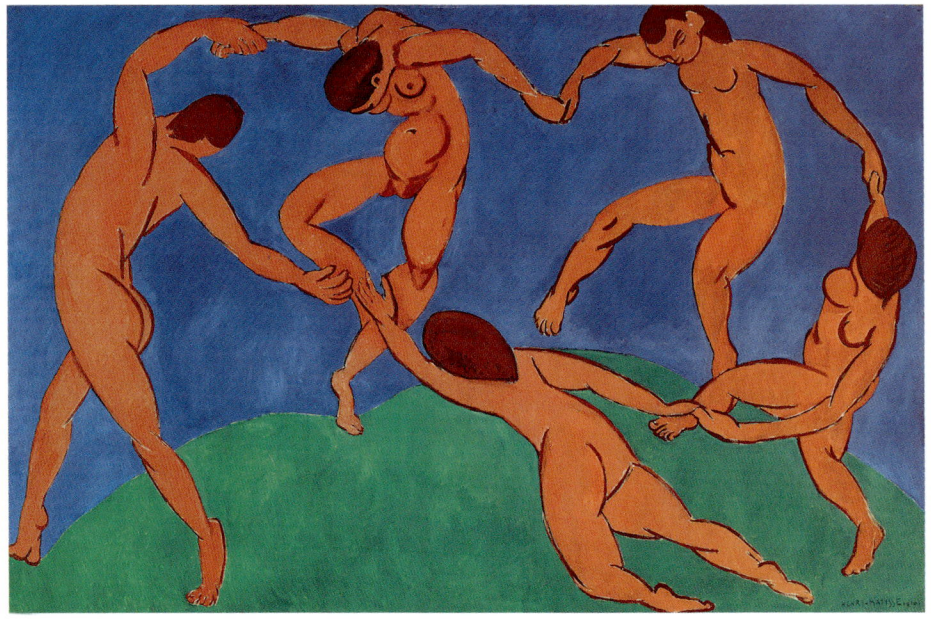

The Dance, 1909/1910

Alongside Pablo Picasso, Matisse was a giant of modern art. He remained a trailblazer par excellence who propagated an art in which reason, simplicity and clarity appear to be distilled into a single form. Using the means of line and colour, he sought a "harmony analogous to that of musical composition", as he once wrote. The pure essence of colour and the line transformed into an arabesque are the two elements that keep his images as flat as an ornamental drawing. His oeuvre culminated in his decorations for the chapel in Vence, consecrated in 1951, and in his minimalistic late cut-outs.

31 DECEMBER

ARTIST INDEX

Caillebotte, Gustave, *Skiffs*, 1877, National Gallery of Art, Washington, DC, 19 Aug.

Calder, Alexander, *Red Petals*, 1942, Arts Club of Chicago, 22 Jul.

Calle, Sophie, *Blind #14, from the series "The Blind"*, 1986, Art Institute of Chicago, 9 Oct.

Cameron, Julia Margaret, *Girl, Ceylon*, 1875–1879, 11 Jun.

Campi, Daisy, *Fair in Paris*, 1926, private collection, 3 Feb.

Caravaggio, *Cupid as Victor*, 1601/1602, Staatliche Museen zu Berlin, Gemäldegalerie, Berlin, 29 Sep.

Carr, Emily, *Kispiox Village*, 1929, Art Gallery of Ontario, 13 Dec.

Carracci, Agostino, *Portrait of a Woman*, undated, Metropolitan Museum of Art, New York, 16 Aug.

Carreño de Miranda, Juan, *Figures of Monks*, undated, Metropolitan Museum of Art, New York, 25 Mar.

Carriera, Rosalba, *Air, from the series "Allegory of the Four Elements"*, 1746, Staatliche Kunstsammlungen Dresden, Gemäldegalerie Alte Meister, Dresden, 7 Oct.

Carrington, Leonora, *Self-Portrait*, 1937/38, Metropolitan Museum of Art, New York, 6 Apr.

Casorati, Felice, *Apples*, 1930, Galleria Nazionale d'Arte Moderna, Rom, 4 Dec.

Cassatt, Mary, *The Boating Party*, c. 1893/1894, National Gallery of Art, Washington, DC, 22 May

Cell, Jennie, *Butchering Day*, c. 1955, Smithsonian American Art Museum, Washington, DC, 20 Oct.

Cellini, Benvenuto, *Salt Cellar*, 1540–1543, Kunsthistorisches Museum Wien, Kunstkammer Wien, Vienna, 3 Nov.

Cézanne, Paul, *Still Life with Apples and a Pot of Primroses*, c. 1890, Metropolitan Museum of Art, New York, 19 Jan.

Charlemont, Hugo, *In the Rose Garden*, 1906, private collection, 18 Mar.

Charpentier, Constance Marie, *Melancholy*, 1801, Musée de Picardie, Amiens, 4 Apr.

Chassériau, Théodore, *The Two Sisters*, 1843, Musée du Louvre, Paris, 20 Sep.

Chirico, Giorgio de, *Mystery and Melancholy of a Street*, 1914, private collection, 10 Jul.

Christo and Jeanne-Claude, *Wrapped Reichstag, Berlin*, 1971–1995, 13 Jun.

Cocteau, Jean, *Self-Portrait*, c. 1954/1955, private collection, 5 Jul.

Corinth, Lovis, *Self-Portrait at His Easel*, 1914, Bayerische Staatsgemäldesammlungen, Neue Pinakothek, Munich, 21 Jul.

Corot, Jean-Baptiste-Camille, *Bridge and Mill near Mantes*, 1860–1865, Bayerische Staatsgemäldesammlungen, Neue Pinakothek, Munich, 16 Jul.

Coustou the Elder, Guillaume, *Hippomenes*, 1711/1712, Musée du Louvre, Paris, 29 Nov.

Cousturier, Lucie, *Still Life*, undated, Christie's Images Ltd, 19 Dec.

Daguerre, Louis, *Louis-Jacques-Mandé Daguerre (1787–1851)*, c. 1844, 18 Nov.

Dai-chien, Chang, *Lady Li*, 1943, 10 May

Dalí, Salvador, *The Persistence of Memory*, 1931, Museum of Modern Art, New York, 11 May

Daubigny, Charles-François, *Landscape near Auvers*, c. 1860–1870 (?), Bayerische Staatsgemäldesammlungen, Neue Pinakothek, Munich, 15 Feb.

David, Jacques-Louis, *The Death of Marat*, 1793, Musées Royaux des Beaux-Arts de Belgique, Brussels, 30 Aug.

Deacon, Richard, *What Could Make Me Feel This Way (A)*, 1993, Sprengel Museum Hannover, 15 Aug.

Degas, Edgar, *Woman Ironing*, c. 1869, Bayerische Staatsgemäldesammlungen, Neue Pinakothek, Munich, 19 Jul.

Delaunay, Robert, *The Eiffel Tower*, 1910/1911, Museum Folkwang, Essen, 12 Apr.

Delisle, Guillaume, *Map of the World*, 1775, Bibliothèque Historique de la Ville de Paris, 28 Feb.

De Maria, Walter, *Installation of Walter De Maria's "The 2000 Sculpture"*, 1992, Los Angeles County Museum of Art, Los Angeles, 1 Oct.

De Niro, Robert, Sr., *Robert De Niro in his studio in New York*, 1982, 3 May

Denis, Maurice, *Madonna and Child (The Kiss)*, 1902, Museum Folkwang, Essen, 25 Nov.

Derain, André, *View of Collioure*, 1905, Museum Folkwang, Essen, 10 Jun.

Devéria, Achille, *Carnival*, 1830, National Gallery of Art, Washington, DC, 6 Feb.

Domenichino, *Penitent St Jerome*, seventeenth century, Städel Museum, Frankfurt am Main, 21 Oct.

Doré, Gustave, *Christ with the Two Disciples Going to Emmaus*, 1866, 6 Jan.

Dou, Gerrit, *The Prayer of the Spinner*, c. 1645–1650, Bayerische Staatsgemäldesammlungen, Alte Pinakothek, Munich, 7 Apr.

Dubuffet, Jean, *Ontogenesis*, 1975, Musée des Beaux-Arts, Le Havre, 31 Jul.

Duchamp, Marcel, *Bottle Rack*, 1914/1964, private collection, 28 Jul.

Dufy, Raoul, *Nice, Festival of Lou Mai*, 1947, Galerie Beyeler, Basel, 3 Jun.

Duplessis, Joseph, *Christoph Willibald Gluck at the Spinet*, 1775, Kunsthistorisches Museum, Vienna, 22 Sep.

Eakins, Thomas, *William Rush Carving His Allegorical Figure of the Schuylkill River*, 1876/1877, Philadelphia Museum of Art, 25 Jul.

Eames, Charles, *Charles Eames and his wife, Ray, working together*, 1975, 17 Jun.

Eitoku, Kanō, *Cypresses*, c. 1590, National Museum, Tokyo, 16 Feb.

Ekong, Afi, *Afi Ekong at work*, 1962, 26 Jun.

Eliasson, Olafur, Installation photograph of Olafur Eliasson's *The weather project*, the fourth Unilever Series commission, Turbine Hall, Tate Modern, 16 October 2003–21 March 2004, London, 5 Feb.

Elout-Drabbe, Mies, *Portrait of a Girl*, undated, 4 Mar.

Emin, Tracey, *My Bed*, 1998, lent by the Duerckheim Collection 2015, Tate London, 3 Jul.

Ensor, James, *Still Life in the Studio*, 1889, Bayerische Staatsgemäldesammlungen, Neue Pinakothek, Munich, 13 Apr.

Etty, William, *Seated Youth with a Staff*, *c.*1815, National Gallery of Art, Washington, DC, 10 Mar.

EXPORT, VALIE, *Tap and Touch Cinema*, 1968, Niklaus Stauss Collection, Zurich, 17 May

Feininger, Lyonel, *Gelmeroda IX*, 1926, Museum Folkwang, Essen, 17 Jul.

Flavin, Dan, *Untitled, from the series "To European Couples"*, 1966–1971, Heiner Friedrich Collection, Traunreuth, 1 Apr.

Forbes, Elizabeth Armstrong, *The Minuet*, 1892, Penlee House Gallery and Museum, Penzance, 29 Dec.

Foujita, Tsuguharu-Léonard, *The Arrival of Westerners in Japan*, 1929, Maison du Japon, Cité Internationale Universitaire de Paris, 27 Nov.

Fragonard, Jean-Honoré, *The Swing*, 1767, Wallace Collection, London, 5 Apr.

Freud, Lucian, *A Young Painter*, 1957/1958, private collection, 8 Dec.

Friedrich, Caspar David, *Monk by the Sea*, *c.*1808–1810, Staatliche Museen zu Berlin, Alte Nationalgalerie, Berlin, 5 Sep.

Funke, Helene, *Three Girls*, 1915, Lentos Kunstmuseum, Linz, 3 Sep.

Fuseli, Henry, *The Nightmare*, 1790/1791, Freies Deutsches Hochstift/Frankfurter Goethe-Museum, Frankfurt am Main, 7 Feb.

Gabashvili, Gigo, *Old Tbilisi*, 1885, Georgian National Museum, Shalva Amiranashvili Museum of Fine Arts, Tbilisi, 9 Nov.

Gabo, Naum, *Linear Construction in Space No. 4*, 1958/59, Kunsthalle Mannheim, 5 Aug.

Gainsborough, Thomas, *Mr and Mrs Robert Andrews*, *c.*1750, National Gallery, London, 14 May

Gallen-Kallela, Akseli, *Kullervo's Curse*, 1899, Ateneumin Taidemuseo, Helsinki, 26 Apr.

Gaudí, Antoni, *Sagrada Familia, Barcelona*, since 1882, 25 Jun.

Gauguin, Paul, *When Will You Marry?*, 1892, Rudolf Staechelin'sche Familienstiftung, Basel, 7 Jun.

Gego, *Sin título (Tamarind 1893)*, 1966, Los Angeles County Museum of Art, Los Angeles, 1 Aug.

Gerhardi, Ida, *The Singer (Madame de Riau)*, 1903, LWL-Museum für Kunst und Kultur, Westfälisches Landesmuseum, Münster, 2 Aug.

Géricault, Théodore, *Irascible Artillery*, *c.*1814, Bayerische Staatsgemäldesammlungen, Neue Pinakothek, Munich, 26 Sep.

Giacometti, Alberto, *The Hand*, 1947/1948, Christie's Images Ltd, 10 Oct.

Gillray, James, *Characters in High Life*, 1795, Metropolitan Museum of Art, New York, 13 Aug.

Giordano, Luca, *A Cynical Philosopher*, *c.*1650–1653, Bayerische Staatsgemäldesammlungen, Alte Pinakothek, Munich, 18 Oct.

Godefroid, Marie Eléonore, *The Sons of Marshal Ney*, 1810, Staatliche Museen zu Berlin, Gemäldegalerie, Berlin, 29 Jun.

Goldin, Nan, *Self-Portrait on New Year's Eve, Malibu, California*, 2006, Marian Goodman Gallery, New York/Paris/Los Angeles, 12 Sep.

González, Julio, *Homme cactus II (Cactus Woman)*, 1939/1940, Staatliche Kunsthalle, Karlsruhe, 21 Sep.

Goya, Francisco de, *The Third of May 1808*, 1814, Museo del Prado, Madrid, 30 Mar.

Granet, François-Marius, *Light Effects in the Ruins*, *c.*1820, Petit Palais, Musée des Beaux-Arts de la Ville de Paris, 17 Dec.

Greuze, Jean-Baptiste, *Charles Claude de Flahaut (1730–1809), Comte d'Angiviller*, 1763, Metropolitan Museum of Art, New York, 21 Aug.

Gris, Juan, *Fantômas*, 1915, National Gallery of Art, Washington, DC, 23 Mar.

Grosz, George, *The Pillars of Society*, 1926, Staatliche Museen zu Berlin, Nationalgalerie, 26 Jul.

Guardi, Francesco, *Regatta on the Giudecca Canal*, *c.*1784–1789, Bayerische Staatsgemäldesammlungen, Alte Pinakothek, Munich, 5 Oct.

Günther, Ignaz, *St Peter Damian*, *c.*1762/1763, St Peter and Paul, Rott am Inn, 22 Nov.

Gursky, Andreas, *Charles de Gaulle*, 1992, Städel Museum, DZ Bank Kunstsammlung, Frankfurt am Main, 15 Jan.

Guston, Philip, *Untitled*, 1971, private collection, 27 Jun.

Guys, Constantin, *Four Girls, 1800s*, nineteenth century, 3 Dec.

Hackert, Jacob Philipp, *Cave of St Francis*, 1801, Museum Folkwang, Essen, 15 Sep.

Hanım, Mihri Müşfik, *Portait of a Young Man*, undated, Sabancı Üniversitesi Sakıp Sabancı Müzesi, Sakıp Sabancı, 26 Feb.

Haring, Keith, *Untitled*, 1989, Christie's Images Ltd, 4 May

Hassam, Childe, *The South Ledges, Appledore*, 1913, Smithsonian American Art Museum, Washington, DC, 17 Oct.

Hatoum, Mona, *Impenetrable*, 2009, Mathaf: Arab Museum of Modern Art, Doha, 11 Feb.

Hepworth, Barbara, *Sculpture with Colour (Deep Blue and Red)*, 1940, Presented by the executors of the artist's estate 1980, Tate Modern, London, 10 Jan.

Hermann-Paul, René Georges, *Salon of the One Hundred*, 1895, High Museum of Art, Atlanta, 27 Dec.

Hicks, Sheila, *Window II*, 2009, Addison Gallery of American Art, Phillips Academy, Andover, 24 Jul.

Hidalgo, Félix Resurrección, *The Indigenous Boat*, 1876, National Gallery Singapore, Hervé Champollion Collection, 21 Feb.

Höch, Hannah, *The Mosquito Is Dead*, 1922, Staatliche Museen zu Berlin, Alte Nationalgalerie, Berlin, 1 Nov.

Hockney, David, *A Bigger Splash*, 1967, acrylic on canvas, 242.5 × 243.9 × 3 cm (96 × 96 × 1 1⁄8 in.), Tate Modern, London, 9 Jul.

Hodler, Ferdinand, *The Night*, 1889/1890, Kunstmuseum, Bern, 14 Mar.

Holzer, Jenny, *France – Paris (75) 1st Arrondissement: The Louvre Pyramid (04 – 09)*, 2009, 29 Jul.

Horn, Rebecca, *The River of the Moon*, 1992, private collection, Barcelona, 24 Mar.

Husain, Maqbool Fida, *Couple with Small Child*, 1960, National Art Gallery, New Delhi, 17 Sep.

Ingres, Jean-Auguste, *La Grande Odalisque*, 1814, Musée du Louvre, Paris, 29 Aug.

Israëls, Jozef, *Children of the Sea*, 1872, Rijksmuseum Amsterdam, 27 Jan.

Jacobsen, Robert, *Earthly Nourishment*, 1954, Moderna Museet, Stockholm, 4 Jun.

Jawlensky, Alexej von, *Abstract Head: Last Light*, 1925, Museum Folkwang, Essen, 13 Mar.

John, Gwen, *A Young Woman in Blue*, c. 1914/1915, Christie's Images Ltd, 22 Jun.

Johns, Jasper, *Three Flags*, 1958, encaustic on canvas, overall: 77.8 × 115.6 × 11.7 cm (30 5⁄8 × 45 1⁄2 × 4 5⁄8 in.), 50th Anniversary Gift of the Gilman Foundation, Inc., The Lauder Foundation, A. Alfred Taubman, Laura-Lee Whittier Woods, and purchase, acc. no. 80.32, Whitney Museum of American Art, New York, 15 May

Jordaens, Jacob, *The Satyr and the Peasant*, c. 1620/1621, Bayerische Staatsgemäldesammlungen, Alte Pinakothek, Munich, 19 May

JR, *Giants, Kikito, US-Mexican Border*, 2017, 22 Feb.

Kabakov, Ilya, *Life and Work of Charles Rosenthal*, 1999, private collection, 30 Sep.

Kahlo, Frida, *Diego on My Mind (Self-Portrait as Tehuana)*, 1943, Jacques and Natasha Gelman Collection, Mexico City, 6 Jul.

Kandinsky, Wassily, *Romantic Landscape*, 1911, Städtische Galerie im Lenbachhaus, Munich, 16 Dec.

Kaprow, Allan, *Portrait of Allan Kaprow*, 1971, 23 Aug.

Käsebier, Gertrude, *Alfred Stieglitz*, 1902, J. Paul Getty Museum, Los Angeles, 18 May

Kauffmann, Angelika, *Self-Portrait of the Artist Hesitating between the Arts of Music and Painting*, 1792, Pushkin State Museum of Fine Art, Moscow, 30 Oct.

Kelly, Ellsworth, *Window, Museum of Modern Art, Paris*, 1949, Musée National d'Art Moderne, Centre Pompidou, Paris, 31 May

Khedoori, Rachel, *Untitled*, 2005, 20 Nov.

Klee, Paul, *Fire at Full Moon*, 1933, Museum Folkwang, Essen, 18 Dec.

Klein, Yves, *Blue Sponge Relief (Little Night Music)*, 1960, Städel Museum, Frankfurt am Main, 28 Apr.

Klimt, Gustav, *Portrait of Adele Bloch-Bauer I*, 1907, Neue Galerie New York, 14 Jul.

Kline, Franz, *Untitled*, 1953/1954, Museum Folkwang, Essen, 23 May

Klinger, Max, *Portrait of a Roman Woman on a Flat Roof in Rome*, 1891, Städel Museum, Frankfurt am Main, 18 Feb.

Klint, Hilma af, *The Ten Largest, No. 7, Adult, Group IV*, 1907, Hilma af Klint Foundation, Stockholm, 26 Oct.

Kokoschka, Oskar, *Dresden, Augustus Bridge with Figure from Behind*, 1923, Museum Folkwang, Essen, 1 Mar.

Kolig, Anton, *Recumbent Man*, 1918, Kunstmuseum Stuttgart, 1 Jul.

Kollwitz, Käthe, *The Parents, sheet 3 from the series "War"*, 1921/1922, Städel Museum, Frankfurt am Main, 8 Jul.

Koons, Jeff, *Balloon Swan (Blue)*, 2004–11, Van Ham, Cologne, 21 Jan.

Krieghoff, Cornelius, *Following the Moose*, c. 1860, Brooklyn Museum, 19 Jun.

Kubin, Alfred, *Death*, 1926, 10 Apr.

Kusama, Yayoi, *Infinity Mirrored Room – Love Forever*, 1966/1994, Ota Fine Arts, Tokyo/Singapore/Shanghai, 22 Mar.

La Farge, John, *The Fish or The Fish and Flowering Branch*, c. 1890, Museum of Fine Arts Boston, 31 Mar.

Labille-Guiard, Adélaïde, *Portrait of Louise-Elisabeth of France and Her Son Ferdinand*, 1788, Musée National des Châteaux de Versailles et de Trianon, 11 Apr.

Lange, Dorothea, *Migrant Mother*, 1936, Oakland Museum of California, 26 May

Laserstein, Lotte, *Russian Girl with Compact*, 1928, Städel Museum, Frankfurt am Main, 28 Nov.

Lassnig, Maria, *Self-Portrait with Monkey (Beloved Forefathers)*, 2001, Städel Museum, Frankfurt am Main, 8 Sep.

Lechner, Alf, *Alf Lechner with one of his sculptures*, 1969, 17 Apr.

Lehmbruck, Wilhelm, *Fallen Man*, 1915/1916, Bayerische Staatsgemäldesammlungen, Sammlung Moderne Kunst in der Pinakothek der Moderne, Munich, 4 Jan.

Lely, Peter, *Study for a Portrait of a Woman*, 1670s, Metropolitan Museum of Art, New York, 14 Sep.

Lempicka, Tamara de, *The Telephone II*, 1930, private collection, 16 May

Overbeck, Gerta, *Young Girl*, 1934, Frank Brabant Collection, Wiesbaden, 16 Jan.

Pajou, Augustin, *Ideal Female Heads*, undated, J. Paul Getty Museum, Los Angeles, 19 Sep.

Parmigianino (Girolamo Francesco Maria Mazzola), *Madonna and Child with a Monk*, c. 1530, Bayerische Staatsgemäldesammlungen, Alte Pinakothek, Munich, 11 Jan.

Parreiras, Antônio, *Seascape*, 1902, Pinacoteca do Estado, São Paulo, 20 Jan.

Parsons, Betty, *Il Oglala*, 1979, Collection of Beth Rudin DeWoody, 31 Jan.

Peale, Raphaelle, *A Dessert*, 1814, National Gallery of Art, Washington, DC, 17 Feb.

Peiffer Watenphul, Max, *Grand Canal with View of Santa Maria della Salute in Venice*, 1947, private collection, 1 Sep.

Perry, Lilla Cabot, *Lady with a Bowl of Violets*, c. 1910, National Museum of Women in the Arts, Washington, DC, 13 Jan.

Pfrang, Erwin, *Untitled*, 1990, Bayerische Staatsgemäldesammlungen, Sammlung Moderne Kunst in der Pinakothek der Moderne, Munich, 23 Oct.

Picabia, Francis, *The Cacodylic Eye*, 1921, Musée National d'Art Moderne, Centre Pompidou, Paris, 22 Jan.

Pirosmani, Niko, *Chicken and Cockerel*, 1904, Georgian National Museum, Tiflis, 5 May

Pollock, Jackson, *Painting (Silver over Black, White, Yellow and Red)*, 1948, Museé National d'Art Moderne, Centre Pompidou, Paris, 28 Jan.

Pontormo, Jacopo da, *Alessandro de' Medici*, 1534/1535, Art Institute of Chicago, 24 May

Popova, Lyubov, *Painterly Architectonics*, 1917, Sepherot Foundation, Liechtenstein, 6 May

Poussin, Nicolas, *Apollo and Daphne*, c. 1627, Bayerische Staatsgemäldesammlungen, Alte Pinakothek, Munich, 15 Jun.

Poynter, Edward, *A View of the Arno*, Florence, 1874, National Gallery of Art, Washington, DC, 20 Mar.

Primaticcio, Francesco, *Dance of the Hours*, c. 1547/1548, Städel Museum, Frankfurt am Main, 30 Apr.

Procter, Dod, *Morning*, 1926, Tate Gallery, London, 21 Apr.

Puvis de Chavannes, Pierre, *Study of a Sleeping Woman*, c. 1867, Art Institute of Chicago, 14 Dec.

Ratkowski, Anne, *Still Life with Children's Shoes*, 1945, Museum Kunst der Verlorenen Generation, Salzburg, 3 Mar.

Rauch, Neo, *Star*, 2001, Städel Museum, Deutsche Bank Collection, Frankfurt am Main, 18 Apr.

Rauschenberg, Robert, *Breakthrough I*, 1964, Museum Folkwang, Essen, 22 Oct.

Ray, Man, *Le Violon d'Ingres*, 1924, 27 Aug.

Redon, Odilon, *Woman with Wild Flowers*, c. 1900, Hermitage, St Petersburg, 22 Apr.

Rego, Paula, *Untitled No. 4*, 1998, 26 Jan.

Reinhardt, Ad, *Abstract Painting, Number 33*, 1963, oil on linen, overall: 152.7 × 152.7 cm (60 1/8 × 60 1/8 in.), 50th Anniversary Gift of Fred Mueller, acc. no. 80.33, Whitney Museum of American Art, New York, 24 Dec.

Rembrandt van Rijn, *Self-Portrait as a Young Man*, 1629, Bayerische Staatsgemäldesammlungen, Alte Pinakothek, Munich, 15 Jul.

Reni, Guido, *Assumption of the Virgin*, c. 1638/1639, Bayerische Staatsgemäldesammlungen, Alte Pinakothek, Munich, 4 Nov.

Renoir, Pierre-Auguste, *Lise with a Parasol*, 1867, Museum Folkwang, Essen, 25 Feb.

Richter, Gerhard, *Portrait of a Young Woman, from the cycle "18 October 1977"*, 1988, Museum of Modern Art, New York, 9 Feb.

Riley, Bridget, *Gentle Measure*, 1982, Kunsthalle zu Kiel, 24 Apr.

Rivers, Larry, *History of Matzah: The History of the Jews, 1982–84*, 1984, Yale University Art Gallery, New Haven, 17 Aug.

Rivière, Henri, *The Trocadéro*, 1900, Staatliche Museen zu Berlin, Kunstbibliothek, Berlin, 11 Mar.

Rodin, Auguste, *Crouching Woman*, 1880/1882, Bayerische Staatsgemäldesammlungen, Neue Pinakothek, Munich, 12 Nov.

Rodchenko, Alexander, *Pioneer with Horn*, 1930, 5 Dec.

Rosso Fiorentino, *Madonna and Child with Saints* (detail), 1518, Galleria degli Uffizi, Florence, 8 Mar.

Rothko, Mark, *Untitled*, 1960, Adriana and Robert Mnuchin Collection, New York, 25 Sep.

Rousseau, Henri, *The Dream*, 1910, Museum of Modern Art, New York, 21 May

Rozanova, Olga, *Suprematism*, undated, Sprengel Museum Hannover, Kurt und Ernst Schwitters Stiftung, 21 Jun.

Rubens, Peter Paul, *The Reconciliation of the Romans and the Sabines*, c. 1625, Bayerische Staatsgemäldesammlungen, Alte Pinakothek, Munich, 28 Jun.

Runge, Philipp Otto, *The Hülsenbeck Children*, 1805/1806, Hamburger Kunsthalle, Hamburg, 23 Jul.

Ryman, Robert, *Classico IV*, 1968, Solomon R. Guggenheim Museum, New York, 30 May

Sadr, Behjat, *Untitled*, 1974, Musée National d'Art Moderne, Centre Pompidou, Paris, 29 May

Saïd, Mahmoud, *The Port of Beirut*, 1954, Dalloul Art Foundation – Modern and Contemporary Arab Art, Beirut, 8 Apr.

Saint Phalle, Niki de, *Black Dancing Nana (Big Black Dancer)*, c. 1968, private collection, 29 Oct.

Sansovino, Jacopo, *Palazzo Corner della Ca' Granda, Venice*, engraving by Luca Carlevarijs, 1703, Fondazione Ugo Da Como, Lonato del Garda, 2 Jul.

Sardeau, Hélène, *Hélène Sardeau models an American Venus*, undated, 7 Jul.

Sargent, John Singer, *Madame X (Virginie Amélie Avegno Gautreau)*, 1883/1884, Metropolitan Museum of Art, New York, 12 Jan.

Savage, Augusta, *Augusta Savage with Her Sculpture "Realization"*, c.1938, 29 Feb.

Schadow, Johann Gottfried, *The Princess Group (Princesses Luise and Friederike of Prussia)*, 1795, Staatliche Museen zu Berlin, National-galerie, Berlin, 20 May

Schindler, Emil Jakob, *Cypresses near Zara*, c.1887/1888, Albertina Museum, Vienna, 27 Apr.

Schlemmer, Oskar, *The Dancer (The Gesture)*, 1922, Bayerische Staatsgemäldesammlungen, Sammlung Moderne Kunst in der Pinakothek der Moderne, Munich, 4 Sep.

Scott, Kathleen, *Kathleen Scott working on a statue*, 1912, Veneranda Biblioteca Ambrosiana, Milan, 27 Mar.

Scully, Sean, *Red Star*, 1990, Museum Folkwang, Essen, 30 Jun.

Seelos, Gottfried, *Bergisel*, 1880, Österreichische Galerie im Belvedere, Vienna, 9 Jan.

Senefelder, Alois, *Printing Press / Stone Printing, Lithography*, 1818, Staatliche Museen zu Berlin, Staatsbibliothek, Berlin, 6 Nov.

Serra, Richard, *The Matter of Time*, 1994–2005, Guggenheim Museum, Bilbao, 2 Nov.

Seurat, Georges, *A Sunday on La Grande Jatte*, 1884/1886, Art Institute of Chicago, 2 Dec.

Shapiro, Joel, *Untitled*, undated, Israel Museum, Jerusalem, 27 Sep.

Sher-Gil, Amrita, *Group of Three Girls*, 1935, 30 Jan.

Shonibare, Yinka, *Nelson's Ship in a Bottle*, 2010, National Maritime Museum, London, 9 Aug.

Sieverding, Katharina, *Capillary Dynamolysis III*, 1997, Städel Museum, DZ Bank Kunstsammlung, Frankfurt am Main, 16 Nov.

Silvestre, Louis de, *Chevalier de Bavière*, 1707, Bayerische Staatsgemäldesammlungen, Alte Pinakothek, Munich, 23 Jun.

Sirani, Elisabetta, *Madonna and Child with the Infant St John*, undated, Galleria dei Dipinti Antichi della Cassa di Risparmio di Cesena, 8 Jan.

Sirry, Gazbia, *The Teacher*, 1954, Dalloul Art Foundation – Modern and Contemporary Arab Art, Beirut, 11 Oct.

Sívori, Eduardo, *Spring*, 1914, Museo Nacional de Bellas Artes, Buenos Aires, 13 Oct.

Slevogt, Max, *Self-Portrait*, c.1929/1930, Bayerische Staatsgemäldesammlungen, Neue Pinakothek, Munich, 8 Oct.

Smith, Kiki, *Virgin Marie*, 1992, Pace Gallery, New York, 18 Jan.

Smithson, Robert, *Spiral Jetty*, 1970, Rozel Point on the northeastern shore of Great Salt Lake, Utah, 2 Jan.

Sorolla, Joaquín, *Girls on the Beach*, 1908, Museo Sorolla, Madrid, 27 Feb.

Soto, Jesús Rafael, *Pénétrable de Chicago*, 1971, Museum of Contemporary Art Chicago, 5 Jun.

Sparhawk-Jones, Elizabeth, *The Shoe Shop*, 1911, Art Institute of Chicago, 8 Nov.

Spranger, Bartholomeus, *Entombment*, undated, 21 Mar.

Stella, Frank, *Getty Tomb (First Version)*, 1959, private collection, 12 May

Sterne, Hedda, *NY, NY No. X*, 1948, Tate Gallery, London, 4 Aug.

Stieglitz, Alfred, *Margaret Prosser's Clasped Hands in Lap*, 1933, Metropolitan Museum of Art, New York, 1 Jan.

Strand, Paul, *Abstraction, Bowls*, 1916, J. Paul Getty Museum, Los Angeles, 16 Oct.

Strij, Jacob van, *Landscape with Cattle Driver and Shepherd*, c.1780–1785, Rijksmuseum Amsterdam, 2 Oct.

Stryjeńska, Zofia, *Seasons: July–August*, 1925, National Museum, Warsaw, 13 May

Stuck, Franz von, *Sin*, 1893, Bayerische Staats-gemäldesammlungen, Neue Pinakothek, Munich, 23 Feb.

Sutherland, Graham, *Roses*, 1950, Christie's Images Ltd, 24 Aug.

Tagore, Rabindranath, *Rabindranath Tagore*, c.1935, 7 May

Tamayo, Rufino, *Woman in Grey*, 1959, Solomon R. Guggenheim Museum, New York, 26 Aug.

Tanguy, Yves, *The Lovers*, 1929, Museum Folkwang, Essen, 5 Jan.

Tanning, Dorothea, *A Little Night Music*, 1943, private collection, 25 Aug.

Tatlin, Vladimir, *Counter Relief, 1915,* reconstruction of 2008, 28 Dec.

Taylor, Al, *Untitled (Without Riggers)*, c.1998/1999, David Zwirner Gallery, New York / Los Angeles / London / Paris / Hong Kong, 2 Mar.

Teniers the Younger, David, *Tavern Scene*, 1643, Bayerische Staatsgemäldesammlungen, Staats-galerie Neuburg, 15 Dec.

Tessai, Tomioka, *Scene Inspired by the Scrolls of Frolicking Animals and Humans*, 1890s, Metropolitan Museum of Art, New York, 25 Jan.

Thomkins, André, *Sugarloaves*, 1971, Kunstpalast, Düsseldorf, 11 Aug.

Thöny, Wilhelm, *New York, Manhattan with Crane*, Österreichische Galerie im Belvedere, Vienna, 10 Feb.

Thorvaldsen, Berthel, *Epitaph for Johann Philipp von Bethmann-Hollweg, Rome*, 1813–1832, Liebieghaus Skulpturensammlung, Frankfurt am Main, 19 Nov.

Tiepolo, Giovanni Battista, *Adoration of the Magi*, 1753, Bayerische Staatsgemäldesammlungen, Alte Pinakothek, Munich, 5 Mar.

Tischler, Manina, *Phoenix*, 1972, Österreichische Galerie im Belvedere, Vienna, 11 Sep.

IMAGE CREDITS & ARTIST COPYRIGHTS

.sammlung.pinakothek.de/de/artwork/A9xIyOeLWv (last updated on Apr. 2, 2025) 5 Mar., URL: https://www.sammlung.pinakothek.de/de/artwork/bwx0jyqGm8 (last updated on Aug. 28, 2023) 19 May, URL: https://www.sammlung.pinakothek.de/de/artwork/Dn4Zy5vGaK (last updated on Aug. 24, 2023) 18 Oct., URL: https://www.sammlung.pinakothek.de/de/artwork/gR4k3Xg4Ee (last updated on Oct. 17, 2023) 14 Aug., URL: https://www.sammlung.pinakothek.de/de/artwork/gR4kR1vGEe (last updated on Jan. 23, 2025) 11 Jan., URL: https://www.sammlung.pinakothek.de/de/artwork/jpxepgB4J7 (last updated on Mar. 31, 2025) 15 June, URL: https://www.sammlung.pinakothek.de/de/artwork/jpxeV1vLJ7 (last updated on Aug. 28, 2023) 10 Dec., URL: https://www.sammlung.pinakothek.de/de/artwork/ma4dgdaGrO (last updated on June 19, 2023) 23 June, URL: https://www.sammlung.pinakothek.de/de/artwork/PdxzEoZ4w5 (last updated on April 1, 2025) 4 Nov., URL: https://www.sammlung.pinakothek.de/de/artwork/wq4jX0qLWo (last updated on Aug. 24, 2023) 28 June, URL: https://www.sammlung.pinakothek.de/de/artwork/Y0GR916LRX (last updated on Aug. 28, 2023) 15 Apr., URL: https://www.sammlung.pinakothek.de/de/artwork/y7GE1PmGPV (last updated on Feb. 29, 2024) 15 July, URL: https://www.sammlung.pinakothek.de/de/artwork/ZKGPV62xgA (last updated on April 14, 2025) 5 Oct.

Bayerische Staatsgemäldesammlungen – Neue Pinakothek, Munich, URL: https://www.sammlung.pinakothek.de/de/artwork/01G1BpA4kE (last updated on June 19, 2023) 11 Nov., URL: https://www.sammlung.pinakothek.de/de/artwork/5RGQ16vGz3 13 Apr., URL: https://www.sammlung.pinakothek.de/de/artwork/6kLaEKXL8V (last updated on Nov. 29, 2024) 14 Nov., URL: https://www.sammlung.pinakothek.de/de/artwork/ApL8qN7GN2 (last updated on Jan. 22, 2025) 23 Feb., URL: https://www.sammlung.pinakothek.de/de/artwork/Dj4moVbL5A (last updated on April 7, 2025) 21 July, URL: https://www.sammlung.pinakothek.de/de/artwork/gR4k3694Ee (last updated on Dec. 5, 2024) 26 Sept., URL: https://www.sammlung.pinakothek.de/de/artwork/jWLpOQ6xKY (last updated on June 19, 2023) 16 July, URL: https://www.sammlung.pinakothek.de/de/artwork/k2xn7W5LPd (last updated on June 19, 2023) 15 Feb., URL: https://www.sammlung.pinakothek.de/de/artwork/ma4dlRj4rO (last updated on Dec. 12, 2024) 4 Oct., URL: https://www.sammlung.pinakothek.de/de/artwork/Qm45J95xNo (last updated on June 19, 2023) 24 Sept., URL: https://www.sammlung.pinakothek.de/de/artwork/QrLW3qXLNO (last updated on Oct. 17, 2024) 8 Oct., URL: https://www.sammlung.pinakothek.de/de/artwork/z9pL3DjGeb 12 Mar., URL: https://www.sammlung.pinakothek.de/de/artwork/ZnxwPj7LXg (last updated on Dec. 5, 2024) 19 July

Bayerische Staatsgemäldesammlungen – Sammlung Moderne Kunst in der Pinakothek der Moderne, Munich, URL: https://www.sammlung.pinakothek.de/de/artwork/Qm45p2qGNo (last updated on Nov. 29, 2023) 4 Sept.

Bayerische Staatsgemäldesammlungen – Staatsgalerie Neuburg, URL: https://www.sammlung.pinakothek.de/de/artwork/OrLbkwyG1V (last updated on April 9, 2025) 15 Dec.

Belvedere, Vienna 9 Jan., 11 Sept.

Blauel Gnamm – ARTOTHEK 4 Jan., 12 Nov.

Bottrop, Josef Albers Museum, Museumszentrum Quadrat, © The Josef and Anni Albers Foundation / VG Bild-Kunst, Bonn 2025 19 Mar.

bpk / Addison Gallery of American Art, Phillips Academy / Art Resource, NY, © VG Bild-Kunst, Bonn 2025 24 July; adoc-photos 18 Nov.; Alfredo Dagli Orti 17 Nov.; Angelika Platen 23 Aug.; Bayerische Staatsgemäldesammlungen, © Cy Twombly Foundation 25 Apr.; © Erwin Pfrang, courtesy Galerie Jahn und Jahn 23 Oct.; Buffalo AKG Art Museum / Art Resource, NY, © VG Bild-Kunst, Bonn 2025 2 June; CNAC-MNAM / Adam Rzepka, © Succession Brâncuşi – All rights reserved / VG Bild-Kunst, Bonn 2025 19 Feb., Philippe Migeat, © The Jacques & Yulla Lipchitz Foundation 22 Aug.; Gemäldegalerie, SMB / Jörg P. Anders 29 June; Kunsthalle Mannheim, Leihgabe des Landes Baden-Württemberg seit 1984 / Cem Yücetas, The Work of Naum Gabo © Nina & Graham Williams / Tate, 2020 5 Aug.; Kupferstichkabinett, SMB / Dietmar Katz, © VG Bild-Kunst, Bonn 2025 15 Oct.; Jörg P. Anders 7 Dec.; Los Angeles County Museum of Art / Art Resource, NY, © Fundación Gego 1 Aug.; © The Estate of Walter De Maria 1 Oct.; National Portrait Gallery, London / Richard Cockle Lucas 24 Oct.; Nationalgalerie, SMB / Friederike Labahn 20 May, Jörg P. Anders, © Estate of George Grosz, Princeton, N.J. / VG Bild-Kunst, Bonn 2025 26 July, Jörg P. Anders, © VG Bild-Kunst, Bonn 2025 1 Nov.; Smithsonian American Art Museum / Art Resource, NY 9 Dec.; © Estate of Jennie Cell 20 Oct.; Sprengel Museum Hannover / Michael Herling / Aline Gwose, © Richard Deacon 15 Aug.; Staatsbibliothek zu Berlin 6 Nov.; Städel Museum, © courtesy Galerie EIGEN + ART, Leipzig/Berlin und Zwirner, New York / VG Bild-Kunst, Bonn 2025 18 Apr.; The Art Institute of Chicago / Art Resource, NY, © VG Bild-Kunst, Bonn 2025 11 Dec.; Jacopo Pontormo 24 May; The Solomon R. Guggenheim Foundation / Art Resource, NY, © VG Bild-Kunst, Bonn 2025 30 May; © D.R. Rufino Tamayo / Herederos / México / Fundación Olga y Rufino Tamayo A.C. / VG Bild-Kunst, Bonn 2025 26 Aug.

Bridgeman Images 12 Jan., 22 Jan., 21 May, 11 July; © Salvador Dalí, Fundació Gala-Salvador Dalí / VG Bild-Kunst, Bonn 2025 11 May; CR Number: 53-02, © The Estate of Francis Bacon. All rights reserved / VG Bild-Kunst, Bonn 2025 28 Oct.